Italy Since 1800

The Present and the Past
General Editors: Michael Crowder and Juliet Gardiner

These books provide the historical background necessary for a proper understanding of the major nations and regions of the contemporary world. Each contributor illuminates the present political, social, cultural and economic structures of his nation or region through the study of its past. The books, which are fully illustrated with maps and photographs, are written for students, teachers and general readers; and will appeal not only to historians but also to political scientists, economists and sociologists who seek to set their own studies of a particular nation or region in historical perspective.

Titles already published

Australia   *John Rickard*

Modern China: A History (Second Edition)   *Edwin E. Moise*

Russia: The Tsarist and Soviet Legacy (Second Edition)   *Edward Acton*

Italy since 1800: A Nation in the Balance?   *Roger Absalom*

Italy since 1800

A Nation in the Balance?

Roger Absalom

LONGMAN
London and New York

Longman Group Limited,
Longman House, Burnt Mill,
Harlow, Essex CM20 2JE, England
and Associated Companies throughout the world.

*Published in the United States of America
by Longman Publishing, New York*

First published 1995

ISBN 0 582 02772 1 CSD
ISBN 0 582 02771 3 PPR

British Library Cataloguing-in-Publication Data

A catalogue record for this book is
available from the British Library

Library of Congress Cataloging-in-Publication Data

Absalom, Roger Neil Lewis.
    Italy since 1800 : a nation in the balance? / Roger Absalom.
       p. cm. — (the Present and the past)
    Includes bibliographical references and index.
    ISBN 0-582-02772-1 (csd). — ISBN 0-582-02771-3 (ppr)
    1. Italy—History—20th century. 2. Italy—History—19th century.
I. Title. II. Series.
DG568.5.A27 1994
945' .08—dc20
                                     94-11465
                                        CIP

Set by 14 in 10 on 12pt Sabon
Produced by Longman Singapore Publishers (Pte) Ltd.
Printed in Singapore

Contents

List of Illustrations

Preface

The underlying objective of this presentation of the way in which the past of Italy has a bearing on the present is to explore the nature and implications of its inhabitants' success in coping with the contradictions of the country's political and economic situation, and of its social structure, and to attempt an explanation of how that success is related to the making and repeated remaking of the Italian nation-state and of Italian society through the major episodes of crisis since Bonaparte's conquests began the tortuous process whereby the idea of a united Italy became a political reality. Recent developments illustrate all too clearly that this process has still not reached its final resolution and that fault-lines dating from the initial phases of the country's formation still indicate a fundamental instability.

No claim is made for original research, although some comments upon the resistance and the immediate post-war period are informed by my research in relation to other projects. The approach has been to present both the main lines of historical development and the main interpretations put upon them. It is hoped that the result will be of some help to students and others confronting the Italian paradox of a country in the top ten of economic success and endowed with a rich artistic and intellectual culture, but burdened with a political and administrative system remarkable mainly for its corruption and inefficiency. No definitive answers can, of course, be given, but it is hoped that this review of Italy's recent past will help in the formulation of the right questions.

Thanks are due to many colleagues and friends who have read various drafts and commented helpfully upon them, to Juliet Gardiner and Longman who have been unfailingly sympathetic at moments of difficulty, and above all to Patricia Absalom for her endless patience. It goes without saying that the shortcomings of the book are entirely the responsibility of the author.

Roger Absalom

Acknowledgements

The publishers would like to thank the following for their permission to reproduce illustrative material:

Bibliotheque Nationale, Paris/Giraudon-Lauros/Bridgeman Art Library, London, for plate 1.1;
Istituto Geografico De Agostini, Milan, for plates 1.2, 3.4 and 10.1;
Archivio Editore Torino for plates 1.3, 3.1, 3.2, 3.3, 3.5, 3.6, 4.2, 4.3, 4.4, 5.1 and 5.2;
Mary Evans Picture Library for plates 2.1 and 4.1;
Laterza, Rome, for plates 5.3, 6.2, 7.3 and 8.2;
La Pietra Editrice Srl, Milan, for plates 5.4, 6.1 and 7.1;
Farabolafoto, Milan for plate 6.3;
Publifoto Milano for plates 7.2, 8.2, 8.3, 9.2 and 10.2;
Cambridge University Press for plate 8.1, by permission of the Syndics of Cambridge University Library;
Dr David Ellwood for plate 9.4;
Marzia Malli, Milan, for plate 11.5;
Rex Features Ltd for plate 12.2;
The Associated Press Ltd for plate 13.2;
and Professor Harry Hearder for his assistance in tracing elusive prints.

The publishers would also like to thank The Estate of Italo Calvino and Wylie, Aitken & Stone, Inc. for granting permission to print a translation of an article by Italo Calvino.

Whilst every effort has been made to trace the owners of copyright material, in a few cases this has proved to be problematic and so we take this opportunity to offer our apologies to any copyright holders whose rights we may have unwittingly infringed.

Chapter 1 ....

The origins of modern Italy: The dream of reason and the dream of unity

This book is about the significance we can assign to the strengths and weaknesses of one of the major partners in the European Union. It explores them from a historical point of view, tracing the roots of the present in the past, and the difficult and often paradoxical routes followed by the 'makers of Italy', and the victims of their nation-building efforts, to the present condition of the country, its society, politics and economy. In particular, in attempting to identify and characterise the nature and implications of the success of Italians in coping with the material and cultural contradictions of their country's geopolitical and economic situation and of its social structure, the book will focus its attention on the specific form taken by the modern nation-state in the area now usually coloured green on the map of Europe, and how the inner logic of its formation and its deep structures impinge on Italians today.

One starting-point must be that, despite all the peculiarities for which its political life is notorious, Italy works – if only just. Over the last two centuries the Italian 'nation' has been 'remade' politically at least five times, and perhaps is about to be refashioned yet again. But, in another sense, little really seems to have changed during this period: deeply ingrained habits of mind and patterns of behaviour centred upon the single-minded pursuit of the interests of the individual, the family and the 'clan', still dominate Italian 'civil society'. There is a basic paradox here: it is almost as if the Italian people prefer to deal with the stresses and strains of modern life without reference to a wider collectivity, as if the need to carry the burden of their institutions and leaders is not just expensive and uncongenial (as electorates may frequently feel in any part of the world), but an imposition upon them from without and from above which they would gladly throw off altogether.

As with any attempt at historical explanation of a current situation, inter-pretation cannot be dispensed with, even at the outset. A set of 'facts' cannot simply be deployed as the cause of a particular course of development, for

Map 1. Italy : Regions and Provinces.
After David Hine *Governing Italy: the Politics of Bargained Pluralism* (OUP, 1993), p. vii.

'facts' embody interpretations. Such a 'fact' is already contained in the concept of 'a process of modernisation', which is the basic question addressed by this book: how the people of the peninsula and islands called 'Italy' arrived, via a tortuous process of repeated crises punctuated by stagnation, at a point where, economically, they have outstripped other apparently better-endowed countries, including the United Kingdom, while indulging in at least one change of régime and 44 changes of government since 1943.[1] For the outside world, at least, 'Italy' is, in the 1990s, a political and economic reality to be reckoned with, despite all its contradictions. At the same time, it often seems almost as impervious to conventional political analysis as Japan, another recently fashioned constitutionally democratic nation-state, which shares Italy's peculiarity of never, apparently, being able or willing to practise democracy as an alternation of parties in power, however blatantly corrupt (and worse) its ruling party is proven to be.

As one of the two great political and cultural power-houses of the 'classical world', and as a centre of a self-aware population, Italy has a special place at the very origins of our continent's distinctiveness. To be thorough in a retrieval of its developmental path into modernity it would probably be necessary to trace out the whole of its history from the Roman Republic of classical times onwards, through the barbarian invasions, the centuries-long struggle between the Eastern Christendom of Byzantium and its Western rival based in Rome, the conflict between the latter and the Holy Roman Empire, and the dynastic wars between Normans, Hohenstaufens and Angevins for possession of the peninsula, its resources and its trade.

The social self-awareness of its populations, though formed over a considerably longer period, is not, however, essentially any older than that of the other distinct population groups of the European continent, and the lineages of contemporary Republican Italy as a polity may largely be found within the last two centuries. It therefore seems reasonable to take as our starting-point the moment in European history, between the eleventh and the fifteenth centuries, when some at least of the familiar nation-states of today first became recognisable units, and brought with them the relative political stability which was a condition for the emergence of the *homines novi*, the 'new men' who took the roles of adventurers, explorers, soldiers of fortune, but also capitalist bankers, manufacturers, traders, and even prelates and princes.

The process was slow, uneven and spasmodic, but in the Italian peninsula, which was then divided into five large and many small sovereign states constantly at odds or at war with each other and most of which were

---

1. The term 'modernisation' is used throughout this book to denote the historical development of the economic and political systems commonly assumed to be typical of the advanced industrialised world. The connotations of the term naturally vary greatly between its users, whether politicians, social scientists or historians, and for many of the latter it is a highly problematic concept.

subdivided into several smaller semi-autonomous mini-states frequently tempted or driven into rebellion, it was more rapid and generally more intensive than elsewhere in Europe. There were simply more opportunities available for the mixture of aristocratic attitudes and entrepreneurial skills which usually characterised the 'new man'. The situation was made even more complex by the presence in the peninsula of the Pope, spiritual leader of Christendom but also a great temporal prince in his own right, as the ruler of much of central Italy. Around the Papacy there was constant intrigue and unstable alliances were continually being formed between the supporters and the adversaries of the Papal power, both in the peninsula and further afield.

The diplomatic and military dimensions, although endlessly complicated by theological dispute and problems of princely succession, were historically the least significant aspect of the tensions and pressures which prevailed at all levels of the social structures in the states of Italy. It was not the constant ebb and flow of territorial boundaries nor the rise and fall of particular self-made princely houses which determined the economic success of the new capitalists, but the growing opportunities for trade in goods and financial services which, despite wars, plagues, piracy, crusades and persecutions, dominated the thoughts of the 'new men' from the time of Dante onwards. War and economic advantage often, in practice, went together: the Republics of the Genoese and Venetians in particular were able, by aggregating their skills in war, in navigation, in commerce and in banking to dominate the western and eastern basins of the Mediterranean.

Equally, however, 'new men ' without powerful states behind them, and often of humble social antecedents, were able not only to amass great fortunes, but also to rise in the social scale, to acquire by benefactions the approval of their fellow citizens, and even to become, by their economic success, politically powerful. The inhabitants of Lombardy gave their name to banking throughout Europe, pursuing the dangerous trade of lending money to monarchs. Perhaps more historically significant, however, was the success of men such as Francesco di Marco Datini, the 'Merchant of Prato', who, through the fortuitous survival of a massive archive of the fourteenth century ledgers (always headed 'In the name of God and of profit'), letters and contracts in which he preserved a complete record of his life and times, has become one of the most intimately accessible figures of the period when parts of Italy seemed to be anticipating a mercantile culture which was not to become general in the rest of Europe for centuries. Yet there is something unmistakably modern about him:

> avid for gain, determined to become rich, never satisfied with what he
> has acquired (a fortune which would seem substantial even in our own
> time), suspicious of his factors, his employees, his servants, his
> peasants, a dogged worker both by day and by night [...] irascible and
> imperious, he was also perpetually anxious, ever dreading that some

misfortune might fall upon him: any of his ships that was delayed might have been sunk or become the prey of the Saracens.[2]

What is particularly significant about men like Datini is their seeming imperviousness, in their working, gainful lives, to the pervasive teachings of the Church, whose vision of the meaning of the universe as the detailed working out of God's purposes in every human life reigned supreme, and which sternly forbade all forms of usury, enjoining the faithful to think ever of the life to come.

It was not that 'new men' such as Datini neglected religious observance, and even piety, nor that they did not care about their immortal souls: Datini was always troubled about his spiritual health. Yet though anxiety, 'the canker that ate all joy away', and which made them so much the precursors of our time, was never far from their thoughts, in material terms they very successfully lived double lives, reconciling the imperatives of both God and profit with apparent ease.[3] The model of behaviour and attitudes which can be discerned in them still continues to adapt itself to the changing circumstances of the Italian peninsula.

This admirable ability to come to terms with the contradictions between the spiritual and the material worlds appears well before the period usually referred to as the Italian Renaissance, which is generally dated from the mid-fifteenth century. Despite war, famine and plague, modern capitalism, or at least some of its principal attributes and attitudes, took root in the peninsula over a century earlier: in Dante's Florence, there were already large textile factories and a recognisable factory working class to go with them, as well as independent artisans, shopkeepers, merchants and bankers, while in the Po valley plain Europe's first system of canals and locks was already installed.

It can be said, in fact, that to a considerable extent the Renaissance, which in Italy was almost entirely an expression of secular and refined aristocratic values, was an attempted refeudalisation and ran counter to further development of technology and the reorganisation of production of the types specific to capitalism, which necessarily involved loosening the ties with agriculture of sectors of the population, technical rationalisation, the formation of investment capital and the freeing of markets. It is, of course, an open question whether, in the thirteenth and fourteenth centuries, the technical conditions for any further diffusion of the embryonic capitalism represented by men such as Datini were yet present either quantitatively or qualitatively, and the arrest of the processes by which they made their fortunes may not therefore have been inevitable. We need not, however, settle this rather hypothetical dispute before we can acknowledge that the economic changes which affected social structures and social attitudes in parts of the Italian peninsula between the

2. Luigi Einaudi, preface to the Italian edition of Iris Origo, *The Merchant of Prato*, Peregrine Books, Harmondsworth, 1963, p. 21.
3. Ibid. p. 12.

twelfth and fifteenth centuries, must have radiated to other parts of Europe and left permanent residues of unsatisfied aspiration to upwards mobility both at home and abroad.

Conventionally, the Renaissance in Italy is not characterised as a turning-point in economic and social history so much as in the realms of culture and ideas: it was the moment when the classical world of Greece and Rome were called in by scholars not, as it was in the medieval concept, to confirm the superiority of the Christian world-view, or at best as mere antecedents for the latter, but to question its subordination of this life to the next. *L'uomo è la misura di tutte le cose*, the phrase so often used to sum up the essence of Renaissance thinking, expresses not only the content but the method, being borrowed from Plato, who attributes it to a still earlier philosopher.[4] Later Italians were to look back upon the half-century down to 1492 as almost a golden age. This was especially so for Florentines, one of whom, writing amidst the troubles of the following century, recalled:

> The city was in perfect peace, the leading citizens were united, and their authority was so great that none dared to oppose them. The people were entertained daily with pageants and festivals; the food supply was abundant and all trades flourished. Talented and able men were assisted in their career by the recognition given to art and letters. While tranquillity reigned within her walls, externally the city enjoyed high honours and renown.[5]

That with the Renaissance there was indeed a justly celebrated flowering of all the arts and sciences, the former now profoundly influenced by models sought in the real, or imagined, classical world, and that artists and inventors in the Italian peninsula were setting the pace for all Europe, should not obscure the fact that the later part of the period saw the population of Italy subjected increasingly to war and pillage and its élite thrust back into conformist religiosity. From 1490 onwards the states of the peninsula were constantly invaded, or allied themselves with invaders, while their rulers sought to save themselves or to settle scores with their enemies.

The invaders came from all quarters, but the two most persistent were the French and the Spaniards (in unholy alliances with Germans and Swiss), both seeking to appropriate not only the rich spoils of what was then Europe's most prosperous and economically advanced area, but also the control of the centre of Christendom itself, the Papacy, in order to be able to deploy its ideological power in their own expansionist, dynastic cause. The Papacy itself

---

4. Plato, *Theaetatus*, 160d, Loeb, citing Protagoras; the usual English translation is 'Man the measure of all things'.
5. The writer was Francesco Guicciardini, whose *Storie fiorentine*, appeared in 1510, (cited in E. L. Scarano (ed.), *Francesco Guicciardini. Opere*, UTET, Turin, 1970, p. 98); also cited in H. Hearder and D.P. Waley, *A Short History of Italy*, Cambridge University Press, Cambridge, 1963, p. 85).

was in the hands of a succession of larger-than-life figures, of whom the best known was Alessandro Borgia. All the great cities of a country marvelled at as 'the land of a hundred cities' suffered in the conflicts which kept the whole peninsula in miserable turmoil for almost 70 years, and two of the greatest were subjected to unprecedented sieges and sack by the invading armies: Rome was looted, pillaged and half destroyed in 1527 by uncontrolled armies of German and Spanish troops, while Florence, where the ancient Republic had been briefly re-established, after a year's siege during which Michelangelo had acted as director of fortifications, underwent a similar fate at the behest of the Pope in 1529. By 1559, when a final settlement was reached between the warring parties, the only path for personal advancement for ambitious and talented inhabitants of the peninsula was to become trusted servants and agents of foreign rulers, or to make their fortune abroad as courtiers or *condottieri*.

For the next century and a half, with the partial exception of the ancient Republic of Venice, the peninsula declined from its former cultural pre-eminence to become a poverty-stricken backwater dominated by religious obscurantism and the Holy Inquisition. Even if men of huge talent still arose and made their contributions to world culture, nowhere was it possible to write and speak with the freedom of spirit which had characterised the three centuries from Dante to Machiavelli. It was no accident that Italy's greatest contribution to the arts in this period was in music, with the development of opera from the polyphony which had reigned in the Renaissance period. In architecture, too, great distinction was achieved in the period of the baroque. Only in the case of a great philosopher and a great scientist, did the Renaissance spirit of speculation and enquiry seem briefly to revive, but Giordano Bruno, who envisaged a plurality of worlds, was burnt at the stake, and Galileo Galilei, who confirmed the heliocentric system, was forced to recant.

The cultural decline was paralleled by a long economic immiseration, as the period of '*Spagna spugna*' ('Spain the sponge') dragged on. The economy of Italy was subordinated to the needs of the Spanish empire, which, despite its possession of the immense treasure houses of Latin America had, by the end of the sixteenth century, lost much of its vitality through reliance on the supply of precious metals from its colonies. Although Italy possessed none of these, its mainly subsistence agriculture was squeezed to the maximum to extract money-income for the local and Spanish exchequers, without the slightest consideration for any form of improvement. The population grew, and with it, hunger.

Although Spain remained the hegemonic power in the peninsula for almost two centuries, its control of Italy grew progressively less effective as its own military strength declined and the grandees who had taken lands and station there became, inevitably, more concerned with their own interests than with those of the world empire of which they were nominally a part. The decline of Spain, in Italy as elsewhere in the world, put temptation in the paths of the other major expansionist dynastic powers of the continent, the France of Louis XIV and the Turkey of the Ottomans. The fate of the Italians was once again to be settled by the struggle of rivals for their control. With the death of the last Spanish Habsburg king in 1700, the struggle became one between the huge heterogeneous Austrian empire and the French.

The vestigial independence of the remaining Italian-ruled components of Italy was further reduced in the course of this contest, the chief beneficiary being the Pope, but one of them, the half-Italian Duchy of Savoy led, exceptionally, by an able ruler, took the opportunity provided by its control of the Alpine passes from north and west to assert itself as an independent force in the area, with a redoubtable army of its own.

With the Treaty of Utrecht (1713) Italy's patchwork of historic states was used as a toy box of prizes to be distributed to reward the winners or console the losers, without regard to the wishes or interests of the inhabitants. Thus it was that, for example, Sicily was separated from Naples and assigned to the Duke of Savoy, who became its king for seven years before being forced to exchange it for the even less-developed and congenial island of Sardinia. The Sicilians now found themselves ruled by the less sympathetic Austrians, until the Spaniards returned in 1734 after the reconquest of Naples by Don Carlos, whose Bourbon kingdom was to last until it was overthrown by Garibaldi in 1860. That the Sicilians might be allowed to rule themselves did not occur to anyone.

The Spaniards, if little loved, were at least familiar rulers and the Sicilians might even have counted themselves relatively lucky compared with Italians in other parts of the peninsula who now found themselves under the heavy-handed Austrians, the ferocity of whose troops was legendary. A period of Teutonic rule began for some of the peninsula's most lively and enterprising populations which was to renew the traditional dislike of the 'barbarians from the north' inherited from medieval times and to become a dominating factor in popular attitudes for over two centuries.

Rule by Austrians continually reminded the inhabitants of Italy of how little independence they enjoyed and how little regard was had for their interests. Yet to the north, and particularly in Lombardy, it nevertheless brought, from the mid-eighteenth century onwards, benefits of rational administration and a tax system which encouraged intensive and profitable farming, which the Spaniards, after the Bourbon restoration in Naples and Sicily, completely failed to match, and which only one Pope (Pius VI, in the last 20 years of the century) ever sought, feebly, to imitate in his extensive, and increasingly centrifugal domains, now stretching from Bologna to include all of central Italy with the exception of Tuscany.

Under the Austrians the first coach road was opened over the Alps, linking Vienna directly to its north Italian domains, and to the states and statelets as far south as Florence which were ruled by relatives or protégés of the Habsburg dynasty. Free ports were opened all round the coast, from Trieste to Leghorn, enabling Italian agriculture to benefit from the period of exceptional European prosperity which marked much of the eighteenth century. One consequence was a rise in the price of land and a massive increase in the rural population (hand labour still comprising the basis of production), while the cities ceased to grow or even shrank.

It was in the relatively independent Grand Duchy of Tuscany that the improving trend of the rest of Europe, led by Holland and England, had the greatest impact across the whole political and social spectrum and the Enlightenment of the later eighteenth century produced what in many ways were its finest practical effects. When the Austrian Emperor's brother Leopold of Lorraine became its ruler in 1745, he brought with him much of the glow of that effort to 'cultivate the garden' of the world and embarked upon a series of reforms which made Tuscany in many ways the most civilised country in Europe: secret trials, torture and capital punishment were abolished, vaccination was introduced, the navy sold and the army disbanded. Leopold encouraged the great landowners to study the scientific principles of a rational agriculture, and to contribute to their application on their own estates, and in 1753 the peninsula's best-known and most influential society of scholar-improvers, the Florentine *Accademia dei Georgofili*, was created by them.[6] Equality of taxation based on a fair land-registration survey and the sequestration of incomes from vacant ecclesiastical offices were popular reforms.

Although for some decades the interest of the landowners was aroused by technical innovations and rationalisation of land use, their dominant preoccupation remained to keep the peasant class (which signified over 90 per cent of the population) in moral and economic subjection. This was achieved through refinements of the system of *mezzadria*, which was esteemed as much for its value as a method of social control as for that of being a productive system capable of generating marketable surpluses.[7]

Although the intellectual, and above all the literary-artistic life of Venice and Piedmont, the other two independent states in the peninsula with significant political and economic weight, were also touched by the Enlightenment and its values, here the rulers made no attempt to apply the principles of D'Alembert's *Encylopédie*, even though the whole vast bulk of its volumes was translated and published in Italy within a few years of their appearance in France, and quickly became extremely influential among the educated classes the length of the peninsula. Even in conditions of censorship, repression,

6. Sadly, this illustrious relic of the Enlightenment in Tuscany was demolished, and the 40,000 historic volumes of its library mostly destroyed, in the bomb-explosion of June 1993 which killed five people and also badly damaged the Uffizi gallery. At the time the bomb was attributed to the *mafia*, possibly acting on behalf of disgruntled southern politicians and/or in connivance with 'deviant' members of the intelligence services. A year later there were still no leads to the perpetrators.
7. *Mezzadria*, or share-cropping, became widespread in central and northern Italy from the twelfth century.

backwardness and ignorance, the intellectuals of the peninsula had themselves thrown up a whole succession of serious scientists, from Spallanzani and Algarotti to Volta, economists and historians from Genovesi to Muratori, Verri and Giannone, and philosophers, from Vico, whose *Scienza nuova* seems to anticipate Hegel and even Marx, to Beccaria, the theorist of penal reform.

The achievements of Venetian and Piedmontese thinkers, painters, architects and writers bore comparison with any of their time in Europe, from Canaletto, Tiepolo and Guardi to Denina, Goldoni and Alfieri, but, in diametrically opposed ways, the societies to which they belonged failed almost completely to rise to the challenges of the age. Venice continued to live almost entirely on its past glories, attracting visitors from all over Europe to its artistic treasure-house – and to the orgiastic and anarchic rituals of its legendary carnival. But its shrunken oligarchy of rulers were not inspired by visions of a dynamic future, they were merely terrified by them. They clung to the forms of the past in every respect: Venice's hinterland was kept without roads and deliberately divided into a series of economically watertight compartments, each with its own internal customs barriers designed to ensure that trade was only with the capital. Their foreign policy 'seemed to have no aim but to camouflage the existence of the Republic, and all their acts seemed dominated by [a] *terreur de l'avenir*' [dread of the future].[8]

Piedmont, in contrast with this picture of total decay of the political structure, had become the earliest example in the peninsula of a centralised, absolutist and aggressive state ruled by a predatory dynasty. Although Vittorio Amedeo II had guided his country through the War of the Spanish Succession as part of the alliance against Louis XIV, and Carlo Emanuele III, his successor had picked the winning side to join in two later wars of succession, leaving Piedmont in possession of considerable extensions to its territory, the royal model they adopted was that of Louis XIV, and not any anticipation of the 'Enlightened Despots' who ruled much of Europe, and parts of Italy, from the mid-century onwards. Piedmont was a strongly militarised state, its aristocracy brought to heel as great servants of the monarch, its rising middle class incorporated into a *noblesse de robe* of able administrators, and its population as a whole possessed of a sense of national identity which made it capable of disciplined and efficient action. As the century proceeded, dissent was first discouraged and then forcibly repressed, religious conformity enforced, censorship made so rigid that almost no hint of the tides of new thought running strongly elsewhere could here be sensed. The best and most original minds were driven into peevish exile, and Turin became 'the stolid barracks of Italy', as distinct in its intellectual climate from the rest of the peninsula as if it were at the other end of Europe. Even the shock of defeat and dismemberment by the armies and ideas of the French Revolution did not completely wipe out the

---

8. Giuliano Procacci, *A History of the Italian People*, Weidenfeld & Nicolson, London, 1970, p. 147.

deep social and cultural effects of this long-term experience of identity and autonomy, and in some respects may have reinforced the popular attachment to the values which they had generated. It was an apprenticeship that was to enable Piedmont to take the lead in the events of the next century which no other state in the peninsula, whatever its other endowments, could match.

There can thus be no question that, throughout the eighteenth century, national unification came well down the moral and political agenda of the educated minority of those living in the Italian peninsula. The main business of the *illuministi* (the term for those Italians who in the *età dei lumi* or Age of Enlightenment became intellectual converts to the rationalistic doctrines of the philosophers of north-west Europe, from Locke to Voltaire and from Adam Smith to the 'physiocrats') was, in their own opinion, to overcome prejudice, superstition and ignorance, for the 'light' by which they were guided was, precisely, that of reason. Insofar as they considered national sentiment at all (to speak of 'nationalism' would be anachronistic), they regarded it as one aspect of the forces of darkness against which their efforts were directed. In a real sense, their allegiance lay elsewhere: to concepts of mankind rather than to the tribes into which it was divided by history and custom.

By the mid-eighteenth century, in any case, with so many centuries experience of fragmentation under foreign rule, 'illuminated' Italians would have looked in vain for any realistic prospect of national unification brought about from within the peninsula.

At the same time, of course, they could not be unaware of the long rhetorical tradition in Italian literature, stemming from Petrarch, Italy's greatest poet after Dante, and from Machiavelli, which deplores the subjection of Italy to foreign conquerors, to the refrain of *fuori i barbari!* (out with the barbarians). Yet even this tradition did not point unequivocally to a concept of a united Italy – a single state ruled by a single sovereign power, but was, rather, a convention which permitted the poet or political theorist to promote the dominance of one existing source of secular or religious power within it, Petrarch favouring the Roman demagogue Cola di Rienzo, and Machiavelli the Spanish Pope's son Cesare Borgia. The outcome of these contradictory tendencies was, in the thinking and writing of the intellectual élite, a purely abstract concept of Italy embedded in a series of overwhelmingly particularistic regional cultures, almost all of them incorporating direct or indirect subservience to foreign power.

As for the non-intellectual mass of the population, its only allegiance beyond its immediate masters was to the vision of the universe offered by a highly conservative Church which, though decreasingly influential politically in the wider world, remained, for all the existing power-holders in the peninsula, an essential mechanism of social control of the peasantry upon which their own relative privilege depended. This cultural situation led to a new 'diaspora' of Italian intellectuals, artists and craftsmen, whose talents found a ready market in the more prosperous or more imperially ambitious capitals of the rest of Europe: St Petersburg, still one of the most handsome cities in the world, was almost entirely designed and adorned by architects and craftsmen brought from Italy, reviving a tradition going back to the fifteenth century, when two of the four cathedrals in the Kremlin had been designed by Italian architects.[9]

The Age of Reason was, of course, a notion in men's minds rather than a political and social reality. It was also an age of the maximum use of slaves and serfs, of meaningless dynastic wars, of institutionalised corruption, whether parliamentary or absolutist, of a large-scale re-entrenchment in most of Europe of aristocratic power and privilege: for good reason it was the greatest age of satire.

Although, as we have seen, the abstract concept of a dynastically-based national unification had been part of Italian literary culture since the Middle Ages, it had never seriously affected the policies and actions of the Italian states. Even when, late in the century, Italian intellectuals such as Pietro Verri started to promote the ideal of such a unified country more systematically, particularly through the production of 'advanced' journals such as *Il Caffè*, which electrified the Milanese élite in the 1780s, it was seen primarily as the consequence of catching up with, and imitating, the richer and more powerful European states: in Italy at this time, rationalism was the precondition of nationalism. 'Improvement' was thought to be possible within the existing framework of civil and political society and considered to be a preliminary to any attempt to go beyond it. The possibility would depend upon the breaking down of the existing obstacles to all forms of economic and cultural mobility (notably the free movement of goods, persons and ideas between the states of the peninsula).

In Italy, such 'enlightened' intellectuals believed, the essential reforms, whether political, economic or social, would have to come from above. By civilising the rulers, one would civilise their subjects, even if those absolute rulers who sympathised with the notion of 'reform' did so primarily because they wished to make the processes of administration more efficient, raise their revenue from taxation by adopting rational criteria and removing economic privileges from the aristocracy and the Church, enabling them, ultimately, to make their writ run more effectively.

In practice, Italy was most affected by 'enlightened despotism' in the areas directly ruled by the Habsburg Empire, or dependent upon it, and thus it was Lombardy, Parma, Modena, Lucca, and Tuscany which derived the greatest benefit from the tendency. The basic problem posed by this situation for Italian reformers such as Pietro Verri was that the Habsburg Empire was an essentially non-national state. Although the Habsburgs well realised that a condition of successful reform was a measure of recognition of regional identities, they sought to achieve this result by incorporating the non-Germanic

---

9. Ridolfo Fioravanti, a Bolognese, in 1479 designed the Uspensky Sobor (Cathedral of the Assumption); a second Kremlin cathedral was the work of the Milanese architect Alvesio Novy.

élites into their administrative and military bureaucracies rather than by encouraging the development of distinctive political institutions.

However great the benefits to its subjects achieved by the rationalisation of administrative and taxation systems, they were always offset by the inter-ethnic conflicts between the subject peoples of the Empire on which the latter's coercive power ultimately depended: the inhabitants of most of the economi-cally advanced parts of the peninsula thus found themselves under a military occupation whose agents were mostly Czechs, Slovaks, Croats and Hungarians enlisted in the imperial army, while Italians would find themselves serving the Empire in areas remote from Italy.

It became increasingly apparent to Italian reformers that the outcome of collaboration with Habsburg despots, however enlightened, would be a per-manent compression of a specifically Italian identity rather than a gradual evolution towards political autonomy and self-reliance. Moreover, much of the benefit of agricultural improvement and tax reform would be siphoned off to maintain the splendour and extravagance of the imperial court in Vienna.

Yet any appeal to popular discontent among the minority of urban craftsmen and the vast majority of poor peasants was out of the question, since these were largely under the sway of conservative social forces (the landed gentry and the priesthood) determined to resist reform from any quarter, while the middle classes of merchants, manufacturers and independent farmers were far too few in numbers, too divided in ideas and loyalties, and too afraid of social turmoil which might disrupt a highly and rigidly stratified society, to become the focus of an effective campaign for political autonomy at regional level, and still less at a national level which was still a pure abstraction.

Thus the prospects for any far-reaching assertion of Italian identity in any form were clouded by the objective conditions of division and subordina-tion even in those parts of the peninsula where economic rationalisation, with its encouragement of native enterprise and self-awarenenss, had been most effective.

Into this essentially stalemated situation burst the ideas of the French Revolution, the ideas first of 1789, and then the more extreme version of 1792. Not far behind the ideas, and the ferment they brought to men's minds, came the armies of a conquest differing radically from those of Spain and Austria in previous centuries, for the armies of Napoleon Bonaparte, whether he was Consul or Emperor, were as much agents of social as of military and political change. Northern Italy was among the first areas to come within the range of the unprecedented combination of military and ideological power represented by the French 'nation in arms'. It is also worth noting that Napoleon's interest in Italy was not merely that of a French invading general, later emperor: he was himself a native of an island, Corsica, where Italian was the common tongue, and his own early political universe had been that of the passionate struggle for liberty of Pasquale Paoli, which had made the latter one of the most popular figures in Italy. Corsica had become French and was sharing in the Revolution, but it was still an Italian land by language and tradition:

Figure 1.1 The 'Nation in Arms' exemplified for Italians: Napoleon enters Milan at the head of the armies of the French Republic.
(GIR63427) The Entry of the French into Milan, 25 floreal, 4 Annee (May 15th 1796) after A C H Vernet (1758–1836).

---

what more natural, then, than to bring all three elements together in Italy?

For the next 20 years, from the first French invasion in 1794 until the downfall of Napoleon in 1815, the north and centre once more became a theatre of battle for every warring army but Italy's own – for none existed.

By the autumn of 1798 the map of Italy, with the exception of the islands and Venetia, showed it to be entirely under French control, directly by annexation or occupation, or indirectly by a French puppet government (the Ligurian Republic based on Genoa, the Cisapline Republic, comprising Lombardy, and Emilia-Romagna, and the French-dominated Duchies of Parma and Lucca). But the following spring a Russian army dislodged them all, except in Genoa, while Napoleon was marooned in Egypt after Nelson's destruction of his fleet at the Battle of the Nile. It took him just a year to set out on his next Italian campaign, during which he reconquered most of the north and centre, large portions of which were formally made part of the French Empire when Napoleon proclaimed himself emperor in 1804. Two years later the French seized Venice (adding it to the Cisalpine Republic, now renamed the Kingdom of Italy) and settled their score with the Bourbons, installing successive relatives of the Emperor as Kings of Naples, where their reign was, strangely, long remembered as a kind of golden age.

The last act of this melodramatic period was the collapse of the whole artificial fabric constructed by Napoleon. With his defeats in Russia and at

Leipzig, the relatives whom he had installed as rulers of the Kingdoms of Italy and Naples vainly sought ways to survive without him, should it prove necessary, by making deals with the Allies. Neither of them dared to risk seeking the support of their subjects through constitutional means.

Just as eagerly as Italy's reform-minded intellectuals had welcomed and propagated the French-led Enlightenment, they rallied to the cause, and absorbed the outlook, of the French Revolution, which in its initial stages seemed to promise the full implementation of the ideals of the Age of Reason. Although this promise was in reality quickly dashed, as Robespierre's attempt to enthrone his version of 'Reason' ended in his own death by 'Madame Guillotine', the power of the Revolution to attract a whole generation of European intellectuals previously stifled by whatever form of the *ancien régime* had frustrated their commitment to political and social improvement, scarcely waned as the armies of the Consulate, the Directory and ultimately the Empire of France defeated those of all the powers ranged against them in the cause of restoration, and then began to fill the vacuum left wherever the old régime had crumbled.

Despite the doubts of the older devotees of Enlightenment such as Pietro Verri who wrote that 'We are immature and not yet worthy to live under the reign of Virtue', a younger generation of enthusiasts for liberty, equality and fraternity, whose favourite reading was the works of Jean-Jacques Rousseau, and who gladly called themselves *giacobini* in imitation of the French Jacobins, quickly appeared in every part of the peninsula, conspiring with the French representatives (and often subsidised by them) to bring the Revolution to their own lands. The first of these was archetypal: a descendant of Michelangelo called Filippo Buonarroti, he moved from Pisa to Corsica to publish a periodical entitled *Il giornale patriottico* as the mouthpiece of his Jacobin convictions and four years later he was appointed Commissioner of the French Republic in part of occupied Italy.[10] In 1794–95 there were attempts to overthrow established authority in Bologna, Palermo and Sardinia. Their young leaders, often students in their early twenties, were quickly caught and executed, for their fervour was only matched by their lack of any sense of the real possibilities for social change that could exist within a population of peasants and urban poor so fragmented, so accustomed to priestly and aristocratic rule and so culturally impervious to any form of communication that this tiny, city-bound élite of zealots could possibly direct to them.

There is no doubt, however, that the latent energies of this mass could indeed be aroused. But it was not the Tree of Liberty, by which the Paris mob and their Jacobin leaders had symbolised their conquests, that was to take root in the fertile soil of the millenarianism which always underlay both its long

---

10. Buonarroti later fell foul of the French Thermidorians and after a period in prison joined the Conspiracy of the Equals of François-Émile Babeuf, from which he graduated to *carboneria* and *Giovane Italia*.

patience and its sudden anger. The peasant and bandit armies led by Cardinal Ruffo and Fra Diavolo from Calabria to the reconquest of Naples for the Bourbons in 1799, only five months after the Parthenopean Republic had been declared, and the 'Army of Arezzo' of the 'Maid of Valdarno', whose members believed they were commanded by a saint and a madonna, massacred Jews, Freemasons and *giacobini* mercilessly, to the war-cry of 'Viva Maria': these were the popular forces which came to the surface when the old order faltered, and which brought to Italy 'a *Vendée* without [...] a genuine revolution'.[11] It was a revelation which was to recur, and still be ignored by the élite and its political class, for a further century and a half.

Other revelations, during this time of troubles for the peoples of the Italian peninsula, and equally indicative for the future, were the vindictiveness exhibited by the old rulers whenever they were restored, and their dependence on support by foreign powers whose interest in Italy was usually less than altruistic. In Naples, 'the flower of Neapolitan virtue and intellect' was hanged, shot, sent to the galleys or exiled by the King and Queen who had returned with their ally against the French, Nelson: their leader, Admiral Francesco Caracciolo was hanged from the yard-arm of the English flagship.

Italy's experience during the period was traumatic from every point of view. Long-established authority was swept aside and replaced by manufactured republics and kingdoms whose only *raison d'être* was the pursuit of French national or Napoleon Bonaparte's dynastic interests. Moreover:

> The brutality and irreligion of the soldiery, the spoliation of the treasures of art which the French *savants* carried out with such zeal and thoroughness, were only equalled by the insatiable rapacity of the civil and financial experts who followed the victorious army and descended like vultures upon each prostrate government in turn.[12]

The financial and fiscal policies of all the governments in fact remained geared to the needs of the French war machine and the policy of continental blockade against England: in the Kingdom of Italy alone, in 1802, 60 per cent of revenue went to military expenditure by the French, although Europe had been at peace for a year.

Yet French, or French-dominated, rule was not without its benefits, both direct and paradoxical. The 14-year period of Napoleonic government, with blanket imposition of French administrative structures (the system of *départements*) and civil law (the *Code Napoléon*), the radical simplification of taxation and internal and external customs barriers, the stimulation to large areas of manufacturing of the insatiable demand for military supplies and the effects on popular consciousness of universal military service in a modern and successful army made it possible for a larger proportion of the middle and

---

11. Giuliano Procacci, *A History of the Italian People*, p. 261.
12. H. Hearder and D. P. Waley, *A Short History of Italy*, p. 115.

upper classes to envisage an Italy constituted as a nation-state comparable to those which had for centuries dominated it by force or the threat of force. The construction of such a nation-state for the first time appeared a concrete rather than a merely abstract prospect even if at this time there was not even the hint of a consensus on how such a goal might be achieved. It was not unjustified that perhaps the finest ode upon the death of Napoleon Bonaparte in 1821 was penned by one of Italy's greatest writers of the century, Alessandro Manzoni, who with historical justification saw him as a figure whose presence in the world had left it radically and irreversibly changed.[13]

Much of the latent intellectual and political energy that had for so long remained unused in the élites of the peninsula now began to be channelled in this direction, but the process was far from unproblematic. The complications of the diverse historical formations within Italy to some extent explain this: the long-term tensions between regions and sub-regions, between north and south, between town and country, could not be reduced by attempts to focus attention on a political aim still totally incomprehensible to the socially archaic mass of the population. The latter, especially the peasantry, had indeed been mobilised, as we have seen, during the Napoleonic period, but at a different level of cultural and political awareness, and in the cause of counter-revolution. To harness the two forms of energy in the same cause was to prove an insoluble problem for many generations to come.

The only level at which the aspirations of the élites and the masses were linked was their resentment of the French and all those who had been their willing tools. The systematic rapacity and brutality of Napoleonic rule had quickly discredited the *giacobini* and disillusion was followed by resentment and by passive resistance to the swingeing taxation, conscription and summary requisitions which characterised it. After Napoleon's defeats in 1812–15, there was general acceptance of the idea of a Restoration as the guarantee that French domination was ended for ever. Despite Metternich's scornful dismissal of Italy as a mere 'geographical expression', there was far less acceptance, among the educated fraction of the population, of the reimposition of the irrational mosaic of the pre-1795 Italian states, with its unequivocal consequences of permanent economic and political subordination to the Great Powers of northern and central Europe.

The change that had occurred was most sharply highlighted by the new attitude to Habsburg rule of the intellectuals, and the professional and middle classes in general, of those areas most directly subject to Vienna after 1815 (Lombardy, Venetia, Emilia-Romagna and Tuscany). Whereas they had eagerly cooperated with the Habsburg 'enlightened despots' Maria Theresa and Joseph II, their opposition to Austrian rule and influence was now virtually

---

13. Alessandro Manzoni, author of the classic historical novel, *The Betrothed*, was also a notable poet; his ode upon the news of Napoleon's death 'Il 21 marzo, 1821' is perhaps the nearest in any language to a fitting tribute to his career.

universal and was reflected in the proliferation of secret sects and conspiratorial societies, such as the *Carbonari* in the south, the *Federati* and the *Adelfi* in the north, and even stranger organisations in the Papal State, whose purpose, however confusingly expressed in blood-curdling oaths and elaborate initiations, was to drive the foreigner from 'Italian' soil.

Although opposition to the Restoration in northern Italy was almost universal among the educated, the educated remained a tiny minority of the population and hostility to foreign rule was the only unifying factor: ex-*giacobini*, ex-Bonapartists, supporters of the Papacy's temporal power, romantics and rationalists could not possibly agree on any positive programme of action, let alone a political strategy. Their attempts over the next 15 years to overthrow restored legitimist rulers were uncoordinated. Though amateurish conspiracies proliferated, they were always put down easily by Austrian or local troops. Justly celebrated in grand opera by composers from Verdi to Puccini, their martyred heroes achieved none of their declared aims, merely providing fodder for the executioners and gaolers.

Martyrs were, nevertheless, precisely what was needed to nourish the idealism of the younger generation which had not lived through the stirring times of the French revolutionary epoch nor thrilled to the mould-breaking conquest of Napoleon. An intense, though generic, national sentiment was also fostered by the literary movements of the time, in which the influence of German romantic nationalism was strongly present. But although this amalgam of national sentiment and popular resentment of foreign rule came to dominate Italian high culture, it remained, in relation to the general population, a minority phenomenon, and if the Quadruple Alliance of the Great Powers which had imposed the restoration upon Italy had not, after the Whig victory in the English parliamentary elections of 1832, started to crumble, Italy's road to national independence might have been even longer than it proved to be.

The 'classic' conditions for social, as opposed to political, revolution were by no means present. Much of the peninsula was still almost totally pre-modern in economic terms: fields were tilled with wooden ploughs, epidemic diseases such as typhus and cholera frequently decimated the population of the towns, few of which possessed even a rudimentary sewage system or supply of clean water. In the countryside, especially in the remoter parts, even a wheeled cart was a novelty.

Popular mentalities were in harmony with the state of economic development and social conditions. The great majority of the population lived on the land, largely outside the money economy, and permanently on the verge of starvation: the only possible way for the mass of the people to accumulate the wealth to move upwards in the social hierarchy was, literally, to practise highway robbery (and its practitioners rarely survived long enough to invest their gains in property, even if they could have escaped notice when doing so). The rural social hierarchy itself was steeply pyramidical and rigidly exclusive

Figure 1.2   The archetypal peasant extended family of nineteenth-century Italy.

of mobility from below. In the towns, most manufacture was strictly controlled by artisan guilds which were difficult to penetrate by outsiders. It was no accident that, as an increasing number of lower-class women were driven into menial work in order to supplement family incomes, the number of babies abandoned at foundling homes almost doubled in some large towns.[14] The strategic safety-valve of emigration as yet scarcely existed. The mechanisms of social control by brutal repression on the one hand and religious terror and consolation on the other were everywhere effective enough to maintain social order whatever the degree of popular suffering and deprivation.

The great majority of the peninsula's inhabitants were thus permanently trapped at the socio-economic level into which they were born, most commonly in forms of economic subsistence activities: agriculture, primitively equipped extractive industries, precarious fishing for restricted local markets. Most were usually near the boundary between survival and total penury, with all the penalties upon health, life-expectancy, personal autonomy and social mobility implied thereby. They were profoundly ignorant of the world beyond the bounds of their parish, and the folk wisdoms to which they had access and which comprised a rich store of survival stratagems, legitimated endurance

---

14. Cf. Marzio Barbagli, 'Marriage and the family in Italy', in John A. Davis and Paul Ginsborg (eds), *Society and Politics in the Age of the Risorgimento*, Cambridge University Press, Cambridge, 1991, pp. 122–7.

rather than rebellion. Their condition of poverty and cultural deprivation did not, therefore, of itself lead to much popular sympathy for the ideals and idealists who preached the cause of Italian nationhood.

This lack of response among the oppressed masses was not only due to the heavy repressive apparatus of their rulers, whether Austrian, Papal or Bourbon, nor only to the life-long psychological pressure exerted by the Church, but it also reflected the wide difference in the models of the 'good life' entrenched in the various popular cultures. The peasantry, in whichever of the forms of inescapable economic bondage its members found themselves (varying from *mezzadria* in the north and centre to day-labouring on the great estates of the south), had a pre-political vision of peace, plenty and justice dispensed by a benevolent and absolute ruler, whose nationality was simply irrelevant. When driven to desperation they had recourse not to revolution but to a vengeful banditry.[15] Their consolations were those of heartfelt observance of the rites of religion and the community of family, clan and locality. The urban poor of pre-industrial towns such as Naples had these, and also a limited measure of access to the takings of organised crime. Neither category could be regarded as readily aroused for a social revolution, far less for a mere rotation of authority in the name of a, to them, largely meaningless national entity.

The traditional middle class of the pre-*Risorgimento* states consisted of the small minority, mainly town-dwelling, of professional men and other caterers to the needs and tastes of the wealthy: lawyers, apothecaries, doctors, shopkeepers, and independent artisans working, often on commission, for the propertied class. They had little or no economic motivation to risk their comfortable livelihoods, and their political interests were in order and stability. The only sub-categories of the middle classes who could be stirred by thoughts of national unity and independence were the minority of natural adventurers: younger sons without prospects, students, frustrated young officers with no wars to fight, and above all by the increasingly numerous class of men with professional qualifications who were excluded from careers in public administration and the law by the policy or whim of their absolutist rulers.[16]

The majority of those who joined the conspiratorial forms of Italian nationalism of 1817–31, when revolutions were attempted successively in the Marches, Sicily, Piedmont, Bologna, the Papal State and Modena were thus not the materially oppressed, but came from the most enlightened families of the aristocracy and the 'middle orders'. After the tragic failures of their

---

15. 'Ah, Sirs! If I'd known how to read and write, I'd have exterminated the human race', was how one bandit expressed his motivation as he was about to be executed (cited in F. Molfese, *Storia del brigantaggio dopo l'Unità*, Feltrinelli, Milan, 1964, p. 132).

16. In the areas ruled by Austria, many salaried posts, particularly in the judiciary and the police, were reserved for non-Italian subjects of the Emperor, while in the still semi-feudal south, they could only be obtained by personal petition to the ruler, with rare success by those outside the 'magic circle' of the already privileged. Cf. Adrian Lyttleton, 'The middle classes in Italy', John A. Davis and Paul Ginsborg (eds), *Society and Politics in the Age of the Risorgimento*, pp. 217–50.

attempts, thousands of the best and brightest of this Italian élite were executed, flogged, gaoled or exiled. Inspired by this example of sacrifice, a new generation of would-be revolutionaries came to the fore, led by Italy's 'greatest patriot', Giuseppe Mazzini.

The son of a Genoese doctor, he was a *Carbonaro* at an early age, but he quickly became alienated from the melodramatic rituals and rhetoric which were *Carboneria*'s stock in trade. Exiled to Marseilles, with a few companions as youthful as himself, he founded a new patriotic society entitled *Giovane Italia* (Young Italy), specifically limited to those under 40 years of age, and embarked upon a lifetime of revolutionary and nationalist agitation, conspiracy and rebellion, much of which he spent in hiding, under arrest or in exile.

Mazzini was the first and perhaps the most influential of the strategists of the *Risorgimento*, as the movement for Italian independence and unity came to be called. His strategy was never practical, but at least it was consistent and based upon a philosophical rather than a merely sentimental conviction of the necessity for the creation of a nation-state in the peninsula. The phrase in which he encapsulated his doctrine was 'Thought and Action', meaning political education leading to rebellion, in the cause not only of the traditional aims of liberty and independence from foreign and domestic oppression, but also of Italian unity, a far more problematic concept in the circumstances of the time. To his contemporaries, his programme proved to be immensely influential and persuasive, at least to the extent that it polarised opinion and crystallised it around certain key issues.

At the same time, however, Mazzini's approach was so lacking in political pragmatism and so wrapped in cloudy notions of Italian primacy that it often disabled his followers from deciding upon practical action while providing his enemies and detractors with ample scope for dismissing him as a dangerous agitator, and the police with regular opportunities to penetrate and defeat his conspiracies, with severe consequences for his followers.

His impracticality was compounded by his intransigent republicanism, based on a total commitment to the ideals of 1789, which, though it may have anticipated the Italian settlement of 1946, was wholly inappropriate in the circumstances of the country's nineteenth-century political and ideological configuration. He also had, and inspired in his followers, a quasi-religious faith in the 'mission' of Italy to free itself and to set an example thereby to all oppressed nations. Although (despite a few clumsy attempts by the King during the 1860s to manipulate his movement for his own ends) Mazzini's tactics remained to the end those of conspiracy and insurrection in the name of overthrowing tyranny, he also appreciated the importance of creating a unified climate of opinion which favoured radical change. From the moment in 1831 when he founded *Giovane Italia*, he was concerned to create what he termed an 'apostolate' which would propagate as openly as conditions allowed an explicitly Italian national doctrine, based on that 'unity of religion, language

Figure 1.3 A glimpse of the 'social question': a shackled inmate of a lunatic asylum in Venice, 1886.

and customs' which distinguished each nation from all others and conferred a specific national character on all its inhabitants.

His approach differed most significantly from that of the *Carbonari* in that it hinged upon an appeal to 'the people', and he bitterly criticised the revolutionaries who had preceded him for their narrowly 'aristocratic' concept of revolution from above, and for their distrust of the 'people'. The two concepts of 'the people' certainly differed greatly, although the *Carbonari* had reason enough to distrust 'the people' of the Papal State whose addiction to the cause of *Sanfedismo* (in effect the vigilantes of the Pope) had led to the murder of many among them. Mazzini was, in any case, himself quite inconsistent about the role of the people in his strategy for revolution. While his aim was to create, through the work of the 'apostolate', an explosive political atmosphere whose energy would be released by the insurrectionary gesture of a select band of determined revolutionary activists, and while he accepted that this concept implied that for his movement to succeed it would have to find a way to exploit the political potential of the 'social question', or the fundamental economic injustice of existing society, he resolutely refused to include in his programme any promise of redistribution of the land, the issue precisely which was at the root of the social question, and bitterly denounced the advocates of class war. For Mazzini, all Italians, irrespective of class and property, were impoverished and oppressed, and all were therefore included in his amorphous notion of 'the people'.

In practice, this attitude made it impossible realistically to tap the revolutionary potential of the peasantry, which formed the vast majority of the population. But in this imprisoning rhetoric there also appears the starting-point of an ambiguously left-wing radical position which, with the *nazionalisti* and the Fascists in the next century, came to define Italy as a 'proletarian nation' whose woes and backwardness were all attributable to the denial by other nations of Italy's rightful share of the world's wealth.

Mazzini's movement was the first truly political one in Italian history, providing an example of single-minded self-sacrifice in the cause of revolutionary nationalism, but it was essentially impractical and unproductive in the conditions of the time and during a lifetime of conspiracy all his attempts at insurrection failed ignominiously. A series of such abortive attempts in 1833–34 and the subsequent repression led Mazzini to report, by February 1836, the break-up of *Giovane Italia*, and this was followed by his own flight to 11 years of exile in London.

It was not long, however, before two other political strategies for the achievement of liberty, independence and unity were being proposed, both of much greater influence on the actual course of the events which led to 'the making of Italy' in the critical period 1848–60.

The two approaches had in common the beliefs that, firstly, Italy already possessed a natural basis for, and potential leadership of, the movement for independence and unity, and secondly, that the movement could only succeed if some at least of the major powers of Europe took a benevolent attitude towards it. They differed substantially, however, in their analysis of the specific constraints and optimum policies in relation to both and gave conflicting answers to the practical questions of which Prince in the existing Italian states should be the standard-bearer and chief organiser of the struggle, and which of the European powers were more likely to assist the movement to achieve its goals.

The so-called neo-Guelph policy (indicating that it hinged upon the role of the Papacy, the Guelphs having been the Papal faction in the Middle Ages), was based on the ideas put forward by the Piedmontese politician Vincenzo Gioberti in his *Of the Moral and Civil Primacy of the Italians*, first published in 1843. The essence of Gioberti's proposal, which was taken up enthusiastically by wide sectors of the educated classes, was to bring about a confederal union of the existing Italian states, under the chairmanship of the Pope, with Piedmont, the only truly sovereign state in the peninsula and the only one with a tradition of serious military power, acting as its principal defender. Austria would, it was hoped, accept compensation for the loss of its Italian provinces in the form of further territorial gains at the expense of the declining Turkish Empire which still extended over most of the Balkan peninsula.

This was a fundamentally impractical strategy, for none of the protagonists round which it revolved were remotely willing to accept the roles assigned them: the Papacy was much more interested in retaining or recovering its influence outside Italy than within it, and the Papal State was in any case the most backward region of the peninsula, while Austria had no intention of giving up the rich provinces of Lombardy and Venetia for problematic gains in the poverty-stricken Slav lands. As for the great mass of peasants, whose main concern, however primitively expressed, was the 'social question', the project had little appeal, since the existing rulers of Italy had no incentive to compromise on the crucial issues of economic justice for the landless underclass.

One feature of the strategy did, however, make more political sense: the reliance for military power on the one state which possessed it, the Kingdom of Savoy, for it was self-evident that no nation-state could be created without the capacity to win its independence by force of arms if necessary, and then defend it. The same consideration was at the heart of the second strategy whose concept now developed among the politically aware. Initially no more than a Piedmontese group within the neo-Guelph current of opinion, the so-called *moderati* were mainly practical men with administrative experience and a keen sense of the real constraints which were likely to bear down upon the economic and political process of unification. It was no accident that the first intervention in political debate of the man who was to become the main architect of unity, Count Camillo Benso di Cavour, was about the benefits of railway construction:

> If the future has in store for Italy a happier fate, if, as one may hope, this fair land is destined to recover its nationhood one day, it can only be as the result of a new European settlement or as the outcome of one of those great upheavals, of those events which to some extent are providential, upon which the ability to move a few regiments with more despatch which railways might afford us could have no influence.[17]

---

17. Cited in Giuliano Procacci, *History of the Italian People*, p. 287.

Such cautious pragmatism was unlikely to enthuse many while Gioberti's grand design swept all before it during the 1840s, appearing in 1846–47 even to have found the Papal champion it needed in the newly-elected Pope Pius IX, who almost miraculously, seemed to fit the neo-Guelph prescription for a reforming and activist role of the Papacy in a controlled political reordering of Italy.

A wave of expectation swept every state in the peninsula: reforms, modelled on the French constitutional monarchy of 1831 but less sweeping, were granted everywhere except the Kingdom of Naples, and in January 1848 the population of Palermo rose in revolt to demand autonomy for Sicily. The Bourbon garrison was expelled and the King conceded a constitution. But this was only the beginning of much more dramatic events: in February 1848, a Republic was proclaimed in Paris, and by mid-March rebellions had broken out in Hungary and Austria itself. Within a few weeks the legitimist order created throughout Europe by the post-Napoleonic settlement of 1815, and maintained for over 30 years by the Habsburg Empire, had finally crumbled, apparently beyond recall.

Thus in 1848, only two years after Cavour had penned his prophetic words there occurred precisely one of those great upheavals which he had seen as a possible key to the problem. In that *annus mirabilis* of revolution, when, with the exception of Russia, the whole of Europe from Berlin to Palermo erupted in political, social and national rebellions against the existing order, Italy went through particularly traumatic experiences of turmoil, repression and invasion. The dangerous vacuum of power created in Italy by these events gave both the revolutionaries and the *moderati* among Italian nationalists an unparalleled opportunity to put their theories into practice, with universally disastrous results.

After this, however, the moment came when the natural path to Italian independence and unity seemed inevitably to pass through a step-by-step absorption by Piedmont of other parts of Italy, for after the débâcle, as we shall see, it was the only state with a native royal house, an effective army, and some diplomatic weight in Europe, even if its king was to be forced to abdicate to avoid the military occupation of his country. The way that this first war of the *Risorgimento* began, the direction it took and the options it left for those who were striving for Italian unity, were to have profound consequences for the further course of Italian history.

The making of Italy by diplomacy, politics and war

It was the year 1848 when Karl Marx and Friedrich Engels published the *Communist Manifesto* in which they proclaimed that the historical moment had arrived for the revolution of the proletariat and the overthrow of the capitalist system and the bourgeois state, declaring the latter to be 'no longer compatible with society'. Yet the revolutions which spread through much of Europe in that year and the next resembled much more the events of 1789 than they anticipated those of 1917. Outside England a recognisable 'proletariat' could hardly be said to exist anywhere in Europe, and nowhere did it yet form a majority of the population of a country. A few large cities such as Paris, Naples and Vienna contained hundreds of thousands of the classic 'urban poor' who could usually be counted upon to take to the streets when their chronic desperation was sufficiently exacerbated by a worsening of their economic conditions and by appropriate demagoguery, but the political awareness of the great majority of the population, even in the most economically advanced countries was still rooted in an archaic imagery of retributive justice against tyrants rather than being a reflection of a programme for the transformation of the existing social and economic order into something qualitatively superior. The exploited class in every country except England was still predominantly the peasantry, whose capacity for rebellion could never be overlooked but which was still far from being culturally prepared to understand and apply the message of the *Communist Manifesto*.

It is equally questionable whether the underlying impulse to the revolutions of 1848 came from the class, the bourgeoisie, which the authors of that pamphlet somewhat prematurely thought had already exhausted its historical function. On the contrary, despite the fact that by the mid-century the middle classes in a few parts of Europe had become the most economically powerful group in society, there was little evidence that they were also politically ready and motivated to conceive and mount a substantial challenge to the dynastic political systems reimposed in the aftermath of the Napoleonic adventure. In the event, the leadership of the attempts, in 1848 and later, in Western and Southern Europe to overthrow the existing political order was provided by small groups of idealistic intellectuals, many with aristocratic rather than bourgeois connections, overwhelmingly concerned with the agenda of national independence rather than that of social upheaval. Even in France, the supposed heartland of the triumphant bourgeoisie and the hotbed of socialist agitation, the outcome of the French Revolution was not the triumph of the manufacturing and commercial classes over the landowning interests. Still less was it the victory of the proletariat. Rather it amounted to the reassertion, for the span of another generation, of the curious blend of populism and autocracy invented by the first Napoleon and now imitated, albeit with less bravura, by his nephew, Louis Napoleon, first as President of the Second French Republic, and then, after his *coup d'état* of 1851, as Emperor. Paradoxically, a decade later, he was to become one of the protagonists of the unification of Italy.

The point is made in another way by the course of events in Italy itself during what is usually termed the 'First War of the *Risorgimento*'. The protagonists of this politically muddled, militarily disastrous and economically counter-productive display of idealism and heroism were the small élite of revolutionary-romantic intellectuals which had been formed in the great debate of the previous years about the strategy for achieving national unification. Popular involvement, though genuine enough where it occurred, was confined to the conscripts sent by Piedmont and the other Italian States and the populace of the cities under siege. It scarcely touched the mass of the peasants, although some of them helped the fleeing remnants of what they always called the 'rebels' to survive, nor was it promoted by the small emergent class of entrepreneurs, although many of them certainly hoped to gain by any success of the movement.

Even if it had been the case that industrialisation might be the proximate cause of social revolution, in Italy the phenomenon was still so patchy, and so limited in its political influence, that the bourgeoisie's immediate agenda was one of mere survival against the more rapidly industrialising competition in England, France and Germany.

Such temporary successes as the sporadic uprisings throughout the Italian peninsula did achieve were at least as much due to the temporary eclipse of the Habsburg empire, busy contending with rebellions in Vienna and Budapest, as they were to any real military impact made by Italians in arms. For over a year and a half, between January 1848 and August 1849, in every state in the peninsula, whether directly ruled by Austria or not, rebellion was followed by ugly repression and the harsh restoration of Austrian dominance or its satellite governments. There was no lack of heroic ardour, but all the real sinews of war were missing on the Italian side. Military incompetence was everywhere compounded by ideological confusion, and the only relatively hard-headed political vision for a viable convergence of the states of Italy which would not hold back the progress of the industrialising north, the federalist plan advanced by the Milanese philosopher Carlo Cattaneo, was howled down by the clamour

SWITZERLAND AUSTRIA-HUNGARY

SAVOY

K

LOMBARDY

VENETIA

Po R. • Milan

Padua • Trieste

Verona

Turin

Venice • Fiume

PIEDMONT PARMA

R. Po

Genoa

• Ferrara

Bologna • Comacchio

MODENA

ROMAGNA • Ravenna

Nice

San Marino

i n g d o m o f

Florence •

Pisa

A D R I A T I C

D A L M A T I A

Venetian ○ *Territory*

TUSCANY Urbino

• Ancona

(PIEDMONT)

Siena

MARCHES • Castelfidardo

Elba

PAPAL

STATES

S E A

CORSICA

(France)

UMBRIA

Rome •

S a r d i n i a

N

Gaeta

A

Naples • ◌ BENEVENTO

(Papal State)

• Bari

P

SARDINIA

L

TYRRHENIAN

SEA

E

**Kingdom
of the
Two Sicilies
1860**

S

Palermo

▲ Aspromonte

• Calatafimi

SICILY

MEDITERRANEAN SEA

0   50   100

miles

Map 2. Italy at the time of Unification.
       After J M Scott *Italy* (Ernest Benn, 1967), p. 49.

for unity at all costs. It is hardly surprising that 'making an 1848' remained in the popular mind principally as a phrase used to describe a situation of total chaos and confusion: *'fare un quarantotto'*.

The spark that ignited the powder-keg came, paradoxically, from the election of a little-favoured candidate for election to the Papacy after the death of the reactionary Gregory XVI in 1846: a stalemate between another reactionary and a more liberal candidate much favoured by the Roman populace led the conclave to the compromise election of the little-known and decidedly uncharismatic Cardinal Giovanni Mastai-Ferretti, who took the name of Pius IX. Without ever intending to do so, this Pope was to become first the reluctant standard-bearer of the movement for a unified Italian state, and then, in the perception of its rulers, the greatest single threat to its survival.

A month after his election, Pius declared the customary amnesty to political prisoners. It was seized upon by those made expectant by the Giobertian vision of a confederal Italy unified under the auspices of a reforming Pope which had gained such currency in the mid-1840s. As the news of the amnesty spread, demonstrations of wild enthusiasm spread across the peninsula, and even the Mazzinians, convinced that Pius could only disappoint the false hopes his accession had aroused, not only joined in the celebrations, but organised more, inserting political demands into the cries of the crowds. Pius, half flattered and half intimidated by the clamour around his name, in March 1847 proclaimed concessions: a less rigid censorship of the press and the creation of a state council of laymen to advise him on civil affairs. The examples spread to Florence, and then to Turin, whose governments signed an agreement to form a customs union. The Austrians, sensing that the movement was already infecting their domains of Lombardy and Venetia, reinforced the military presence which was the most resented aspect of their domination, a move which in turn sparked off riots and protests in Milan.

The south remained, however, apparently immune to the excitement aroused by these events and expectations: under the Bourbon Ferdinand II, the Kingdom of Naples, which had included Sicily for over 100 resentful years, had not bent to the winds of change and had granted none of the limited reforms initiated by rulers further north. In January 1848 the population of Palermo rioted and drove out the Neapolitan governor and by the end of February the whole island, except for Messina, had been taken over by an unlikely alliance of rebels united only by their resentment of Neapolitan rule. Trying to forestall the spread of this agitation to the mainland, Ferdinand hastily granted a constitution modelled on the French constitution of 1830 which set up the so-called bourgeois monarchy; within a few weeks Florence, Turin and even Rome had followed this example, although only the *Statuto* of Carlo Alberto of Piedmont was to be maintained after 1849 (with important implications for the future of the Kingdom of Italy after 1861). These constitutions all provided for a bicameral parliament elected on a franchise limited to those paying substantial taxes, and the setting up of a citizens' militia.

29

When news of these developments and of the uprisings in Paris, Vienna and Budapest were followed by that of Metternich's resignation and exile, the radicals and revolutionaries in Milan and Venice felt their moment had come. In Milan, between 19 and 23 March, a veritable popular insurrection led to the famous '*cinque giornate*' ('five days') of street fighting which dislodged the Austrian garrison of the redoubtable General Radetzky, while the Venetians accepted the surrender of their Austrian garrison on 22 March.

In the special character of these very successes, however, lay the seeds of the subsequent disastrous failure of this first attempt to unify Italy by military means. Whereas the new and largely untried leaderships of the imitations of 'bourgeois monarchy' were essentially bringing revolution from above, with either little popular participation or merely the temporary effervescence of excitable plebs, in the regions directly ruled by Austria there was no alternative to driving out the foreigner if any concessions were to be won, and this cause was far more powerfully able to engage the committed support of a far wider social spectrum. Thus in both the areas mentioned, but most especially in Lombardy, not only were the common people of the capitals willing to become actively engaged in the struggle, but those of the other towns and of the countryside also often rallied effectively to the cause.

Although the Piedmontese army, led in person by Carlo Alberto and soon joined by contingents from Tuscany, the Papal state and Naples, crossed the Ticino under the Italian tricolour flag on the day that the Milanese, led by their Council of War (in which the federalist Carlo Cattaneo was a dominant figure), drove the Austrians from their city, the approach to Italian independence of the rulers of all the Italian states involved in the intervention differed profoundly, both among themselves and above all from that of the groups which had successfully carried out the insurrections. While the Milanese and the Venetians wanted independence as the basis for unity under a completely revised constitutional order, the interventionist states either wanted something very different, or did not know what they wanted except to be part of a millennial event. Within a month the Pope had withdrawn his support from the making of Italy, declaring that as the pastor of all Catholics he could not support strife between them, and had thus at a stroke demolished the neo-Guelph project of Gioberti. A fortnight later Ferdinand II regained absolute control of Naples, effectively ending the liberal experiment there, although it took him from May 1848 to March 1849 to restore Neapolitan rule over Sicily.

Tuscany, Rome and Naples had, however, never been serious military protagonists in the struggle, despite the heroism of some of their soldiers such as the Neapolitan General Pepe, who disobeyed his orders to return to Naples after Ferdinand II's counter-revolution and went on to fight for the Venetian Republic. Only Piedmont could field an army at least potentially able to defeat a weakened Austrian power. Carlo Alberto had declared that '*l'Italia farà da sé*' but in fact, none of the Piedmontese generals were really a match for Radetzky, despite an early minor victory at Goito at the end of May. The latter,

Figure 2.1 *L'Italia farà da sé* (Italy goes it alone): Carlo Alberto leads his army to defeat by the Austrians at the battle of Custoza, July 1848.

however, was politically useful for it strengthened at a critical point the hand of the Piedmontese in their effort to persuade the Milanese and the Venetians to accept the annexation of their territories by the Kingdom of Piedmont, ostensibly as a necessary step on the road to Italian independence, but in fact in pursuit of their basic aim of territorial and dynastic aggrandisement. The dispute over whether to accept the holding of plebiscites for 'fusion' with Piedmont, even with the proviso that no final decision on the constitution of Italy would be taken until the war was over, split the leaders of the Milanese rebels and led the most prominent of the radical democrats, Cattaneo, to withdraw from the struggle in disgust.

After the ephemeral Piedmontese success at Goito, Radetzky regained the initiative and defeated his enemies comprehensively at the battle of Custoza at the end of July. Carlo Alberto retreated to Milan, not in order to deny it to the Austrians but to forestall any attempt by its citizens to take their defence against reoccupation into their own hands while he was negotiating an armistice with Radetzky on the basis of which he vainly sought to persuade the Austrians to make a compromise peace which would leave Piedmont with some modest territorial gains.

Piedmont was now also losing the political initiative: with the collapse of the Giobertian project for unity under the Pope and the fading of hopes of a heroic military conclusion to the first attempt at independence, further south the Mazzinian idea of creating an all-Italian elected assembly to conduct the war and to make a constitution embracing the whole peninsula began to gain ground, first among the radical democrats in Tuscany, who led the new ministry formed in Florence in October, and then, far more dramatically, in Rome itself. Here on 15 November a minister in the Papal government was assassinated by Mazzinian sympathisers and a few days later Pius IX fled to the Neapolitan fortress town of Gaeta. Equally alarmed by developments in Tuscany, Leopold joined him a few days later. Even in reactionary Turin, the democratic and liberal backlash against the conduct of the war forced Carlo Alberto in December to call on Gioberti to become Prime Minister. Although he proclaimed his intention to root out the supporters of a 'little Piedmont' policy known as the *municipali* and initially supported the movement for an all-Italian democratic assembly, he was nevertheless soon caught up in an intrigue to restore Leopold II to his throne by force of Piedmontese arms, a plan which alienated both the King and the democrats in the Turin parliament and lost him his post within two months.

In Rome, meanwhile, the triumphant radical democrats, led by Mazzini, now in full charge after the elections following Pius IX's flight, declared Rome and the whole Papal State once more a Republic. Carlo Alberto attempting to regain the initiative for Piedmont and the interests of his dynasty, responded with a desperate gesture: he broke the armistice with Austria and flung his army against the now well-prepared Radetzky, who had restored a draconian Austrian rule throughout Lombardy and all Venetia except the city of Venice itself.

Within a month Radetzky had destroyed the Piedmontese army at Novara and Carlo Alberto having lost all save his honour, abdicated in favour of his son Vittorio Emanuele II, who at once sued for whatever peace terms he could obtain: in effect, he undertook to withdraw unconditionally from the independence movement and to renounce all territorial claims. One thing only was saved from the wreckage of his father's ambitions: the constitution known as the *Statuto*. At least in Piedmont some form of parliamentary government was able to continue and the talents of the man who was ultimately to forge the political unity of Italy, Cavour, could find some scope to develop.

The Roman Republic of Mazzini and his supporters did not last long. In April, with the pretext that he was merely trying to reconcile the Italian liberals with their Pope, Napoleon III sent an army to occupy the Holy City. For over two months it was fiercely and skilfully opposed by the citizens' militia (10,000 men to oppose the Great Powers of Europe) commanded by Garibaldi, but the outcome was never in doubt and Pius IX was duly restored to his throne. Garibaldi and the remnants of his army set out to march to Venice, the last redoubt of the independence movement, but soon became hunted men, although their red-shirted leader himself made a legendary escape from capture, eventually reaching safe refuge in Tuscany.

The Austrians, having disposed of the main opposition in the northern plains, were now free to resume their role as the military policemen of all Italy: in May 1849 an Austrian force restored Leopold II to his throne, and in August, after yet another heroic but futile defence, they retook Venice, the last outpost of Italian liberty. Once again, as in the period of 1817–31, 'enthusiasm, intelligence and vision had proved no substitute for guns'.[1] The fateful *quarantotto* had perhaps proved that Italy could not be kept the same but it did not clearly foreshadow what it would become, nor how and when.

The one positive outcome of the Italian events of 1848–49 was that crucial lessons had been learned by the few soon-to-be-influential men who had kept a sense of proportion about the real possibilities of success of the Italian movement for liberty and independence during the traumatic years which separated the accession of Pius IX and his return from exile to a Papal State which had virtually become a French protectorate.

Hindsight allows the historian to single out Cavour as the most important of these, but at the time few could have foreseen that the real driving force behind the making of Italy over the next 12 years would be this French-speaking Piedmontese aristocrat, rather than the prophet of national independence, Mazzini, who had for a few months presided over a refounded Roman Republic, or the 'Hero of Two Worlds', Garibaldi, the only Italian soldier to show himself able to defeat foreign generals.

Cavour has been accused of opportunism and even of cynicism, but an equally objective description would present him as a political realist who appreciated the direction in which economic development must proceed if a basis for an independent nation-state was to be created and also understood very well the domestic and external political constraints on any feasible strategy to achieve that goal. As an enlightened conservative his main objective was to overcome the disadvantages of Italy's late and uncertain start as a significant factor in the European order, doing the minimum necessary for success in each phase rather than aiming at a total and apocalyptic transformation of the situation. His prediction, in 1844, that Italy could only achieve independence if there occurred a 'new settlement' between the powers or 'a great commotion', reflected a lifelong perceptiveness about the options that were really available for a small power committed to a large enterprise.

Cavour's analysis was, of course, not the only one that a political realist might have made at that moment of defeat. Despite the defeat of Mazzinian republicanism and the deflation of the neo-Guelph vision, in the decade that followed the first war of the *Risorgimento* some of the leading figures still saw

---

1. H. Hearder and D. P. Waley, A Short History of Italy, Cambridge, Cambridge University Press, p. 141.

the unification of the country as being inseparable from a political revolution of a populistic type, and a few were convinced that it was inseparable from a decisive resolution of the 'social question', the emancipation of the 'most oppressed' strata of society, notably the southern peasantry.

Adopting a counter-factual approach for a moment, it is also worth noting that one of the most intriguing 'ifs' of Italian history is what might have occurred if the 'forgotten solution' to the problem of how to reconcile the goal of liberty with that of national independence, which was powerfully advanced over the next decade, most notably by Cattaneo, had actually won the support of the decisive members of the Italian political élites and led to a federal Italy of autonomous democratic states not dissimilar to the Switzerland in which the Milanese political philosopher was spending his remaining years in exile.[2] His campaign was, however, severely handicapped by his enforced absence from the active political scene, in contrast with Cavour, who between 1852 and 1861, with only one gap of six months, was Prime Minister of Piedmont and then of Italy. The logical power of the federal idea may be gauged by Cavour's own conviction for many years prior to the crisis of 1860 that a great measure of regional and local autonomy would be essential in the new Italy he was working for. Being an opportunist in ideas as much as in policies, he eventually judged that such a concept might reduce the capacity of Piedmont to give a decisive political and military lead when the time was again ripe for action, and was in any case too complex and cerebral to generate the wide and ardent commitment which would be needed.

Even more radical alternatives to Cavour's approach were suggested by two socialist thinkers, Giuseppe Ferrari and Carlo Pisacane, who rejected Mazzini's reduction of all other political and social questions to the single issue of independence for a unified nation. They, unlike Cattaneo, were thorough-going revolutionaries and, anticipating 'proletarian internationalism' and 'Maoism' respectively, believed that the 'social question' (i.e. the gulf between the privileged few and the excluded many) was in fact the key to the problem of both independence and unity. Although Mazzini remained the focus of the republican nationalist movement, there was thus now significant dissent to the left as well as to the right of his ideas, which was yet another factor enabling Cavour to dominate the next phase of the *Risorgimento*.

After the heroic fiasco of 1848–49, however, the initiative in politics was clearly no longer in the hands of the 'democrats', whether federalists or centralisers, but passed to the '*moderati*' (who, though utterly opposed to radical social transformation, can hardly be called 'conservatives', given the massive political changes they wanted to bring about). These were led by

---

2. Cf. M. A. Tyler, 'A Dissenting Voice in the *Risorgimento*: Angelo Brofferio on Mid-Nineteenth century Piedmont', in *Historical Journal*, 33, 2 (1990), pp. 403–15. Cattaneo did not return to Italy even after unification: although he was elected a deputy in the first parliament of the Kingdom of Italy, he never took his seat in it.

Figure 2.2 A new boot for old shoes. Cavour to Vittorio Emanuele II: 'Push hard, it has to give way right down to the toe! It will fit you like a glove!' (Satirical cartoon by Florentine cartoonist Sanesi in *Il lampione* of 15 May 1860).

Cavour and his Lombard, Emilian and Tuscan equivalents such as Marco Minghetti in Bologna, Marquis Giorgio Pallavicino Trivulzio in Milan, and Baron Bettino Ricasoli in Florence, who were mostly cautiously liberal members of the aristocracy, though without Cavour's political skills.

They aimed at a modern secular state (modelled on the contemporary political system of England) extending to north and central Italy, to be achieved with the general consent of the Great Powers and therefore without any tincture of social revolution. Though in favour of constitutional and institutional change, they wanted only the most limited form of popular participation, on a franchise restricted to men of substance. If the changes they wished to bring about constituted a revolution at all, it was to be imposed from above and not permitted to erupt from below.

Although Cavour, a 'cross between Sir Robert Peel and Machiavelli',[3] was careful never to make explicit public declarations of his strategy for achieving his overall objective of unification, its main lines can be deduced from his policies and actions: firstly, the insertion of Piedmont into the European balance of power as a guarantor of a peaceful, orderly and above all non-revolutionary unification which would promote and not undermine continental stability; secondly, the creation of a consensus among the whole of the educated classes of society in favour of Italian unity.

3. Denis Mack Smith, *Italy. A Modern History*, University of Michigan Press, Ann Arbor, 1959, p. 23.

Cavour's essential strength as a practical statesman was his pragmatic attitude to means and, sometimes, to ends. Although in 1848 he had briefly agreed with Carlo Alberto's policy of non-reliance on outside help in the struggle for Italian independence, he had no difficulty in absorbing the main lessons of the calamities of the following two years.

The first of these was that Piedmont could not hope to be the protagonist of unification while its political and economic life was stagnant and backward: the first essential was therefore to bring his country into the mainstream of European development by adopting a policy of free trade and investment in infrastructures, notably railways, and in manufacturing industry. He brought in modernising reforms of the army and judiciary. An admirer of the British parliamentary model, he made the deputies in the Turin parliament speak from their seats and not from a rostrum, thus encouraging a business-like and interlocutory attitude in them. At the same time, however, he positively discouraged the development of a two-party system with alternation in government, preferring a permanent (and ten-dentially corrupt) 'connubium' of all the centrist and 'moderate' forces in politics, in line with his lifelong conviction that the only basis for effective action was 'an honest *juste-milieu*' which would marginalise extremists of both left and right.

Cavour's second principle was that Italy could not be made by its own efforts in a Europe dominated by the great hegemonic powers of France and Austria unless one of them, by diplomacy or war, or by both, could be brought into play to offset the other. The third, equally important, was to understand the importance of ideas and idealism in the struggle without ever expecting them to be effective in a vacuum of state power.

The instruments he was to use in the pursuit of the two latter goals were both diplomatic and conspiratorial. Firstly, he undertook a prolonged, subtle and single-minded diplomatic campaign to use every opportunity to make a united Italy attractive and even necessary to the one major continental power, the France of Louis Napoleon, which had a permanent interest in offsetting Habsburg influence, while giving enough reassurance to other Great Powers which would be opposed to any renewal of upheavals of the 1848 type to ensure that they assumed a benevolently neutral stance in the case of armed conflict between a Franco-Piedmontese alliance and Austria. Secondly, Cavour was not prepared to see a repetition of the fatal disunity of 1848–49 and therefore wanted to ensure that the moral and political, as well as the military and diplomatic, leadership of the movement for unity and independence was firmly in the right hands: those of sound, loyal and determined men who had no interest in abetting a social revolution. With this in view, he promoted the creation of the *Società Nazionale Italiana* a 'respectable' conspiracy of moderate liberals in north and central Italy intended to create the political and psychological conditions for political unification without social disruption, and under Piedmontese leadership.

The first turning point in Cavour's diplomatic strategy was reached in 1854, after he had been in office for two years. France and Britain in that year went to war with Russia over a series of issues relating to the declining power of the Turkish Empire in the Balkans and Russian expansionism at its expense. French and British forces landed in the Crimea in March and laid siege to Sebastopol. Piedmont had no quarrel with Russia, but Vittorio Emanuele and Cavour nevertheless seized upon the chance for their country to play a part on the international scene as a way of putting the Italian question on the agenda. In January 1855, 10,000 Piedmontese troops were despatched to the Crimea, fought in a minor battle with success, and secured Piedmont a place at the Congress of Paris in 1856, where, with the vigorous support of Lord Clarendon, the British Foreign Secretary of the day, Cavour achieved his objective of forcing the problem of Italo-Austrian relations on to the attention of the major European powers.

From Paris Cavour brought nothing concrete back to Turin, but he had impressed Louis Napoleon, Emperor of the French, himself an inveterate plotter who was already thinking of provoking war with Austria. Two years later 'the two arch-conspirators of Europe',[4] met secretly at Plombières in French Savoy to work out their joint strategy for driving Austria from Italian soil. Returning once again to Turin apparently empty-handed (for no treaty had been signed), Cavour nevertheless hurried on his preparations for war, not only strengthening the regular army but also, in order to give an 'Italian' dimension to the conflict, semi-officially raising a volunteer force headed by Garibaldi (a strange bedfellow in that he was the hero of the defence of the Roman Republic, but now to command an army raised by the King of Piedmont). Cavour was especially concerned that popular enthusiasm in the Austrian-occupied regions might wane because of the far more enlightened policy being carried out there since 1857, after the retirement of the 91-year old Radetzky: Lombards and Venetians were again beginning to prosper under an administration which, though strict, was notoriously more efficient and more honest than any other in the peninsula.

One more difficulty was, however, still to be overcome. Getting wind of the Franco-Italian plot, the British and the Russians pressed for a negotiated solution through another Congress of the Great Powers. Fortunately, the Austrians insisted upon impossible conditions for their participation. The Powers then demanded that Piedmont accept disarmament, and even Napoleon was forced by his own hostile public opinion to acquiesce in this demand. Cavour refused to disarm before the Austrians did so, and the latter once again came to his rescue, issuing an ultimatum which was in effect a declaration of war. Napoleon now had his *casus belli* and his armies poured into Piedmont to repel the invading Austrians and in less than a month had inflicted a severe defeat upon them at the battle of Magenta. The second war

---

4. H. Hearder and D. P. Waley, *A Short History of Italy*, p. 148.

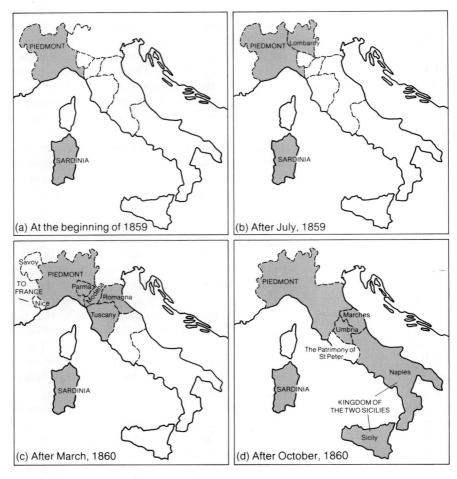

Map 3. The process of Italian Unification.
   After Derek Beales *The Risorgimento and the Unification of Italy* (Longman, 1981), p. 77.

of the *Risorgimento* thus began, this time with the main condition for military success apparently well secured.

The second arm of Cavour's policy for unification, which had only been created in 1857 when the long process of his diplomacy was on the point of succeeding, was now brought into play (to the surprised displeasure of Napoleon). While working to obtain French support, he tried to make sure that in all the Austrian-ruled or Austrian-dominated regions and states of the peninsula the *Società Nazionale Italiana*, his network of grandees committed to national unification, moved to seize power and organise plebiscites for annexation by Piedmont, while also acting to rein in the other major conspiratorial network, that of Mazzini.

The *Società Nazionale Italiana* had recruited many of those members of the educated classes who had previously been Mazzini's followers but who had turned away from him on account of the tragic failure in 1857 of an attempted insurrection in Calabria which he had supported. But it failed to put down roots among the common people, even though it was led by Daniele Manin, the hero of the defence of Venice, and Garibaldi himself lent it his name, despite his Republican convictions. Cavour believed that the *Società Nazionale Italiana* would be able to provide the mass popular uprisings in Austrian-ruled and dominated areas which he had promised Napoleon as a means of assuaging public concern in France about the legitimacy of his intervention. In the event they largely failed to materialise, prompting Napoleon to comment indignantly that 'only by showing one is ready to fight can one prove one's worthiness to become a nation', and leaving Cavour to complain bitterly that 'patriotism has so far produced very feeble results'.[5]

After news reached them of the Franco-Piedmontese victory at Magenta the princes of the Austrian-protected states (Tuscany, Modena and Parma) nevertheless fled to safety, and the Austrian garrisons in Bologna and Ancona (still part of the Papal state) had to withdraw to rejoin the main armies further north. Without informing Napoleon, Cavour at once sent Royal Commissioners to try to hold the vacant states until the peace settlement, while the patrician conspirators of the *Società Nazionale Italiana*, whose calls for insurrection had gone unheeded by the populace, devoted themselves more successfully to orchestrating popular demand for annexation to Piedmont, and resistance to any return of the exiled rulers. Napoleon refused, however, to countenance any Piedmontese military occupation of the duchies.

Meanwhile, on the battlefield, events appeared to be moving decisively towards a complete triumph for the Franco-Piedmontese project: less than two months after Napoleon had landed at Genoa, the Austrians were again defeated in the second major battle of the campaign, at Solferino. French losses were heavy, Prussia was massing forces on the Rhine, and Cavour having shown himself to be as unrelenting as he was deceitful in pursuing Piedmontese

---

5. Denis Mack Smith, *Cavour*, Methuen, London, 1985, p. 169.

interests in central Italy, Napoleon now decided unilaterally to make peace with the Austrians without consulting him.[6]

Under the hastily concluded peace terms agreed between the Austrian and French Emperors at Villafranca the two superpowers reached a distinctly unsatisfactory compromise: Austria was to cede Lombardy to France (which would then, humiliatingly, pass it on to Piedmont as a mere satellite), a hypothetical federation of Italian princes was to be set up (although the exiled rulers should not be restored by force), and otherwise the *status quo* would prevail. France would renounce the annexation of Nice and Savoy, which was to have been the main reward for its intervention.

When the terms of the settlement agreed over his head were made known to him, Cavour, purple in the face and breathing with difficulty, 'seemed almost to have lost his mind'.[7] After quarrelling passionately with the King, calling him a traitor, he resigned, although he did not leave office before sending instructions to his supporters in the *Società Nazionale Italiana* to keep control of the central Italian states at all costs. Villafranca, despite the acquisition of most of Lombardy, was a set-back which invited comparison with the events of a decade earlier, and Cavour's enemies in Turin were exultant that 'artful, adroit, unscrupulous and audacious as he is, he has been used, outwitted, played with, and made a tool of by one more artful, more unscrupulous, more audacious, and very much more profound than himself.'[8]

Such a judgement was premature. Napoleon soon found himself profoundly embarrassed at home by his failure to derive any advantage for France from the war, while Britain made it clear that it would support Piedmontese annexation of the central Italian states. The new government in Turin, inexperienced and naïve, floundered in uncertainty and Vittorio Emanuele II, was forced to bring Cavour back as prime minister only six months later.

Rested and refreshed, and by now bored by his enforced holiday from power, if not from intrigue, Cavour at once pulled the necessary rabbit out of his diplomatic hat by arranging plebiscites for annexation, by Piedmont and France respectively, of the areas which they coveted. Overwhelming majorities, at least partly engineered by bribery and bullying, created political facts with which not even Austria could argue and before Easter 1860, Piedmont had been extended to include all of the modern regions of Tuscany and Emilia-Romagna, while Savoy and Nice opted to be absorbed by France. Garibaldi could never forgive Cavour for his disregard of the population's real wishes in his native town of Nice, where the manipulation of the vote was particularly blatant, but was soon able to return the compliment by a legendary feat of conquest which left Cavour for a critical moment completely at the mercy of events.

---

6. Vittorio Emanuele II was, however, a passive party to the negotiations and appeared quite willing to accept an outcome in total contradiction with the policy he had agreed with his own ministers. Cf. ibid, pp. 173–4.

7. Ibid, p. 174.

8. Ibid. p. 175, citing John Daniels, the United States minister in Turin.

Figure 2.3 Whetstone-holder with carved head of Garibaldi, united Italy's only true 'local hero'.

Garibaldi had taken a distinguished part in the 1859 campaign as the commander of a small force of volunteers sent to harry and distract the Austrians in northern Lombardy, but he was always kept far from the main fields of battle by the Piedmontese general staff in case he was too successful and sparked off a popular insurrection (as Cavour had initially hoped he would). After Villafranca, he became the magnet for idealistic volunteers from all over Italy as he began, with the covert personal support of Vittorio Emanuele, to prepare for an expedition to liberate the south of the peninsula, starting with Sicily.

Even Cavour did not, however, anticipate the actual course of events when matters finally came to a head in May 1860.

In April the inhabitants of Palermo had once more risen against the oppressive rule of the Bourbon kings and had sent envoys to Garibaldi asking for his help. Because Garibaldi was the only authentic national military hero so far produced by the *Risorgimento*, it was not possible for Cavour and his government publicly to take stern measures to prevent Garibaldi from responding to the Sicilian invitation, which coincided with their own strategy for forcing the pace of unification. The most they could do was to try to sabotage his preparations in various ways. When he sailed from Genoa on 6 May 1860 in two dilapidated steamers with no more than a thousand red-shirted volunteers (the legendary *Spedizione dei mille*) few expected he would succeed, and Cavour was still attempting to prevent his ever arriving in Sicily by ordering his arrest should his vessels enter Piedmontese and Sardinian waters. The leaky armada reached Marsala on 11 May and four days later engaged the much stronger Neapolitan army in the first battle of the campaign. To the cry of '*qui si fa l'Italia o si muore*' ('here we make Italy or we die') Garibaldi led his little army to a famous victory at Calatifimi. Four days later, joined by several thousand Sicilian guerrillas, he brilliantly captured Palermo. By the end of July 1860 the whole island was in his hands and he was preparing for an invasion of the mainland part of the Kingdom of Naples.

These astonishing military successes were also of the greatest political consequence: they put Cavour and Vittorio Emanuele on the defensive and both thrilled and alarmed the whole of Europe. The French in particular were worried that Garibaldi, whose anti-clericalism was particularly rabid, would not stop at the conquest of Naples but press on to take the greatest symbolic prize, Rome itself, precipitating an extreme reaction among the French clericals, strengthening the hand of Austria and threatening once again to set Europe ablaze with social revolution.

Garibaldi himself had little political sense ('a heart of gold and the brains of an ox', as one of his contemporaries put it) and no conception of how greatly the unification of Italy must still depend upon the friendship of France. On the contrary, he was determined at all costs to continue his conquest as far as Rome, turn out the French garrison and himself proclaim Vittorio Emanuele King of Italy on the Campidoglio hill, where the ancient Roman generals were accorded their triumphs. It soon looked as though he might achieve at least the military aspect of his goal, for by 6 September, after being everywhere welcomed by cheering crowds, he entered Naples. Cavour's attempt to forestall this triumph by a 'respectable' seizure of power there by his supporters in the *Società Nazionale Italiana* had failed completely, clearly demonstrating the superior charisma of the 'Hero of Two Worlds'.

Cavour's political skills, with a little help from the delay to Garibaldi's progress northwards by the unexpected resistance of the remnant of the Neapolitan army at the battle of the Volturno, proved equal even to this situation. He persuaded Vittorio Emanuele to order the Piedmontese army to advance southwards through the Papal State in order to come between

Garibaldi and his last objective, while at the same time reassuring Napoleon that no invasion of Rome itself, far less any social revolution, would be permitted. The Papal army was quickly beaten and the Piedmontese army interposed itself between Garibaldi and the Pope. Cavour also used the delay to manoeuvre the Hero into accepting the usual plebiscite for annexation to Piedmont, which produced the usual crushing affirmative vote among the enfranchised men of property, although it was not at all clear how far it was a vote for absorption into a greater Piedmont or simply an expression of admiration for Garibaldi. By mid-October the King and Garibaldi could meet at Teano so that the latter could hand over the half of Italy he had conquered, and be told that he and his army were no longer required. Naïvely noble to the last, Garibaldi would accept no honour nor reward except a bag of seeds to plant on the rocky island of Caprera to which he now retired.

Cavour himself remained in Turin throughout these heady months and never visited any of the territories then added to the Kingdom. During the eight months that followed he devoted himself to the business of providing a constitutional outcome to the process of unification (Vittorio Emanuele was proclaimed King of Italy in February 1861) and planning the policies of pacification and education which were already so clearly necessary in the aftermath of unity. In the first week of June 1861, however, his health was so undermined by years of overwork that he became seriously ill and within a few days 'one of the greatest patriots that have ever adorned the history of any nation' was dead.[9] Whether this accolade was justified or whether Lord Acton was nearer the mark in describing Cavour's life as 'a triumph of unscrupulous statesmanship', it is also worth bearing in mind the judgement of a later analyst:

> Cavour had the professional diplomatist's exaggerated view of things
> which led him to overestimate difficulties and to indulge in
> conspiratorial excesses and in prodigies of subtlety and intrigue
> (which were largely elaborate balancing-acts). In any case Cavour
> acted mainly as a party man. Whether in fact his party represented the
> deepest and most durable national interests [...] is another question.[10]

---

9. The problematic accolade was bestowed by Lord Palmerston, speaking in the House of Commons, before Cavour's death, cited in H. Hearder and D.P. Waley, *A Short History of Italy*, p. 156.
10. Antonio Gramsci, *Quaderni del carcere*, edited by V. Gerratana, Einaudi, Turin, 1975, Q1924.

Chapter 3 . . . .

The 'historic compromises' of the Liberal State

In an often-quoted aside in the aftermath of the proclamation of Vittorio Emanuele as King of a united Italy, Massimo D'Azeglio, Piedmont's first Prime Minister after the catastrophe of 1849 and subsequently an influential publicist on behalf of the independence movement, had remarked that 'Italy is made, now we must make Italians'.[1] He was expressing a well-founded apprehension shared by many Italians at the time: for the most part the state now denominated as 'Italy' had been created for their own ends by a derisory percentage of the population and the great mass of its inhabitants had little or no sense of belonging to a 'nation'. The newly-crowned monarch did not follow the example of James VI of Scotland and I of England but, with typical petulance, refused to relinquish his Piedmontese title as the second of his name, becoming Vittorio Emanuele II, King of Italy. He summed up his own scornful attitude to his subjects early in his reign when he remarked that 'There [are] only two ways [...] of governing Italians, by bayonets and by bribery'.[2] Cavour himself did not dissent from such views.

Not even the personal magnetism of a Garibaldi could 'nationalise the masses': even before he handed over his conquests to Vittorio Emanuele his men had to be sent to repress peasants in Sicily and Irpinia who had massacred the local 'liberal' gentlemen.[3] In any case, for the first few years of the new régime, he was an absentee from constitutional politics, preferring to try for a

---

1. Cited in C. Seton-Watson, *Italy from Liberalism to Fascism, 1870–1925*, Methuen, London, 1967, p. 13.
2. Citation from the Clarendon Papers in Denis Mack Smith, *Italy and its Monarchy*, Yale University Press, New Haven and London, 1989, p. 43.
3. Half a million people turned out to cheer Garibaldi on his visit to London in 1864, a crowd never remotely matched anywhere in Italy. Cf. D. Beales, 'Garibaldi in England: the politics of Italian enthusiasm', in J. A. Davis and P. Ginsborg (eds), *Society and Politics in the Age of the Risorgimento*, Cambridge University Press, Cambridge, 1991, pp.184–216.

repetition of his Sicilian exploits in two armed attempts to invade the Papal State and seize Rome. Both were defeated and followed by harsh repressive measures. There were no other politicians among the élite ruling group who could begin to match the Hero's capacity to overcome the barriers to mutual communication with the common people, still less win their trust, in the cause of rallying them to the new order.

The populations of the historic states of the peninsula for the most part did not even share a common language and were still divided by fierce ancestral rivalries, even at the level of the educated classes. Although Italy was no longer Metternich's 'geographical expression', the task of creating a common national identity from its widely differing, and tendentially incompatible, regions and histories was still to be adequately defined, let alone addressed. Not only a journey of almost 1,000 miles separated Milan and Turin from Palermo: they were also separated by centuries of disparate experience.

Even the basic question of where the capital city of the new realm should be was itself fraught with divisive emotions: when, as a way of moving closer to Rome, the parliament chose in 1864 to transfer the seat of government to Florence, there were bloody riots in the streets of Turin, and the same resentment surfaced among the Florentines 12 years later when, in 1870, Rome finally became the capital of the country.

A still greater problem than these cleavages was the abyss which now separated the new nation-state not simply from the Papacy, but from the Church, the main institution of civil society throughout the peninsula. Pius IX became even more implacably hostile to 'the triumph of disorder and the victory of the most perfidious revolution' represented by the *Risorgimento* when the Piedmontese army, with the flimsiest of pretexts, occupied much more than half of his domains, leaving him only the narrow strip of the 'patrimony of St Peter', in effect Rome and its immediate malarial hinterland.

For the first 18 years of what is usually referred to as the 'Liberal State', Pius ignored all attempts to bring about a reconciliation between Church and state and pursued a relentless vendetta against it and all its works, excommunicating all politicians and civil servants who supported legislation to limit the prerogatives of the Church. In 1864 he issued the Syllabus of Errors, in which all forms of 'progress, liberalism and modern civilisation' were formally condemned as the work of the Devil, and in 1870, after declaring himself to be 'the prisoner of the Vatican' he proclaimed the doctrine of Papal infallibility, following this up with the decree of *Non expedit* which effectively forbade practising Catholics from participating in the Kingdom's political life in any way. The clergy, at his instigation, fostered and supported rebellious peasant movements in the south, and preached subversion to the urban poor of the north. It was hardly surprising that many of the *moderati* suspected an unholy alliance between extremists on the left and the Papacy, a fusion of the Red and the Black conspiracies against the survival of the new state.

Figure 3.1 The 'brigand' Tamburini after his capture. The northern 'pacification' of the south was far more costly in lives than all the wars of the *Risorgimento*.

There is a clear linkage between all these difficulties and the fundamental problem besetting the governments of the new régime, conventionally known as the '*destra storica*' ['the historic Right'], which inherited Cavour's achievement. For over 15 years the succession of well-intentioned but second-order politicians, far too much influenced by Vittorio Emanuele's impulsive interventions and imperatives in foreign policy, sought first to consolidate and then to complete the political unification of the country. Although they had succeeded in adding Venetia and Rome to it by the end of their first decade in power, they were never able to get to grips with the deeper problem of the economic, social and cultural mismatch between its main components. Sometimes referred to as the 'southern question', sometimes as the 'social question', it was and is the breeding ground of all that has been and remains negative in the historical experience and current situation of unified Italy.[4]

The multiple dualisms which persisted for at least a century were, of course, partly a legacy of the long experience of division, conquest and exploitation, and of uneven development already analysed. But they were exacerbated by the way in which the country was unified politically from above and, in the experience of the great majority of the population, from outside. To most southerners the experience was indistinguishable from harshly rapacious colonisation by a foreign country, which introduced a totally new set of laws and regulations governing every aspect of civil society, in the name of free trade substituted shoddy and over-priced imports for the familiar products local handicrafts and industry had previously provided, imposed ruinous and unaccustomed levels of taxation, conscripted the young into its army, and added insult to injury by the propagation of contemptuous attitudes towards them. Though railways and public buildings were constructed, the benefits to the local economy were limited by the fact that the government funds invested in the work went to northern contractors.

But even regarded from the point of view of advantages to the more developed north, the bargain cannot be said to have been a good one, for the south, against the almost universal expectations of northern politicians from Cavour onwards, turned out to be anything but the treasure house of exploitable resources, needing only a dose of rigorous administration, that they had imagined it to be. On the contrary, its over-populated towns and countryside bred delinquency and revolt on a massive scale: between 1861 and 1865 a Piedmontese army of 100,000 men was needed to suppress, in fighting which left more dead than all the wars of the *Risorgimento*, the endemic so-called 'brigandage' of the former Bourbon kingdom, while in Sicily, as the *mafia* continued to dominate the western half of the island, in 1861 alone some 25,000 young men took to the hills to evade conscription. It was not long before the

---

4. The 'south' is understood to mean all the former territories of the Kingdom of Naples, comprising the modern regions of Abruzzo, Molise, Campania, Basilicata, Puglia, Calabria and Sicily.

Piedmontese, like the Bourbons before them, found they could not suppress the *mafia* by force and in effect formed an alliance with it to maintain social order at the cost of political and economic favours to the 'men of honour'.

The network of corruption then established soon reached as far as Rome, in a pattern still all too familiar. This was, however, only one aspect of the price the north paid for its policy of 'piedmontisation' of the south: others, perhaps even more grievous in the long run, were the growing preponderance of southerners recruited as civil servants and politicians, bringing with them an administrative and political culture based on the exploitation of public office for private ends, and the unceasing draining away by emigration of the most enterprising and vigorous elements in the southern population while a fatalistic dependency culture spread among those remaining.

Though to some extent these negative characteristics of southern society reflected the specific unpurged forms of feudalism which was the Bourbon legacy, they were consolidated and made more rather than less pervasive by the style of rule adopted by the representatives of the Liberal State. The latter were the Prefects of the new provinces, and their subordinates, whose primary responsibility was to maintain order at all costs. Given the paucity of the administrative and police resources at their disposal they could not risk alienating the one class prepared, for its own reasons, to support them in the society over which they now ruled: this was the class of landowners of the great estates, the so-called *latifundia*, and the informal network of their parasitic hangers-on and agents: 'the one element of stability on which they could rely against counter-revolution and social upheaval'.[5]

The pious hopes of northern liberals that opening up the south to trade and introducing modern institutions and impartial government would soon sweep away any remnants of feudal attitudes and practices, transform the economic base of society and enable the mass of peasants to escape the crushing burden of extreme immiseration, could not possibly be fulfilled, for the basic assumption underlying them was the existence of a middle class comparable to that which was providing merchants, bankers, manufacturers and intellectuals to the expanding economy of parts of the north. In practice the suppression of feudal obligations and customary rights in the south produced an intensification both of economic exploitation by the local *signori* and of social tension between the few 'haves' and the mass of 'have-nots':

> The propertied classes enjoyed absolute economic power; in addition, local government, justice and the administration of charity were in their hands. They decided local taxation which was frequently of an unashamedly class character. Only they possessed the vote. The deputy was their creature, and to secure his support in parliament governments were prepared to turn a blind eye to the grievances of the

5. C. Seton-Watson, *Italy from Liberalism to Fascism, 1870–1925*, Methuen, London, 1967, p. 24.

peasantry [...] The prefect was reduced to the status of 'a diplomatic agent' accredited by a 'foreign' government to the local potentates.[6]

The most hated effect of unification for the southern peasantry was the opportunity that the new dispensation gave to the big landowners to acquire common lands and to traffic in them, and the consequent loss of age-old associated rights of pasture, gathering and woodcutting, which were often their only margin of survival. It seemed no less than 'an act of brigandage' connived at by the government.

Thus the south from the first conditioned the long-term political development of the north in unwitting exchange for such social and economic 'modernisation' of the south as the north was able, tardily and unevenly, to provide. It was not a transaction that at any stage had obvious benefits for either, in terms of development, but it became unavoidable once the decision was taken to create a centralised unitary nation-state.

It hardly needs to be said that this was not at all the outcome which the makers of Italy had planned. A few particularly shrewd and reflective observers from the north, including one future prime minister of the country, as early as the 1870s, had clearly understood the implications of this flawed relationship but their critique of the results of unification had limited political resonance and no political effect at the time it was published.[7] On the contrary, the sporadic rebellions and riots of the peasants in the south, often with the encouragement of local clergy, in protest against the appropriation of common lands and in the north against the infamous grist-tax were ruthlessly suppressed and attributed simply to agents of Bourbon counter-revolution and to clerical and/or radical agitation.

This was a pattern of response which was to persist, with only minor variations, well into the post-1945 Italian Republic: manifestations of economic desperation, albeit with some tincture of political rhetoric, are invariably officially attributed to the activities of 'subversives' and 'agitators', or even to organised crime and the *mafia*, and never to the failure of the state to address fundamental problems of social and economic deprivation.

In other ways, however, more positive results were achieved by the *destra storica* in its efforts to create a modern nation-state on the territorial basis created by the Piedmontese conquest of the peninsula in 1859–61.

The characteristics essential to such a state are territorial integrity, political and administrative cohesion, economic development, cultural unity

---

6. *Idem.*
7. For example the work of Leopoldo Franchetti and Sidney Sonnino, *Inchiesta in Sicilia*, first published in 1877. Both authors were conservatives politically, but their report had a considerable impact and initiated the scientific discussion of the problems of the south which has continued ever since. The flavour of their views may be judged from Sonnino's famous 1880 remark that 'the tax gatherer and the policeman are the only propagators of the religion of patriotism amongst the brutalised masses of our peasantry'.

and international respect. Progress was made in some of these areas, most notably in that of rounding out the boundaries of the Kingdom, even if the manner of its achievement reflected little credit on the country's military prowess or diplomatic skills. In 1866 a tactical alliance against Austria was concluded with Bismarck's Prussia which enabled Italy to acquire Venetia (but not Trento or Trieste, as planned) after Austria's historic defeat by the Prussian army at Sadowa, despite the fact that the land and naval battles fought by the Italians, at Custoza and Lissa respectively, resulted in Italian routs. In 1870, when Bismarck engineered a war against Napoleon's Second Empire, although most Italians sympathised with France and Garibaldi raised and led a volunteer force to fight with the Third Republic, the Italian army was at last in a position, ingloriously unopposed, to seize the Papal enclave and Rome itself without serious international repercussions.[8]

It may also, perhaps, be regarded as a formal success of government policy that the newly-unified state was equipped with an administrative system in keeping with its centralised, bureaucratic character. The Piedmontese *Statuto* was applied to the new state without amendment except for the title of the monarch, enabling the latter, in the shape of Vittorio Emanuele, to enjoy a very large measure of both affirmative and veto power, particularly in relation to foreign policy.

Most of his prime ministers, being of a similar autocratic bent, were happy enough to rule largely by decree, by-passing the parliamentary legislative process. It may also have been the case that such an autocratic style was the only one consistent with the nature of the state which had been set up. Even before Cavour left the scene, all thought of administrative decentralisation had been abandoned in favour of the prefectorial system whose deficiencies in the newly-added territories have already been alluded to. Only in the last 20 years has there been any serious concession to regional autonomy, but even now the greatest threat that most Italian politicians of all persuasions can detect in the electorate is that of a demand for genuine devolution to regional governments.

Certainly the least successful sphere of government activity in the period in question was the economic. Under the *destra storica* the standard of living of the mass of the Italian population fell steadily from an already low level. The government had but one aim in view in fiscal matters, to balance the budget at all costs. The need to do so was starkly clear: in 1866, when Venetia was added to the overloaded Kingdom, expenditure exceeded revenue by 60 per cent and only the most draconian measures seemed to be appropriate. The Finance Minister of the day, Quintino Sella applied a policy of 'economy to the bone' to pay off the accumulated debts incurred through unification, from the cost of the Crimean intervention to the loss of the Italian fleet at Lissa. Since the royal prerogative, under the *Statuto*, was to fix the budget for the armed forces without reference to parliament, and since Vittorio Emanuele

---

8. Ecuador was the only country which sent a note of protest.

50

remained determined to conduct the foreign policy of the country by means of war and the threat of war, this meant that the taxation levied from an already semi-pauperised population had to be steeply increased. In the period 1862–80 tax revenue more than doubled in a situation of slow and uncertain economic growth, so that the Italians became the most heavily taxed people in Europe and received the least in return. The taxes were, moreover, uniformly regressive in nature, so that the poorest paid the highest proportion of their income.

The effects of these burdens were compounded by recourse to the so-called *corso forzoso*, that is the issue for domestic purposes of paper currency with no backing in precious metal, which enabled the government to use the country's whole stock of precious metals to pay its debts but also in practice meant that Italian manufacturers dependent on the import of raw materials found it harder to obtain credit abroad for needed supplies.[9]

Generally speaking, the reliance on free trade as a formula for stimulating economic growth had negative effects, killing off formerly protected industries and depressing the inefficient agriculture of the south without bringing in any stable foreign investment to fill the gaps. Such foreign capital as was invested was sucked into the politically salient (but economically irrelevant) infrastructural sector (railways in particular, but also armaments and public works) which the state had heavily to subsidise to stave off their bankruptcy.

The thesis that the reduction in the living standards of the peasant masses which occurred during the first decades of Liberal Italy was essential in order to generate a surplus which could be applied to industrial development and modernisation of infrastructures has little basis in fact. Agriculture became more labour-intensive rather than less (at starvation wages for a growing mass of dispossessed tenant or independent small peasant farmers) and the improved surplus from favourable conditions in the international market for Italian agricultural produce was not ploughed back either into industrial development or into amelioration of agricultural technology. All in all it was a formula for minimum benefits and maximum social tension. The latter could only be regulated by coercive methods, since the consensus-creating mechanisms of the Church were now being denied to the state authorities, or even deployed against them. Any potential for consensus that might be gradually generated by the tentative movement towards a common national culture deriving from a common system of public education, and the collateral effects of mass conscription in a national army, was therefore significantly reduced.

The 'hegemony of the north', which really meant that of Piedmont, had become by 1876 strengthened and largely unchallengeable in political and administrative terms, but was underpinned almost exclusively by coercive power rather than by the consent of the governed, which could only have

---

9. The measure also had the positive effect of causing exports to rise because the currency was depreciated; it also encouraged Italians to invest at home rather than abroad, but not necessarily in the risky ventures of manufacturing industry.

accumulated if the unification had brought real benefits to them. For the latter to have been acquired, however, real economic gains would have had to be created by more efficient forces of production (improved technology and skills) and then diffused among the working population, which would have implied considerable changes in the relations of production (the rules and conventions governing who has and who does what).

The policies adopted by the *destra storica* tended to constrain the factors of greater efficiency as much as they prohibited any modification of the pattern of distribution of benefits, with the consequence that Italy, unlike Germany, its northern analogue as a nascent nation-state, could not achieve a 'kick-start' in industrialisation. Even when, between 1896 and 1912, the process of economic modernisation finally became more intensive, the underlying structural conditions of Italian society were still unpropitious to an even development, with far too great a proportion of the potential energies and enterprise present in the population (especially in the agricultural sector) still locked into the archaic, or at best stagnant technologies, attitudes and social practices which continued to typify the class system.

Could the *destra storica* and its successors, as some historians have asserted, have done more, and done it sooner, to foster industrialisation and the creation of a homogeneous and dynamic market economy? The answer to this exercise in counter-factual history depends on the definition we use of what precisely Italy's economic disadvantages were. Clearly some of the supposed material prerequisites of industrialisation were in short supply: coal

Figures 3.2/3.3 Economic development: the effect of industrialisation is reflected in the contrast between the engineering technology displayed in the Milan exhibitions of 1881 and 1898.

and metal ores are two obvious cases. Equally significant, as we have seen, was the inability, for political and diplomatic reasons which forbade contagious social upheavals, to address the structural and technological problems of the agricultural sector of the economy (still by far the largest in terms of both output and workforce), nor, by the same token, to offset their potential for social conflict by means of the traditional methods of consensus formation. The social system which guaranteed order also guaranteed the perpetuation of the conditions of economic backwardness by preventing any real movement of surplus labour from farm to factory. All these factors were present in the 'southern question', which was, precisely, the particularly acute form assumed by the unevenness of such development as did occur: the south grew less industrialised as the north developed its industries.

Several generations of Italian historians have concluded that the sum of these failures can best be understood as a 'revolutionary opportunity wasted' (the revolution in question being a 'bourgeois' breakthrough into economic and political modernity). According to this view, whose best-known exponent was the hero-figure of Italian communism, Antonio Gramsci, the land could have been forcibly redistributed to benefit the poor peasants, creating higher levels of consumption and therefore a more dynamic internal free market, which in turn would have generated surpluses to be invested in industry and allowed the transfer of surplus agricultural labour to the factories.

For the *destra storica* this could not have become a thinkable proposition, since the theoretical assumptions of their economic policy were essentially those of Adam Smith's 'invisible hand', whose beneficial effects were to be the outcome of the untrammelled accumulation of private capital allowed to pursue its own interest in the market-place. Equally it would have required the government to plan and execute much of the necessary process of industrial development, with direct incentives to encourage specific, and therefore planned, initiatives: another negation of the free market.

The thesis also contained highly negative implications specific to the precarious politics of the new Kingdom: the competition for state-controlled resources with the military establishment led by the monarch, and the political risks of alienating the power-holders in the south. Their traditional private interests and privileges had to be preserved, however great a hindrance to economic progress they might be, as a precondition for the maintenance of social order, and even of the survival of the state itself, should the disgruntled *signori* of the south decide to back the counter-revolutionary designs of the Vatican. The fragile political compromise between northern élite and southern landowners excluded any radical change in either the forces or the relations of agricultural production, and hence of the national economy as a whole.

It must be added, too, that the concept of the missed opportunity for revolution in the 1860s was, for Gramsci, at least as much a speculation about how the Italian labour movement had missed its chance for a Soviet-style revolution in 1919–22 as about anything that occurred half a century earlier.

A balanced hindsight would perhaps incline rather more to the view that a re-run of either 1789 or of 1917 has never been on the agenda of Italian history. Ironically, it would have been the men of the *destra storica* who might well have been justified in applying to Italy the words Karl Marx used to describe the situation in mid-century Germany:

> Side by side with the troubles peculiar to modern life, we have [...] a number of troubles handed down from the past, the outcome of the pursuance of antiquated methods of production, with their train of anachronistic social and political conditions. We suffer, not only from the living, but also from the dead. *Le mort saisit le vif!*[10]

The moral strength of the *destra storica* had derived from the dedication to constitutional liberties, at least in theory, which it had inherited from Cavour and its principal achievement, as we have seen, had been the virtual completion of unification, despite military weakness and frequently inept diplomacy. Its main political difficulties had been due to its inability to deliver the economic benefits which would have defused the extreme social tensions stemming from the complex structural dualisms of the new nation-state, and they were mightily compounded by its failure to bring the Church into the area of consensus-making.

By 1871, however, it had at least sanitised, for international purposes, the rift with the Vatican by the Law of Papal Guarantees which unilaterally provided the Pope and the Church with both a regular income (which was never drawn) and the diplomatic status and privileges of a sovereign power. Even though the Vatican never recognised this law and a formal relationship was only created between it and the Italian state in 1929, in practice it created generous conditions for a peaceful coexistence, falling rather short in this respect of Cavour's offer in 1861 of 'a free Church in a free state' (which certainly did not imply a permanent subsidy to the Pope, nor the continuing discrimination against any religion except Catholicism).

The *destra storica* not only completed the territorial unification of Italy but also centralised its administration and established an effective, if thoroughly unpopular, system of tax collection. Although always repressive, and sometimes ruthlessly so, of popular movements tending to public disorder, it nevertheless usually maintained respect for the liberties of individuals to think, speak and write, and for the most part its exponents were men of rigid personal standards and of an exemplary honesty in public life that has rarely been matched by any subsequent ruling group.

Paradoxically, however, the very fact that the budget had finally been balanced triggered a widespread demand in parliament for a less sternly

---

10. Karl Marx, *Capital*, Preface to Vol.I, 1867, J. M. Dent & Sons Ltd, London, 1974 p. xlix; the legal sense of the phrase in French ('the heir-at-law inherits as of right') is that the legacies of the dead encumber the actions of the living.

moralistic approach to public affairs and the majority of the *destra storica* crumbled overnight before the discontent of an unholy alliance between southern deputies who had long felt excluded from any but the most subordinate role in the structure of power and, among the government's nominal supporters, conservative malcontents from northern constituencies who were alarmed at the possible financial consequences of a bill then before parliament to nationalise the entire Italian railway system in an attempt to give it some financial stability and the public a more reliable service. In 1876 the *destra storica*, the main lines of whose economic and political action had been already defined by Cavour, ran out of parliamentary steam only two days after its last prime minister, Marco Minghetti had finally achieved its ultimate goal of balancing the budget.

The King then called upon the leader of the moderate left, Agostino Depretis to form a government. He did so amidst a feverish exultation among both the radicals and the representatives of the most reactionary southern interest, some of whom, ominously, he included in his first ministry. Six months later, fresh elections were called and by the exercise of blatant pressure and cajolery, through the prefects, almost all of whom were pliant new men, a crushing victory was gained over the *destra storica*, which never returned to power. Depretis, aptly nicknamed by his critics 'the Walpole of Italy', then dominated Italian politics for the entire period of the *sinistra storica* until 1887.

Despite the domestic and foreign achievements of the *destra storica* in consolidating the new Kingdom, the framework of constraints upon economic and political action by the government in the Italian Liberal State remained essentially unaltered. The structural and conjunctural factors which limited what the ruling group could actually do, by way of fiscal arrangements, education and diplomacy, and the ideological and cultural conditioning which defined what its members thought was possible, generally changed only at the margin, and in certain respects significantly worsened.

It is always necessary to keep these factors in mind when using the terminology of Western politics in relation to Italy. Terms commonly used in referring to groups and tendencies opposing the policies of the Italian Liberal State, or opposing the system as such, must be understood in their specific Italian meanings: 'Moderates' must be understood as deeply conservative, usually aristocratic, politicians whose main purpose was to frustrate the perilous revolutionism of Mazzini and Garibaldi, while 'democrats' were those who favoured an extension of the franchise but still with major exclusions (illiterates, women, non-taxpayers) and who were not by any means necessarily agreeable to allowing 'popular opinion' to determine policy (after all, a large majority of the population might well have voted to undo the *Risorgimento* and restore the temporal power of the Papacy).'Radicals', sometimes regarded as coterminous with the 'Extreme Left', had as their main aim in political life the abolition of the monarchy, which they regarded as the precondition of the forging of a truly popular Italian nation, while 'Liberals' were those who accepted the hybrid Piedmontese-Bourbonic centralising state, made a religion of free trade, and feared above all a Papalist *revanche* and any enfranchisement of popular strata which might threaten their monopoly of power.

Italy's exploitable material resources were not plentiful and often already over-committed: in the south the ruthless deforestation of the mountains, which was one of the results of the sale of Church and common lands was already preparing a cruel legacy of irreversible environmental blight. Any better use of its human resources was blocked or severely hampered by the massive illiteracy (over 80 per cent in the south) and lack of technical skills of the bulk of the population.

This framework of domestic constraints left governments with almost no room to manoeuvre. There was no margin available for transferring resources to areas of greatest developmental need and still less for humanitarian purposes. The 'historic compromise' between north and south was at best a regulated antagonism rather than an alliance for necessary change, and the dominant motive for any transfer of resources to the south by state investment or subsidy took the form of piecemeal responses to political blackmail by local power-holders there. These men had a stranglehold on politics because of the extremely limited nature of the franchise: less than 2 per cent of the population was entitled to the vote until 1882, when the proportion increased to 7 per cent (compared with over 25 per cent in France, over 20 per cent in Germany and 8 per cent in England at the same period). In practice, whether because of the *Non expedit* or simply because of apathy, less than half the electorate cast a vote, and it was a simple matter for local magnates to influence the outcome to their liking by the exercise of threats and promises: thus just over half a million male voters, dominated by a few thousand influential men, determined the fate of 25 million Italian subjects.[11]

Not all of the ruled were prepared to accept this authoritarianism and corruption. Beside parliamentary opposition from incorruptibles on the right and intransigent republicans or radicals on the left, extra-parliamentary opposition not only to the government but to the 'system' as such grew rapidly, often taking the form of conspiracy and insurrection under the influence not just of the ageing and discredited Mazzini but of foreign agitators who saw in Italy an ideal terrain for putting their theories of spontaneous revolution into practice. The best-known among these 'stirrers-up of strife' was undoubtedly the exiled Russian aristocrat Mikhail Bakunin who between 1864 and 1867 spread his romantic gospel of insurrectionary anarchism throughout the peninsula, leaving behind him a number of rivals to Mazzini's organisation. By 1872 the Italian police believed him to have some 32,000 followers and in 1874 he attempted to stage an insurrection with a few hundred peasants in Bologna: rather typically, it ended as soon as the police appeared on the scene.

---

11. To be qualified to vote, one had to be male, over 25, able to read and write and pay a minimum of 40 *lire* a year in direct taxes.

More lasting was the influence of those of his disciples who then moved away from the futile tactics of 'revolutionising the peasantry' which he had advocated and were instrumental in founding the Italian socialist movement, one of the most prominent among them, Andrea Costa, being elected as the first Italian socialist deputy in the parliamentary elections of 1882.[12]

Revolutionary anarchism did not die out, however, and its assassins continued to claim victims among statesmen and crowned heads (including Vittorio Emanuele 's successor) for decades to come. If a régime may be judged by the quality of the opposition it creates for itself, neither the *destra storica* nor the *sinistra storica* had any reason to feel satisfied.

Emigration was virtually the only safety valve available to release some of the social tensions which might otherwise have led even greater numbers to feel attracted to political extremes. Between 1870 and 1890 some two and a half million Italians went seasonally or permanently abroad to seek work, the proportion of those not returning from mostly trans-Atlantic destinations rising steadily during the period from about one quarter to well over half. Most of the emigrants in this period were from the north and centre of the country, particularly from the Veneto region but by 1890 the proportion of long-term emigrants from the south was increasing rapidly, foreshadowing the almost apocalyptic figure of some eight million inhabitants of the peninsula who were unable to get a living in their own country in 1901–13. It has been calculated that over the half-century following unification, the net permanent loss of population to Italy was 4.5 million people.

It should be added that, in economic terms, this tide of emigrants was by no means a negative factor: not only did they remit very large sums to their relatives left at home, increasing the per capita income of the south by one third, providing a welcome boost to consumption and even to investment there, but their departure from the domestic labour market caused wages to rise and induced employers to seek in technological investment rather than in intensification of labour the remedy for their falling incomes. Emigrants who returned after making a better living abroad than they could have dreamed of at home often brought new ideas and new patterns of personal behaviour back with them, and in general these provided positive models for those who had not been in contact with modern ways.

The cost in human suffering and trauma was also very great and emigration could never be more than a palliative to the structural problems of the Italian nation-state. In the period of the *sinistra storica* the economic benefits were relatively limited and the main value of emigration was simply that it reduced the probability of revolution.

---

12. Marx described the Italian supporters of Bakunin as 'a rabble of *déclassés*, the dregs of the bourgeoisie... lawyers without clients, doctors without patients and without any knowledge of medicine, billiards-playing students, commercial travellers and clerks, and above all gutter-press journalists of dubious reputation'.

In effect the rulers of Liberal Italy were hemmed in on every side: their sole priority was to maintain the precarious balance between the mutually antagonistic forces within the new ruling class, between the modernising north and the archaic south, in order to contain the pressures threatening the system as a whole. The political space between the immiseration of the peasant mass and the intransigence of the potential leaders of a popular reaction to it was so narrow that it bred a parliamentary and executive practice of *immobilismo*, a repressive paralysis of policy behind a smoke-screen of high-flown political rhetoric.

Though the advent to power of the *sinistra storica* under Depretis was hailed as a 'parliamentary revolution', it amounted in reality to a continuation by other means of the policies of stabilisation and consolidation of the *destra storica*. What was new was the style of legitimation and the techniques of manipulation which Depretis adopted in parliament to hold together the mutually hostile components of his majority by recruiting support among the opposition.

Announcing that 'We are a progressive government and if anyone wishes to transform himself and become progressive, if he wishes to accept my very moderate programme, can I reject him?' he was able to secure his hold on power for over a decade. Quickly becoming known as 'transformism', this approach to politics enabled him to command a permanent majority by constant wheeling and dealing with all the deputies prepared to compromise principles in order to gain local or personal advantage from the spoils of power.[13] An unlooked-for result was the so-called 'meridionalisation' of the civil service, because very often the favours accorded consisted of advancement for large numbers of the kinsfolk and clients of southern *signori* who had neither training nor aptitude for the work and saw their appointments as no more than an invitation to prey upon public funds. The system was locked into place by the electoral reform of 1882 which had the effect of giving a permanent majority in parliament to deputies from the south.

A fringe of intransigents on left and right soon made the word transformism into a term of abuse and a synonym of corruption and lack of principle, but most saw it as a necessary reworking of Cavour's 'connubium' with the opposition in the Piedmontese parliament which enabled 'a great new national party' of the centre to emerge and dominate Italian politics in the name of

---

13. Cf. Giuliano Procacci, *A History of the Italian People*, Weidenfeld & Nicolson, London, p. 337: 'Assuring the government of an adequate majority in parliament either by a preliminary deal with leaders of the opposition and by then absorbing them into the government as ministers, or by favours granted to deputies in return for support, or by combining both methods.' A contemporary definition was provided by Gaetano Mosca, Italy's best-known political theorist of the time: 'The Chamber of Deputies is becoming a partial and artificial representative of the country [...] Its members represent only a collection of basically private interests, whose sum total is far from comprising the public interest.'

continuity and stability, and above all to ensure that no rifts would occur in the 'moderate centre' which might provide opportunities for the extreme left to advance.

The stagnant political life which was the correlative of transformism was unlikely to become a propitious environment for fostering the economic changes which were essential if Italy was even to begin to make up the ground which separated it from the states which had already industrialised, or even keep pace with those, such as Germany, which were also latecomers but were making far more rapid strides in that direction.

The economic stagnation, however, was much less a sign of lack of political will to bring about improvement than the reflection of an intractable situation. Italy was perhaps the most disadvantaged of the latecomer industrialising nation-states of Europe in terms of natural resources and accumulated debts from the long struggle to achieve and consolidate its political independence. Moreover, its ruling élite did not (and could not) possess the theoretical tools for framing an economic policy which might have mitigated the effects and lessened the delays imposed by those material disadvantages, since they were still to be invented: they were operating in the age of Samuel Smiles and not that of John Maynard Keynes.

The basic model of development available to them was the classical free market/free trade example of England (which it should be remembered was only fully in place, at enormous human cost, in the 1840s). In this model, the state merely 'holds the ring' but does not interfere in economic processes except, in certain limited circumstances, to foster infrastructural development, such as ports and railways. The assumption underlying it is that the mere existence of a domestic free market induces practical men (entrepreneurs) to maximise their profits by greater competitiveness. It also induces those with capital to invest (rentiers) to risk that capital in the most promising industrial prospects. A further assumption is that the domestic market cannot be truly free unless trade with external competitors is also free. The dominant principle is that governments should only take such action in economic matters as will assist in the creation of a situation of 'perfect competition', in which the 'invisible hand' maximises benefits to both producers and consumers.

In practice, of course, no government can allow such 'perfect competition' to develop totally without regulation and it was no accident that the first industrialised nation-state, Great Britain, was also the first to introduce legal control of working conditions in a series of Factory Acts. In international trade, moreover, the firstcomers held most of the aces and their advantage over those nation-states which were at an earlier stage of industrialisation was likely to be maintained or increased rather than diminished by free trade. For a country such as mid-century Italy, the penalties for latecomer status were virtually impossible to overcome because even if they benefitted relatively during times of boom, as soon as the trade cycle brought a slump in demand they fell even further behind their more efficient competitors.

Another model was available, although the classical economists appeared to have demolished its theoretical basis long before. Their weakness was, however, to underestimate the power of nation-state politics to determine developmental paths irrespective of logical long-term interests. According to this second model, the state intervenes in economic matters to build and protect domestic production, using such devices as subsidies, ownership and control of specific industries created by investing state revenues in their establishment and activity, and tariff barriers to protect weak or inefficient domestic producers against foreign competition. In such ways, it would be assumed, economic development might be hastened and/or directed to 'national' needs, and dependence on actually or potentially unfriendly or unreliable sources of supply might be avoided. The dominant principle here is that the political independence and economic strength of individual nation-states in the world market are intimately linked: the ultimate logic being that, if a nation-state is to prosper, the country concerned must achieve total economic self-sufficiency, either controlling its external markets by force or able to forego them because domestic resources can supply all its needs. Seventy years later, Benito Mussolini proclaimed this type of economic independence, which he called autarky, to be the goal of the Fascist régime.

The drawback, as the outcome of Mussolini's policy was to reveal all too starkly, is that most nation-states do not possess natural resources adequate to make them self-sufficient and they are therefore drawn into a struggle to secure markets and supplies by colonial conquests and/or internecine wars, whether purely economic or military.

If a nation-state adopts a variant of the second model discussed above, foreign policy considerations loom large in the calculations of its rulers, sometimes to the detriment of its domestic concerns and interests. This was the case with Liberal Italy after a decade of relative quiescence under Depretis.

By the mid-1880s it was clear that the reliance on a basically free-trade policy in economic matters was doing little to bring about the industrialisation of the country. This was revealed and compounded by the effects on native industry and agriculture of the major European depression of that period. The former's ability to withstand foreign competition was extremely limited because of a low level of technology while the latter, being very labour-intensive and inefficient, could not respond to the flood of cheap grain arriving from America and Russia without further reduction of peasant incomes, which were already below subsistence levels. Labour unrest on the land was becoming endemic and more violent, and this tendency was abetted by the increasing proportion of the agricultural labour force which was reduced to the condition of day-wage labourers.

In political terms the web of compromises and favours on which Depretis had relied to control parliament began to unravel as the extremes in politics found more favourable terrain. On the right, encouraged by the monarch, there was increasing pressure for draconian solutions to dam the tide of social unrest, and for a more authoritarian style of government to muzzle those agitating for greater popular participation. On the left, now that the old parliamentary left of Mazzinian and Garibaldian deputies had been 'transformed', the radicals and socialists outside parliament increasingly sought to call into question not merely the policies but the very existence of the constituted authority which excluded the mass of the population from any participation in politics except by means of riot and brigandage. Although Bakuninist anarchism faded quickly as a mass movement, it was clear that a solid basis was being formed for a militant and effective labour movement to emerge and for the first time Marxist influences began to permeate the thinking of the régime's most determined opponents.

The man who emerged as Depretis's successor was Francesco Crispi, a Sicilian who in 1860, after a long apprenticeship as a revolutionary Mazzinian agitator, became one of Garibaldi's closest associates in the conquest of his native island, and for a while was its 'dictator' in succession to Garibaldi himself. Recognised by friend and foe alike to have great ability, he nevertheless remained intransigent in his opposition, first to the *destra storica* and later to the *sinistra storica*, joining the so-called 'pentarchy' of prominent members of the rump of the *destra storica* who were the leading opponents of transformism and its corrupting influence. His reputation had been badly tarnished by a scandalous remarriage but nevertheless, as Depretis's health and grasp of power waned in 1887, Crispi was made Minister of the Interior, and upon Depretis's death in the same year, was invited to become Prime Minister, as a man whose *Risorgimento* pedigree could not be doubted but who was also very clearly a man of order and strong government, whose loyalty to the *Statuto* and the monarchy was no longer in question.

The situation of the country when the self-styled 'man of destiny', Francesco Crispi, took office was problematic and its ability to lift itself out of backwardness far from certain. A master of florid patriotic rhetoric which enabled him to stifle parliamentary criticism and with the brutal self-confidence deriving from his status as the last politically active strongman of the *Risorgimento*, Crispi believed he had the formula which could lift Italy's economy out of recession while maintaining the existing social and political order intact. His three-point plan involved the imposition of high tariffs and the application of strategic subsidies in order to protect and build up home industry and agriculture, the exemplary harsh repression of extra-parliamentary political protest, and the creation of an Italian colonial foothold in Africa.

Crispi intended by these means to forge a new 'historic compromise' between the emergent northern industry, the holders of financial power (principally the banks, which were following the German model of using their capital to secure a controlling interest in industry and commerce), and the established power-holders, whether traditional landed gentry or capitalist landowners, in the agrarian sector of the economy, which was still by far the largest in terms of all conventional measures notwithstanding its profound dysfunctionality as a system of production.

Crispi had no understanding of economics and very little of diplomacy. Nor did he have any genuine political strategy to achieve modernisation by enabling the leading social and economic rôle in society to be seized by the northern industrialists. His essentially unoriginal policies were borrowed from other European powers and applied without any serious theoretical underpinning to show that they were appropriate to Italy's problems. Rather than being the outcome of a cool analysis of the facts of Italy's case, they derived from the considerations of political manipulation implicit in Crispi's authoritarian and bullying approach to his fellow-countrymen, anticipating Mussolini's attempts, a generation later, by force and fraud to dragoon them into acceptance of short-term simplistic solutions to complex long-term problems. The outcome of his domination of Italian politics for over a decade was to anticipate the inevitable bankruptcy of such an approach, creating ugly precedents of extreme social division, political polarisation, military disaster and, perhaps most ominously of all, sowing the seeds of an aggressive and irrational nationalism in a political culture which was already too apt to develop a sense of rancorous grievance at an inferiority perceived as the fault of others rather than its own.

This is not to say that a wiser and more balanced application of the social and economic policies espoused by Crispi would not have benefitted the country. Steps to broaden the participation in active politics of the social élites and to 'transform' the unruly and dissident classes of peasants and urban poor into supporters of the Liberal State by a more systematic use of both coercive repression and economic co-option through social legislation, fiscal equity and the prospects of colonial settlement, were not untimely in themselves. In particular, a measure of protection and state subsidy for Italian industry and encouragement of a more rational agriculture were clearly needed to offset the stagnation from which the economy was suffering.

But the former required sensitive and persuasive diplomacy, of which Crispi had almost no notion, and the latter could only result from significant challenges to the prevailing pattern of ownership and labour relations on the land which would in turn imply the creation of a new politics departing from the historic compromise between north and south discussed earlier. Protectionist policies applied over the 20 years following Crispi's ascendancy undoubtedly did have positive effects on certain industrial sectors such as mechanical engineering, shipbuilding and chemicals, but their immediate effects were particularly hard on southern agriculture and resulted in increased social unrest: a dangerous mixture of economic and colonial rivalry with France, particularly in relation to Tunisia, led to a tariff war far more damaging to Italian interests than to French ones, and discrimination not only against Italian agricultural exports to that country but also against inoffensive Italian emigrants to it who found themselves to be the targets of popular hostility and

63

Figure 3.4 The environment of the urban poor: a *basso* in Naples, 1914.

riotous violence. In Sicily, in 1892, the hitherto uninfluential small urban groups of socialists suddenly found themselves at the head of a millenarian mass movement of peasants and sulphur workers numbering several hundred thousand reduced to destitution by the tariff war with France and by United States competition: Crispi, returning after a brief absence from office, typically responded by declaring a state of emergency and sending 40,000 troops to put down a supposed separatist plot which existed only in his own rhetoric.

The victims of these repressions joined a long series of martyrs of what the opposition called 'proletarian massacres' which marked the whole decade. In 1897, attempting to stem the tide of opposition to his crude and violent political methods, Crispi tried to suppress the rapidly growing socialist movement and had its leader, Filippo Turati arrested, along with hundreds of other leading opposition figures both within and outside parliament.

Despite the 'proletarian' terminology adopted by the left in general, and in particular by the Italian Socialist Party, which was founded by the amalgamation of various workers' parties and movements in 1894, there were profound differences between the Italian 'labour movement' and those of other more industrially advanced European countries. In Italy any invitation to the 'workers' by the social-democratic intellectuals who formed its leadership to 'cast off their chains' was in practice an appeal to a highly differentiated ocean of oppressed peasants, not to factory workers and uprooted urban poor (as, for example, in England). The revolution they needed, though rarely wanted, would have been against the 'parafeudal' relations of production still predominant in Italy rather than against the barely embryonic exploitation of capitalist relations of production.

There were also important cultural differences between the grass-roots reality of Italian socialism and that of the forms of political socialisation experienced by the working class in Protestant countries where varieties of traditional legitimation of upwards social mobility could be deployed against the property-owning classes. In Italy the world-view propagated by the clergy remained essentially a reactionary one of an unchanging and scarcely changeable social order only to be tempered by fortitude, thrift and charity. Even the promulgation by Pope Leo XIII in 1891 of the famous encyclical on the social question *De Rerum Novarum*, which inspired many among the lower clergy to set about the establishment of a Catholic alternative to Socialist and trade-union forms of militancy, was reined back a decade later by a Papal interdict on the activity of these Catholic 'social modernists', although its concerns remained a major current, first in the Italian Popular Party, the Catholic party which was founded in 1919, and again in 1943, when it was restarted under the title of Christian Democracy.

The origins and development of both the ideas and the structures of what had become known by the turn of the century as the *movimento operaio*, in effect the Italian Labour Movement, cannot be understood except in the specific context of the options and constraints issuing from the period of the

Risorgimento and the Liberal State. It is no accident, in a country where most citizens only encountered the state in the form of the tax-collector and the recruiting sergeant, that it developed in specific antagonism to the concept and practice of 'national unity' so embodied. Rejection of the apparatus of the 'modern state', to wit the centralised, bureaucratic and heavily authoritarian version created by the *destra storica* and sustained and in some important ways strengthened by the *sinistra storica*, went hand in hand with rejection of the cultural justification for it in the various versions of nationalism advanced as a fundamental legitimising principle by left and right alike, even when offered in the guise of 'patriotism'. In this sense the persistent internationalism of the socialist opposition to the Liberal State was the refusal to cooperate in any way with those forces in Italy which, in however arbitrary, muddled and cynical ways, were after all seeking to bring about by political means the industrialisation of the country and thereby to modernise its economy and social arrangements.

Despite its bloodthirsty calls for the humbling of the mighty and its resounding protests at the injustice and inequity inflicted on the exploited and dispossessed, it was a historically backward-looking, even reactionary response. Examined dispassionately, the famous episodes of popular revolt which formed the sustaining mythology of the Italian Labour Movement for a century or more (brigandage, grist-tax rioting, the Carrara quarrymen's insurrections, the millenarian Sicilian agitations of the 1890s) have far more in common with the Gordon Riots, Luddism and Captain Swing in England, or the *Vendée* in France, than with the explicitly political actions of the French Revolution, or even Peterloo and the Chartist Movement. They were not demands for a due participation in the enterprise of remaking society and sharing in the fruits of change ('progress') but a chaotically violent rejection of change as such, without any alternative vision of the future to offer except a backward-looking dream of an archaic utopia, without *signori*, without armies, without taxes.

Viewed in this perspective the internationalism and subversive rejection of all 'national' and 'bourgeois' authority by the Italian Labour Movement appears at best ambiguous. Though the Socialists took over much of the symbology and rhetoric of Bakuninism and later of Marxism, their antipathy was not to the 'bourgeois' state, but to the state as such. And in this it was clearly convergent with the root and branch critique of capitalism emerging from the Catholic social movement in the same period of rapid proselytisation of the masses who could play no part in the Italy of the Liberal State. Although the Vatican, whose principal interest always lay in underpinning and legitimising the dominant position of the traditional power-holders in agrarian society, soon took steps to discipline the radical leaders of the social movement, the élite of the Liberal State, for their part, were in no doubt that this phenomenon was a subtle prolongation of the Papacy's non-recognition of and noncooperation with its attempts to modernise Italy. In the two decades preceding the First

World War the increasing nationalistic overtones of workers' movements in other parts of Europe, even though their leaders officially preached the doctrine of worker internationalism, contrasts sharply with the 'anti-nationalism' of the Italian Labour Movement. The strength and the ambivalence of the feelings which underlay this political position presented a challenge to successive Italian governments and ultimately to the Liberal State itself.

Crispi himself was driven from office in March 1896, first by well-founded accusations of embezzlement and then by the dramatic failure of his attempts to colonise Abyssinia and the destruction at the battle of Adowa of an Italian army from which he had demanded an impossible military triumph. But the policies of authoritarian rule which he had introduced were not immediately abandoned, being continued for the next two years by a series of undistinguished but highly conservative ministries.

By May 1898 the whole country had broken out in disorders, with nearly half its provinces under martial law: the culminating episode was bloody riots in Milan when troops used artillery against socialist demonstrators, killing almost a hundred, for which King Umberto I awarded their commander a high military honour and lavished praise upon his service 'to our institutions and to civilization'. A month later the King appointed a 'cabinet of Generals', led by General Pelloux, which attempted in 1899 to pass a law restricting public liberties and effectively banning 'subversive' opposition groups.

When filibusters from the Left nevertheless prevented the passage through parliament of the law providing for legal suppression of opposition, the cabinet, egged on by the increasingly authoritarian monarch himself, tried to impose it by Royal Decree, only to be frustrated once again when the High Court declared such a measure unconstitutional. The cabinet resigned in the expectation that elections would renew its authority and provide it with a mandate to take a strong line but even the restricted electorate of men of property had by now had enough of the vicious circle of violence and repression and returned a parliament dominated by the moderate left, led by the indecisive but incorruptibly liberal elder statesman Giuseppe Zanardelli and the determined and wily rising star among the younger generation of politicians, Giovanni Giolitti, who together formed a 'government of reconciliation'. A week later King Umberto I, who had once admitted that the social question kept the monarchy 'sitting on the edge of its throne' was assassinated by an Italo-American anarchist, with the paradoxical result of strengthening rather than undermining the wave of public revulsion against a style of government that seemed to reflect a preference for relying upon authority rather than social consent.

In every way the turn of the century represents a watershed in the development both of the Italian economy and of the Liberal State itself. The policies of Crispi had brought the state into the leading role in the economy. His attempt to accelerate economic growth through protection, subsidy and colonisation was, however, accompanied by neglect of the 'social question'.

Figure 3.5 The state as political repression: troops firing on demonstrators in Milan in 1898.

By contrast the policies of Giolitti, Crispi's most significant successor in the period preceding the First World War aimed, while maintaining the state's economic leadership, to restore social peace by means of a series of social and political reforms which would be capable of winning the support of the hitherto intransigent adversaries of the state itself: the nascent labour movement and the Church.

In one sense, evidently, this was a return to the classic pattern of 'historic compromise', founded upon 'bayonets and bribes' which had been the basis of the precarious survival of every Italian government since unification of the country, and which had found its most complete expression in the transform-ism of Depretis. But Giolitti's new edition of the technique was undoubtedly the most far-reaching and the most successful in providing a framework for a new cycle of industrial growth and political restructuring. The more far-sighted northern politicians, in the light of the negative results of the authoritarian methods adopted by Crispi and his immediate successors in the 1890s realised that exploitation of the possibilities of economic advance deriving from protectionist policies was inextricably linked to the 'social question', and that the need was for a strategy of social consensus rather than one of social confrontation reliant upon state coercion and repression.

This meant creating a dialogue and a *de facto* social contract with the industrial working class which was rapidly forming by 1900 in the so-called 'industrial triangle', the favoured area with good communications and access to foreign markets which lay between Turin, Milan and Genoa. It was also understood by them that the 'contract' would have to be extended to the industrialised peasantry which by now formed a significant proportion of the rural population in the north of the country as a consequence of the rationalisation of agriculture and the introduction of monocultural production, especially on land being reclaimed between Emilia-Romagna and the Po delta.

Giolitti, who sat in the Italian parliament for 46 years from 1882, having begun his career in politics in the very year of the unification of his country, was probably the most able and far-sighted statesman produced by the Liberal State, rivalling Cavour in the boldness and subtlety of his thought and conduct. His first public offices were under Depretis, and in Crispi's first ministry he served as Treasury Minister. He soon fell out with Crispi, however, because of the latter's impetuous decisions, for the style of which the pragmatic Piedmontese Giolitti felt considerable distaste. His own first experience as Prime Minister, for 18 months in 1892–93 ended disastrously in a bank scandal. Although this was the responsibility of previous governments, and notably that of Crispi himself, who had suppressed a report on the illegal dealings of the Banca Romana, Giolitti was the one who was vilified by a hysterical press and hounded from office, despite the fact that once the scandal broke he had acted decisively to clean up the mess, enabling Crispi to return to office in the guise of the saviour of the nation's honour.

Giolitti's unpopularity among the political class of the day was certainly related to the programme of social reform and fiscal justice which he proclaimed, for even at this stage he had realised the growing urgency of the 'social question' if Italy was to overcome its problems as a latecomer nation. His declared aim was to improve the conditions of the urban working class, and in Turin he went to some trouble to forge links with their emerging organisations. But he was driven from office before any of the concrete measures proposed in his programme could be enacted: it was a lesson in political backstabbing that he did not forget, for during his main periods of office over 13 of the next 20 years he perfected the political arts of isolating and destroying his rivals and enemies, and of ensuring his own succession whenever there was a crisis.

Giolitti used the prefect system of provincial administration to ensure his success in three successive elections (1904, 1909 and 1913). His dominance of parliamentary politics throughout this period enabled him, albeit with pragmatic caution and using the device of strategic resignation in favour of much weaker or less skilled politicians, to enact a series of measures which ensured the right of workers to organise, peaceably protest, agitate and strike, while also consolidating the prosperity and confidence deriving from the first phase, between 1896 and 1906, of the spectacular, if belated, industrial revolution in the north of Italy. His greatest single achievement was, however, the great Electoral Reform law which, in time for the 1913 elections, extended the franchise from 3 million to 8.5 million. Undoubtedly intended to be the keystone of the general consolidation of the Liberal State at which he aimed, the paradoxical outcome of its introduction was the resignation of his government in favour of a rigid southern conservative who was to take Italy in a radically different direction, bring social and political polarisation to a point of paroxysm, and ultimately the downfall of the Liberal State itself.

Yet Giolitti's 'grand design' had been, precisely, to ensure that the authoritarian solution to Italy's problems would never again be tried. His ultimate goal was to form a broad consensual centre which would extend to the reformist wing, led by Turati, of the Socialists on the left and to the political Catholics, led by Gentiloni on the right. To this end he had wooed the moderate leadership of the fledgling parliamentary Socialist Party and, although unable to bring them, as he had hoped, into actual coalition with him, had succeeded in gaining their support for his trade union legislation. When, consequent upon his war for the conquest of Libya, the leadership of the Socialists was seized in 1912 by the extreme 'maximalist' wing of the Party led by Mussolini, and Giolitti was left without essential parliamentary support, he had also sought to tempt the Catholics, who were increasingly active in local politics, into formally entering the arena of national policies.

It was his apparent final triumph in the latter direction which led to his downfall. With the hard-nosed pragmatism typical of his political style, he had made an unofficial deal with the Catholic political leaders to have the *Non expedit* by which the Church forbade the faithful to become involved in the political life of the Italian Kingdom, lifted from over half the constituencies in the country in preparation for the 1913 elections on the new, extended franchise, to ensure that his Liberal candidates would be backed by the new Catholic electorate, and thus prevent a massive Socialist advance. By this manoeuvre he planned to strengthen the moderate leaderships of both factions against more extreme elements both inside and outside the parliamentary spectrum, while making both of them dependent on his mediation.

Although the Catholics had not yet formed a distinct political party, they were already well organised in a broad front of supporters of the Church's social policies known as the Catholic Electoral Union. Its leader was Count Ottorino Gentiloni and the revelation in an anti-Giolittian newspaper that the deal, to which the journalist had given the name of the Gentiloni Pact, had led to the election of 228 supporters of government who had pledged to promote the Church's 'seven commandments' on civil liberties, divorce and other social issues, created outrage among the intransigent secularists of the Radical Party who had until then consistently supported Giolitti.

Their withdrawal of support reflected not only their own dismay at what they regarded as an ultimate exercise in disreputable transformism but the rejection of 'Giolittism' as such by an unholy coalition of extraparliamentary extremists, sea-green incorruptibles of left and right such as the historian Gaetano Salvemini and the future leader of the Catholic Popular Party, Don Luigi Sturzo, the fire-eating jingoists of the Italian Nationalist Association, and righteously indignant southern politicians who could see the prosperity gap between north and south steadily widening, alongside his traditional adversaries of the parliamentary right. The lethal ingredient in this mixture of opposites was, however, less the distaste for Giolitti's political manipulations, than the rejection of consensus politics as such and the accumulated resentment of Italy's status as 'the least of the great powers'.[14]

Although the application of policies designed to achieve the consensus Giolitti was seeking had been accompanied by over a decade of relative social peace and economic advance, it must be stressed that the situation was far from homogeneous across the country or even within single regions, and the underlying political polarisation which derived from the continuing co-existence of a 'real' and a 'legal' Italy, separated by stark differences in living standards, both material and cultural, was not greatly affected. The economic advance of the north was counter-balanced by the stagnation of the south, and the tensions resulting from the gap between classes and cultures were beyond the control of any government whose social base was as narrow and whose political base was as unstable as those of Giolitti's administration.

The 'leap forward' which his policies brought to northern industry inspired not emulation but resentment in the south. The basic dualism of Italian political culture rapidly reasserted itself as the compromises of the new-style transformism, on which his parliamentary and popular support depended, began to fall apart in the period 1912–14. Firstly, his political support was eroded by indignation among an influential sector of the educated middle class both against his frequent recourse to the gerrymandering and corruption on which his power in the south relied, and which had earned him the title 'Minister of the Underworld', and against what, when he formed the unannounced tactical political alliance with the Catholics, was regarded as a cynical betrayal of the secularism which was the historical legacy of the *Risorgimento*.[15]

The same sector was then also shocked by his apparently cynical resort to the high-risk policy of international destabilisation over the Italian annexation of Libya, while no compensating support was gained by the piecemeal and haphazard conduct of the war with Turkey which ensued. On the contrary, Giolitti was derided by the very Nationalists emerging on the right wing of politics whose influence he had intended to weaken.

---

14. Cf. R. Bosworth, *Italy, the least of the Great Powers: Italian Foreign Policy before the First World War*, Cambridge University Press, Cambridge, 1979.
15. He was characterised as such by the prominent southern historian and *meridionalista* Gaetano Salvemini in a famous critique of corrupt electoral practices entitled *Il ministro della malavita*, published in 1909.

Figure 3.6 Apprentices in colonialism: Italian officers viewing executed Libyan rebels, 1912.

Thus, despite having an overwhelming majority of deputies ready to vote for him in parliament as a result of the electoral pact he had made with Gentiloni, Giolitti decided that the moment had come to move out of the limelight. In March 1914 he resigned, as he had done twice before during moments of unpopularity, in 1906 and 1910, allowing a prominent member of the opposition to become Prime Minister for a few months until he was ready to bring about his downfall and return to power. He undoubtedly had the same intention on this occasion, when in effect he allowed a second-rank conservative, Antonio Salandra, to take office.

Salandra's government, as Giolitti had doubtless calculated, was soon floundering among growing social and political difficulties amounting to a general crisis of confidence in the political system. In June, police fired upon a worker demonstration, killing six men. A general strike was called in the Romagna and the whole region seethed with insurrection for a week, which entered history as 'Red Week', with occupations of municipal buildings, more dead and wounded, and even the declaration of Republics in two major towns. On 3 August, however, the First World War broke out and the Italian political situation took on a completely new complexion as all the pre-existing tensions and cleavages in political and civil society merged into a general and intense polarisation between those in favour of Italy's intervention in the war and those against it. All political parties and movements, from the Socialists to the Catholics, were split over the question. Only the *nazionalisti* were undivided on the need to intervene, although even they differed as to which nations Italy should side with.

Salandra, well aware of the difficulty he would face if he joined the powers, Germany and Austria, to which Italy was still allied under the Triple Alliance which had been renewed only 18 months earlier, proclaimed neutrality in the conflict and declared that Italy's war aims must be those of 'sacred egoism' (i.e. 'put Italy first'), which offended some of the fanatics on both sides, and caused a diplomatic storm. By the end of the year, however, he had opted, in agreement with Vittorio Emanuele III, to bring Italy into the war on the side of Great Britain and France, thus abandoning Italian undertakings to the Central Powers. To obtain promises of adequate recompense from Britain and France required a further six months of secret bargaining and it was only at the beginning of May 1915 that the Italian government denounced its pact with Germany and Austria and was thus free to go to war against its former partners. To be in a position, however, to carry this decision through in the face of the intensely anti-militarist mood of the great majority of the population was quite another matter for a politician such as Salandra whose beliefs and political style were those of an uncharismatic authoritarian conservative and who had virtually no popular following in the country.

Finally, Giolitti's public caution over the question of Italian intervention in the First World War, and his irresolute attitude in May 1915 when he was in a position to prevent it his country becoming involved in what Pope Benedict

XV denounced as the 'pointless slaughter', finally undermined his reputation as the most skilful statesman of his day.

The First World War, which was to prove the greatest mobilising event in modern Italian history, and the ultimate cause of the final collapse of the Liberal State, was an event for which the country was in no sense prepared.

When Giolitti had come to power in 1900, the first impact of Italy's industrialisation had combined with the end of the world trade recession of the late 1890s to create a more optimistic mood among both rulers and ruled. Dreams of imperial glory and socialist utopia subsided (though did not entirely disappear) and all the most active social and political groups adopted strategies of improvement and reform in a climate of hope created by constantly increasing prosperity. Between 1896 and 1914 industrial production almost doubled, national income rose by 50 per cent and investment in industry by 300 per cent. Cheap electrical power from hydroelectricity in the north allowed Italian engineering and light industry to compete successfully in foreign markets and to maximise their initial advantage of cheap labour.

The political system was able to a much greater extent than previously to respond positively to the almost universal desire for orderly development: the first generation of Italian parliamentarians were largely supplanted by new men, while a strictly constitutional King, Vittorio Emanuele III, with considerable popular appeal, came to the throne and moderated the pressure upon political life from the industrial-military complex of generals, admirals and arms manufacturers. The leading figures in politics were now the pragmatic and unrhetorical group led by Giolitti himself, which skilfully used its primacy to maintain a decisive parliamentary majority. The reform of the banking system in the 1890s and the relative even-handedness of the public authorities in labour disputes had ensured over a decade a stable economic and social framework for growth and the steady diffusion of wealth and education. By 1911 illiteracy in the north was less than 20 per cent and in favoured Piedmont had fallen to 11 per cent. In the south, however, over half the adult population was still unable to read and write.

This persistence of illiteracy in the south is an indicator of the basic weakness of the apparent stability of *giolittismo*: in fact the north–south gap was widening rather than narrowing and the even balance of the 'historic compromise' between northern industrialists and southern landowners began to be undermined by the north's increasing dominance of economic and political life.

Socialists, clericals and conservatives all fished, for their different reasons, in these troubled waters. Although Giolitti could count on Socialist parliamentary support for his social reforms and on Catholic acceptance of a general strategy for creating social peace, neither group was prepared to recognise fully the legitimacy of the Liberal State, particularly in relation to the monarchy. Their diffidence and hostility to the state itself gave leverage to the anti-Giolittian conservatives in parliament who by 1910 were once again demanding a vigorous repression of dissent and 'subversion' and a more aggressive foreign policy to capture markets and raw materials, and forcibly to mobilise the masses in pursuit of 'national' goals conceived in terms of Italy's status as a Great Power. Only the massive outward flow of 3.5 million emigrants from the backward areas of the south to the New World kept social unrest from becoming even more politically explosive.

Even though Giolitti's version of *trasformismo* was intended, by means of a controlled process of participation through the co-option of leaders, to overcome the division of Italian political life into three hermetic groups, his political skills were, ultimately, a disadvantage to him. While he saw the *ad hoc* deals he did with Socialists and Catholics, and the plagiarism he practised in relation to their programmes of social reform, as merely a form of political good housekeeping, the groups he thus outwitted or manipulated felt their leaders were being corrupted. The 'men of principle' within them saw in his practices only an immoral attempt to bribe the leaders to acquiesce in a system which should be rejected *en bloc*. Both the intransigent revolutionaries in the Socialist party ('maximalists' because they insisted upon the fulfilment of the whole programme of socialism), and the young 'integralists' of the Catholic movement (who would not settle for anything less than policies totally inspired by 'Christian values') were ready, respectively, to cry 'traitor' at any sign of collaboration with 'the class enemy' or 'the forces of materialism'.

Giolitti's assumption that both the anti-system groups could gradually be won over to the Liberal State as a political system by a series of inducements, and that in the process their militancy would diminish, excluded the possibility that their real political motives might actually be incompatible with the very pillars of the system: monarchy and rights of property. At the same time the flexibility he had shown towards their demands for concrete reforms in the field of labour law, welfare and universal suffrage could be dismissed by intransigents as corrupting bribes and by conservatives as Trojan horses which undermined the coherence and the power of the state.

Despite his unassailable majority in parliament, an increasing gap opened up again between the *paese legale* and the *paese reale*, the constituted authorities and civil society. It was upon this gap that his most dangerous adversaries seized: when Giolitti sought, by undertaking a fresh colonial venture in Libya, to apply his policy of 'enticing the extremes towards the centre' to the ultra-nationalists and their industrial backers he was spurned by the *nazionalisti*, who dismissed it as a great imperial opportunity (to dismantle and take over large parts of the Turkish Empire) betrayed by a penny-pinching caution typical of 'the old political gang', while what was really needed were men of true imperial vision. In parallel contempt the 'maximalists' of the Socialist Party were given an invaluable opportunity to denounce 'militaristic, predatory capitalism' and to expel those Socialist parliamentarians who had dared publicly to express patriotic sentiments.

There was a measure of justice in the criticism levelled by the *nazionalisti*: though Giolitti had shown himself to be the most far-sighted Italian leader since the death of Cavour, he treated war as merely an extension of political administration rather than an occasion when only inspirational politics, not cool calculation, would suffice to inspire the sacrifices necessary to success. This became even more painfully clear in his pusillanimous response to the cataclysm of the First World War, when he suggested that Italy take diplomatic advantage of the situation without becoming actively involved in the hostilities. His passivity at the moment when lesser men were plunging Italy into a bloodbath without any clear idea of what it might achieve thereby, reflected precisely the most that his country was capable of after 50 years of statehood.

Thus at the end of Giolitti's period of dominance his policies and tactics had created greater polarisation, not greater convergence. Those who had collaborated with him had been fatally weakened within their own groupings while the political initiative had passed to the authoritarian and maximalist left and its mirror-image on the imperialist and corporatist right. Parliamentary opportunism, which had been the terrain on which Giolitti had been able to outmanoeuvre all his rivals and enemies for so long, now gave way to the politics of principle. For those whose interests were threatened by it, the open espousal of violent revolution in the cause of the 'international proletariat' by the Socialist Party could only be adequately met by an equally intransigent response in terms of the reaffirmation of the supremacy of the state, a hierarchical social order to reassert discipline, and above all a national mission to become an imperial power which would enlist the enthusiastic support of the masses destined to benefit from Italy's conquest of 'a place in the sun'.

Giolittian low-key wheeling and dealing in a devious quest for social and political compromise seemed to offer little prospect of defence for the rights of property and status compared with the well-presented and apparently 'progressive' package so confidently put forward by the *nazionalisti*. That this should be the case was no accident, but rather the outcome of a specific set of structural flaws in the Liberal State itself which had rendered it particularly vulnerable to the temptation to resolve tensions at home by playing for higher stakes abroad. It was a tendency which was to play an increasing, and ultimately determining rôle in the subsequent course of Italy's development.

From Liberal State to Fascism

Despite the major changes in the world balance of power and the rapid growth of the major imperialisms through colonial expansion in the period 1850–1914, Italian foreign policy remained entirely Eurocentric during the first 30 years of the existence of the unified state. From Cavour to Crispi, 'legal' Italy asserted itself outside Europe only in token fashion and as a hanger-on of the major colonising powers, as when Cavour offered in 1861 to join in the suppression of the Chinese peasant revolt known as the 'Boxer Rebellion'. Although the *sinistra storica* tried unsuccessfully to condition the expansion of French control into Tunisia and Morocco, and gratefully accepted a minor supporting rôle in the British hegemony over Egypt, Sudan and East Africa, 'real' Italy's presence in the outside world was much more effectively established by the rising tide of permanent emigrants to New World destinations, who on the whole tended to develop a far more deeply felt patriotism towards their new nations than to their country of origin.

In Europe itself the concept of the unification and independence of Italy as an assertion of the revolutionary nationalism of peoples, with its implications of democratic popular sovereignty and consequent impulse to societal reform, against the dynastic settlement of the Congress of Vienna in 1815, met with total defeat in 1848-49. Italy did not 'go it alone' as Carlo Alberto had proudly proclaimed it would, precisely because it represented at the time a revolutionary threat to the existing social order throughout Europe and it was unthinkable for the Piedmontese monarch, as the prime representative of 'throne and altar' in the peninsula, to compound his dynastic war against Austria by throwing in his lot with the revolutionary republics set up in Rome and Venice.

Crispi was later to denounce what he termed 'the diplomatisation of the *Risorgimento*' but in fact, as Cavour had rightly perceived, Italian unification against the wishes of one of the Great Powers of Europe could only be brought about with the active support of at least one of the others and with the general blessing of the rest. After 1848–49, the key to unification was the resurgence of an effective French counterweight to the Austrian hegemony established by the Treaty of Vienna, and the possibility of reassuring the other major powers that a united Italy under Piedmontese control would prevent the country from reverting to a hotbed of social-revolutionary influence and would establish, on the contrary, a socially conservative, unthreatening and unambitious European state with its own native ruling class capable of maintaining a more durable political stability than could be guaranteed by Austrian policing.

Although this condition was met, if barely, by Cavour's powers of persuasion, recognition of the new kingdom was, with the exception of Britain, far from immediate or ungrudging. Austria only formally acknowledged its existence when forced to do so by Bismarck's military triumph in 1866, and even France, under Louis Napoleon, was as late as 1870 still trying to promote a triple partition of the country (Piedmont-Lombardy, Papal state, Bourbon Kingdom of the south). Even the uninvolved powers did not give Italy formal recognition until 1867, thereby acknowledging at last that it had become part of a new 'concert of Europe'.

During the first decade of its life as a nation-state Italy was generally regarded as a French protectorate and the claims put forward that, because it had the sixth largest population it should be treated as 'the sixth Great Power' of Europe, especially if spiced with Mazzinian rhetoric about Italy's historic civilising mission, fell on deaf ears abroad. Despite the sacrifice of blood and treasure by the French in the cause of Italian unification in 1859–60, many of the most ardent Italian supporters of the same cause saw in the intervention of Napoleon III no more than an exercise in the dynastic power politics of a reactionary tyrant, greedy for territorial gain (Nice and Savoy) and determined to protect the Papal state.

Cavour and the *destra storica* had, of course, fully realised the debt that Italy owed to French support, and friendship with France remained the basis of their foreign policy. Yet the failure to 'redeem' the Italian-speaking areas of Trent and Trieste in the war of 1866 continued to rankle and was compounded by fear of Austrian domination of the Adriatic as the Habsburg Empire extended its hold over the Balkan peninsula. The result was a permanent source of tension in domestic political life between the anti-French sabre-rattling demagogues whose Mazzinian watchword remained *Austria delenda est*, and those with the responsibility for avoiding foreign disputes which the country could not hope to win, and anxious to overcome the suspicion abroad of Italy's presumed hidden foreign policy agenda of 'redemption' of Italian lands and hegemonic ambition in the Mediterranean.

From the first, Italian foreign policy revealed the profound mutual conditioning of domestic and foreign situations which were to mark the country's history as a nation-state. The only rational foreign policy for a weak and vulnerable country was one of measured neutrality, to cultivate powerful friends while avoiding provocation to probable enemies: 'always independent, but never isolated' as the Kingdom's first foreign minister put it.[1] But the only clear choice as a friend was Britain, a country whose interests largely lay beyond Europe and whose tradition was to avoid entanglements with any continental power. On the other hand, whatever historic debts might be owed and acknowledged, the mere existence of an Italy which might attempt to thwart French ambitions southwards and eastwards was already a permanent provocation to one of its stronger neighbours, and its very existence was an affront to Austria, a multinational empire whose power it had successfully defied in the name of the self-determination of nations.

From the point of view of finding a counterweight to the latter, Italy needed a powerful continental friend, but the only possible combination was with the new German Empire created by Bismarck after the defeat of the French in 1870 and the downfall of Louis Napoleon. But was it possible for an Italy created by French sacrifice in the cause of Liberty to envisage an alliance with a nation whose natural sympathies would inevitably tend towards an accord with the other great German-speaking power, and which was therefore increasingly likely to become a bastion of European reaction? At the very least, persuading Italians still intoxicated with the rhetoric of the *Risorgimento* to accept such an alliance was bound to be risky for domestic political alignments, and would also tend to weaken the prestige of the monarchy since it would inevitably, in a dynastic age, be forced to take a leading public rôle in the matter. The risks were compounded by the universally changed perceptions of international relations when the Mediterranean ceased to be a backwater and became the world's chief waterway between west and east.

Until 1869, Italy's importance in the wider calculations of other European powers was relatively limited, but in that year, with the opening of the Suez Canal, the situation was transformed, for the country now lay across the most important trade route in the world. Consequently, the other powers increasingly sought to woo or coerce the Italians into a rôle of permanent peaceful subordination to their interests and to resist any manifestation on their part of foreign policy assertiveness. A second critical factor related to the country's geographical location also came into play as the power of the Turkish Ottoman Empire in continental Europe and north Africa began to wane and the major European powers sought to fill the vacuum in ways that suited their interests, by territorial accretion, support of local nationalisms, and economic and cultural penetration. Italy, which had a window upon the Balkans as well as upon the north African littoral, thus became the object of the foreign policy of other powers, while at the same time, despite its economic and military weaknesses, its governments increasingly sought to become protagonists in the wider trends of European expansionism in those areas.

---

1. This was Emilio Visconti-Venosta, a Garibaldian volunteer in 1848 who switched his support to Cavour during the 1850s; he was foreign minister in the governments of the *destra storica* for almost a decade.

Thus, before the country possessed the material and cultural resources to play a great power rôle in Europe, it was already being tempted to try to become the arbiter of the European disputes of far greater powers and to participate in the 'scramble for Africa'. Its new geopolitical importance in the calculations of other countries and the unresolved complexities of the vision of its own ruling élite concerning the rôle it should play in the world led Italy into involvement in the growing polarisation between France and Germany which overshadowed continental diplomacy throughout the 40 years preceding the First World War.

The involvement was not simply that of ambitious or ideologically inspired politicians: it went hand in hand with the ruthless determination of Vittorio Emanuele II and Umberto, his successor in 1878, to retain and exploit to the full the wide powers of initiative and expenditure in diplomatic and military matters conferred upon them by the *Statuto*.[2]

The extent to which these powers might affect the choices possible within the other realms of policy can easily be grasped if one considers that even after the 1860s, when the military costs of unification and pacification absorbed in some years over 60 per cent of the state budget, Italian military expenditure accounted for 18–25 per cent of the taxation revenues between 1870 and 1890. The Ministers of the armed forces were invariably generals or admirals personally appointed by the sovereign and had a personal allegiance to him as their supreme commander. Italian prime ministers had therefore no real control of that portion of the national budget and, in diplomacy, were reduced to acting as the obedient tools of the monarch even when they regarded his policies as mistaken or worse.

Thus the goals and methods of Italian foreign policy during this period developed within a determining context of external and internal pressures the responses to which were usually inappropriate and on occasion tragically costly to the country. In pursuit of a more prominent rôle on the European stage, a 'defensive' Triple Alliance against France, Italy's traditional if overbearing friend, was concluded in 1882 with its traditional enemies, the Austrians and the Prussians. This was renewed and strengthened twice during the period up to 1915, and eventually bound Italy to come to the aid of either of its partners, or at least remain benevolently neutral, in the event of any war in which the latter were involved, with a pledge of territorial compensation for Italy in the event of victory. At the same time, however, there was a move to

---

Figure 4.1 Italy's first reversal of alliances: the Italian King greets the German Kaiser in a pact against France, Italy's traditional ally.

2. The *Statuto* stated the situation as follows: 'The king alone has executive power. He is the supreme head of the state, commands all the armed forces by sea and land, declares war, makes treaties of peace, of alliance, of commerce, but giving notice of them to the two Houses *as far as security and national interest permit* [author's italics].'

hedge this bet by concluding a neutrality pact with France in 1902 and by cultivating good relations with Britain and Russia, the three powers which formed the counter-availing Triple Entente in the years preceding the First World War.

The objective was that Italy should become a decisive factor in all their calculations and therefore be offered inducements to take action or remain inactive in the case of conflict. This policy, which Mussolini was later to call 'the policy of [being] the last straw', was intended to make Italy feared and respected but in practice it had the opposite effect, for it highlighted the lability and lack of principle of Italian foreign policy at the same time as it revealed the country's intrinsic lack of military power to back it up.

After 1870 Italian domestic politics were increasingly affected by foreign policy considerations: the effort of modernisation (in effect to harmonise the development of industry with the bureaucratisation of the state) was more and more directed to the creation of the military and naval resources and the unthinking loyalty to the *patria* which were needed to underpin the 'great power' rôle forced, or so it was thought by the ruling élite, on the country by its strategic importance. The overall domestic effect of the pursuit of these policies was to increase the polarisation between those who demanded greater 'discipline' (i.e. rigid social and political control of the masses) as an indispensable condition of the survival of the Italian state in a world of stronger predator nations, and those who wished to diffuse the benefits of unification and modernisation as a condition for solving the problems of social and economic backwardness in Italy.

The essential choice confronting the successive rulers of Italy, both left or right, was whether to act as if Italy were already an industrialised and militarily formidable country, or to acknowledge its relative weakness and act accordingly. The policy of bluster was generally adopted not only in order to create a false impression of defensive capacity in the minds of potential aggressors, but mainly in order to overcome the population's suspicion or indifference towards the state and win it over to the 'Idea of the Nation' (*l'Idea nazionale*, as the extreme right-wing nationalist movement dubbed its newspaper founded in 1911). The alternative was an apparently pusillanimous public calculation of relative advantage in foreign affairs which had limited appeal to romantic intellectuals reared on the mythologised, and largely mythical, glories of the *Risorgimento*.

The extraparliamentary opposition, and in particular the Socialist Party, had a completely different perception of, and prescription for, foreign policy: 'proletarian internationalism', expressed in the slogan 'The workers have no fatherland'. Although this became an article of faith for the millions of Italians who identified with the Socialist programme, it could have no attraction for the men of the Liberal State loyal to a militaristic dynasty. The unworldly pacifism of the Socialists in this respect was largely matched by that of the Catholic-led peasant movement which was already gathering mass support in several regions, even if the Catholic middle classes and their political leaders, and a large section of the hierarchy, were not opposed to war as such if it advanced the interests of the universal Church both at home and abroad.

The attraction of an aggressively nationalistic stance was that it provided an apparently superior compromise between the political realism suited to a world increasingly dominated by the militarism of potential friends and foes and the unfinished agenda of the *Risorgimento*: the political unification of the country and the 'nationalisation of the masses'. The supreme crisis of this struggle for the soul of the Italian people between 'interventionists' and 'neutralists' was to come in the months between August 1914 and May 1915 when the stark issue that could not be avoided was whether to join in the First World War, and if so on which side. But long before those fevered months, the battle lines between the two fundamentally differing visions of what stance Italy should adopt in foreign affairs had been clearly drawn, in the disputes between free-traders and protectionists, between the cautious realism of those who were content with *Italietta* (little Italy) and those who had visions of an imperial destiny, between those who would opt for a measured balance of 'independence always, isolation never', and those who wanted a policy of national self-assertion in line with territorial extent and population size.

In the 40 years following Crispi's first government, European and world tensions stemming from the unrestrained pursuit of national interests became increasingly sharp until they came to a head in the unprecedented slaughter of the First World War. For Italy during this period, four basic strategies were being proposed, by those working within the framework of the Liberal State and those outside it, all of them marked by a fatal disproportion between the ends projected and the means available to achieve them.

The first strategy, attempted by Crispi himself, was a costly and tragic failure: to imitate the imperialism of greater European powers in the corners of Africa not so far colonised by others, he embarked upon an ill-prepared and vastly ambitious plan to create an Italian empire in the Horn of Africa. With the benevolent approval of the British, Italy had acquired a trading station in Eritrea in 1885 and had gradually thereafter secured it by unopposed occupation of its hinterland. In 1889 the boundaries of this incursion towards the inland empire of Menelik II were regularised in the Treaty of Uccialli, but two years later Menelik denounced it because the Italians were claiming that it gave them rights of protectorate over his empire. In 1895 frontier incidents led to an attempted advance by an Italian army without a declaration of war. The Italian commander, vastly outnumbered and with uncertain supply lines, wanted to retreat, but Crispi, desperate for a political success abroad to stem the tide of opposition at home, ordered him to attack, with the result that for the first time since Hannibal an African army destroyed a European one, the Italians losing almost half their army in the débâcle. The revulsion at home swept Crispi from office, and exacerbated social and political tensions to the point where the monarchical *putsch* of 1898–1900 could be attempted.

The second strategy, which commanded general assent in the first decade of the twentieth century, was to look inwards to the needs of Italy as an industrialising power, encouraging the rapid development of a diffuse capitalism. For success, this approach required a foreign policy which deliberately kept Italy out of the international limelight and on the sidelines of disputes as far as possible, and a cutback in armaments. Its heavy-handed pragmatism had the political disadvantage, however, of neglecting the frustrated romanticism of the Italian political tradition (shared by both left and right) and not providing any outlet for the enthusiasm and idealism of disaffected young middle-class intellectuals nor, on the other hand, clear-cut alternative goals for the major industrial groupings and monopolies which had previously relied for their profitability on large-scale weapons procurement by the state.

The third, purely hypothetical, strategy was that being put forward by the parties representing the workers' movement. It proposed, as a consequence of a supposedly imminent world proletarian revolution, the dismantling of the nation-state in the cause of the international solidarity of the working class. It had, of course, no influence on practical politics, but it did have the collateral effect of helping to keep the middle classes in a state of apprehension about the future course of events should serious concessions be made to the demands of the Socialist and Revolutionary Syndicalist parties, and thus encouraging the pursuit by certain groups within the 'bourgeoisie' of policies which would somehow harness the political awareness and latent energy being generated by the 'social question' among the unenfranchised workers and peasants to a 'new imperialism' based on the concept of a division of existing nation states into 'plutocratic' and 'proletarian'. Italy, of course, was regarded in this vision of things as one of the underprivileged countries in the latter category.

This fourth strategy, which ultimately prevailed and became one of the major components of Italian Fascism, was in complete opposition to all the previous approaches to foreign policy adopted by the Liberal State. Its presupposition was that Italy could only fulfil its destiny as a potential 'Great Power' if a new kind of state replaced the existing one. The new state, in contrast with the Liberal State whose fundamental principles were those of liberty and equality (even if the practice fell far short of the theory), would be based on hierarchy and discipline, a command system which would be capable of imposing the sacrifices needed to bring about an intensification of the industrialisation and rationalisation of the economy to support a programme of foreign conquest and colonial expansion.

This was, essentially, the programme of the Italian *nazionalisti* ('nationalists' in the extreme sense, verging on jingoism) who began to exert a crucial influence on political life and thinking from the end of the first decade of the new century. In 1910 their most prominent figures, Enrico Corradini and Alfredo Rocco began to publish their newspaper *l'Idea nazionale* which propagated effectively their populist-conservative concept of Italy being restructured as a corporative commonwealth, a producers' society, composed of a citizenry of proletarians all imbued with an intransigent patriotism. Borrowing heavily from the popular rhetoric of the socialist movement, their guiding concept in the campaign to win over the workers to this vision was the idea of Italy as the supreme example of the 'proletarian nation', that is a nation whose labour would continue to be exploited by richer ('plutocratic') nations until it carried out a 'revolution' and seized power (and resources) for itself by imperial expansion.

There is no doubt that the *nazionalisti* reflected a far-reaching sense of national mortification which had accumulated because of the long series of unmitigated failures in the country's attempts to join in the colonisation of Africa and to counter Austria's expansionism in the Balkans. In this sense 'imperialist sentiment in Italy developed out of the need to compensate for failure rather than to celebrate success'.[3] It was in the long shadow cast by that failure that the *nazionalisti* developed their most original and successful concept: the transfer of the idea of universal class struggle as the motor of history from the domestic to the international context. As a 'proletarian nation', Italy's inadequacies and backwardness could be attributed to exploitation by foreigners who had conspired to exclude her from the banquet of colonial conquests. But Italy was 'young and virile' (was her population not growing faster than that of France and Britain?) and could therefore be expected to pull herself up by her own efforts which would finally release her 'revolutionary energy'.

The association between colonial conquest, the cult of youth and dynamism, and the self-assertion of the oppressed and exploited classes was functional to the mobilising power of *nazionalismo* and later of Fascism into which it soon flowed: struggle, conflict and war became perceived as a law of history while social reconciliation and international peace were not only a cowardly and petty-minded acceptance of national weakness but also a refusal of any attempt to better the lot of ordinary Italians. Social justice became conditional, for this rising tide of opinion, upon victory and conquest in the struggle between nation-states in a new age of imperialism.

The *nazionalisti* were viscerally anti-socialist precisely because they saw the Socialists as the main protagonists of anti-national and anti-militarist sentiment among the working classes and thus as the supreme obstacle to the realisation of their programme. What they wanted above all was for Italy and Italians to be tempered by war and battle in the struggle between nations (which they saw as a natural extension of the Darwinian concept of the 'survival of the fittest'), rather than in a war between social classes to achieve a world-order which would supplant the nation-state altogether.

Typically, Giolitti, the master-schemer of Italian politics in this period of the Liberal State, sought to instrumentalise the rise of extreme nationalism as

---

3. Adrian Lyttleton, *The Seizure of Power: Fascism in Italy 1919–1929*, Weidenfeld & Nicolson, London, 1973, p. 16.

part of his strategy to 'transform' all extremisms by incorporating them into a complex and permanent mosaic of compromise at the centre of political life for the purpose of promoting steady and cautious reform. In this perspective they represented a useful counterweight to the extreme left, which had come to dominate the Socialist Party in the country (although not in parliament, where the reformist wing of the Party was predominant), and the even more extreme Syndicalist movement, which promoted general strikes as the main weapon of revolutionary education for the working classes and, with its anarchist connections, seemed to represent a continuation of the Bakuninist tradition of total insurrectionary violence against the state itself. What even Giolitti, for all his shrewdness, failed to perceive was that the two extremes he thought could be deployed against each other would in fact converge in a glorification of violence as the mainspring of political activity in both the domestic and foreign spheres.

It is evident that the development of Italian foreign policy under the Liberal State reflected the successive phases of the attempt to build a 'modern' nation and thus always had a close connection with the underlying features of domestic politics, particularly the waxing and waning of the concepts of transformism and 'return to the *Statuto*' as the basis of parliamentary life.[4] Although always capable of arousing strong feelings at home in relation to the stereotypes of the various rôles assigned to France, Britain, Austria and Prussia in the mythologies of the *Risorgimento*, its impact abroad was limited until the Libyan adventure of 1911–13 threatened to destabilise the whole balance of power in continental Europe.

Perhaps the most problematic issue of interpretation in relation to the foreign policies of the Liberal State is whether the constraints and pressures exerted by its more powerful neighbours and friends throughout the first half-century of its national existence were really a significant factor in determining the genesis of the 'Fascist solution' to the country's problems of relative backwardness. If the major powers in the world, especially Britain, had done more to facilitate Italy's colonial expansion and had heeded its diplomatic voice more attentively in the councils of Europe, would this have served to defuse the time-bomb of Fascism which was being prepared by the fatal mixture of protectionism and extreme nationalism?

Figure 4.2 Coming off the fence: Italian troops march across the frontier of their Austrian ally, May 1915.

---

4. The call for a 'return to the *Statuto*, was stigmatised by its opponents as a call for the dilution, or even the liquidation, of democratic parliamentary government, but the men of principle who supported it, notably Sidney Sonnino, were not so much opposed to the idea of a parliamentary régime as to its domination by factions and its distortion by *trasformismo*: the attraction of the monarch being unfettered in his choice of ministers was that he might therefore choose those above party and influence.

On the other hand, if the powers had conceded Italy the status its political élite desired for it, but was too weak to impose, would not that simply have encouraged the extremists to demand still more? This is what appears to have happened during the 1930s, when Britain in particular sought to detach Mussolini from the ideologically-based link with Nazi Germany. Some Italian historians have speculated intensively in this counter-factual fashion, as if attributing Italy's later delinquencies to an unhappy and deprived childhood. Tracing the development of Fascism, however, probably requires a less simplistic metaphor, and it is at least as persuasive an interpretation of this period of Italy's modern history to look for the roots of Fascism in the multiple dualisms already noted which dominated the country's social and political structures and its political culture. Such a more balanced view would see Fascism as the outcome of domestic cleavages and tensions of which the foreign policy of the Liberal State was a reflection as much as a cause.

Whatever the interpretation of the long-term trends may be, the Italy that entered the First World War on 24 May 1915, against one, but not both, of its former partners in the Triple Alliance, switching its allegiance overnight to the powers of the Entente (at the time, Britain, France and Russia), was a contradiction in terms. Its armed forces were numerically large, but badly equipped, trained and led, experienced only in war and repression against fellow Italians; their commanders looked for their authority to their caste and their king, not to the elected representatives of the people and its government, which in practice had no control over the high command; its population was mainly composed, on the one hand, of credulous, peace-loving pre-industrial peasants and simplistically militant socialist proletarians, and on the other, of a substantial emergent lower-middle class of shopkeepers and professionals who, combining a sense of social inferiority with a fear of being driven back into a lower socio-economic status, were particularly vulnerable to nationalistic rhetoric. Its political tradition and administrative culture were a compound of compromise and corruption at the top and coercion at the base. In short, it was largely unprepared to confront the stress and the sacrifice of heavily armed mass warfare of the kind which had already been revealed in France as the essential character of the war that was to change the face of Europe.

Even the ways in which the Italian intervention was planned and executed were a summation of all the negative features of the country's experience in the previous half-century. Ignoring the baleful long-term consequences for Italy's public image, there had been months of secret diplomacy to prepare the overnight switch in Italian allegiance from one great-power grouping to the other, and to draw up in the secret Treaty of London the list of diplomatic and territorial gains, at the expense of weaker third parties, to be acquired by Italy once victory was achieved. Salandra and Vittorio Emanuele III in effect plotted behind the scenes to compel a parliament whose majority was firmly against Italian involvement to accept a vital national commitment in the making of which the elected representatives of the people had had no hand. The majority of the latter were still firmly neutralist, and their opposition to intervention was reinforced by the news of a successful Austrian offensive against the Russians, and the bloody failure of the attempt to seize the Dardanelles through the landings at Gallipoli.

Although for a moment it seemed possible that parliament would resist the pressure and Salandra actually offered his resignation (a majority of deputies even left their visiting-cards symbolically at Giolitti's house in Rome), the impossibility of leaving the Crown exposed to political defeat persuaded all alternative candidates for the premiership, including Giolitti himself, to refuse to form a neutralist government.

The sequence of political events in May 1915 was particularly complex and the pace extremely hectic. The period is often referred to as 'The Radiant May', a reference to the response to the resignation of Salandra's government and the possibility that the King might call back Giolitti in the form of mass demonstrations mounted by the interventionists and the atmosphere of frenzied patriotism created by the charismatic speeches of the poet Gabriele D'Annunzio. There was an orgy of patriotic posturing, with lurid oaths and public kissing of Garibaldian swords in a re-run of the *Risorgimento* myths often bordering on the farcical.

In fact, since it was known that the King was committed to war and would abdicate if the government drew back from it, none of the constitutional politicians, including Giolitti, was prepared to take over and the King was therefore formally justified in refusing Salandra's resignation. In the meantime, however, the interventionists at both extremes of politics had taken command of the streets on a brief tide of unthinking popular enthusiasm for war, setting an ominous precedent for this type of political mobilisation. Salandra was then able to receive a massive majority vote for full powers for war. Only Turati spoke against the motion and almost to a man the Giolittian neutralists voted for the government.[5]

On 23 May an official ultimatum was sent to Austria, and the following day the Italian army launched the first of the eleven offensives on the north-eastern front which over the next two and a half years would cost it 200,000 dead for a maximum advance of 12 miles, to be annulled in three deadly weeks in October 1917 when the Austro-German army routed the Italians at Caporetto and swept almost to the gates of Venice.

The Piedmontese General Cadorna, the Italian Commander-in-Chief, who stubbornly pursued a tactic of massed infantry attacks against entrenched

---

5. Salandra later claimed that the whole sequence of events was a plot to overawe parliament, but it is more likely that he simply took advantage of the hysteria whipped up by others. The episode and its implications are well-summarised and discussed in C. Seton-Watson, *Italy from Liberalism to Fascism, 1870–1925*, Methuen, London, 1967, pp. 440–50.

positions in the belief that a breakthrough could thus be achieved which would open the way for a 'war of movement', planned to fight two major battles and be in Vienna within two months. Three weeks after hostilities began he was complaining to Salandra of the unpreparedness of the army he had already commanded for a year and prophesying that a total war economy would have to be installed if he was to achieve his objectives by the end of the following year. By the end of October 1915 his army of one million men had already lost 25 per cent of its strength in dead and wounded, and had achieved no significant advance. Understandably, a serious problem of morale could already be discerned. Cadorna's response was to sack hundreds of senior officers and insist upon the most draconian field punishments for cowardice or surrender: hundreds of his own men were executed, or simply shot by their officers as they fled from the battle.[6]

Cadorna was technically the most competent general the Italians had, but his attitude to a war of attrition in which his own side was ground down even more terribly than the adversary's and his unconcealed scorn for politicians, for journalists, and for any welfare or other morale-boosting measures for the troops was worthy of his inflexible predecessors of the wars of the *Risorgimento*; it was yet another revelation of how the post-unification history of the country had failed to 'make Italians' of the great majority of his fellow inhabitants of the peninsula, nor to dissolve the contempt of the rulers for the ruled.

It is true that a few thousand young and idealistic middle-class interventionists volunteered for duty, and many of these fought heroically. They were, however, deeply distrusted by the professional officer-corps which was in charge of the war and almost none were allowed to qualify for a commission. Among them was Mussolini, once the young lion of the Socialist Party and the editor of its newspaper *Avanti!*, now an extreme interventionist with a newspaper of his own *Il Popolo d'Italia* (paid for largely by French Secret Service subsidies and contributions from armaments manufacturers). He still claimed to be a Socialist, now asserting that the war would provide the supreme revolutionary opportunity and should therefore be supported by the proletariat. Not surprisingly, his request for officer training was vetoed at the highest level.[7]

By the autumn of 1915 the volunteers were either dead or disillusioned; in any case their contribution to the military effort was bound to be negligible. The peasant conscripts thought they were mad, their officers tended to send them on the most dangerous missions. Propaganda in favour of the war was regarded by the officer corps, and by Cadorna in particular, as being just as

---

6. Cadorna complained bitterly that the penal code did not allow him to apply decimation to whole units, but it was used nevertheless on a number of occasions.
7. Mussolini was invalided out of the army in February 1917 after being accidentally wounded in his buttock by an Italian mortar-shell splinter.

distasteful and lacking in military seriousness as propaganda against it, and until late in 1917, when Cadorna was dismissed, even the high command's own communiqués were not systematically passed on to the troops.

Such considerations were equally a matter of indifference to the government of Salandra which, by mid-September 1915, was beginning to panic about the financial implications of the long war of attrition which both Cadorna and Vittorio Emanuele were now convinced would be inevitable. Taxes were increased but could not possibly meet the enormous costs of the armaments demanded by Cadorna: only a deficit finance scheme of vast proportions, with all its dire implications of inflation and long-term national indebtedness, could possibly yield the immediate cash needed.

The initial febrile enthusiasm for the war had rapidly declined and the idea of trying to drum up wide public support for it by publicity and propaganda was as alien to the élitist conservatives who were in office as it had always been since unification. In any case the only medium then available for such a campaign was the press, itself an élite cultural phenomenon and largely unread by the mass of potential conscripts whose level of literacy was problematic. It was another legacy of the way in which unity had been achieved and consolidated that no tried and tested channel of communication between 'legal' and 'real' Italy had yet been created. The only newspaper that was not entirely in the élitist mode was *Avanti!*, which continued to preach an unremitting neutralist abstentionism from any 'bourgeois' war.

As Salandra struggled to keep the war going without the consent either of the parliament or the people, the parliamentary neutralists began to revive, notwithstanding their overwhelming vote for the war only six months earlier. The impediment to any return to power of their leader, Giolitti, was not however capable of being removed, short of an abdication on the part of Vittorio Emanuele. Giolitti could probably have returned to office as a war leader at any time between December 1915 and June 1916, and was perhaps the only Italian figure who might have played the rôle of popular leader in the style of a Lloyd George or Clémenceau, but he was not prepared to run, on behalf of his less competent political enemies, a war of which he disapproved. His hostility to Salandra and his foreign minister Sidney Sonnino was only matched by that of the *nazionalisti*, who, disillusioned and frustrated by the bloody stalemate at the front, and conveniently forgetting that a year earlier they had called for full support of the Central Powers, now railed against the government for fighting 'a mean little war of its own' instead of cooperating fully with the Entente Powers in a total war against Germany as well as Austria.

By December 1915 there came the first wave of concerted criticism of the conduct of the war, led by interventionists who had actually experienced conditions at the front. They publicly attacked Cadorna's 'big push' strategy of attacking *en masse* along the whole eastern front, and his neglect of the welfare of the troops (described in a report after his eventual dismissal in 1917 as 'mystical sadism'). Even in the cabinet there were critics of Cadorna who wished him to be summoned to attend a war planning meeting at which they could impose their alternative strategy of attacking on a limited front in the hope of achieving a penetration in depth of the enemy defences. But when Salandra adopted this suggestion himself and asked the King (who was, of course, the only person authorised to give orders to the military) to act upon it, Vittorio Emanuele simply ignored him and Cadorna continued to plan further mass offensives to be launched in the spring of 1916.

Before he was ready, however, the Austrian commander launched what he contemptuously called a 'punitive expedition' from the north which for a few days appeared to threaten the Italian army with being cut off completely. Once more summoned to Rome, Cadorna again refused to come, adding insult to injury by submitting a one-page report hinting that he might have to withdraw his armies from the eastern front to defend Venice. The King still refused to take any action against Cadorna, the darling of the interventionists, and this encouraged the *nazionalisti* in parliament to turn against Salandra whose government was voted out of office on 10 June 1916 amidst a hail of criticism for not declaring war on Germany as well as Austria and thereby letting its allies down.

Salandra's Liberal-Conservative ministry was replaced by a 'government of national unity' led by a 78 year-old political mediocrity, Paolo Boselli, the 'father of the house', whose personal view of his own appointment to lead the country was that it was 'a piece of tomfoolery'. His government, designed to still all criticism by making all factions responsible for it, included token representation of all the main political groupings, even including a Catholic, a Republican and two renegade Socialists who had joined the interventionist cause. With such an assortment of discordant views within it, it reflected perfectly the irrelevance of any government of politicians in a war of such dimensions and costs, conducted virtually as a private matter by the King and his Commander-in-Chief.

Only one of the cabinet dared to challenge this arrangement, the Socialist Leonida Bissolati, who at 58 had been one of the first volunteers to go to the front, where he had distinguished himself in combat. He had been expelled from the Socialist Party in 1912, after Mussolini had declared him a traitor to the proletarian cause in a powerful speech, and had then founded a Reformist Socialist Party which had become the focal point for many of the 'left interventionists'.

Despite his support for the war, Bissolati remained a man of the left and saw his appointment as Minister without portfolio as an opportunity to demand the democratisation of its conduct, calling for a public enquiry into the military unpreparedness which had led to the near success of the Austrian *Strafexpedition* of May. Cadorna's fear of politicians was not diminished by Bissolati's war record: his response was to refuse to have any dealings with the Cabinet except through the Minister of War and to insist on a total ban on all demands for any kind of enquiry into his conduct of operations. Boselli surrendered abjectly, while Bissolati became one of Cadorna's most obsequious adulators. It was further proof, if any were needed, that the war itself was now the only motor of Italian politics.

This effect was equally apparent in the areas of political life which had stood aside from the war and what Salandra had described as the 'national idyll' of patriotic enthusiasm. The Socialist Party had adopted the slogan 'No support, but no sabotage', leaving itself with the worst of both worlds: it was neither able to benefit from the currents of patriotic sentiment which continued to suffuse a significant proportion of the middle classes, nor to assume the leadership of the currents of militant disaffection inspired in the urban working class by the hardships and sacrifices imposed by a war economy, nor even represent effectively the alienated suffering of the mass of peasant conscripts and their families. *Avanti!* continued to present the conflict as purely a clash between rival capitalist imperialisms whose ultimate outcome was bound to be a world revolution of the international proletariat which would sweep away the old order and install the brotherhood of mankind. This imprecise perspective made it possible to hold together most of the various currents in the party: the revolutionaries ('maximalists') could believe in an imminent violent revolution while the reformists, led by Turati, could continue to believe that the great change could occur without resort to violence because the capitalist system would simply collapse under the weight of its contradictions. Only an extreme left faction, led by men who were later to found the Italian Communist Party, tried to implement the promised revolution when in August 1917 they staged a rebellion in Turin against the cost of living and the war. Troops were brought in to restore order and did not hesitate, despite being peasant conscripts who had experienced the horror of the trenches, to fire upon their proletarian brothers. It was an episode that might be seen, with hindsight, as a significant turning-point, not in the irresistible rise of revolution but rather in the 'nationalisation of the masses'.

The Catholics responded to the war almost as incoherently as the Socialists, the lower clergy frequently sharing the patriotic urges of the middle class, and invariably lending the comforting power of religion to alleviate the psychological traumas inflicted on the troops by the appalling conditions at the front. At the same time, however, Pope Benedict XV, deeply concerned that Italy, whose legitimacy the Vatican still contested, was at war with Austria, Catholicism's staunchest supporter, repeatedly urged all belligerents to put an end to 'the suicide of Europe'. In August 1917 he sent a note to both sides pleading with them to desist from the 'pointless carnage': it was not well received by either, and provoked furious denunciation from the Italian interventionists.

In the war zone scarcely an echo of these attitudes and events reached the combatants themselves. Until the end of 1917 not only had there been no attempt to keep the troops informed even of the progress of the war in which they were involved, but Cadorna, sensing 'the rising tide of their

disgruntlement', made it his business to repress forcibly any activity which might affect what he regarded as 'military seriousness', in other words the fatalistic resignation of his men to their wretched conditions and unexplained sacrifice. He thought the biggest danger to the war effort, and the likely cause of the repeated failure of his army to achieve the big breakthrough, was the 'subversive propaganda' which he believed was undermining the men's morale. That they might be weary of being used as pure cannon fodder evidently did not occur to him. The idea of organising a pro-war propaganda campaign to counter the supposed organised rumour-mongering and sabotage (of whose existence no evidence was ever found) had been resisted by Salandra in case it spread alarm among the civilian population that the war might after all not be the short and decisive one for which he hoped against hope. Morale-building measures at the front were confined to the provision of brothels in the rest-areas and a plentiful supply of *grappa* (a crude and fierce peasant brandy) before attacks were ordered: the soldiers called it *benzina* (motor fuel).

Besides the pointless sacrifice of lives inflicted by a high command which refused to believe the evidence of the experience acquired, on all the fronts of the war, that mass attacks against artillery and entrenched machine-guns could never succeed, thousands were killed or crippled by frostbite, cholera and typhus. Medical facilities were far more limited than in France and sanitary conditions were appalling. The order that not a yard of ground won should ever be abandoned meant that Italian front line trenches were often half-way up a mountainside so that the Austrians could attack them effectively by simply rolling boulders downhill.

The litany of the ineptitude and failure of the Italian ruling élite, in a war of its own choosing, could be continued almost to infinity, but it would be far from reflecting adequately the underlying developmental reality of the experience, at all levels of society, and of its effects upon the outlook and participative capability of the Italian people. In a real sense it was the first mass-mobilisation for a common purpose of most of the disparate elements which had been bundled together in the making of Italy as a nation-state.

This mobilising process was uneven: in particular, the mass of peasant conscripts, though fighting with the fatalistic endurance which their class had displayed for millennia, could not at this point be regarded as a 'people in arms' in the way that the soldiers of the French Revolution and Empire had been. Paradoxically, the mass-mobilisation did not achieve its full psychological effect until after the disaster of Caporetto in October 1917, when the German army first came in force to the assistance of the Austrians and employed, with brilliant success, a new tactic to break the Italian front, and advance some 80

Figure 4.3   Facing defeat: Italian military police herding deserters after Caporetto.

Figure 4.4 The war is over: an Italian soldier who survived it.

miles in less than three weeks.[8] The battle destroyed much of the Italian army, threatened to knock Italy out of the war and perhaps undo the *Risorgimento* itself.[9] French and British divisions had to be rushed to the aid of the reeling Italian army, which was attempting to stem the tide by mass decimations among the leaderless retreating troops, and the Austro-German army (hampered in any case by the logistical problems of supporting an unexpected headlong advance) was held on the River Piave line 20 miles east of Venice. The river gave its name to the only widely sung pro-war song: all those previously popular among the rank and file troops had been songs of despair and homesickness.

It was at this point that the First World War finally became a genuinely national war, and at the same time gave birth to one of the mystifications by which the post-war development of Italian politics was crucially influenced and around which post-war politics were to polarise: the belief that the Caporetto disaster was the result of 'defeatism' and a 'soldiers' strike' provoked by subversive Socialist and Catholic propaganda against the war. That there was no factual basis for this belief reinforced, if anything, its currency: what explanation other than sabotage could possibly account for a disaster on this scale, after the nation had thrown all its resources into the struggle?[10]

A further reinforcement of the myth derived from the emergence, as a direct result of the large-scale invasion of Italian territory by the ancestral enemy, of the first wave of genuine popular support for the war, now perceived as a *defence* of a hard-won national identity rather than a political adventure imposed by the *signori* on their unwilling subjects. The sentiment, by a psychological mechanism peculiar to a repressed sense of inferiority, was read back into the situation prevailing prior to the disaster: with the *patrie en danger*, few were prepared to admit they had previously harboured doubts about the necessity and the legitimacy of the war.

---

8. The new tactic, tried out first on the Eastern Front and later employed successfully in the last German offensive in France in 1918, was to secure a rapid breakthrough on a small sector of the front by the use of gas in a night attack and then to rely upon highly mobile machine-gun companies to enfilade successive lines of support trenches. By not relying on massive artillery bombardments prior to the attack total surprise could be achieved. One of the German junior officers who took part in the Caporetto operation was Captain Erwin Rommel.

9. The scale of the disaster at Caporetto can be judged by the statistics: the Italians lost some 40,000 men dead and wounded, 300,000 prisoners were taken, 350,000 Italians deserted, and 400,000 refugees fled westwards, leaving some 1.5 million civilians under enemy rule.

10. Some colour was certainly given to the myth by post-war Socialist boasts of having had a hand in bringing about the defeat at Caporetto, and by the rhetoric of much of the Socialist Party throughout the war, such as the denunciation of contributions to the Red Cross as 'oxygen for the war' and calls for 'revolution by defeat'. But there is no evidence that any of this affected the behaviour of the troops at Caporetto who, when outflanked and left without orders, simply did the most sensible thing and retreated as fast as they could.

Equally paradoxical was the bracing effect of Caporetto on Italian resistance both at the front and in the rear: the inept Boselli government of national unity was replaced by one led by two former protégés of Giolitti, Vittorio Emanuele Orlando and Francesco Nitti, who believed in the Wilsonian principle of national self-determination as the basis for the post-war settlement abroad and a new, more democratic and socially just settlement at home based upon a fully proportional electoral system. Cadorna was dismissed and replaced by a commander less dedicated to massed frontal assaults, new tactics were developed, including the creation of an élite corps of specialised commando-type assault regiments, known as *arditi*, capable of reproducing the kind of surprise achieved by the Germans at Caporetto, an orchestrated pro-war morale-boosting propaganda campaign (larded with promises of land for the landless in post-war Italy) was directed at the troops, now better clad, better equipped and better armed as a consequence of the total economic mobilisation finally achieved on the home front, and at last buoyed up by a sense that what they were doing at the front was appreciated by public opinion at home, and that there was a government in power determined to do something for them once the war was over.

The Fascist movement and the seizure of power, 1919–1925

The final year of the war on the Italian front saw a series of renewed attacks by the Austro-German forces against the well-prepared defences along and behind the River Piave: their initial small gains were, however, eliminated by successful counter-attacks and by the summer of 1918 the whole war machine of the multi-ethnic Habsburg empire was beginning to unravel. A final 'hunger offensive' in the mountains north of Venice was beaten back in August, partly because of the excellent intelligence provided by the growing number of deserters from the discontented Croatian, Slovenian, Czech and Romanian units whose loyalty to the Habsburg Emperor had frayed beyond repair. But General Diaz, Cadorna's ultra-cautious successor, still felt unready to attack and it was only in October 1918, on the anniversary of Caporetto, that he ordered a general offensive. After a few days' resistance the Austrian front crumbled and the Italian campaign was concluded with the victory of Vittorio Veneto, achieved against an army whose disintegration was already well advanced for internal reasons.

Nevertheless, it was in military terms a decisive outcome, yielding almost half a million prisoners, and to a considerable extent restored Italian military pride, which had been badly eroded by the previous course of the conflict. It appeared to leave Italy for a time in a position to assert itself as the dominant power in much of the Balkan peninsula, where the two great Empires, the Austrian and the Turkish, which had historically held sway there, had both been eliminated almost overnight. Yet, although the disappointed interventionists would never admit as much, Italy's diplomatic leverage was in practice somewhat less in 1919 than it had been in 1914–15, precisely because of the changes in the balance of power which the country's intervention in the war had helped to bring about. Anticipating such an outcome, the wilder spirits among the interventionists had already raised the cry of 'mutilated victory' in November 1918, contributing another crucial myth to the general public perception of politics in the post-war period.[1]

Further military adventure was, however, the last thing most Italians, in common with the conscripts of all Europe, wanted at this point: except for the professional military caste and the dedicated *nazionalisti*, the sacrifices had already been too great and the price too high for the dubious benefits of 'making Italy great'.

The comradeship of suffering in the trenches between peasant and artisan conscripts on the one hand, and middle-class junior officers and non-commissioned officers on the other, which for the first time in Italian history had brought a partial bridging of the social and cultural divisions between classes, was now augmented by a sense of common cause which had previously been lacking and which provided potentially new identifications, outside class allegiances, which were to complicate post-war political and ideological trends. Both parties to such an identification were likely to feel far more hostility to those who had, by luck or favour, stayed clear of the battle, in reserved occupations exempt from military service because of their essential technical skills, or simply by dodging the draft, than they did to one another. In the mind of the peasant or unskilled urban conscript, all of them were now likely to be regarded as shirkers or war profiteers.

Such sensations were too often powerfully reinforced by the experience of home leave, when many conscripts found themselves ostracized by former friends and comrades in political and economic struggle in trade unions and their peasant equivalents, the Socialist and Catholic *leghe*. For their part, junior officers felt disgusted by the blatant profiteering and high living of the *nouveaux riches* industrialists and middlemen who had benefitted from the extraordinary, chaotic and inflationary boom of the war years. This had almost doubled industrial production and real profits while concentrating ownership in fewer and increasingly powerful hands. At the same time real wages were reduced by over one third and more than half the able-bodied agricultural labour-force was conscripted or moved into the towns to work as unskilled labour in the booming war industries. It was not surprising that a popular slogan of the interventionist left in the immediate post-war months was a call for the confiscation of war profits. Nor was it surprising that peasant women invading the cities to protest at the price of bread attacked factory workers whom they regarded as profiteers, and that the professional urban middle-class owners of small country properties deeply resented the fact that, when inflation forced them to sell them off in a buyer's market, the purchasers who appeared were peasants whose capacity for self-provisioning in wartime had enabled them to save enough to buy them out.

These developments redefined the social and political polarizations

---

1. The phrase first appeared in an article by Gabriele D'Annunzio published on 24 November 1918.

which had characterised Italian public life prior to the war, between the *paese legale* and the *paese reale*, between town and country, between haves and have-nots, between advanced industrialised north and backward agrarian south, and between nationalism and internationalism as the basis of solidarity and identification. But they did not fundamentally blur them, still less overcome them: on the contrary, in many respects the accumulated tensions of Italy's remote and recent past were intensified by the experience of wartime sacrifice and dislocation, and of post-war instability. The tensions were, moreover, compounded, in the shanty towns and urban slums of these precariously industrialised workers, by the dissolving of the social cements of centuries of patriarchal social structures and their accompanying habits of mind.

These tensions were magnified by the experience of the First World War both at the front and behind the lines. The effects of the war dominated consciousness: a casualty list of 800,000 in three and a half years of conflict, with over half a million dead. Demobilisation was slow and the disaffected majority of soldiers fretted about what kind of Italy they would return to: those with left-wing sympathies with an envious eye on Russia, where the Bolsheviks had seized power and were fighting desperately to keep it, those on the right feeling embittered at what they regarded as a criminal waste of their sacrifices.

The polarisation of social classes, of political argument, of public attitudes was also intensified at every level: tolerance and gradualism, whether that of the Turatian reformist Socialists or of Giolittian Liberals and Democrats, were at a discount. Italians who were in any way politicised increasingly believed in, and looked for, draconian measures and decisive actions, for final showdowns, whether by the aroused masses seizing power in a Bolshevik-type revolution, or by new élites thrusting aside the effete political class which still clung to an outdated and unconvincing contraption of parliamentary government.

For a brief period in 1919 the latter was nevertheless the focus of most political hopes and actions. Orlando, who was still Prime Minister at the moment of military triumph, failed to reap the fruits of incumbency. Although Italy had, in the end, played a valiant and honourable rôle in the Allied victory, the removal of the Habsburg and Turkish empires and the concentration of Allied statesmen on the problems of German reparations and the new threat from the East stemming from the Bolshevik Revolution led to a relative indifference to the question of Italy's rewards in the post-war settlement. Indeed the secret diplomacy which had secured Italy's intervention by the Treaty of London now rebounded on the ambitions of the leaders who had conducted it.

The Bolsheviks had published the embarrassing full text of the Treaty, revealing the expansionist policies of the Italian government which had concluded it. The American President, Woodrow Wilson, was making much of the running in the negotiations at the Paris Peace Conference on the basis of the principles of national self-determination and collective security through an international organisation (the League of Nations) enshrined in his famous 'Fourteen Points'. Not having been a party to the Treaty, he would not endorse the commitments made under it, particularly the cession to Italy of the port of Fiume (now Rijeka), which was the only good deep-water harbour available to the new state of Yugoslavia which was then emerging from the wreckage of the Austrian hegemony of the western Balkans, and whose consolidation was considered essential by the great powers in order to underpin regional security.

In April 1919 Orlando and his foreign minister Sonnino walked out of the Conference in protest at the general indifference to Italian demands. They gained nothing by doing so and returned to Rome empty-handed, to general discontent at their performance. In June Orlando resigned, and was succeeded by Nitti who brought in a new electoral law based on fully proportional manhood suffrage. In November, after the first elections held under its provisions, he continued as Prime Minister of a broad coalition dominated by Giolittian Liberals and the new Catholic party, which took the name Italian Popular Party. Despite the hankerings of Turati and the Reformists, the Socialists would not accept the invitation to participate.

This was not, however, the classic Giolittian coalition. The largest party in the Chamber of Deputies, with 156 seats, was now the Socialist Party, and the Popular Party topped the hundred. The Liberal strength relied almost entirely upon the customary manipulation of the southern electorate, for most of their former supporters in the north, convinced of the inevitability of the defeat of the traditional party of order, had preferred to abstain.

Despite their apparent triumph, the 'outsider' parties were in no way parties of government, having no clear idea of what to do with their electoral success. The Socialist Party, indeed, publicly proclaimed its Leninist disbelief in parliamentary democracy, declaring it to be no more than a bourgeois deception of the workers, and refused to join any government. The Popular Party was prepared to do so, but was far from fully integrated into national political life, nor sure of its policies. The Vatican gave it only lukewarm support, fearing that it would compromise the position of the Holy See if it gave its blessing to Catholics who had accepted in full the legitimacy of the usurping Italian state. It was also fearful of the growing influence of the militant Catholic peasant leagues in the north and of the spread of forcible occupations of great estates in the south by landless peasants looking to the Popular Party for representation. The last thing the Vatican wished to see was a Catholic party dedicated to radical social reform.

The apprehensive middle classes lost faith in traditional parliamentary politics as the necessary vehicle for the advancement of their interests at a point when, in all probability, a reaffirmation of their usefulness as a means to bring about concrete political and social reforms might have created a historical perspective which did not lead to authoritarian solutions. The dangers they perceived in the Socialist Party as the agent of their violent revolutionary expropriation were illusory, for that party had no policy except to await the 'inevitable explosion of the contradictions of capitalism': despite such rhetoric, 'the maximalists were not seriously revolutionary, nor the reformists seriously reformist'.[2] The state and its organs of coercion at no time lost control of the situation in relation to labour unrest or left-wing revolutionary activity in the post-war period, not even in April 1920 when Factory Councils of workers modelled on the Bolshevik Soviets, and led by Antonio Gramsci and Palmiro Togliatti, the future leaders of the Communist Party, took over the main industries in Turin and Milan in protest against management plans for radical restructuring to meet peacetime conditions. Indeed, it was precisely at that moment that Giolitti, who had returned to office on a programme of reconciliation and reform, showed how effective was the pressure the state could apply through the mere threat of force backed by a willingness to bargain. The sit-down strikers were isolated and defeated without a shot being fired.[3]

The 'occupation of the factories' was not, however, widely perceived at the time as a harmless and limited episode of undirected worker militancy against the reassertion of management control. Its reception by the Italian public is a good illustration of the way in which political perceptions had been distorted by the prevailing myths (including those fervently propagated by the would-be revolutionaries): virtually everyone on the left and a significant proportion of those in the centre and on the right (for a few days even Mussolini, by then the most prominent leader of the revolutionary right) were convinced that the occupation of the factories signalled the onset of a Soviet-type revolution in Italy. Yet, if the classic definition of a revolutionary situation is taken as a benchmark, there was no possibility of revolution in Italy at the time: the forces of order were far from mutiny; there was virtually no contact between the occupying workers and the peasants, who constituted the majority group of the exploited; ex-servicemen of all classes had been seriously alienated from the cause by the sectarian manifestations of neutralism during and after the war. Nevertheless, something akin to a 'great fear' seized the middle classes, for the occupations, as Gramsci himself ruefully reflected years later,

> damaged vested interests, upset entrenched opinions, aroused dreadful hatreds even among the easy-going, awakened from their passivity social strata which had been stagnating in rottenness; they created, precisely because they were 'spontaneous' and no one would take responsibility for them, the 'general panic', the 'great fear' which were bound to unite the forces of repression in a ruthless drive to stifle them...[4]

---

2. Giuliano Procacci, *A History of the Italian People*, Weidenfeld & Nicolson, London, 1970, pp. 410–11.
3. The best account of these intriguing events is Paolo Spriano, *The Occupation of the Factories 1920*, translated and introduced by Gwyn A. Williams, Pluto Press, London, 1975.
4. Antonio Gramsci, *Passato e presente*, Einaudi, Turin, 1951, p.60.

If revolution from the left was not really on the agenda, the overthrow of constitutional order from the right certainly appeared to be. The discontent of the dedicated *nazionalisti*, however, soon brimmed over into far more threatening actions. In September 1919 Gabriele D'Annunzio, the agitator-poet who had helped to precipitate the intervention in May 1915, led a column of several thousand fanatics and mutineers to seize the port of Fiume, whose post-war status had still not been settled at the Paris Peace Conference, and which was therefore undefended.[5] Welcomed as liberators by the minority ethnic Italian population of the town (but not of course by the Croats and Hungarians who formed the majority), they set up a surreal 'Regency', with D'Annunzio as its charismatic leader. His main achievement was to keep the townsfolk for some 15 months in a state of perpetual excitement by means of constant parades, fanfares, speeches from the balcony of the city hall, and publication of dramatic manifestos and programmes, which in many ways anticipated (or were imitated by) the doctrines of Fascism and the Corporate State which Mussolini's acolytes were later to develop.

D'Annunzio's only real chance of success in his attempt to repeat this application of rhetoric to politics on the model of the 'radiant days' of May 1915, would have been to use it to precipitate an immediate military takeover of the whole of Italy. But it was by no means certain that the army was yet disaffected enough to join in the adventure. On the other hand, D'Annunzio and his supporters, despite some early attempts to woo the revolutionary wing of the Socialists and to persuade Lenin to recognise his mini-state, feared that any such revolt would get out of hand and result in a revolutionary process outside their control, for they too were far from immune from the 'great fear' (which for some, of course, was the great hope) then blocking any chance of progress to stability in Italian domestic politics. This error of judgement enabled first Nitti and then Giolitti to cut off support for the 'Regency', and successfully negotiate, by the Treaty of Rapallo of November 1920 with the newly-founded Kingdom of Yugoslavia, a general Adriatic settlement favourable to Italian interests, making Fiume a Free State and consigning the Italian inhabited port of Zara and some Adriatic islands to Italy. Finally, with one

---

Figure 5.1 The land to those who work it: Sicilian peasants returning to their village after the occupation of a *latifondo* in 1920.

---

5. D'Annunzio's 'legionaries' consisted, apart from the army mutineers (whose mutiny had been aided and abetted by their officers), of a curious mixed bag of extreme left-wing agitators drawn from the anarcho-syndicalist sects which had played a considerable rôle in fomenting a series of unsuccessful general strikes some ten years earlier and from the so-called 'futurist' followers of the poet Marinetti whose declared intention was to rid Italian culture of all its legacies of the past, from Dante onwards. The best account is probably Michael Ledeen, *The First Duce: D'Annunzio at Fiume*, Johns Hopkins University Press, Baltimore, 1977.

Christmas Eve salvo from an obedient cruiser, D'Annunzio's grandiose charade was brought to an ignominious end.

Mussolini was not at the centre of the Fiume episode. His newspaper, *Il Popolo d'Italia*, though no longer subsidised by French Intelligence funds, had found new backers among right-wing industrialists who foresaw a useful rôle as strike-breakers for the ex-service toughs he controlled. While writing moving editorials in support of D'Annunzio's legionaries, Mussolini had also channelled into the coffers of his movement most of the donations made in response to the paper's appeal for contributions. His articles, though fulsome in praise of the 'warrior-poet', usually managed to suggest that D'Annunzio's supporters were either hopeless idealists or mere adventurers without a real plan, and when Giolitti brought the comedy to an end, he did no more than lament its failure without suggesting any practical help could be given the 'legionaries' during the final crisis.

If Mussolini did little to help D'Annunzio, he clearly learned a great deal from the latter's failure, realising that however many sympathisers there might be among the professional military, this was not enough to overthrow even a weak government. It was necessary to have trained fighting men loyal only to him. From then on he developed his Fascist movement.

The word Fascist was derived from the *Fasci di combattimento* founded in confusion in a disused crypt by Mussolini in March 1919. Initially it seemed to be an insignificant minor sect confined to Milan, with only a few hundred members ready to follow him into action for the sake of a contradictory and populistic programme combining the rhetoric of both nationalism and of socialism with a resort to roughneck tactics in the streets against the leader's former comrades on the left. From then on, however, he developed this force into a private army inside the country. Between the creation of his movement in March 1919 and October 1922 when he became Prime Minister, the number of his disciplined and armed *squadristi* (the name given to members of the *Fasci di combattimento* in rural areas of the north and centre) rose from 800 to 200,000. From D'Annunzio Mussolini also learned how useful highly coloured but meaningless slogans, ceremonies, uniforms, oaths and music could be in persuading people to follow and obey him. The Fascist black shirt, sash and fez-type hat were all taken over from D'Annunzio's 'legionaries'.

Despite the wartime influx of large numbers of unskilled workers into the towns of the north, and the spiralling inflation resulting from the huge gap which had opened up between state revenues and expenditure, the standard of living of the urban working-class had not been reduced as far as that of the middle classes, particularly the employees of the state on fixed salaries and those whose income largely depended on rents from property or land, increases in which had been strictly controlled below the rate of inflation. While the factory workers, during the first post-war year of economic boom, were still able to exert considerable economic leverage against employers by the threat of, or resort to, industrial action, the professional middle classes and the small rentiers saw themselves being rapidly reduced to penury by inflation. Their economic distress was accompanied and compounded by their fear of being 'declassed', of losing their relatively superior social status.

The social dykes seemed equally threatened in the countryside. In the fertile plains of the north, where large-scale monocultural agriculture of grain, sugar-beet or livestock was the rule and the agricultural labourers' militancy drew upon a pre-industrial tradition of sabotage of property and personal violence against oppressive landowners and their servants, it was becoming highly dangerous to challenge the power of the organisations known as the *leghe* (peasant 'leagues'), whether nominally affiliated to the Socialists or to the Popular Party. In the south, where the 'great estates' predominated, promises of 'land to those who work it', lightly made during the war, were now coming home to roost, with widespread occupations of unused or under-used land belonging to the *latifondi*, usually led by returning peasant conscripts who had learned how to stand up for themselves in the trenches. Processions of thousands, under red or white banners, seized and distributed the land. In both north and south the *leghe* took over the organisation of labour hire on the big estates, insisting that the maximum number of men be employed irrespective of economic requirements and that all be paid the official minimum wage set by themselves. If a landowner tried to undercut them by employing desperate labourers at lower rates he was likely to find his barns ablaze, his cattle or sheep hamstrung or poisoned, and his labourers driven away by bullying or ostracism. To the chagrin of the landowners, the authorities frequently confirmed the land seizures under a decree issued by the Popular Party Minister of Agriculture Achille Visocchi.

A further result of this tide of land hunger was that many of the more nervous landlords in the northern plain, convinced by the 'great fear' that revolution and collectivisation of the land were imminent, decided to sell up at a time when land prices were at rock bottom. Almost overnight there appeared a new class of small peasant proprietors, attentive only to generations of unsatisfied longing for a farm of their own and unconcerned by the Socialist Party's abstract promise of collectivization. After all, were they not poor peasants, too? In most cases, despite some wartime savings accumulated from low rents and higher prices for produce in the absence of sea-borne imports, they had had to go deeply into debt in order to buy the land and worked it on minimal resources, except for the super-exploitation of their own family's labour-power. Such 'landowners', however humble their social extraction, could be relied upon to defend their newly-acquired or extended property at all costs.

A great deal of this pressure from the peasants could be attributed to the narrowing of emigration opportunities, particularly to the USA, where post-war labour unrest by the so-called 'wobblies' (International Workers of the World) and the consequent 'Red Scare' had led to the imposition of very restrictive quotas for immigration from Europe. As the post-war boom turned into deep recession, the most restless and discontented among the peasants, including many demobilised soldiers, were caught up by the growing unemployment among field labourers, while many peasant proprietors were overtaken by the removal of wartime protection from cheap foreign agricultural products and forced to sell their farms. The natural solidarity between these two groups was, however, turned into mutual hostility by the increasing insistence of the Socialists on the need to end all forms of private property in land, and its classification of the working owner-proprietors as capitalist enemies of the working class just as dangerous to the interests of the landless labouring majority as the owners of the great estates.

While the potential for social conflict increased exponentially in these conditions, the parliamentary political class seemed powerless to get the situation under control. Though parliament still contained men of great administrative ability and political acumen, such as Nitti and Giolitti, they were severely limited in the exercise of their talents by the unreliability of any parliamentary majority that could in practice be formed from the deputies willing to take part in a coalition. Most of the latter had nothing in common except a wish to share in the spoils of office.

Although almost one third of the deputies belonged to the Socialist Party, the majority group (the so-called maximalists) refused on principle to enter any coalition with any non-socialist party, a condition deliberately chosen to prohibit any such participation since its members were confident that the whole 'capitalist system' and its 'bourgeois parliamentary institutions' were on the point of collapse and their own rôle was to hasten the process by making the country ungovernable. The Popular Party deputies, while willing in theory to participate, had adopted policies which tended to preclude optimal solutions: they distrusted the Liberals profoundly, as freethinkers and anticlericals, and refused outright to serve under Giolitti, thus baulking the one man who might still have had the capacity to restore public confidence in the parliamentary process. Five prime ministers in three years pursued only short-term policies amidst a growing insubordination by public servants, particularly the officer caste, many of whom publicly flaunted their support for the right-wing terrorism which was increasingly being deployed against the left-wing extra-parliamentary challengers of the established social order.

It was a situation in which a determined and well-organised parliamentary opposition should have revelled. But constructive opposition with a view to alternation in office was precisely what the Socialist Party was at first unwilling, and soon unable, to provide. In January 1921 the party split into three, reflecting the factions whose interminable quarrelling had paralysed it politically for almost 20 years. On the right there was the Turatian Reformist Socialist Party, now willing to join a coalition, but not invited to do so; on the left there was the self-consciously Leninist Italian Communist Party, dedicated to becoming a party of professional revolutionaries; in the centre was the rump of the former Socialist Party, now totally in the hands of the maximalists, whose proud boast, encapsulated in the headline of a leading article in *Avanti!* was 'Always alone against the rest'. It is hardly surprising that the party's strength in parliament had declined, by the end of 1922, to fewer than 50 deputies.

The former close collaboration between the Socialists and the main trade union organisation, the General Confederation of Labour, quickly became a dead letter because of the abuse of the general strike weapon which was frequently employed, at the instigation of the party. Under the undivided leadership of the maximalists, *Avanti!* constantly used blood-curdling language about the doom decreed by history upon Italian capitalism and its lackeys, but they had no concrete plan for causing a revolution to break out or even for taking control of one which occurred spontaneously in accordance with their constant predictions.

At the other end of the political spectrum, between 1919 and 1921, as the Socialists split and dithered, and as the other parliamentary parties bickered and manoeuvred, there was a growing convergence of forces on the right which intended, and were increasingly able, to impose their will by direct means. The frightening, if empty, rhetoric of the left, and the real spontaneous militancy and resort to direct action of workers and peasants, combined with the resumption of the sleazy compromises of transformism by the political cliques perceived as responsible for the 'mutilated victory', provided ample scope for the indignation which was the stock-in-trade of the extreme right groups, prominent among which was the one led by the vituperative ex-Socialist journalist, Benito Mussolini.

Although the political and economic inadequacies of the Liberal State were now being starkly revealed, these alone would not have sufficed to bring such figures as Mussolini or D'Annunzio to power, for they were still widely perceived by respectable opinion, however discontented with the state of affairs it might be, as men without a stake in society and therefore untrustworthy. Mussolini in particular was distrusted because, in the initial period of the Fascist movement he had adopted radical slogans (designed to attract support away from the Socialists, with which he had then assumed he would have to compete if he was to seize power through revolutionary means) about setting up a Republic and confiscating 80 per cent of war profits. That this situation was reversed within four years of the end of the war, with Mussolini becoming the champion of the respectable middle classes and easily outdistancing the Socialists in terms of popular support, is a clear indicator that the violent pursuit of anti-Socialist objectives nevertheless was acceptable to the groups in society with access to power within the existing system: industrialists, landowners, opinion-makers, armed forces and police, even within the monarchy itself.[6]

---

6. Although Vittorio Emanuele III personally disliked Mussolini, regarding him as a plebeian upstart, his cousin the Duke of Aosta and his mother Queen Margherita both had strong Fascist sympathies.

Figure 5.2 Agriculture under Fascism: hand-reaping near Rome under the watchful eye of the bailiff, 1925.

These forces were able to play upon widespread and genuine fears for the future of property. In 1920 the Red Army was at the gates of Warsaw while in Hungary, almost on Italy's doorstep, Bela Kun's Soviet-style Republic seemed to be a portent of things to come. The occupation of the factories and of land, though in practice successfully contained by government action, gave rise to wide demands for a 'strong government' which would curb the discontented, restrain the rise in wages, subsidise the reconversion of industry and agriculture from their wartime footing, and raise tariffs to protect home producers. Within this process Mussolini's *Fasci di combattimento* abandoned their original pseudo-maximalist platform and adopted virtually wholesale the demands of the industrialists and landowners for comprehensive state protection of the rights of property. Their campaign of violence against the Socialist Party's assets and leaders, which had initially been regarded by respectable opinion as no more than another internecine dispute between left-wing extremists, was increasingly perceived as a legitimate exercise in collective self-defence by the beleaguered middle classes.

Seen within this context, it is clear that the ultimate triumph of Fascism in Italy, often interpreted as the outcome of one exceptional individual's lust for power, reveals an intimate and profound linkage between superficially contradictory trends. Mussolini's trajectory from maximalist Socialism to

110

right-wing totalitarianism was no more than the natural progression of a strong, if erratic, personality able to follow and exploit the deep trends of an imperfectly modernised nation-state. A glance at his early career suffices to confirm this view.

Mussolini had emerged from the ranks of the chronically unruly peasants and artisans of the Romagna region in the years before the war as an agitator and organiser of remarkable verbal dexterity and belligerence. His blacksmith father had been a Bakuninist anarchist, a free thinker and a republican. After completing a training course as an elementary school teacher (at the instigation of his mother, who was one herself) followed by six months as a bored village schoolmaster, the young Mussolini cast about for a way to express the vague but intransigent idealism transmitted by his father. To avoid military service he emigrated in 1902 to Switzerland and, after a number of casual jobs, became a trade union organiser among the Italian seasonal labourers there, getting himself expelled from the country after leading a strike of bricklayers. He read widely, being particularly attracted to the ideas of Vilifredo Pareto, the theorist of the political élite, Georges Sorel, the theorist of the revolutionary general strike, and of Friedrich Nietzsche, the inventor of the 'superman'. On his return to Italy he was called up as a conscript, and despite his theoretical anti-militarism enjoyed his period of service in the *Bersaglieri*. After his release in 1906 he took another teaching post near Genoa and also began writing articles for the left-wing press.

When news of his past caught up with him, he was dismissed from his post and then returned to his birthplace at Predappio where he quickly became involved in a strike of agricultural labourers and got fined for threatening behaviour. He was now writing regularly for various left-wing journals and in 1909 found a post as full-time organiser and journalist for the Socialist club in the town of Trento, which at that time was still part of the Habsburg empire. Here he was constantly in trouble for his anticlerical articles and his preaching of violent revolution. Within a year the Austrians had expelled him from their territory.

Back in the Romagna once more, Mussolini was appointed Secretary to the Socialist Party in Forlì and editor of its local paper. Within a few months he had been nicknamed 'the madman' because he called strikes on every possible occasion: strikes against war, strikes against the King, against the price of milk, against the imprisonment of strikers in Argentina, culminating in a two-week regional general strike against the Libyan war which earned him a four-month gaol sentence.

These feats made his mark on the left wing of the Socialist Party, and after leading the denunciation before the 1912 Party Congress of the reformists, and particularly of the handful who had supported the Libyan war, he was elected to the national Executive Committee of the Party. A few months later, at the age of 30, he was appointed editor of *Avanti!*. He was greeted as the rising star of Italian socialism by Lenin himself.

Mussolini's views on patriotism, religion, parliamentary government and the use of revolutionary violence, were far more extreme than those of most of his Socialist Party contemporaries, even those who called themselves maximalists. His advocacy of terror against men of property appalled them. But his zeal and energy, his indifference to material rewards and good living, and his journalistic flair in handling the clichés of revolution impressed them even more.

Mussolini's editorship of *Avanti!* was a great success: his brand of leading article, full of sarcasm and slashing attacks upon enemies inside and outside the Party, quickly quadrupled the paper's circulation. He was therefore disappointed when, standing in the 1913 elections under conditions of manhood suffrage, he only received a handful of votes in the town, Forlì, where he was well known. He did his best to maximise the impact in his home region of Romagna of the events of 'Red Week', which he hailed as the start of the Revolution. Rushing out to head a demonstration in Milan, he was clubbed unconscious by the police, but still believed the great day had come and appealed through *Avanti!* for the trade unions to declare a general strike throughout Italy in support of the Romagnoles. This proved a dismal failure, confirming the limitations of worker solidarity in the conditions of the Italian Liberal State.

When war broke out in 1914 Mussolini was still trying to retrieve his credibility after these setbacks, whose only result had been to make his name widely known as a dangerous revolutionary firebrand. As editor of *Avanti!* it was now his task to expound the Socialists' line about the war, which was that of total opposition to Italian involvement. Mussolini, though far from a pacifist, had no difficulty in espousing this view since at first it appeared that Italian intervention, under the Triple Alliance, would be at the side of Austria, a country he hated intensely after his experiences in Trento. In an editorial in *Avanti!* he wrote

> let there arise from the depth of the proletarian multitudes one single
> cry, and let that cry be repeated in every street and square in Italy:
> 'Down with the War!' The day has come for the Italian working-class
> to keep faith with the old slogan: 'Not a man! Not a penny!'
> Whatever may be the cost!

A month later, however, he was having serious doubts about Italy standing aside from this terrible clash between, as he saw it, the old and the new, the forces of conservatism and empire on the one hand and those of nationalism, of peoples struggling for their independence on the other. If Italy remained neutral the Italian working class could not benefit from this necessary experience; moreover, having just failed in its first serious attempt to make a revolution, how could the working class let slip a chance to throw the capitalist system into the melting-pot of a war as a result of which it would be in a much stronger position to seize power? Mussolini began to advocate these views in his editorials, openly calling upon the Socialist Party to declare itself in favour of intervention on the side of England and France (he did not mention Tsarist Russia, the third member of the Entente Powers, and the antithesis of progressive democracy), because this would shorten the war or permit Italy to 'dictate terms to both sides'.

The Socialist Party, having just held a national 'peace ballot' to emphasise its opposition to intervention, could not accept this line. At the next meeting of the national Executive Committee, Mussolini found himself in a minority of one and had to resign his editorship of *Avanti!*. A month later, to unanswerable accusations that he had been bribed, Mussolini was able to set up a new paper, *Il Popolo d'Italia* with the financial backing of five of the most important Italian industrialists who stood to gain greatly by Italian intervention. It was an immediate success, for it was the only paper to espouse unequivocally the interventionist cause. Mussolini's invective was irresistible to those who were agitating for war and a few months later the French Secret Service began subsidising it as well.

Mussolini was expelled from the Socialist Party at a meeting well described as 'a moral lynching'. With prophetic intensity he responded: 'You think you are getting rid of me. You are wrong. You hate me because you still love me!' In August 1915 Mussolini was called up but was never in any serious fighting. In February 1917 he was wounded in an accident and invalided out of the army: with these laurels as a war hero, he returned to the editor's desk at *Il Popolo d'Italia*.

For a few months after the end of the war Mussolini's star appeared to be waning: subsidies for *Il Popolo d'Italia* dried up and there seemed to be no obvious space he could occupy on the left of the political spectrum. His initial post-war platform, as we have seen, merely confirmed the public view of him as an irresponsible rabble-rouser, as did his exploits as the leader of a gang of roughneck ex-servicemen ready to howl down the democratic interventionist Leonida Bissolati at a meeting in support of President Wilson's peace plans, and burn down the premises of his former newspaper *Avanti!*. Totally rejected by the electorate in the 1919 elections, his followers numbered a mere 800 at the end of that year, although the readership of his newspaper was very much greater.

With the cynical pragmatism that was his hallmark until late in his career Mussolini rapidly shifted his ideological ground to espouse the cause of industrial and economic modernisation and, by the same political token, the platform of the great war industrialists of the north which in essence was one of discipline for the workers and freedom (and state subsidies) for the employers. This programme quickly attracted powerful backers, not only for Mussolini's own *Fascio* in Milan but also for the many other Fascist chieftains who were emerging elsewhere and for the time being were only in a loose association with him, since Fascism was still officially at this point a 'movement' and not a party. Reduced to its essentials, what these backers were paying for, and what the Fascists were increasingly able to persuade the middle classes to believe they needed, was a form of 'protection' not very far removed from its criminal equivalent.

Even before Fascism was installed as a régime Mussolini was able to organise alternative 'trade unions', membership of which guaranteed a job in a time of high unemployment: an attractive prospect compared with being called out constantly on political strikes. This tactic produced a growing switch in membership away from the unions affiliated to the Socialist Party; declining membership rapidly diminished their bargaining power. Although, as we have seen, the 'occupation of the factories' of August 1920 was far from being the prelude to revolution, Mussolini and his backers made sure that fear of revolution should not subside by themselves, staging violent attacks upon Socialist Party offices, town councils, trade-union halls and upon prominent individuals of any persuasion who spoke out against such tactics. By autumn 1920 this strategy had netted some 25,000 members for his movement, giving it the basis for transformation into the National Fascist Party in November 1921, by which time the party had 250,000 members, many of them refugees from the Socialists.

Throughout late 1920 and 1921, columns of lorries packed with black-shirted toughs, armed with bludgeons and often with firearms, would descend on centres of Socialist Party local power, ransack premises, beat up and humiliate local officials of the party (by forcing them to drink large amounts of castor oil), often leaving numbers of dead and seriously wounded victims behind them. For the most part the forces of order looked the other way, or even facilitated these raids. The Queen mother publicly expressed her approval of what she called 'giving the workers some stick', and even Giolitti dismissed Fascist resort to systematic violence in June 1921, when he was forming his last government, as 'necessary letting off of steam', since he was still hoping – once the 'steam' had been let off – to be able to cajole the newly-elected Fascist leader into some form of coalition government which he would be able to dominate as he had in his pre-war heyday.

Mussolini was privately warned off the idea by his unruly provincial henchmen, known as the *ras* (tribal chiefs), who made it clear that they would rebel if he accepted Giolitti's invitation. He declared that he would only join a coalition which he could himself lead on his own terms. The Fascist terror campaigns had, at least in the areas where opponents had been most numerous, some of the characteristics of a civil war and had resulted, by the time Mussolini came to office as Prime Minister in October 1922, in some 2,000 fatal casualties, yet it was not by violence alone that success was achieved. The middle classes certainly wanted the worker's movement led by the Socialists not just defeated, but crushed, and Mussolini had obliged. They also required, however, to feel morally and intellectually comfortable about what was being done, and only a minority of them as yet shared the Fascist cult of violence. This was something that Mussolini realised clearly from the first and why his movement cannot be regarded as merely a repetition of the previous authoritarian repressions which had been applied since the *Risorgimento*. Its originality lay precisely in its construction of an elaborate, if internally contradictory, ideology, incorporating in pompous language all the panaceas and shibboleths of the newspaper-reading respectable middle classes, justified by respect for property, patriotism and, above all, 'history' – Mussolini's favourite word – yet going beyond the re-legitimation of the established order by proposing the vision of a complete rejuvenation of society and a new morality to go with it. Although this vision was not fully elaborated until nearly two decades later, it was already promised and adumbrated before Mussolini came to power. At its centre was a shrewd appeal to youth, to vigour, to an undefined modernity. Symbolically, the Fascist hymn began with the words 'Youth! Youth! Springtime of Beauty!'

By early 1922, through this combination of force and the prospect of ideological innovation, Fascism had come to dominate the political life of the country and thenceforth its leaders always retained the initiative. It had created a state within the state, with its own laws, armed forces and even its own passports. With this increase in Fascism's extra-legal apparatus of private power and the dawning realisation that the Socialists had ceased to be a threat, the danger for Mussolini was that the middle classes would take fright at the Frankenstein monster they had conjured up, and recoil from its embrace. It was the opponents of Fascism that came to his rescue. Both the Socialists and what remained of the Liberal establishment played directly into Mussolini's hands, the former by calling a general strike in July 1922 in protest against Fascist violence when it no longer had enough support to make it effective, and the latter by trying to compete with the Fascists as the true guardians of law and order against the tide of Bolshevism, a contest which they could not possibly hope to win. It is significant that the main Liberal newspaper, the *Corriere della Sera*, only voiced criticism of Fascist terror tactics after Mussolini had taken office as Prime Minister, at which point it was a simple matter for him to have Luigi Albertini, the editor, removed from his post.

The general strike of July–August 1922 in fact provided the Fascists with a perfect opportunity to pose as the guarantors of civil peace: they took over the trains and the trams and made sure the rest of the population could get to work unhindered. It also provided a pretext for the continuation and intensification of the terror campaign combined with a change of tactics in parliament. Since elections called by Giolitti in June 1921 the Fascists had had 34 deputies, led by Mussolini himself. He now joined forces with the Socialists and the Popular Party to bring down the administration of Luigi Facta, the last of a series of increasingly feeble centrist Prime Ministers, and then continued to use his votes to delay the formation of a new government as long as possible, since the power vacuum was greatly to his advantage in legitimising the resort to extra-parliamentary coercion to 'restore law and order'.

By September 1922 Mussolini felt strong enough openly to declare that

he intended to take power, if necessary by force, and began to make ostentatious preparations for a 'March on Rome'. In an age before opinion polls no one had any real idea of the extent of determined support for Fascism nor of the potential sources of disunity within it. But it was known that its strength was increasing continually, and naturally Mussolini used every means available to confirm the impression that it enjoyed much wider support than was really the case and that its victory was inevitable. At the same time his propaganda machine continued to magnify the supposed threat from the revolutionary left.

Only one hurdle was left to surmount: the allegiance to the monarchy of the officer caste which, despite the Fascist sympathies of many officers, was still fundamentally unshaken. Some high-ranking officers shared their sovereign's distaste for the blustering vulgarity of the Fascists and particularly of Mussolini, who had never renounced his republican beliefs; the commander of the Rome garrison was known to be itching to teach the rabble a lesson, once a state of siege was declared to deal with the insurrectionary intention of the 'March on Rome'.

Mussolini recognised the danger to his plans and began to make speeches eschewing any return to his former Socialist convictions, disavowing 'violence as a cult, a doctrine or a sport', and praising 'the very beautiful mission of the Savoy monarchy' (notwithstanding his private opinion that his monarch was 'a pipsqueak'). It was also hinted that if the King seriously opposed him, he might be replaced by his Fascist cousin, the Duke of Aosta. Once Vittorio Emanuele was reassured that his throne would be safe in Fascist hands, he refused to sign the proclamation of a State of Emergency which would have enabled the Army to deal with the 25,000 rain-sodden, mainly unarmed and increasingly demoralised Fascists encamped on the approaches to Rome and sent Mussolini a telegram asking him to form a government.

It was, paradoxically, only two days after Mussolini had been named as Prime Minister that the Blackshirts actually walked into Rome. The rest of the 'March on Rome' was largely a propaganda stunt, despite a few prefectures in central Italy being taken over by local Fascists with the connivance of civil servants anxious to secure their future careers. False reports of massive Blackshirt concentrations were spread, and a few telegraph wires were cut to confirm the impression of a grave crisis of the state. But the Blackshirts had orders not to return fire if the Army moved against them and Mussolini himself conducted the whole operation from a point conveniently near the Swiss border, just in case he should need to make a quick escape.

In effect the 'Fascist Revolution' was an invited *coup d'état*. In this sense it was perfectly in line with the unscrupulous covert manipulation of public

Figure 5.3 Italo Balbo, the Fascist *ras* of Ferrara, leads a 'punitive expedition' against the Socialists of Parma.

life which had characterised the Kingdom of Italy since its inception. It represented no more than the reassertion, under new management, of the traditional balance of social power, disguising with an exaggerated rhetoric the contradiction between the need to repress and the desire to reassure. It is a measure of the degree of this continuity with the past that Mussolini, at the head of a party of 34 deputies, was able to remain undisturbed in office for more than two years longer before finally implementing the first irreversible steps towards the permanent monopoly of power which was his aim. It was equally significant that in the interval his adversaries were incapable of finding within the constitutional framework of the Liberal State the means necessary to prevent him from achieving it.

Mussolini's first moves, on becoming Prime Minister on 28 October 1922, were all aimed at the permanent consolidation of his tenure of office. By the very manner of his achieving it he had demonstrated that he regarded constitutional forms as no more than items of political furniture among which he could pick and choose at will those which suited this purpose. Two weeks later, in his first speech to the Chamber of Deputies, where his Fascist and *nazionalista* supporters held less than 10 per cent of the seats, he made it abundantly clear that parliament itself was under notice of forcible eviction:

> What I am doing in this hall today is to perform an act of formal courtesy [...] Today it is a fact that the Italian people – the best part of them at any rate – have ousted an administration and given themselves a government without regard to the wishes of parliament [...] I am here to defend the revolution of the 'blackshirts' and to strengthen it to the utmost by attaching it closely to the history of the nation.

> Although I could have abused my victory, I refused to do so. [...] With 300,000 fully-armed young men, ready for anything and almost mystically prepared to carry out my orders, I could have punished all those who defamed Fascism and attempted to depreciate it. I could have transformed this dreary, silent hall into an encampment [...] I could have nailed shut the doors of parliament and formed a government consisting exclusively of Fascists. I could have done these things but I refused, at least for the duration of this initial period.

After reviewing the foreign policy issues facing the country, and reassuring the wartime Allies that he had no intention of abandoning them, he turned to the domestic scene, speaking soothingly of his commitment to the maintenance of law and order, with explicit reference to any hotheads among his supporters who might be tempted to continue the exercise of the illegal violence: 'Constitutional liberties will not be violated; the law will be enforced at any cost. The state is strong and will prove its strength against everyone, even against eventual Fascist illegality.' But at the end he reverted to his earlier threatening approach:

I should like as long as possible to avoid government against the will of the chamber but the chamber must realise its position, which renders it liable to dissolution within two days or two years [...] Let none of our adversaries of yesterday, today or tomorrow deceive themselves as to the brevity of our tenure of power: it would be a puerile and foolish delusion.

By this alternation of bluster and cajolery he easily persuaded the cowed deputies to vote him full emergency powers for a year.

During the next two years Mussolini, confident in his ability to control events now that the political initiative had been permanently bestowed upon him by the King's pusillanimous refusal to oppose him by force, moved steadily to create a Fascist state within the shell of the existing one. Yet he never acted decisively, and probably never intended to do so, in order completely to disarm and disestablish the existing forms of state power. He calculated that he might need to deploy them, or at least threaten to do so to curb the ambitions of his own supporters and particularly of the provincial chieftains of the Fascist movement.[7]

Although there was an immediate purge of the police and the civil service to remove any declared opponents of Fascism, neither at the time nor later was any serious attempt made to delegitimise the monarchy as the focus of the loyalties of the armed services (which, it should be remembered included the *carabinieri*, Italy's main police force responsible for public order). It was, on the contrary, made easy for Fascist sympathisers in their ranks to observe the traditional proprieties respecting the King's pre-eminence. In parallel with the Council of Ministers, a Fascist Grand Council of Fascism was set up with a *Duce*, or leader, as its head. Inevitably Mussolini was declared *Duce* for life. Similarly, the Fascist blackshirted *squadre* who had formed Mussolini's private army were now converted into a permanent National Security Militia, with a distinctive black uniform, whose oath of loyalty was not to the King but to the *Duce* alone: the private army became the army of the parallel Fascist state within the state.

It is impossible to know for certain whether Mussolini intended these mixed political and military arrangements to be a permanent feature of the ultimate political order he was constructing, or even whether there was any overarching grand design. What is certain, however, is that they remained substantially unchanged until the *Duce* was overthrown, with fitting irony, by a royal *coup d'état* 21 years later. Whether by design or not, their function became that of ensuring that Mussolini remained in all situations and eventualities the final arbiter of policy and, very often, of its execution. In foreign

7. The local Fascist bosses, whose influence in the north and centre had often, in the period up to October 1922, been as great or even greater than Mussolini's own, were commonly known as *ras*, a title borrowed from the feudal nobility of Ethiopia against whom the Italians had fought (and lost) colonial wars.

119

affairs, the *Duce*'s explicit policy was to be in a position to 'tip the balance'. For him the art of politics was always to lie in that capacity to play opposing forces off against each other to his own undeclared advantage.

Between 1922 and 1924, nevertheless, parliament could theoretically have voted him out of office. He had partly exorcised this possibility by including in his early cabinets representatives of every party except the Socialist Party and the Communist Party, but by mid-1923 he had, with one pretext or another, rid himself of almost every one of these non-Fascist ministers. He increased his parliamentary strength from 35 to 45 by arranging for a merger of his own blackshirted deputies with the blueshirted *nazionalisti*, and then brought forward a new electoral law, known as the Acerbo Law after its draughtsman Giacomo Acerbo, whereby a party obtaining 25 per cent of the votes cast in a general election was entitled to two-thirds of the seats in the Chamber.

Reluctant to achieve so fundamental a part of his programme by means of normal parliamentary procedures, where his adversaries could in theory combine to reject it, Mussolini tried at first to persuade the King to bring this law into force by decree, but on this occasion the monarch refused to take responsibility for so gross a manipulation of the constitutional proprieties. The *Duce* need not have concerned himself with the possibility of rejection: most of the Giolittian Liberals, the 'constitutional' conservatives, and even a number of the Catholic Popular Party accepted his blandishments at face value, despite the continuing brutality which the Fascist *squadre* were using against distinguished leaders among their groupings who dared to voice any criticism of Mussolini's assault upon the *Statuto*. The bulk of the Popular Party, although increasingly hostile to Fascism and already dubbed by the *Duce* as an 'enemy party', decided to abstain when the Acerbo Law was finally put to the vote, leaving only the Socialist Party, the Communist Party and a handful of genuine Liberals to vote against it. Even if the Popular Party had voted against the second reading of the bill, Mussolini would still have won it by 19 votes, and once it had passed this hurdle, defections and calculated abstentions ensured that it was passed speedily and without significant amendment. Some 200 non-Fascist deputies thus voted themselves out of the next parliament, for the Acerbo Law ensured that 356 Fascists and fellow travellers would be returned.

That the Fascists would receive at least the necessary 25 per cent of the popular vote was by now not doubted by anyone. Every Italian government, between unification and the first post-war ballot in 1919, had successfully manipulated the elections in the south of the country, from which the majority of deputies came. Now, in addition, the Fascists could deploy the threat, and the reality, of widespread intimidation and blackmail during the electoral campaign, as much to prove they still had the monopoly of force as because there was any real risk of electoral failure. In fact the violence was completely unnecessary: when the votes were counted after the elections Mussolini called in April 1924, it was found that his coalition had received some 65 per cent of the votes, so that the composition of the parliament which resulted would have been virtually the same even if the Acerbo Law had not been enacted. The deputies who had helped its passage through parliament had nevertheless calculated wisely in terms of the possibility of continuing a political career, for after his stunning victory at the polls, Mussolini was once again looking over his shoulder at his own unruly, ambitious and potentially disloyal supporters 'of the first hour'. He was thus glad to have a good supply of experienced and pliable professional politicians now sufficiently magnetised by the scale of his success, and the rewards he might be able to offer, to ensure the neutralisation of any threat from those in his party who still harboured ideas of a 'revolutionary Fascism' which might pass beyond his control.

The Fascist violence and the electoral malpractice which had marked the campaign did, however, have a sting in their tail. A week after the new parliament met at the end of May 1924, Giacomo Matteotti, a Socialist deputy who had been one of the most outspoken parliamentary critics of the *Duce* drew up a scrupulous tally of the irregularities and intimidation perpetrated by the Fascists and made them the basis of an hour-long swingeing personal attack upon Mussolini which ended with a call that parliament should declare the election invalid. When he had finished, he turned to his friends and told them 'to prepare the speech to be made at his graveside'.

From the editorial columns of *Il Popolo d'Italia* Mussolini called for something more concrete than a verbal response to this 'monstrous provocation', and a week later Matteotti was seized by a gang of armed men in broad daylight, bundled into a car and stabbed to death. His body was discovered in a wood not far from Rome two months later. The murder was carried out by a group of Fascists organised by one of Mussolini's closest collaborators, and led by a Fascist well known to the Chief of Police; a witness reported the car's registration number, which was in the name of the editor of a Fascist newspaper, and this trail quickly led to the identification of the killers.

Even before these details became public knowledge, Italy had been convulsed by a tidal wave of shock and revulsion. Almost universally it was suspected that Mussolini had himself ordered the killing. For weeks the government was paralysed, Fascists ceased to wear their uniforms and badges, Mussolini's office received no visitors. The judicial system had still not been completely 'fascistised' and as the investigations proceeded it became clear that the evidence led straight to 'the very heart of government', as a leading Liberal critic put it. Indeed, so damning was it that, had Mussolini not enjoyed parliamentary immunity, he would, according to the investigating magistrate's memoirs, himself have been arrested.

Typically, Mussolini both blandished and blustered, on the one hand declaring to parliament that even his worst enemy could not have plotted such an effective way to damage him and promising that justice would be done, on the other warning against any attempt to exploit the situation to attack Fascism as such. On the same day, all sections of the parliamentary opposition of Liberal Democrats, *Popolari*, Socialists, Reformist Socialists and Communists

Figure 5.4 Socialist party fellow-MPs mourn the murder of Giacomo Matteotti by Mussolini's henchmen, June 1925.

(all considerably reduced in numbers since the election) decided to walk out and not return 'so long as grave uncertainty remains concerning the sinister episode'. Thus, belatedly and without any concrete programme, rather less than 20 per cent of the deputies embarked upon what was to be called 'the Aventine Secession'.[8] They believed that Mussolini's days were numbered and that, inevitably, the call would come from the King and the people for a new government that would restore the rule of law. They could agree on no more positive programme than to await this outcome: there was always a majority against any more decisive action, such as the arrest of Mussolini or the calling of a general strike. Vittorio Emanuele refused to listen to their appeals for his intervention to restore the *Statuto*: only if Mussolini were defeated in parliament would he be prepared to move. 'The Aventine therefore went on waiting for a lead from the King, the King waited for a lead from parliament, and parliament was boycotted by the Aventine. The deadlock was complete.'[9]

8. In memory of the tradition of classical Roman politics when the plebs seceded from the Roman assembly on the Capitol and set up an alternative one on the Aventine Hill; in fact the group remained in the parliament building.
9. C. Seton-Watson, *Italy from Liberalism to Fascism, 1870–1925*, Methuen, London, 1967, pp. 654–5.

As the heaps of flowers brought by thousands of ordinary Italians to the spot where Matteotti had been abducted withered, the moral indignation of the public began to wane and turn into apathy, and despite the emergence outside parliament of a genuinely unitarian anti-fascist movement among the younger generation of the intelligentsia and the ex-servicemen, the Fascists began to recover their confidence. Mussolini, encouraged by renewed demonstrations of support from the provinces, once again revealed his mastery of the tactics which had brought him to office and kept him there for two years. Token gestures of moderation such as the announcement that henceforth the Fascist militia would take an oath of loyalty to the King as well as to the *Duce*, and the creation of 53 new senators most of whom were not formally Fascists, were always balanced by veiled or open threats to defend the 'revolution' at all costs. The paralysis of the Aventine secessionists allowed him to play for time. Even when the truth about the murder of Matteotti became public knowledge and a second wave of public indignation again threatened Mussolini's position, the Aventine group continued to await a resolution of the situation by others rather than take the risks of decisive action themselves. The King remained unresponsive to their approaches, declaring the statement by the now convicted organiser of the Matteotti murder, affirming that Mussolini had directly instigated violent action against his opponents, to be 'a lot of nonsense'.

The Fascist leaders, particularly the *ras* who dominated the northern strongholds of agrarian Fascism, despite their public cult of the supreme qualities of their *Duce*, did not entirely trust him to hold out. When one of their number, Italo Balbo, was forced to resign as a General of the National Security Militia because incontrovertible evidence had emerged that he had ordered the beating-up of Socialist supporters acquitted by the courts, a large body of them, led by the ultra-fascist Roberto Farinacci, went to Rome to stiffen his resolution, warning him that they would accept no more scapegoats and demanding he launch the 'second wave' of the Fascist 'revolution'.

In fact, Mussolini had already reached the same conclusion. On 3 January 1925, after three days of organised Blackshirt violence against the persons and property of the opposition, the arrest of more than one hundred of its deputies and the seizure of its newspapers, he defied parliament to impeach him and declared:

> I alone assume the political, moral and historical responsibility for all that has happened [...] If Fascism has been a criminal association, I am head of that association [...] If all the acts of violence have been the result of particular historical, political and moral climate, well then, mine is the responsibility, because I have created that climate by my propaganda from the day of intervention down till today [...] You may be sure that within forty-eight hours [...] the situation will be completely cleared up.

Most of the non-Fascists brought into his cabinet to stem public disquiet after the murder of Matteotti resigned in protest, but Mussolini now felt strong enough to discard the velvet glove and replaced them with hard-line Fascists. Within six months the whole cabinet was 'fascistised', and by October 1926, on the pretext of a number of alleged attempts to assassinate the *Duce*, the last vestiges of political liberty as known in the Liberal State had been extinguished. All political parties except the National Fascist Party were banned and their leaders imprisoned or driven into exile, the remains of the free press were turned into Fascist propaganda sheets, non-Fascist trade unions dissolved, local governments no longer elected but appointed from Rome, and the 'Head of Government', that is Mussolini, enabled to rule by decree without reference to parliament. Significantly, the ultra-fascist Roberto Farinacci was appointed Secretary of the Party a month after Mussolini's declaration of war upon the opposition.

A secret police, deliberately given the mystifying acronym of OVRA, was created to track down and control opponents of what was now proudly claimed to be a 'totalitarian state', reporting their 'crimes' to a Special Tribunal which met in secret and could apply the death penalty (abolished in 1890) to political offences.[10] The only part of the *Statuto* left in place was the King's rôle as Head of State and Commander-in-Chief, a countervailing power only when the Fascist régime was facing military defeat 21 years later.

The finishing touches to the Fascist political structure came in 1928. The National Fascist Party now ran the country, at least in appearance: civil servants, policemen, magistrates and journalists all more or less willingly took their orders from it. Mussolini took steps to legalise this situation by passing a new electoral law which gave the Fascist Grand Council exclusive rights in deciding who should become a deputy or senator in the now powerless parliament, while the Council itself was promoted to a decisive position in the *Statuto*: it was given the power to appoint the *Duce*'s successor 'in case of vacancy', and its advice on constitutional matters was mandatory even where the issues concerned the monarchy itself. Mussolini was by right the President of the Grand Council and appointed all its members. He alone could summon its meetings. He thus acquired, as *Duce*, many of the prerogatives of the King himself, though still within a parallel system, in the other sector of which he continued to function as Prime Minister appointed by the monarch.

---

10. The Special Tribunal judged an average of 2,000 cases a year, mostly of a trivial nature (e.g. insulting the *Duce*) until the end of the régime in 1943. OVRA, according to some, stood for *Opera volontaria repressione anti-fascismo* (implying that it was a vigilante organisation), while others believed the acronym stood for *Opera vigilanza repressione anti-fascismo* (implying that it was an official security service). In fact it relied upon an immense network of bribed informers as well as upon a core of professional policemen and intelligence agents. Denis Mack Smith maintains that the acronym was a deliberate mystification invented by Mussolini to intimidate his opponents.

This was a deliberate political choice on his part, for, at least in theory, it enabled him always to hold the balance of power between State and Party and always to tip the scales in favour of his own survival. In this ambition he was maintaining, in his own brutal terms, a political tradition which had been the unacknowledged principle of every Italian Prime Minister since Depretis, and which was to reassert itself as powerfully, if more subtly, after Fascism had been overthrown. Seemingly totally secure and buoyed up by the support of a population which was at last proud to be both Fascist and Italian, Mussolini had finally seized power.

Chapter 6 . . . .

The Fascist regime, 1926–1945

There was one point in the complex process described in the previous chapter at which the general programme of Fascism in Italy was being generated in specific terms by an unplanned, though explicable, conjunction of social forces and conditions and took the form of specific political and practical behaviour. This was the moment in Spring 1920 when the uncoordinated provincial groupings of *squadristi* actuated the initial thrust of agrarian Fascism. It was here that the characteristic convergence of usually hostile social elements first became a mass phenomenon, bringing together, in conditions of agricultural slump, elements of the most disadvantaged unemployed landless labourers, small peasants with holdings of precarious viability determined nonetheless to resist being pushed into landlessness, and large property owners anxious to defend their vested interests against encroachment by the organised agricultural labourers who formed their main work-force.

Any analysis based on social class would see these elements as profoundly antagonistic to one another yet the *squadre* drawn largely from these groups were the mainspring of the success of Fascism as a political project going beyond a mere chance alliance of forces against the power of the *leghe*. They saw the latter as the real face of the Socialist Party in the countryside, determined to impose its economic and political terms on its adversaries: forcing up wages, threatening small peasant property with collectivisation, and controlling the local labour market to prevent undercutting by the most desperate pre-political fringe of the landless.

The *squadristi* were, however, bound together not just by contingent, and temporary, economic interests in common, but also by a common mythology whose rallying power was the greater precisely because it contained all the contradictions and frustrations of the 'mutilated victory', of the outcome of a war in which unprecedented sacrifices had been endured 'to make Italy great', and to win the prosperity and security which that 'greatness' was supposed to produce.

126

The mythology shared by *squadristi* of all social extractions was the foundation upon which the rapidly developed ideology of Fascism was built. It was not original in any sense, but the combination of its different and contradictory components was a historical 'first'. Liberalism proclaimed the 'Rights of Man' and *Liberté, Égalité et Fraternité* (not to mention Free Trade), Socialism's appeal was to the 'solidarity of the international working class' and ruthless pursuit of the 'class struggle' to achieve emancipation from 'the exploitation of man by man', while the Popular Party drew upon both traditions, binding them together as a form of applied religious faith. Fascism, however, expressed precisely the contrary of all the elements in these value systems, a mirror-image of what its adherents feared. Thus

progress to equality	*becomes*	regress to hierarchy
internationalism	*becomes*	nationalism
class conflict	*becomes*	class collaboration
peace	*becomes*	war
reason	*becomes*	blood
democracy	*becomes*	discipline
human rights	*becomes*	duties to the state
fraternity	*becomes*	survival of the fittest

The list can be extended, with a little ingenuity, to every explicit and implicit moral imperative in the vocabulary of politics, and became the backbone of the official doctrine of the Fascist régime, whose most complete statement is Mussolini's 1932 article on it for the Italian Encyclopaedia.[1] There can be little doubt that the success of Fascism depended not only upon the systematic use of violence but also on the attraction of a functional ideology which supplied impressive-sounding legitimations for its practices as a paramilitary movement. It could draw effectively upon a rhetorical tradition reaching back to the *Risorgimento*, whose greatest exponent had been Mazzini himself: the cult of the nation as the source of all values. Its immediate effectiveness in the period of Fascism's rise to power and consolidation was, however, mainly due to the fact that it expressed the immediate visceral reaction of Italians who felt threatened by the endemic disorder of the post-war period.

Mussolini, in private, was capable of being brutally cynical about his own vocation as leader, defining it on one occasion as being 'to stay in business'. But in public he always made great play with the rhetoric of the supposed 'historical justification' for Fascism, with an uncomfortable echo of the 'manifest destiny' which was used to legitimise the expansionism of the USA in the pre-1914 period. For popular consumption, his propaganda

---

1. Although Mussolini was the signatory, the real author was the philosopher Giovanni Gentile, whose basic doctrine of 'philosophy as a form of action' kept him close to the *Duce* and the régime from 1923 until his death in 1944 before a partisan assassination squad.

Figure 6.1 'Fascistisation': a university graduate is sworn in as a fully fledged Fascist, 1930.

machine reduced the 'philosophy' of Fascism to the ubiquitous slogans with which the public walls of Italy were adorned for 21 years: BELIEVE! OBEY! FIGHT!, and MUSSOLINI IS ALWAYS RIGHT.

Fascism denied the need for and, indeed, the possibility of 'progress' in the old-fashioned sense of movement towards greater freedom and equality, yet itself needed the vocabulary of progress and dedication to ideals. In the early years its very amorphousness, its protean ability to accommodate the discontents of every social group that was frightened or greedy, was the fundamental condition of its success in attracting mass support. When Mussolini came to power his ardent supporters ranged from the Queen Mother, who enjoyed receiving the Fascist raised-arm salute (later adopted by the German Nazis, and inherited by most extreme-right parties ever since) from handsome young Blackshirts, to the officer caste, from industrialists who had grown rich during the war to unemployed factory-workers, from great landowners to landless peasants, from lifelong anarcho-syndicalists to many of the highest in the Church.

But although Mussolini often spoke of the Fascist movement as a disciplined army, and liked to use the vocabulary of military life about it, referring frequently to bivouacs, punitive expeditions and offensives, he had, as we have seen, relatively little control over what the provincial *ras* actually did. Even on his way to Rome to take office in October 1922, he was forced to change his cabinet list several times as successive Fascist notables boarded his train and overruled his choices. It was an early example of the fact that beneath the institutionalised bluster of Fascism and its leader, there was a basic hesitancy which not only reflected Mussolini's own personality but the nature of Fascism as an unstable balance of social forces.

In January 1925, however, it appeared to most Italians that Mussolini was firmly, not to say permanently, in the saddle and that opposition to him had finally been crushed. The overwhelming majority of the population either rallied to the new régime or withdrew into apolitical passivity. When an oath of loyalty to Fascism was introduced for university teachers in 1930, only ten in the whole of the academic world refused to comply: it was a stark example of how most Italians sought to survive for the next 15 years by paying lip-service to a threadbare ideology for which they inwardly felt indifference or contempt. In a real sense, 'living with contradiction' became a consciously chosen way of life.

In the immediate aftermath of the 'seizure of power' in January 1925, four unsuccessful but highly convenient attempts were made on Mussolini's life, providing the justification for a rapid intensification and consolidation of the repressive measures already taken against the anti-fascist opposition. The principal architects of the world's first 'totalitarian' state were two intelligent opportunist ex-*nazionalisti*, Luigi Federzoni, Minister of the Interior until November 1926, and Alfredo Rocco, Minister of Justice until 1932. The work of these two competent jurists enabled Mussolini to keep the intransigent wing of the Party from seizing direct control of the repressive organs of the state (which might have been turned against the *Duce* himself if he should thwart them), while his appointment of Roberto Farinacci to the post of secretary of the Party in January 1925 proved to be a master-stroke in achieving the same general aim. Mussolini personally disliked and distrusted Farinacci and was far from sharing his views about the desirable relationship of the Party to the State. He harnessed Farinacci's ambition by allowing him to embark upon a determined campaign to bring the unruly elements in the Party into a subordinate and disciplined role in relation to the central leadership, and especially to bring to heel the provincial *ras* who were still capable of unleashing gangs of *squadristi*, despite the militarisation of the Fascist militias. When he had served this useful purpose, Mussolini manoeuvred him into resignation, replacing him with a faithful bureaucrat who diligently completed the task by purging any remaining intransigents who were unwilling to conform docilely to the new Party Statute of October 1926, whereby the *Duce* had become the permanent leader of the Party and all Party posts had become subject to appointment, not election.

The net result of this disciplinary campaign was to bring about a fundamental change in the nature of the Fascist Party and the motivations of its adherents. From being the instrument of repression and at the same time the channel for a certain spilt idealism, it became the most obvious route to upwards social mobility for the ambitious middle classes. In 1921–22 as many as one Fascist in three was a peasant or a factory worker, but by the end of the decade the National Fascist Party had become overwhelmingly a party of public employees, professionals and white-collar workers. This was precisely what Roberto Farinacci had predicted; what he had failed to understand was that it was the outcome desired and planned by Mussolini. Its leaders now formed a professional bureaucracy with a particularly marked tendency to reproduce itself, whose allotted task was to 'fascistise' Italians through education, propaganda and social organisation, but not to 'occupy the state' in the way that the Communist Party was doing in the Soviet Union and the Nazi Party would soon do in Germany. In this sense, Fascism was progressively converted into Mussolinism, a system of belief which depended solely upon blind faith in the power of the *Duce*'s charismatic leadership.

The taming of the *squadristi* was a critical turning-point, not only ensuring Mussolini's own permanent tenure of office, but also in reconciling the great majority of fellow-travelling Italians to a permanent cohabitation with Fascism. The raucousness and violence which had brought Mussolini to power were now an embarrassment to the fulfilment of the new roles he wished to assume, as international statesman and as the inventor of a new world-system. His reputation as both of these was now bringing to his door a stream of admirers ranging from Sir Oswald Mosley to George Bernard Shaw and from Juan Perón to Winston Churchill, all of whom saw him as a 'great man', or at least as a great servant of his country. What attracted them particularly was the claim now made that Fascism was in the process of establishing a totally new model of social production and interaction from which the class struggle would be finally eliminated.

This social and economic outgrowth of the establishment of a politically 'totalitarian' state is usually referred to as the Corporate State and its doctrine as corporativism. Its declared objective was to be both revolutionary and socially cohesive, to guarantee economic development and social justice by bringing employers, managers and workers together within the same legal framework which would carefully prescribe the role each was intended to play, while retaining the state's own function as the ultimate arbiter of the national interest.

Corporativism was not invented by the Fascists: part of its appeal was that it had a contradictory ancestry in two movements which at the turn of the century had deeply influenced a wide variety of critics of the Liberal State: extreme Catholic integralism and Revolutionary syndicalism. In his famous encyclical *De Rerum Novarum*, Pope Leo XIII had envisioned a harmonious society in which employers and workers in each area of economic activity would be brought together within 'corporations' whose very existence would overcome social conflict by replacing the class struggle by class cooperation, and reduce political conflict by acting as homogeneous economic constituencies in place of geographical ones which inevitably contained groups whose interests were in conflict.

Similarly, but at the opposite end of the political spectrum, the revolutionary syndicalists, a significant proportion of whom were to rally to Fascism after 1921, had stressed the revolutionary role of trade union solidarity in shaping the social and political forms of the future, a belief that was easily converted into a version of corporativism once they had adopted the thesis that class collaboration in the cause of increased industrial production or 'productivism' ('wealth creation' in the jargon of the 1980s) would best serve the interests of the working class.

In the third influential version of the doctrine prior to its Fascist incarnation, the *nazionalisti*, in a logical development of their fundamental concept of the 'proletarian nation' mobilised for expansion and war, took elements from both the other two, seeing corporativism as the key to the enhancement of the wealth and authority of the nation-state in peacetime and its military capability in war.

Thus the Fascist concept of the Corporate State was inevitably a bone of contention between individuals in the movement, and later in the National Fascist Party, who sought to mould its guiding principles and basic structures to conform with, and confirm, their particular view of what Fascism should lead to. Between 1919 and the 'seizure of power' in January 1925, it was the ex-revolutionary syndicalists such as Michele Bianchi and Edmondo Rossoni who sought most actively to promote the concept, principally through the Fascist Labour Confederation, which Mussolini had set up as a rival to the Socialist Party's allies in the General Confederation of Labour. Unlike the Party zealots such as Farinacci who wished the National Fascist Party to dominate the country, Bianchi and Rossoni, who may be regarded as the 'left wing' of Fascism, believed that the way to achieve mass identification with the fascistised Italian state was to mobilise the masses in a movement of a populistic 'national syndicalism' which would bring worker and employer unions together in 'integrated corporations' designed to control the labour market and labour relations, decide economic policies and act as the channel for popular opinion.

More technocratic Fascists, such as the first Minister for Corporations Giuseppe Bottai, saw corporativism essentially as a mechanism of economic rationalisation and modernisation of the Italian economy, intended to eliminate class conflict, boost production and restructure management, while ex-*nazionalisti* such as Federzoni, who were the representatives of the industrial establishment within Fascism, saw it simply as a way of suppressing labour indiscipline at the workplace.

Until the final banning in 1925 of the free trade unions of the General Confederation of Labour the Fascist Labour Confederation had only limited success in its ambitious programme. This was largely because the employers' main organisation, the *Confindustria* did not like the practical implications of 'integral corporativism': despite the fact that in 1923 it had signed a deal (the so-called Chigi Palace Pact) with the Fascist Labour Confederation giving it

131

sole collective bargaining rights in the workplace in return for an abandonment of 'integral corporativism', neither side had kept its word. After the 'pacification' of 1925, however, support for the Socialist and Catholic unions melted away and the Fascist Labour Confederation was able in October of that year to make a new 'exclusive bargaining rights' agreement with the employers of *Confindustria*.

Rossoni and his supporters now seemed set to triumph, but their vision of the Corporate State quickly faded over the next two years as the Fascist Labour Confederation was effectively muzzled by the Fascist State itself. Under the new labour laws of April 1926 brought in by Rocco (subsequently enshrined in the so-called Charter of Labour of 1927) there was an abrupt end to the notion that Fascism could evolve into a system of equal capitalist–worker partnership. On the contrary, the Fascist unions were turned into direct instruments of state policy, which was to create a system of labour market regulation whose rules and procedures were entirely favourable to the employers, while the union representatives were appointees of the state and no longer elected. The Fascist Labour Confederation was broken up into six separate blocks, each supposedly representing a coherent sector of economic activity, and Rossoni and Fascist syndicalism (not to mention the by now three million members of the Fascist unions) ceased to be a serious force in the internal politics of the régime. Mussolini's formula 'Everything within the state, nothing against the state, nothing outside the state', as applied to corporativism, meant in practice that industrial relations were henceforth a function of a coalition of representatives of Masters, Men and the Public whose real identities revealed a crude domination of the workforce by the employers, backed by the forces of repression the State could command.

A cosmetic appropriation of corporativism was nevertheless maintained for the remainder of the Fascist period. In July 1926 a Ministry of Corporations was created, and this was followed in 1930 by a Council of Corporations which was intended to foreshadow a 'corporative parliament' to replace the now moribund national parliament packed with appointed Fascists and fellow-travellers who spent more time and energy on shouting slogans and singing Fascist songs than attending to legislation (which they had merely to rubber-stamp in any case).

In 1934 the long-heralded 'mixed corporations' were finally set up, covering most areas of economic life, and empowered (in theory) to determine wages and conditions within the area concerned. Finally, in 1939 as the second European war approached, a full-blown Chamber of Fasces and Corporations was established to replace the old parliament completely. The Corporate State appeared, at last, to have become an institutional reality.

The less impressive truth about Mussolini's Corporate State was expressed succinctly by Felice Guarneri, one of the *Duce*'s Treasury Ministers during the period concerned:

Neither the Corporations nor the Minister in charge of them ever put their legal powers to serious use: this was why the only concrete result of the law [setting up the 'mixed' Corporations] was in practice the setting up of a special department to collect the charters, balance-sheets and annual reports of the consortia – which no one ever bothered to inspect, but which poured in in such quantities that they threatened to swamp the office. Eventually the law was revised to the effect that the consortia were excused from sending in their documents 'provided that the Minister of Corporations did not consider them to have an influence on the national production and sales situation'.[2]

The economic effects of the Corporate State were just as much a reflection of the reality behind the façade, as described by the correspondent of *The Economist* in 1935:

> The new Corporate State only amounts to the establishment of a new and costly bureaucracy from which those industrialists who can spend the necessary amounts can obtain almost anything they want, and put into practice the worst kinds of monopolistic practices at the expense of the little fellow, who is squeezed out in the process.[3]

The increasing concentration of economic power in the hands of limited cartels and monopolies was a natural outgrowth of the Fascist policies of state protection of uncompetitive industries and enterprises, and political control of the labour market in favour of low wages and long hours: the net effect of these two factors was that of inhibiting improvements in efficiency and productivity based on the introduction of improved technologies and rationalisation of the productive process, while encouraging price-fixing and intensified exploitation of low-skilled labour.

As may be inferred from Guarneri's acid comments, the Corporate State was readily 'transformed' in the usual Italian fashion. The Corporations were riddled with careerists and hangers-on, while the 'consortia' formed by the large cartels were able to cook their own accounts without benefit of such clergy. Both were fertile terrain for bribery and corruption: once again, 'everything had changed so that everything could remain the same'.[4]

The Corporate State was also a side-show in another sense: Mussolini

---

2. Felice Guarneri, *Battaglie economiche tra le due grandi guerre*, Il Mulino, Bologna, 1988. The bigger industrial cartels were able to keep clear of the army of Fascist officials, snoopers and scroungers that were the reality of corporativism by using a special dispensation in the law which allowed them to designate themselves as 'consortia', responsible for their own documentation.

3. Cited in Gaetano Salvemini, *Under the Axe of Fascism*, Viking Books, New York, 1936.

4. The slightly adapted quotation is from Giuseppe Tommaso di Lampedusa, *Il gattopardo*, Feltrinelli, Milano, 1958; it refers to Garibaldi's annexation of Sicily.

and his followers, particularly the ex-*nazionalisti*, had proclaimed, and perhaps even believed, that Fascism would, through its 'dynamism', be the instrument of Italy's promotion into the league of major economic powers. The real constraints of Italian economic policy were never identified, far less overcome, under Fascism: the incestuous relationship between state finance and heavy industry which had marked Italy's economic development from the time of Depretis onwards, the favouring of certain interest groups such as the landowners and merchant marine and the neglect of others, such as textiles and handicrafts, and the systematic weakening of consumer spending-power through heavy taxation, the revenue from which was used for bailing out inefficient industries. Fascist 'dynamism', expressed through the cult of speed and the advanced technology that went with it, was a fundamental part of Fascist image-making: the régime was lavish with its support for the aircraft-construction industry which seemed to typify modernity. There was, however, no coordinated industrial research and development policy, indeed no clear objective for economic policy at all, but rather the pursuit of uncoordinated targets and symbolic 'firsts', conceived largely with the aim of effective propaganda at home and abroad.

During the springtime of Fascism in the mid-1920s a world economic boom was enough to keep the Italian economy from deteriorating too evidently, but by 1926 serious inflation and balance of payments problems began to make inroads on the régime's credibility. The *lira* came under increasing pressure for a devaluation, which would have been the most appropriate economic response.

Mussolini could not tolerate the political implications of such a step. He insisted upon severe deflationary measures, combined with further tariff protection of inefficient Italian producers, as a matter of national prestige. In 1927, at his personal instigation, the Bank of Italy set the *lira* exchange rate at 90 to the pound sterling, which made Italian goods almost unexportable. Typically, the *Duce* presented this retrograde decision in a military metaphor, as the taking of 'hill 90', while his measures to protect inefficient Italian domestic wheat production and to increase the area under cereals by high tariffs were dubbed 'the wheat battle', with Mussolini himself, shirtless and grimly throwing the sheaves up to buxom peasant girls, in the 'front line' of a field of wheat.

These were the first steps down a road to what the régime referred to as 'autarky': the economic self-sufficiency of a 'warrior nation'. The great depression of 1929–32 led to an intensification of direct intervention in economic matters, characterised by massive state participation in industries large and small. In 1933 a special agency, the Institute for Industrial

Figure 6.2 Fascists on the run: one way of symbolising Fascist dynamism was for the *gerarchi* to run to their tasks.

Reconstruction (IRI), was set up for this purpose, taking over from the over-extended banks the rôle of the channel for the investment of private and public funds. Its activities rapidly intensified and spread, until by 1939 it controlled over 80 per cent of Italy's shipping and shipyards, 75 per cent of iron and 50 per cent of steel production. It is no surprise to discover that these were the industries which had most heavily backed Mussolini's rise to power. By the outbreak of the Second World War, Italian state intervention was second only to Soviet Russian, and much greater than that of Nazi Germany. Other great monopolistic industries were less, or not at all, affected: chemicals and automotive engineering did not require this type of support, being relatively highly mechanised and therefore capable of rationalisation of production.

Although their owners may have disliked the increasingly warlike trend of Italian foreign policy, they were far too compromised by their long-term reliance upon Fascism's system of social control to be able to withdraw support from the régime. Similarly the army of time-serving bureaucrats spawned by the same system, whatever their misgivings about its long-term prospects, were not in a position to abandon their allegiance, however shallow its ideological roots. Both these categories, together with protected industrialists, landowners and agri-capitalists, profited directly and indirectly from Fascism: the far more numerous losers were the share-croppers, tenant farmers, and independent peasants, many of whom had hoped for advantage from Fascism but had received only rhetoric about the supremacy of 'rural values', and the industrial and rural working class dependent on wage-incomes which, between 1925 and 1938, declined in real terms (taking account of some reduction in prices due to deflation) by an average of over 10 per cent as a result of three rounds of wage reductions. Malnutrition became commoner and general dietary standards declined. For Mussolini this was a positive outcome, since lean and hungry Italians would be more aggressive and 'full of hatred', a belief reflected in the régime's anti-British propaganda, which poured scorn on 'the people of five meals a day'.

The social effects of Fascist economic policies were no less debilitating in the long term. A clandestine flight from the land continued, despite draconian administrative measures to circumvent it. Upwards mobility through technical self-improvement was rare, since vocational education was almost non-existent for the shop-floor worker, with the result that educationally qualified skilled labour was always in short supply, and this could only be partially compensated by the ample reservoir of traditional artisanal skills passed down through family and neighbourhood connections. On the other hand, Fascism provided a fertile terrain for lower middle-class careerists, who found unprecedented opportunities to become upwardly mobile within the parallel bureaucracies created by the régime to manage the vast public-sector holdings of the IRI as well as within the new bureaucracy of the Corporate State. A whole generation of pseudo-bureaucrats was thus created whose ethos was essentially that of submission to the political demands of its masters rather than the impartial, if pettyfogging, administration of laws and regulations characteristic of the traditional bureaucracy.[5]

As always under Mussolini's Fascism, appearances usually took precedence over reality. As if to compensate the workers for their low wages and the peasants for their immiseration and confinement to the land, the régime instituted a system of welfare facilities and amenities which were intended to be the focal points of political and social life of every village and city ward, and also channels for the propaganda of Mussolinism. These so-called *dopolavoro* ('after work') centres combined some minimal social facilities (they often had the only bar in the village) with the provision of lending copies of the Fascist press and perhaps the only radio set in the area. In towns the facilities were rather more extensive (and supplemented by the popular provision of cheap seaside holidays), but not different in principle. In many cases the premises had been taken over from the former *casa del popolo* run by the Socialists or the *lega*. For many isolated rural centres, the *dopolavoro* was the only intrusion, into a closed, semi-archaic 'community', of a wider 'society' of which little else was known. Apart from the traditional forms of village socialising (such as the Tuscan *veglia*) at which domestic tasks were shared by neighbours and enlivened by song and story-telling, the *dopolavoro* was, for the half of the Italian population which then lived off the land, the only rival to the Church as a focus of community life, and was correspondingly popular, despite its limitations, with those for whom Communion wine did not suffice as consolation for perennial hardships. Its importance should not, however, be overstated, for those who controlled its tangible, if meagre, benefits were normally the very same local notables whose personal patronage was still a crucial factor for the humble whenever they needed to overcome the vexations of bureaucracy. Thus the *dopolavoro*, too, in practice reflected long-term continuities of Italian society rather than the 'revolutionary' mobilisation claimed for it.[6]

Almost all of Mussolini's most resounding successes prove, on closer inspection, to have shared this fundamental ambivalence in the *Duce*'s conduct of affairs. Just as the taming of his own trade-union movement already described was presented, in the grandiose language of the 'Charter of Labour', as Fascism's abolition of the class-struggle, so the Lateran Accords of 1929, which amounted to a peace treaty between the Italian state and the Papacy after almost 60 years during which Popes had been the 'prisoners of the Vatican', also turned out to be a notable Trojan horse.

---

5. After the fall of Fascism these careerists were easily transformed into the equally pliant servants of the Christian Democrat hegemony: cf. Mariuccia Salvati, *Il regime e gli impiegati*, Laterza, Bari, 1992.
6. For a memorable representation of the failure of Fascism to have any real impact on everyday rural life: cf. Carlo Levi's justly celebrated *Christ Stopped at Eboli*, (trans. F. Frenaye, Farrar, Strauss, New York, 1947); in the big cities the cheap holiday provision was popular, but did not necessarily overcome the negative effects of low wages and intensified exploitation.

Figure 6.3 Church and State reconciled by the Lateran Accords, 1929.

By ending the Church-State feud and creating an all-embracing framework for cooperative cohabitation between the Kingdom of Italy and the
Papacy, the *Duce* appeared to have brought off triumphantly a prize which
had eluded all his Liberal predecessors. To almost universal applause it seemed
to seal the final spiritual unification of the nation. But, as with the residual
prerogatives of the monarchy (which included the 'royal' command of the army
and navy), and the concessions to *Confindustria* and the landowning interest,

the autonomous space left to the Church in social *mores*, education, youth training (the Catholic boy scouts provided an alternative to the various Fascist youth organisations), and above all in the resonance it restored to Papal pronouncements directed essentially at Italians, made it at best a way of sharing power rather than seizing it.

Despite Mussolini's confident assertion that Italy was a 'totalitarian' state which could command the commitment and participation of its population over and above the latter's mere obedience, the persistence, and indeed the strengthening, of these conservative, but autonomous interests, made the claim unreal. Much of the propaganda effort of the régime was directed, vainly, at creating in the Italian man-in-the-street an identity and a set of allegiances whose objective correlative would be in Fascism alone. Thus the insistence on the omniscience of the *Duce* through the ubiquitous slogans of MINCULPOP (the Ministry of Popular Culture, responsible for propaganda activities), the setting up of special training centres to inculcate in the régime's young cadres a supposed 'mystique of Fascism' capable of inspiring a loyalty superior to any other, and the creation of children's and youth organisations which were to be the vehicle for disseminating this transcendent faith, all reflected the incompleteness of the 'totalitarian' character of the régime.

The structural and functional compromises of fully-fledged Fascism had a number of paradoxical effects. Allowed by the régime to consolidate their power, their prestige, their perquisites, and their profits, the parallel upholders of the Fascist social and economic order could play successfully upon the fault lines within a régime articulated between multiple and conflicting hierarchies of state and Party appointees, and between the latter and Mussolini himself, both *Duce* and Head of Government, who could by definition do no wrong. The increase in the *Duce*'s personal authority was a function of their own guaranteed autonomy: the implicit pact was that neither side should challenge the other in the matters which had been effectively devolved to them.

As far as Mussolini was concerned the outcome of this situation was that he had complete control of foreign policy and of all those aspects of domestic policy which did not conflict with the interests of his social partners. In other respects he was, as he once lamented, 'the most disobeyed dictator in history'. He was, however, free to plan national strategies of aggrandisement which would inevitably involve aggressive war, provided that the process enhanced the immediate economic and structural interests of the 'military-industrial complex'. While state revenues continued to swell the profits of the industrialists concerned and the career prospects and prestige of the military and naval officer castes were enhanced by armaments expenditure, no one seriously questioned the aims or the conduct of the policies, even when they were clearly leading to disaster.

There were, certainly, major and minor disagreements between the partners. The King resisted certain forms of 'fascistisation' of the rituals of service life, uniforms, ranks and the like, although he never confronted

Mussolini head-on about any one of them; nevertheless, his mere existence as the formal focus of allegiance for the army and navy was always a veiled threat to Fascism's grip on power.

More importantly, Pope Pius XI, knowing the political impossibility for the régime of any attempt to undo the Lateran Accords, was able to speak out forcefully on matters which from the Church's point of view were of both ecclesiastical and universal concern: control of education, and the institution of compulsory religious instruction in schools, and above all the autonomous existence of the Catholic organisation of laymen, Catholic Action. Politically an extreme conservative and happy to support authoritarian régimes when they appeared to stand for the enhancement of religion and the established order (as during the Spanish Civil War), or the area of Catholic religious hegemony (as with the conquest of Ethiopia and the annexation of Albania), he reacted strongly against Fascist and Nazi attempts to invade the area of spiritual authority claimed by the Church, above all as the guide of individual conscience and personal morality. When Mussolini closed down Catholic Action's youth and university offshoots on the grounds that they were interfering in politics, Pius XI launched a furious attack upon Fascist 'paganism' in an encyclical which rallied the faithful to his cause all round Catholic Europe.

On this occasion Mussolini decided to retreat, although severe restrictions were placed (vainly, in the event) on the Catholic Action youth organisations in an attempt to make them less attractive. Throughout the 1930s Pius XI kept up his running skirmish with the régime's spokesmen, who were no match for him in polemic, and when, towards the end of his reign, Mussolini imposed an imitation of the Nazi régime's racial laws, he denounced them in unequivocal terms as un-Christian and cruel. His successor, Pope Pius XII, as will be seen, tended to be less forthright, but no less determined to maintain as great an autonomy as possible.[7]

Neither the monarchy nor the Papacy constituted any active threat which might destabilise, far less overthrow, the *Duce* and his régime, but they were a constant reminder all the same of the incompleteness of the totalitarian state and of the compromises upon which its power was based. Far from being a classic example of a 'mass-mobilising developmental state' as some political scientists have suggested Italian Fascism proved to be, it was an attempted short-cut to overcoming the disadvantages of latecomer status which relied on improvisation and wishful thinking at the top and passive acceptance lower down. The personality cult of the *Duce* on which the whole ideological effort of the régime was built left Mussolini dangerously isolated from reality at the top of a political structure incapable of conveying to him the realistic appreciations of relative strengths, weaknesses and strategies, upon which a rational

---

7. Mussolini is reputed to have exclaimed, on hearing of the death of Pius XI, 'At last that stubborn old man is dead.'

foreign policy must be based, above all if it proposes to achieve its ends by the threat of war or war itself.

Mussolini's adventures in foreign policy and war, which will be dealt with in the next chapter, merely served to exacerbate these contradictions, but in no sense resolved them. On the contrary, at each turn of events, even those apparently reflecting Fascism triumphant, they were sharpened and the *Duce* was impelled to seek an escape from them by taking an even wilder gamble. Boxed in by his structural compromises at home, he backed his instinct for joining the winning side in the struggle between world systems. Other, cannier Fascist dictators, such as General Francisco Franco whom Mussolini had supported at considerable cost in 'blood and treasure', survived the stresses of the Second World War by hedging their bets and avoiding final commitment. Mussolini, whose régime was the outcome of the way the Italian state had been made and re-made, could not respond in the same way to the popular longing to remain at peace, but plunged Italy into a war it could not sustain in a pathetic attempt to redeem by force the disadvantage imposed by history.

Fascism and aggression, 1934–1945

The course of Italian foreign policy under Mussolini provides a clear, and often melodramatic, illustration of the conflicts which Fascism had fostered or generated both as a movement and as a régime, but which it could not resolve. Insofar as the Fascist régime was both a continuation and an exacerbation of the specific social, cultural and economic compromises which had from the first underpinned the Italian nation-state born of the 'passive revolution' of 1859–61, the catastrophic outcome of Italy's intervention in the Second World War must be seen as the final reckoning imposed by history upon a flawed project. After three years of the 'total war' which the *Duce* had declared to be the destiny and justification of his country's existence, it suffered in September 1943 a collapse which not only compromised that existence, diplomatically, politically and economically, but challenged the Italian nation-state's cultural *raison d'être* as a framework for collective identity. After September 1943 both state and nation had to be re-invented from scratch by those who sought to re-establish the legitimacy of its being.

Although its final causes have to be sought in the Italian nation-state itself, in its need for a compensation mechanism for intractable internal stresses, which in turn were partly a reflection of the country's resource and demographic handicaps, it was in and through the conduct of Fascist foreign policy that this catastrophe was consummated. As we have seen, it was in this field that Mussolini enjoyed his greatest freedom of action once he had command of the machinery of state. In tracing his use of this freedom, however, it would be a mistake to reduce all his decisions to the calculations of a demagogue primarily concerned to consolidate his grip on all forms of domestic power. In foreign policy, too, Italy was constrained by its past, by its geopolitical situation and by its balance of resources, and any Italian government would have had to cope with the effects of these in its attempts to respond to the pressures of national rivalry as they expressed themselves between the wars in the shadow of the Versailles settlement after the First World War.

Although Italy was one of the victorious powers, we have seen how the powerful myth of its 'mutilated victory' became an important factor in the country's post-war politics. Fascist demands for its 'revision' quickly began to be voiced. It was not from defeated Germany, however, that Italy's compensations could be derived, but from her own victorious allies. Long before the outcome of Versailles was known, Mussolini had already stated his basic position. In January 1919 he asserted in the *Il Popolo d'Italia* that

> Italy, just because of its geographical position, which puts it next door to Egypt and the Suez canal, to the Middle East and India, could tomorrow accomplish the task of bringing about the collapse of the British Empire in Asia and Africa.[1]

Three months later he was calling for 'a settlement of accounts between us proletarians and the richest bourgeois nation in the world, Great Britain'.[2] This was a brash and embarrassing formulation of what had long been, and was to remain, a fundamental objective of Italian foreign policy: an adjustment of the balance of power in the Balkans, the Mediterranean and Africa which would comprise a recognition of Italy's status as a great power. Although the post-war Italian pre-fascist governments all nursed the same ambitions, they were also anxious not to offend too greatly their more powerful allies. Nevertheless, the effect of their constant complaints about the injustice of Versailles in practice aligned them with the other major European power, Germany, which could not in the long run accept the constraints of the post-war settlement.

Mussolini's foreign policy was always expansionist even when conducted with a prudent moderation. For long periods the *Duce* was his own foreign secretary, and even when he allowed the ministry to be presided over by others (Giuseppe Bottai between 1929 and 1932, and his son-in-law Galeazzo Ciano from 1936 until Mussolini's overthrow in 1943), he did not relinquish control even over day to day business.

From the first, although completely unversed in diplomatic skills and background knowledge, he was prepared to ignore the advice of his experienced officials. In his first year of office, he burnt his fingers rather badly by ordering the naval bombardment and occupation of the island of Corfu in response to the death of an Italian general, killed on duty on Greek soil while working with a mixed Allied mission engaged in defining the Albanian-Greek frontier. This piece of gunboat diplomacy, although presented to the Italian public as a success for Fascist decisiveness in asserting national interests, proved to be an inauspicious start for Mussolini's personal conduct of foreign policy. It brought in its train the first crisis of the League of Nations, which

1. *Il Popolo d'Italia*, 1 January 1919.
2. *Il Popolo d'Italia*, 20 March 1919.

Italy had just joined (pledging never to resort to force without negotiation) and a consequent reinforcement of the stereotypes of Italian unreliability, particularly in the eyes of the British. In the end the Italians had to withdraw, after Britain had conveyed a veiled threat to dislodge them by force, with a semi-apology and a monetary compensation from the Greek government.

A more solid success was the outcome in 1924 of a negotiation with the new government of Yugoslavia which consigned the Free State of Fiume to Italian sovereignty, thus enabling Mussolini to trump D'Annunzio's ace of 1919. The port was, of course, cut off from its hinterland by this separation and went into permanent economic decline, relieved only by continual subsidy from the motherland. Nevertheless the 'redemption' of Fiume was considered to be a triumph for Italian diplomacy.

There is no evidence that the *Duce* had a consistent and detailed foreign policy strategy during at least the first decade of his régime, but his opportunism and publicity seeking were nevertheless always informed by a diffuse 'revisionism'. Although he had contempt for British and French democracy, he was forced to respect their superior military strength and networks of long-established economic and political influence in the Mediterranean basin and the Balkans. Moreover, he could not adopt the traditional Italian diplomatic strategy of being the outsider capable of upsetting the apple-cart of the balance of power in Europe, unless a balance of power continued to exist. Such considerations undoubtedly played their part in his efforts to stay on good terms with the British, whose foreign secretary of the day, Austen Chamberlain, was an admirer of Mussolini's resounding anti-communism and strong-arm methods of keeping order at home.

The relative warmth of Anglo-Italian relations was, however, a cover for determined Italian efforts to replace French influence in central and eastern Europe by Italian, notably by offering support to the authoritarian régime of Admiral Horthy of Hungary, another 'revisionist' nation-state. Mussolini also encouraged militant right-wing and pseudo-Fascist movements in other Balkan countries, notably the Iron Guard in Romania, and the Croat separatists in Yugoslavia.

It remains an open question for historians whether Mussolini planned to take Italy to war from the moment when his power was consolidated in 1925, or even when he first came to office in 1922. There can be no doubt that the Fascist addiction to violence was not limited to its exercise against domestic opponents, but it seems unlikely that Mussolini, despite his generally revisionist attitude, had any specific plan for a colonial war, still less for a general European conflict, during the 1920s. In 1926, with the friendly acquiescence of the British government, he declared an Italian 'protectorate' over the anarchic state of Albania, which enabled Italy to dominate its economic development thenceforth (the Albanian national bank had its head office in Rome). It was characteristic of Mussolini's improvised and impressionistic approach to foreign policy that he conceived this backward and mountainous province to be an appropriate base for the extension of Italian influence in the Balkans.

A more ominous token of his developing ambitions for foreign conquest was the ruthless suppression of the endemic Berber resistance to Italian rule in Libya, the colony acquired by Giolitti for Italy in 1912. Despite quasi-genocidal measures to repress the Senussi-led revolt in Cyrenaica, it was only in 1931 that it became safe to bring in large numbers of heavily subsidised Italian settlers to begin the fulfilment of the *nazionalista* dream of an African solution to the problem of the south. The fragile prosperity of the colony depended, however, on a continual flow of funds from the Italian treasury, and the policy of *apartheid* applied to the native population ensured that when the colony was invaded by the British in 1940–42, the population rose in their support virtually *en masse*.

By the end of his first decade in office Mussolini was determined to make his mark on history as a world statesman backed by a supposedly formidable military capacity. He frequently boasted of Italy's 'eight million bayonets' and of the Italian air force whose mighty wings could 'blot out the sun', and was particularly irritated by the disrespect for these pretensions exhibited by foreign journalists and commentators not inhibited by Fascist censorship. The half century of contact with Italian emigrants (usually perceived as typically unruly and delinquent) had quickly overlaid the heroic images of Garibaldi and his red-shirts with negative popular stereotypes about Italy and Italians, which presumed double-dealing in diplomacy and cowardice in battle. They had not been erased by the genuine valour and sacrifice of the Italian forces in 1915–18, and the typical image of Fascism as a movement of vulgar upstarts given to posturing in fancy uniforms was, if anything, compounded by the efforts of the Fascist propaganda machine and declarations that the twentieth century was to be 'the age of Fascism' and the organisation of a 'Fascist International', with branches, secretly subsidised by Italy, in many European countries, including Britain. In 1933 the *Duce*'s self-professed disciple, Hitler, came to power in Germany, almost as if to confirm the theory of Fascism as the wave of the future.

Mussolini responded to this situation in a mirror-image of the tactics which had proved so successful in his rise to power at home: by publicly raising the stakes to make himself appear indispensable to any solution, whether peaceful or otherwise, while privately guarding his retreat. His rhetoric on foreign policy now became even more stridently revisionist (despite his being a guarantor of the Locarno Pact of 1925 which renewed and strengthened the guarantees against German *revanche*, and despite his anti-German show of force at the Austrian frontier in 1934 after Austrian Nazis assassinated his *protégé*, Chancellor Dollfuss, in an attempt to precipitate an *Anschluss*, that is Austria's unilateral absorption into a greater Germany).

At the same time, he continued to hedge his diplomatic bets. He signed the 1928 Kellogg–Briand Pact renouncing force as a means of settling international disputes, and publicly supported the League of Nations and disarmament. But at least equally prompted by renewed fears of *Anschluss*, he promoted the 1935 Stresa conference, following up his intervention in the Austrian crisis of 1934, to form, with Britain and France, a common diplomatic front against Germany, where Hitler had just declared that the Versailles limitation of German armaments would no longer be respected, raising once again the threat of a powerful and aggressive Germany at Italy's northern frontier. Ramsay MacDonald, the British Prime Minister, declared that henceforth nothing could come between the three signatories of the anti-German Stresa Declaration of 1935.

This was, however, Mussolini's last real concession to a policy of public equidistance between revisionism and defence of the Versailles settlement. Within six months of having signed it, the *Duce* had committed himself to a course of action which was to lead directly to Italy's involvement as Hitler's main ally in the Second World War.

Characteristically, Mussolini applied his particularly crude and cynical version of 'tipping the balance' to the increasingly tense European situation in order to try to extract concessions from both friends and foes. In return for his support against Germany, he expected Britain and France to give him a free hand in a colonial adventure he had been planning for three years: the conquest of the last remaining independent African state, Ethiopia (then known as Abyssinia). In a notorious exercise in appeasement, the British and French foreign ministers, Sir Samuel Hoare and Pierre Laval, intrigued together to force the Emperor Hailié Selassié to hand over most of his country to the Italians in order to avoid an open conflict. But even this was not enough to satisfy the *Duce*, who wanted a resounding victory in a Fascist war to establish himself as the successor to the Roman Emperors.

Mussolini never lost faith in his ability to rally Italians to his cause by the force of words. For him rhetoric possessed a power to annul inconvenient reality. He was never so buoyantly arrogant as when he stood on the floodlit balcony of his office overlooking Piazza Venezia in Rome, legs astride, arms akimbo, prognathous jaw out-thrust, posturing, gesturing, grimacing, bellowing his latest 'historic speech' to the 'oceanic' crowds bussed in from all over Italy. In such moments he appears to have believed that his power was absolute: 'The crowd loves strong men. The crowd is like a woman... Everything turns upon one's ability to control it like an artist.'[3]

Mussolini greatly disliked being unable to see the crowd he was addressing (he rarely made broadcast speeches) but his effectiveness as an orator on carefully stage-managed occasions cannot be doubted. He could arouse displays of delirious enthusiasm among the massed Fascists below him, who responded to his pronouncements with endless roars of '*Du-ce, Du-ce, Du-ce*'.

The 'daily bath of lies' to which the Italian population was subjected by

---

3. Cited in E. Ludwig, *Talks with Mussolini*, Little Brown, Boston, 1933.

Figure 7.1 'The crowd is like a woman ...': Mussolini at Bologna, 28 October, 1936.

MINCULPOP was all-pervasive. The simplest form of propaganda were the slogans which were painted on the walls of buildings in every town and village in Italy (some faded examples can still be seen).[4] They exhorted Italians to 'BELIEVE! OBEY! FIGHT!' and constantly reminded them that 'HE WHO HAS STEEL HAS BREAD!' that 'BETTER ONE DAY AS A LION THAN 100 YEARS AS A SHEEP!, and that the country belonged to the Fascists (ITALY IS OURS! or simply OURS!).[5]

Newspapers and magazines had of course to reproduce in full the latest 'historic' speech made by the *Duce* or his ministers, but also regularly printed solemn discussions about how to impose a 'Fascist style' on every activity, from tennis to cooking and from architecture to the writing of history. Instructions went out daily from MINCULPOP to every editorial office in the country on

---

4. The 'daily bath of lies' was how Benedetto Croce, Italy's best-known modern philosopher, sought to explain the extraordinary enthusiasm evinced for Fascism by so many Italians, as part of his attempt to exculpate the Liberal State of which he was the ardent defender.

5. Some slogans were unintentionally humorous: 'Boycott foreign words', using the English neologism 'to boycott' (BOICOTTATE LE PAROLE STRANIERE!). Or, painted on a cemetery wall, '*DUCE, WE AWAIT YOU!*'

what stories to play up, what to omit, what to emphasise, what photographs to use. These 'service notes' reveal much about the preoccupations of the Fascist leadership:

> Report that the *Duce* was called back to the balcony ten times.
> Stress that the *Duce* was not in the least tired after four hours on the threshing-machine.
> Do <u>not</u> mention that the *Duce* took part in a folk dance.
> Do <u>not</u> use the phrase 'the *Duce*'s kind heart'.
> Do <u>not</u> print photographs of the *Duce* with monks.
> Among those present at the première of the film 'Benghazi', mention the Minister Pavolini even if he does not attend it.
> Resume the war on flies.[6]

At the next level there were the various journals of 'Fascist culture' such as: 'Fascist Civilisation', 'Hierarchy', 'Defence of the Race', dense with articles of unrelieved turgidity which were read by few but served the purpose of providing a fig-leaf for the intellectual poverty of the ideologues of the régime.

The pinnacle of the edifice were the thoughts of the *Duce* himself as recorded by the privileged journalists allowed access to him. Of particular importance, in the eyes of the régime, was the article in the Italian Encyclopaedia on Fascism which, though signed by Mussolini, was in fact largely the work of the one eminent philosopher, Giovanni Gentile, who had thrown in his lot completely with the régime. In it he gave expression to the fundamental tenets of Fascism as the ideology of an 'Ethical state', a state whose needs were the sole justification for the actions of the individual and whose highest purpose was war:

> The Fascist conception of the state is all-embracing, and outside of the state no human or spiritual values can exist, let alone be desirable. Perpetual peace would be impossible and pointless. War alone brings all human energies to their highest state of tension, and stamps the nations that dare to confront it with the seal of nobility.[7]

Able to manufacture 'public opinion' in Italy to order, he was quite unable to grasp the real constraints it created in the democratic countries, however duplicitous or reactionary their governments might be. News of the attempts to appease Mussolini deeply shocked the British public and Hoare was quickly forced to resign. Anthony Eden, his successor, had made his reputation as an anti-appeaser and he was determined to make a stand against

---

6. A popular joke told the story of an enraged Fascist official upbraiding a Neapolitan fruit-seller found asleep under his barrow with flies all over himself and his wares: 'Why haven't you joined the war on flies?'. 'I did. But the flies won'.

7. Denis Mack Smith, *Italy. A Modern History*, University of Michigan Press, Ann Arbor, 1959, p. 412.

148

the *Duce*'s blackmail. When, in October 1935, without a declaration of war, the Italians launched an all-out attack on Ethiopia, Britain led the moves at the League of Nations to impose limited economic sanctions on the aggressor.

The war was over in a few months: the Ethiopian army, without modern weapons (except for rifles) or training, could do little to resist forces numbering some 100,000 men using bombs, artillery, machine-guns and chemical weapons. On 9 May 1936 Mussolini was able proudly to declare to wildly cheering crowds the formal annexation of the country to the newly-created Italian Empire and proceed with his plans for a colony which would truly reflect the Roman imperial tradition he claimed to have inherited. A network of military roads, and a massive extension to the capital city in the form of a set of ministerial buildings in the grandiose 'Fascist' style were rapidly constructed, to the virtual exclusion of any other infrastructural economic development, and some 130,000 Italian civilians were encouraged, at great expense to the Italian exchequer, to emigrate to the country as settlers and administrators. Ethiopian resistance continued in the countryside, however, and the Fascists dealt with it in gruesomely ruthless fashion, with mass public executions by hanging.

To hold the popular resistance in check the size of the Italian occupation force had to be increased to over a quarter of a million, but Ethiopia did not possess the economic resources needed to sustain it and its continued effectiveness depended entirely on supply lines from Italy, 2,000 miles away, which could easily be severed, as they were in June 1940, when Italy declared war upon Britain. Less than a year later 'Italian East Africa', as Mussolini had renamed the country, was liberated by a small British army taking advantage of the Italian military highways, and the Emperor returned to his capital. Such was the inglorious end of what Mussolini's modern biographer has pronounced to be his 'masterpiece'.[8]

Even at the time, the conquest of Ethiopia seriously weakened Italy's position in Europe. The only country which had wholeheartedly supported the founding of 'Mussolini's Roman Empire' was Germany, whose aid was important in defeating the sanctions imposed by the League of Nations. The price of this was the abandonment by Mussolini of his resistance to *Anschluss* and the arrival of a German army on his northern frontier.[9] In March 1938, after Hitler had forced the Austrians to accept a Nazi as Chancellor, the German army occupied the country at the latter's invitation to the sound of the *Duce*'s assurances that there was no threat to Italy in the annexation which immediately followed.

---

8. Cf. Renzo De Felice, *Mussolini il duce: I. Gli anni del consenso 1929–1936*, Einaudi, Turin, 1974, pp. 758–808. It was, however, a short-lived masterpiece in terms of mobilising popular enthusiasm at home.
9. The best account of Mussolini's empire-building is Denis Mack Smith, *Mussolini's Roman Empire*, Penguin Books, Harmondsworth, 1976.

The League of Nations sanctions, on the other hand, had a consolidating effect on Mussolini's domestic support, giving him a perfect opportunity to appeal to Italian patriotism. He was able to dramatise the situation of Italy as that of a poor but worthy nation being excluded by the rich and satisfied powers from joining the colonial feast. For a few months the Fascist régime enjoyed a peak of popularity and the *Duce* was able to elicit an unparalleled response from millions of usually sceptical Italians: led by the Queen herself, housewives all over the country donated their gold wedding rings to replenish the nation's gold reserves, proudly wearing replacements made of steel. It was Fascism's greatest propaganda triumph. Even some of the exiled opposition declared their support for the *patrie en danger*. The sanctions themselves were politically and economically ineffective, given Germany's support and the fact that the United States did not apply them, since it was not a member of the League of Nations. The only sanction, on oil supplies, which might have seriously damaged Mussolini's war effort, was not used and the British, for all their public indignation against Fascist bullying, did not close the Suez Canal to Italian troopships. The wedding rings were not returned to their owners, and a large number of them turned up in Mussolini's luggage when he was attempting to flee the country in April 1945.

The application of sanctions also provided precisely the kind of justification that Mussolini wanted for his economic policies intended to create 'autarky' for Italy. Imports were to be cut to the minimum, and where possible replaced by home products, however uneconomically, or by *ersatz* substitutes.[10] Exports were encouraged by government subsidies enabling inefficient Italian producers to compete. Worse still, from the point of view of serious military preparation for the coming war planned by the *Duce*, all government spending was to be directed to home industries. Where the latter were insufficient or non-existent, subsidies would be provided for their establishment. These measures encouraged a proliferation of competing speculative suppliers to the armed forces, with highly negative consequences for the standardisation and maintenance of weapons and equipment, and training in their use.

An immediate result of these policies was the necessity to devalue the currency in 1936 because of a growing balance of payments deficit and excessive borrowing. While the main industrial monopolies and cartels,

---

Figure 7.2 A performance to celebrate victory in Ethiopia, 1936. The slogan above the stage reads 'May God damn the English to hell'.

---

10. These were given names ending patriotically in '-ITAL'; thus a wool (*lana*) substitute was called LANITAL. A popular joke during the 1940–45 war was that while the Germans were reduced to eating mouse (*topo*), the more fortunate Italians were to be issued with a new synthetic food called TOPITAL.

particularly those specialising in weapons production, had had no objection to the conquest of Ethiopia, since it immediately increased their profits, doubts now began to creep in about where increasing entanglements abroad and the slavish imitation of the Nazi models of belligerence and racism would eventually lead. The monied classes particularly disliked Mussolini's irrelevant but vexatious measures intended to forge a 'warrior race', such as the suppression of sleeping cars on the railways and the banning of the use of polite forms of address in the Italian language.

Had Mussolini paused to consolidate at the moment of his greatest popularity in April 1936, he might perhaps have been able to preside over a cautiously neutral Italy in 1939–45. The Fascist régime itself might slowly have stagnated into impotence as its counterparts in Spain and Portugal did, or even have slowly evolved into something less ugly and unbalanced. But the *Duce* was temperamentally incapable of withdrawing from the limelight and the easy success of Italian arms in Ethiopia, and of Italian resistance to League of Nations sanctions, undoubtedly fostered his *folie de grandeur*. Within two months of the triumph in Ethiopia, the outbreak of the Spanish Civil War tempted him to commit Italian military forces once again in a war of aggression against a legitimate government.

It has been argued that this move reflected a pondered attempt to increase Italian, and weaken Anglo-French, power in the western Mediterranean. But any such consideration was secondary to the determination to demonstrate within Europe itself the warlike qualities of Fascist Italy, and to put Italy firmly in the forefront of European historical development. The Italian military contribution included hundreds of aircraft, thousands of artillery pieces, tanks, transport vehicles, as well as an army, officially of volunteers, numbering over 100,000 men. Italian submarines attacked merchant ships carrying supplies to the government forces. The Nazi régime also gave large-scale assistance to the Spanish rebels, mainly through its air power, and in this sense the alignments on this side of the Spanish Civil War anticipated the later attempts by Mussolini to wage a 'parallel war' which would demonstrate Italy's equality of status with Germany as the protagonist of a new world order.

After 1936, despite Mussolini's efforts to keep Italy in the forefront of developments, the diplomatic running in Europe was largely made by Hitler, who provoked the Czechoslovak crisis of 1938 which was the occasion for the notorious 'Munich agreement' under which the Czechs were forced to concede to Germany all the areas in which German-speaking citizens were settled. Germany annexed the remainder of the country in the following spring. Following a carefully planned progression of moves, the Nazi leader unexpectedly concluded a non-aggression pact with Stalin which enabled him first to invade and occupy within three weeks half of Poland, and then turn confidently westwards to face the Anglo-French allies.

The *Duce* did his utmost to retain his international prominence throughout this process, but with decreasing success. In 1936 he declared the existence of a 'Rome-Berlin Axis' (around which Europe was presumed to revolve) and joined the German-Japanese Anti-Comintern pact in 1937. He took part in the Munich talks but made no significant contribution to them. Returning to Rome, he was irritated by his restored popularity with the crowds that turned out at every station and roadside, chanting not '*Du-ce, Du-ce*' but '*Pace, Pace*' ('Peace, peace'). In April 1939, piqued by the unannounced Nazi annexation of Czechoslovakia, he sent troops to occupy an unresisting Albania, replacing King Zog with King-Emperor Vittorio Emanuele. He secretly transferred large subsidies to the French *cagoulards* and the British Union of Fascists in the hope of making the French and British governments more sympathetic to his demands. None of this made much difference to the balance of power, although some politicians in both countries, and the British Prime Minister Neville Chamberlain in particular, clung to the belief that Mussolini had enough influence over Hitler to persuade the latter to draw back from armed conflict. Finally, in May 1939, as if to confirm that he was now totally committed to the offensive-defensive alliance with Germany, Mussolini concluded the 'Pact of Steel' with Hitler.

In fact Mussolini, by September 1939, possessed neither the military power nor the diplomatic influence greatly to affect the course of events. As we have seen, between 1936 and 1939 more than half the Italian army was deployed overseas in Ethiopia and Spain and its already weak logistical base was being steadily worn down. When Hitler went to war in September 1939, Mussolini, who under the terms of the 'Pact of Steel' was bound to join in the hostilities, had to send him a message that he could not possibly be ready for war until 1943.

The *Duce*'s embarrassment was compounded by the contrast between the surgical effectiveness of the *Luftwaffe*'s operations in Spain and the performance of his own army, which in 1937 lost the critical battle of Guadalajara to the International Brigade, in which some 4,000 Italian volunteers from anti-fascist exiles and emigrants around Europe particularly distinguished themselves against their blackshirted fellow countrymen. The Fascist response was to pour in still more men and supplies in an attempt to avenge the defeat and restore the régime's prestige, and this too was an ominous anticipation of the way in which Mussolini was to respond to setbacks after 1940, like a gambler whose reaction to losing is always to raise the stakes rather than to cut his losses.

The Italian intervention in the Spanish Civil War had been far from popular. Casualty lists were no longer negligible and the final victory of Franco brought no evident advantage to Italy. Rumours (well-founded) began to circulate widely about corruption and favouritism connected with the family of Clara Petacci, Mussolini's mistress. The newly-imposed official policy of anti-semitism was widely resented as a slavish imitation of a Nazi ideology which Pope Pius XI had only recently condemned in the strongest terms, and was regarded with distaste even by many Fascists, who were well aware that

153

Figure 7.3 Fascist anti-semitism at work: 'This shop is Aryan'.

Italian Jews had consistently been among the régime's most convinced and conspicuous supporters. The costs of war and the economic consequences of autarky were now being felt in the form of a steep rise in the cost of living.

Devaluation and war had, between 1936 and 1939, brought a 30 per cent cut in average spending power, and even within the National Fascist Party voices were counselling against Italian participation in any further warlike commitment. Despite the massive effort to persuade them that, 'for the first time in modern history Italians had given the world a doctrine, a philosophy, a new style of living',[11] whose ultimate purpose was to be found in a totalitarian state capable of successfully waging aggressive war, by the time that Hitler

---

11. Denis Mack Smith, *Italy. A Modern History*, University of Michigan Press, Ann Arbor, 1959, p. 411.

precipitated the Second World War in September 1939, the Italians were as unready morally for a major conflict as, after the wars in Ethiopia and Spain, and the occupation of Albania, they now were logistically. It was therefore with a profound sense of relief rather than disappointment that the Italians greeted the announcement that Italy would remain 'non-belligerent'.

It is equally true, however, that fear of war and dislike of German influence did not in themselves amount to anti-fascism. They must be seen in the context of the mass scepticism, ignorance and gullibility resulting from nearly twenty years of unremitting propaganda, of a resurgence of popular clericalism in relation to the anticlerical atrocities reportedly perpetrated by the government side in the Spanish Civil War and the still strong currents of unreflecting nationalistic aggressiveness among Fascist militants. For the mass of middling Italians, Munich had been perceived as a victory for peace as much as a triumph for Mussolini's insistence on Italy's great power status in foreign policy. Moreover, the 'demographic' argument for an African solution to the European crisis remained attractive not only to Fascist militants and conservative career diplomatists, but also to a mass of peasants and small entrepreneurs: it was a period when the Italian equivalent of 'The Road to Mandalay' became a genuinely popular song.[12]

Between August 1939, when the Nazi-Soviet non-aggression pact was concluded, and May 1940, when the Italian decision to intervene in the war was finally and hastily taken, the *Duce* seemed quite unable to formulate and follow any clear foreign policy line. Hitler had not consulted him about the pact with Stalin, which appeared to fly in the face of the Anti-Comintern alliance which Italy had signed only three months previously, and did not display any enthusiasm for an early Italian participation in the war, a fact which alarmed Mussolini, who talked gloomily of the coming German hegemony of the continent, to Italy's disadvantage.

During this period a number of attempts were made by the Italians, largely at the instigation of Ciano, Mussolini's son-in-law who had been made foreign minister in June 1936 after three successful years in charge of MINCULPOP, to persuade the powers at war to reach a compromise peace. There is ample evidence that Chamberlain had strong hopes that such a deal could be arranged, using the *Duce*'s good offices. Through the Maltese legal councillor at the Italian Embassy in London, and his own security confidant, Joseph Ball, Chamberlain kept a direct line of communication open with Mussolini from July 1937 until March 1940, a fact of which even the Foreign Office was unaware. Eden's successor, Lord Halifax, also kept Ciano's hopes alive through Sir Percy Loraine,

---

12. The song, *Faccetta nera*, remained popular long after the end of the régime. Its flavour is matched well enough by Kipling's lines 'By the old Moulmein Pagoda, lookin' eastward to the sea,/There's a Burma girl a-settin', and I know she thinks o' me;/For the wind is in the palm-trees, an' the temple-bells they say:/ "Come back, you British soldier; come you back to Mandalay". '

the British ambassador in Rome. Both Pope Pius XII and President Roosevelt also made official and unofficial approaches to Mussolini and Ciano with the same purpose in mind, as did two successive French premiers, Daladier and Reynaud, during the German *blitzkrieg* in spring 1940.

It is difficult to judge how serious either Mussolini or his interlocutors were about these approaches. The *Duce* was certainly aware of the relief felt by the majority of the Fascist Grand Council when he declared nonbelligerency. He shared some of their misgivings about German expansionism and the possibility that Italy would be relegated to the margins of Hitler's plan for a new world order. Italian aid (loudly proclaimed, though problematic in actual quantity) to Finland during the winter war of 1939–40 between that country and the Soviet Union, was probably intended to signal this concern to the Germans.[13]

On 5 January 1940 Mussolini sent a long personal letter to Hitler which clearly sought to influence him in the direction of compromise, while at the same time reassuring him of Italy's continued material and moral support until such time as she could intervene militarily. The *Führer* was in any case unresponsive, probably seeing a link between Mussolini's attempt to mediate and the press campaign against the Nazi–Soviet pact the latter had simultaneously unleashed in the Italian newspapers, and sensing a manoeuvre intended to restore Italy's capacity to tip the balance of diplomacy. This impression could only have been confirmed a few weeks later when the Germans discovered that the Italians had deliberately leaked to the Belgians the details of Hitler's plan to invade their country.[14]

Hitler's formal reply was delayed for over three months, and when it finally arrived on 10 March 1940, it ambiguously suggested that Italy could now do most to assist Germany by staying out of the war. Immediately after reading it, Mussolini called in Ciano and forced him to read in his presence a spine-chilling description of 'the night of the long knives' of 1934, when Hitler's close but ambitious collaborator Roehm was brutally murdered, as if to impress upon his son-in-law the risks of any further attempt to detach Italy from Germany. Ciano took the hint. By the end of March, Mussolini had finally decided upon an early intervention, although the actual military dispositions were set in train only on 9 April and the attack on France was not settled until the very end of May 1940.[15]

Finally, on 10 June 1940, Mussolini, having informed his Chief of Staff

---

13. It was claimed that 40 aircraft had been sent, but no record of their receipt appears to exist; cf. Giorgio Bocca, *Storia d'Italia nella guerra fascista 1940–43*, Laterza Bari, 1976.
14. The head of Italian intelligence was working for the German *Abwehr*, providing early access to all Mussolini's machinations, with predictable effects on German-Italian military cooperation; cf. Denis Mack Smith, *Mussolini's Roman Empire*.
15. The only campaign for which the Italian army had planned was an attack on Yugoslavia, which the Germans vetoed because of the unpredictable consequences of Balkan involvement at this stage of the war.

that he 'needed 5,000 dead in order to secure a seat at the peace-table', sealed the fate of his régime and put the survival of his country in jeopardy, by declaring war upon France and Britain.

When the King dismissed and arrested Mussolini on 25 July 1943, not a single Fascist, great or small, made any move to restore him, while popular rejoicing was universal. In the seven years since the proclamation of the Italian Empire, Italy had fallen with increasing rapidity to a nadir of national prestige so profound that it appeared to jeopardise the very existence of the country as a nation-state. Even worse, however, was still to come: 19 months of foreign occupation by armies locked in a slow, grinding battle which inflicted immense damage upon the country's infrastructures and economy at a human cost to the civilian population which left few families untouched. Their misery was compounded by the civil war which raged everywhere in the German-occupied part of the country between pro-Allied partisans and resistance workers and a puppet Fascist state set up by the Nazis in the north.

It will be clear from the foregoing that the Fascist régime was, already in 1940, fundamentally unsound. It was incapable of developing a coherent diplomacy or military strategy, and was politically so fragile that after 20 years of undisputed power its leadership was unable to mobilise its economic and demographic resources to wage effective war. Its weaknesses appear even more evident if we contrast it with what was achieved by the Nazi régime in terms of war production during the same period and subsequently, despite the fact that Germany did not even attempt all-out mobilisation of its resources for war until 1943.

It is beyond doubt that an important factor in Italy's failure to meet the challenge of total war was the dominance of its politics, especially in foreign and military policy, by the *Duce* himself. Despite the propaganda image of a man of inflexible will and unalterable determination, Mussolini was by 1940 vacillating and indecisive. With justice he could lament that he was 'the most disobeyed dictator in history'. But to attribute the failure of Fascism in Italy to its transformation into a 'Mussolinism' characterised by the *Duce*'s many failings misses the essential point that his dominance, based on a comprehensive application of the principle of 'divide and rule' to both the political and the non-political supporters of régime, was itself functional to the survival of the system.

The Fascist régime was, like all its predecessors since the *Risorgimento*, the expression of a series of compromises between northern commerce and industry, southern great estates, a bureaucracy primarily used as a reserve bank of political favours, the Church and the monarchy, and a ruling élite of professional politicians, in this case the *homines novi* of the Fascist movement and those among their predecessors who had been 'transformed' by them. Mussolini had prevailed by skilfully playing them off against each other, not by recruiting their allegiance, nor by curtailing or eliminating their influence and privileges. The régime had no great difficulty in repressing overt or clandestine opposition, since it had taken over and extended an efficient police state; it could not, however, rid itself of the massive centrifugal tendencies implicit in its structure because its own survival depended on keeping them in balance, and therefore in existence.

The *Duce*'s own problematic decision-making style reflected the unresolved tensions and conflicting tendencies generated by this social and political environment. By 1939–40, to judge by the evidence of his private and public statements, the structural incoherence was becoming extreme, leading to periods of profound and paralysing uncertainty, punctuated by irrational decisiveness which was never followed through. Thus the basic aggressive thrust towards imperial expansion inherited from the *nazionalista* programme taken over by Fascism in 1919–22 (itself a compromise between the demands of northern industry and those of the landed interest of the south) is accompanied by the obliqueness and caution of the Italian diplomatic tradition. The pressure for an aggressive foreign policy fully aligning Italy with Germany was intensified by the need to satisfy the expectations created among young Fascist militants by 20 years of propaganda in exaltation of violence, but tempered by a desire to keep intact the military strength which might be necessary to counteract a unilateral German domination of central and eastern Europe which would leave Italy a minor power, and Mussolini with no more to offer the Italians than the Giolittian 'good deal' to be gained by sitting on the fence.

The alternative, an alliance with Britain and France (which Ciano briefly toyed with), was psychologically and ideologically unthinkable for a leader and a régime which had its deepest roots in rejection of Giolittian compromise; moreover to most of the world, in June 1940, the end of the war seemed only weeks or even days away. Wiser statesmen than the *Duce* might well have been tempted to gamble as he did.

In 1939–40 it was a common assumption among both the friends and foes of Fascism that in the preceding twenty years the movement, and then the régime, had genuinely brought about a radical transformation not only of Italy's military capacity, its institutions and economy but also of its people's self-image, now supposedly rooted in a proud national identity. It was widely thought that Fascist Italians would fight, and fight well, out of fierce loyalty to their *Duce*. In short it was felt, even by Churchill, when in his first broadcast to the Italian people in December 1940 he invited them to abandon their leader, that Mussolini was a great man who had done great things for his country.[16]

---

16. 'One man, one man alone, has ranged the Italian people in mortal combat against the British Empire and has deprived Italy of the sympathy and friendship of the United States of America. That he is a great man I do not deny, but that after eighteen years of unbridled power he has led your country to the brink of a dreadful abyss no one can deny. It is one man alone who, against the Crown and the Italian Royal Family, against the Pope and the whole authority of the Vatican and the Roman Catholic Church, against the wishes of the Italian people, who were never keen for this war, has led the successors and heirs of ancient Rome to side with the fierce barbaric pagans' (Winston Churchill, *The Second World War*, Vol. IV. Cassell, London, pp. 327–8).

The extreme exiguity and fragmentation of the domestic, and even the emigrant anti-fascist movement, and the latter's obvious inability to gain significant support even among the sections of the home population worst hit by the effects of autarky, tended to confirm this judgement, as did the tidal waves of popular enthusiasm for Mussolini's defiance of sanctions and conquest of Ethiopia: allegiance to the Italian 'nation' had, it seemed, at last gripped the popular imagination.[17] Although Italian armed assistance to Franco was considerably less popular, it did not appear seriously to have weakened, either politically or materially, a régime enjoying a wide measure of popular support and having, through its supposed 'totalitarian' control of the economy and the media, the means to achieve a rapid and effective mobilisation of resources in aid of its policy objectives.

The fact is, however, that the 'radical transformation' claimed by the Fascists and their foreign sympathisers had simply not occurred. Italian society, whether at the level of the élites, or at that of the mass of the population, was still riven by the same profound dichotomies between 'modern' and 'archaic', between centre and periphery, between lay and clerical, that had afflicted it since unification. The masses were not mobilised by Italian Fascism as they were by Nazism because Italy was still basically the 'disadvantaged latecomer' of modern Europe and the Fascist régime could not risk jeopardising the delicate balance between the many centres of diffused power in the country upon whose continuing mutually opposed interests it relied for its role as arbiter. The demands of any radical modernisation process, involving a rapid, enforced transfer of investment and labour from agriculture to industry, with a consequent heightening of social tensions and disruption of conservative agrarian mentalities, were out of the question for a ruling group such as the Fascists whose underlying aspiration had become, in Mussolini's own phrase, 'to stay in business'.

As for the 'consent' claimed for Fascism by some revisionist historians, it was no more than a continuation of that cynical, patient endurance of defeat and exclusion which is the condition of the poor in backward societies, while that of the élites was in direct proportion to their conviction that the régime could guarantee their privileged status. They applauded the régime vigorously while they prospered, but were ready to abandon it and back a more likely winner as soon as it wavered or showed signs of demanding more than a token *quid pro quo* from them.

Seen in this light, the fluctuations and gambles of Mussolini's foreign policy in 1939–40 are more readily comprehensible. The *Duce* was well aware of the precarious balance of the system over which he presided (but which in its essentials he had not invented so much as refined), and was constantly

---

17. The best-organised of the clandestine anti-fascist groups was the Italian Communist Party: its official historian, Paolo Spriano, calculated that it had probably no more than 800 active members in the country in 1940.

preoccupied with minimising the strains to which it was subjected. At the same time the whole momentum of Italian foreign policy since 1861, to which he had added little more than a veneer of bombast, and his increasing entanglement with the policies of a hegemonic 'greater Germany', forced him to maintain a public image of a warlike, expansionist and revisionist Italy, ready for a final show-down.

In May 1940, with the fall of France and with Britain apparently on the verge of collapse after the fiasco of the Norway campaign, Mussolini sensed an almost miraculous window through which he could escape from these contradictions, make a cost-free propaganda war, yet not upset the domestic apple-cart. He might even gain in reality the power for Italy which he already claimed for it. Ironically, one month before he declared war, the window concerned had been firmly closed and bolted as a result of the 'Norway debate' in the House of Commons, when Lloyd George had so ruthlessly demolished Chamberlain's standing that the way was cleared for Churchill.

The inner logic of Italian foreign policy, which Mussolini took over and embellished with the ideology of *nazionalismo*, was to use the destabilising threat of war to gain Great Power status for Italy within the existing world order. This trend was powerfully reinforced by the increasing pressures for a revision of Versailles which even a non-fascist government would have found it hard to resist.

At the same time, the inner logic of Italian Fascism as a system of social and political control through the maintenance of an existing balance of power meant that efficiency and coordination had to be sacrificed to the protection of the entrenched interests of an under-capitalised and uncoordinated defence industry and an incompetent military caste. Paradoxically, a régime which proclaimed war to be 'the supreme hygiene of history' was inherently incapable of forging the means to wage it.

By 1939 Italian Fascism was already constrained within the logic of an offensive alliance whose aims were bound to run counter to the interests of Italy, but whose hegemonic character effectively made it as dangerous to remain neutral as to intervene.

The point of convergence of these logics is the ultimate gamble that Mussolini decided upon in May 1940: to intervene in the war in order not to have seriously to wage it. Once again it is depressingly clear that Italian Fascism was, in a prescient phrase first used in 1922, 'not a revolution, but a revelation'.[18]

---

18. L. Salvatorelli, *Il nazionalfascismo*, Einaudi, Turin, 1977.

1943–1945 as the turning point of modern Italian history

At one stroke, with the declaration of war on 10 June 1940, Mussolini appeared to have reversed all the negative trends in Italy's, and his own, situation, and at minimum cost.[1] The *Duce* was euphoric. Within a week, despite the universal international odium incurred by what Roosevelt had called the 'stab in the back', the French had sued for peace, while the British were still reeling from the collapse of France and the trauma of Dunkirk. All seemed set for Italy to achieve its maximum foreign policy aims. So sure of the imminent end of the war was Mussolini that he ordered the demobilisation of his army to begin, and he did not even take up the full extent of the territorial concessions in France and its Empire which Hitler had offered when they met in Munich on 18 June 1940.[2]

Thus began the 'parallel war' ('a war not for Germany, not with Germany, but a war alongside Germany') whose outcome was to nullify within six months all the *Duce*'s dreams of an Italian future of conquest and empire.

Although the doubtful morale of the Italian people cannot be said to have precluded Italy's intervention in the Second World War, there can be no doubt whatever that the country's armed forces were in no state to wage it. Mussolini's frequent references to the 'eight million bayonets' he could deploy in support of his aims were blatant propaganda. Italy possessed in 1940 a second-rate navy (lacking a single aircraft carrier and unable to afford live ammunition for firing practice) and a third-rate air force and army, under-trained and badly led. Moreover, the natural resources and technology vital for a modern weapons industry were not available from domestic capacity, and Mussolini's German ally had no intention of equipping the Italians with

---

1. The Italian forces only sustained 631 fatal casualties in the fighting on the French front.
2. This may have been an attempt to ingratiate himself with the French with a view to the creation of a Mediterranean hegemony in which France and Spain would be associated with Italy in barring Hitler's path to Africa. Within weeks he again changed tack and claimed Corsica and all the French North African territories.

any weaponry which might render them less dependent upon the protection of the *Reich*.

In mid-October 1940, Mussolini informed his generals that they were to attack Greece in two weeks time. Whether this unexpected decision was due to pique that, after the German veto on the original Italian plan to invade northern Yugoslavia, he had only learned from the newspapers of Hitler's decision to secure Romanian oil by sending German troops (ostensibly to reinforce the Romanian army) a few days earlier, or whether it was a last desperate gamble to expand Italy's Balkan foothold before the Germans arrived in force, the means to make the attack a success did not exist.[3]

The military and political catharsis was not long delayed:

> From October 1940, Italy suffers a succession of defeats: in Greece, the sinking of part of her fleet at Taranto, defeats in North Africa and then in East Africa. But the political consequences of greatest significance derive from the Greek campaign because it is here that the Germans become fully aware of the extreme weakness of their ally and decide to assume the political and military direction of the war in the Mediterranean [...] And in fact with abandonment of the 'parallel war', Italy's freedom of action also ends. From then on Italy is merely a German satellite.[4]

Within a fortnight the Greeks, whose strength had been underestimated by Italian intelligence by a factor of ten, were threatening to dislodge the Italians from their Albanian bases and drive them into the sea. The Italian setback, after the earlier gloating propaganda claims that Greece had already been defeated, aroused such universal derision of Italy's military capability that even the French customs officers at Menton, despite the memory of their own country's collapse in May, erected a notice reading 'Greeks stop here: you have reached France'. The *Duce* was reduced to unshaven, pallid desperation by the magnitude of the disaster and the ruin of his policy of 'parallel war'. As for the Italians who had believed the propaganda about a walk-over, their feelings were well reflected by an Italian peasant conscript serving in the snow, mist and mud of the Albanian mountains who turned to his officer in consternation and said 'But, Sir, the Greeks are firing at us!'

A month later, on 4 December 1940, the Italian Chief of Staff, Field Marshal Pietro Badoglio, the 'hero' of the conquest of Ethiopia, who had advised half-heartedly against intervention in June but had not resigned, was dismissed by Mussolini. His dismissal marked a significant crack in the edifice of Fascist 'consensus'.

---

3. Cf. Mario Cervi, *The Hollow Legions. Mussolini's Blunder in Greece 1940–41*, Chatto & Windus, London, 1972.

4. G. André, 'La politica estera fascista durante la seconda guerra mondiale', in Renzo De Felice (ed.), *L'Italia fra tedeschi e alleati*, Il Mulino, Bologna, 1973.

It has been suggested that for the three years between 1940 and 1943, Britain's war effort was mainly directed against Italy.[5] If this seems an exaggeration, the converse is demonstrably close to the truth: Italy was broken militarily by a series of defeats at the hands of the British in 1940 and early 1941, both at sea and in Africa. Only the arrival of General Rommel's *Afrika Korps* and the German success in Crete in the spring of 1941 staved off an Italian evacuation of Libya. From November 1940 Italy was unable, despite joining the victorious Germans as auxiliaries in the occupation of Greece and Yugoslavia, to exert any significant influence in the Balkans.

Mussolini's response to each disaster was to commit himself to a greater one: the road from his first defeats in Albania and Egypt led to the almost total destruction of the expeditionary force which he despatched, uninvited, to join the German campaign against the Soviet Union in July 1941. His only principle of action had become that of securing an Italian 'presence', however subordinate and however humiliating, alongside the victorious *Wehrmacht*. The precarious balance of the Fascist hegemony over Italian society was fatally destabilised by this process, and no amount of propaganda was from then onwards capable of obscuring the record of military defeat, the squandering of hundreds of thousands of lives in the snows of Russia, economic dislocation and civilian hardship.[6]

The last months of 1942 and the first of 1943 are usually regarded as the turning-point of the Second World War: this was certainly the case as far as Italy was concerned. After Mussolini had declared war on the United States in December 1941 as a gesture of support for the Japanese attack at Pearl Harbour, few Italians had much faith in the inevitability of victory, for America symbolised in popular feeling both the land of promise and an invincible industrial strength. This sentiment was powerfully confirmed when Hitler's armies were comprehensively defeated by the Red Army at Stalingrad within a few weeks of the British victory over the German-Italian forces at El Alamein. Only days later this disaster was followed up by the Anglo-American invasion of French North Africa. In May 1943 despite the presence of the *Afrika Korps* the Italians were driven from their last foothold in Tunisia, and in July the Anglo-American allies launched a sea-borne assault on Sicily, which was captured within five weeks.

By Spring 1943 members of Vittorio Emanuele's entourage and a group of dissident Fascists led by Giuseppe Bottai, Dino Grandi and Ciano, all recently ousted from the Cabinet, were separately involved in conspiracies to get rid of Mussolini and to ask the Allies for a separate peace. The plot hatched

---

5. Cf. A. J. P. Taylor, *The War Lords*, Penguin Books, Harmondsworth, London, 1976.
6. The rapid erosion of public confidence is fully documented in the increasingly pessimistic top secret reports sent to the *Duce* from all over Italy by his own prefects. Cf. L. Benomini *et al* (eds), *Riservato a Mussolini*, Feltrinelli, Milan, 1974.

in the palace was to make the former Chief-of-Staff of the Italian army, Pietro Badoglio, Prime Minister and then negotiate Italy's exit from the war on terms which would ensure their own survival as the new ruling group. It was less clear what the dissident Fascists were aiming at, apart from the succession to the *Duce*'s position, but they too were convinced that Italy could no longer wage war.

When the matter was put to the King, he hesitated. Although he detested Mussolini, a plebeian upstart who had so often humiliated his sovereign, he still feared for his throne, either at the hands of a Germany enraged by betrayal, or in the course of social upheaval once the coercive apparatus of the régime was disrupted. On the other hand, if he stood aside and the Allies took Rome as quickly as they had taken Sicily, his position might be equally precarious. A heavy Allied air-raid on Rome's suburbs, coupled with the news that at Mussolini's latest summit with Hitler the only decision reached was to carry on the war at all costs (despite Mussolini's original intention to persuade the *Führer* to allow him to withdraw into neutrality), probably clinched the issue.

Getting wind of the Royal plot the Fascist group decided to act first in the hope of getting one of their own number appointed to replace the *Duce*. For the first time in its existence, the Fascist Grand Council was convened without Mussolini's consent. On 24 July 1943, after a marathon sitting, a motion of no confidence in the *Duce* was passed by a large majority and it was resolved to ask the King to take supreme command of the armed forces.

Learning of these moves, Vittorio Emanuele hurried on with his own plan. Badoglio was secretly appointed as Head of Government. On 25 July, Mussolini was summoned to the palace as if to make his usual report to the monarch. As soon as he was in the royal presence he was informed that he was dismissed and as he left the building he was arrested and whisked away in an ambulance, then transferred 'for his own protection' to the prison island of Ponza to which he had sent so many of his anti-fascist enemies in earlier days. His political career was apparently terminated at the hands of the same man who had originally summoned him take office 21 years before. The German embassy confidently predicted a counter-coup by militant Fascists to restore the fallen *Duce*, but the only Fascists who turned up there were seeking Nazi protection: not a single supporter of the *Duce* made even a gesture of defiance, although one faithful journalist committed suicide.

The 45 days which separated the dismissal of Mussolini from the surrender of Italy to the Allies on 8 September 1943 were again a revelation of a political culture and a style of government which had been accentuated but not invented by Fascism, a compound of deception and self-deception, not only relying on the manipulation of events but finding therein its sole legitimation. In the circumstances of Italy's absolute impotence vis-à-vis both its allies and enemies, it was a guarantee of failure for the diplomatic strategy adopted by the new government. At the same time it reiterated the classic repressive response of the Italian State to the possibility of an assertion of popular sovereignty.

Badoglio and Vittorio Emanuele sought deviously to surrender to the Allies without alerting the Germans to their intentions: in his first broadcast to the nation, as the crowds wildly celebrating 'unconditional peace' were surging through the streets toppling statues of the *Duce* and defacing the now hated symbols of his régime, the new Prime Minister announced that 'the war goes on alongside our German allies'. On the home front, apart from formally dissolving the National Fascist Party, his only decisive action was to send troops to fire on strikers and demonstrators. The anti-fascist prisoners of the former régime were released but kept under surveillance, and some former statesmen of pre-fascist times were allowed to resume political activity as a kind of loyal opposition. In order to reassure their Nazi allies, German reinforcements were allowed to continue to flow into Italy, increasing their strength from seven to 19 divisions, ostensibly to assist in repelling any Anglo-American landing on the peninsula, while most of the Italian troops carrying out occupation duties in the Balkans and the south of France were not repatriated. No preparations were made for military resistance to a German takeover.

Meanwhile, a series of secret missions were despatched from Rome to parley with the Allied representatives in neutral Portugal and Spain. None of them had a clear brief to negotiate the 'unconditional surrender' which the Allies were publicly demanding. So devious were the manoeuvrings of the Royal government that it has been suggested that Badoglio, despite having secretly agreed at the end of August to the terms of an armistice dictated by the Allied Supreme Commander, was all along not intending to change sides or even to declare neutrality, but simply attempting to beguile the Allies into revealing their invasion plans so that he could ensure that with German help the invaders could be driven back into the sea. There is little doubt that he was hedging his bets in case the Germans succeeded in repelling the Allied invasion, and engineering a possible non-fulfilment of the armistice terms was part of a game which was intended to allow him to survive whatever occurred.[7]

Whatever the truth of this, at the beginning of the fifth year of the Second World War, on 3 September 1943 the first Allied troops landed on the mainland of Italy and on 8 September 1943, Italy's surrender to the Allies was announced by the latter on the day before the main Allied landing at Salerno, south of Naples. Italian forces were given the ambiguous order to cease

---

7. 'Unconditional surrender' was the policy agreed by Churchill and Roosevelt in January 1943. Its meaning was never clarified and in fact, in the Italian case, the surrender was termed an armistice and hedged about with extremely lengthy economic and political conditions in addition to the military terms. Badoglio's possible duplicity was discussed in Denis Mack Smith's paper 'The Armistice of September 1943', presented to the British-Italian Historical Conference 'Italy and Britain since 1790: Relations and Images', Oxford, 1–3 July 1985.

operations against the Allies and to resist attacks from any other quarter (thus exempting them from any aggressive military initiative against their erstwhile German allies). In Rome there was panic and confusion, but no sign of any preparation to resist German occupation: on the contrary, within a few hours of the announcement Vittorio Emanuele and Badoglio had left the capital to its fate and were fleeing across country to the Adriatic port of Pescara whence they sailed immediately to take refuge at Brindisi, which was already occupied by British troops. Despite their distaste for the incoherent and self-interested conduct of these two old men, the Allies recognised that they were a vital link in the chain of legitimation of the Italian surrender, being the sole remaining legal representatives of the Italian state created by the *Risorgimento* and the only formal guarantee that the Italian armed forces would observe the terms of the armistice. To make assurance doubly sure, heavy pressure was exerted upon them to declare Italy to be at war with Germany, not as an ally (with consequent rights to consultation) but as a 'co-belligerent'. Despite the King's obvious reluctance to accept this basis of future relations with the Allies, he was constrained to sign the declaration of war on 10 October 1943. The whole shoddy strategy of the '45' days, intended to bargain with Italy's withdrawal from the war in order to assure the 'continuity of the Italian state' and to prop up the existing social order, had thus apparently collapsed in ignominy.[8]

For the next 19 months Italy became a field of desperate and muddled struggle between armies, classes, and ideologies in many perversely paradoxical combinations which added to the complexity of a situation whose outcomes no one could foresee, far less command.

On the battlefield itself the contending forces were unusually heterogeneous. On one side the forces of the German *Reich*, an 'alliance' between Germans, Austrians (the latter only incorporated in the *Reich* for four years), and a motley collection of Czechoslovaks, Russians, Ukrainians and Cossacks were joined, within a few weeks of the Italian surrender to the Allies, by the armed formations of Mussolini's born-again Italian Social Republic, an equally uneasy mixture of reluctant conscripts and élite Fascist units.

Fighting its way northward against these defending forces was an even more heterogeneous army, officially known as the United Nations. The British contingents within the Allied Armies in Italy consisted of units drawn from almost every ethnic group then within the British Empire, while the US units included a segregated Negro Division and a Combat Group of Japanese

---

Figure 8.1 Badoglio being escorted by Eisenhower to sign the secret 'long armistice', 29 September, 1943.

---

8. The main gain made by the Allies was the surrender of the Italian fleet, which significantly altered the naval balance of forces for the remainder of the war; Churchill's gratitude for this probably induced him to take a more lenient view of the Badoglio and Vittorio Emanuele than would otherwise have been the case.

Americans. Other contributions, of various magnitude and at different times, were made by Free French units (mainly Senegalese, Algerians and Moroccans), General Anders' Polish Corps, Royal Hellenic Greeks, a Brazilian Expeditionary Force, and a Palestine Jewish Brigade. After a few months the Allies grudgingly allowed an Italian contribution to be made, in the form of Combat Groups equal to some six divisions, drawn from units of the Italian army reconstituted in the south of the country.

These Italians were at least as ill-assorted as their countrymen fighting with the Germans. As well as being merely 'co-belligerents', insult was added to injury by the powerful anti-Italian stereotypes persisting among the Allied military and occupation authorities whose distrust and contempt were expressed at every level.

For the same 19 months, between these fires, the Italian people experienced the traumatising impact of a modern war, whose weight and extent in terms of explosives rained upon the infrastructures of the economy and of civil society, was unprecedented, and far beyond the imaginative capacity of a population whose experience of modernity had not gone beyond the superficial effects of Fascist modernisation. This experience, too, both compounded and contradicted that of the preceding 21 years, adding new polarisations to old cleavages.

The Royal Italian government in the south, though recognised as the signatory of the instrument of surrender, had virtually no influence upon Allied occupation policies at this stage. Until March 1944 the six anti-fascist parties which had emerged in Rome in September 1943 to form a Central Committee of National Liberation claiming to represent the true Italy, refused to have any dealings with it. No one would take an oath of loyalty to the monarch, Vittorio Emanuele, who was almost universally blamed for both the advent of Fascism and the bungled manner of Italy's change of sides, but it was not at all clear whether the Committee's bickering members (dubbed 'political ghosts' by Churchill) could command any added measure of popular support, not to mention enthusiasm.

This situation was in marked contrast with that obtaining in the German-occupied areas of the country. Here, the political and ideological polarisation of the population quickly became more sharply defined, precisely because the oppressive presence of the German army and secret police and of their Republican Fascist surrogates was soon at least as pervasive (and persuasive) as the longing for liberation. A Resistance movement, with both military and political dimensions, quickly emerged and began to engage its enemies as best it could. By December 1943 there was a five-party National Liberation Committee for North Italy whose leaders claimed to have the sympathy and support of the entire population of the north. Major strikes in the industrial cities and growing evidence of the widespread existence of partisan bands, collectively numbering tens of thousands, appeared to prove their point.

In the nature of the situation, the process of organizing resistance in the north had to be carried out without much reference either to the Central Committee of National Liberation or to the King's Government in the south. The separation was partly a reflection of the practical difficulties of consultation across the front line of battle but also expressed some of the profound ambivalence of Italy's history as a unified country. The political and cultural cleavages between the north and the south were, ironically, exacerbated by development of a Resistance movement intent upon forging a new national unity in the name of anti-fascism while itself being deeply divided along all the country's historic fracture-lines in politics, culture and social structures.

The centrality of the Italian Resistance movement of 1943–45 in the process leading to the survival and re-legitimation of the Italian nation-state can hardly be exaggerated. The break with Fascism and the experience of living through a closely and cruelly fought war and civil war left no family and no individual untouched. Some two million Italians were prisoners of war in Allied hands or as German internees; of the hundreds of thousands in Russian hands, few returned. Those who joined the Resistance movement, whether from motives of patriotism, revolutionary commitment or simply to avoid being called up by the re-born Fascist régime in the north, were divided by profound ideological differences which, under the veneer of 'unity of the Resistance', were to limit their military effectiveness and provide a fertile terrain for the fatal disunity of the innovative forces which sought to reshape the country's social and political order in the post-war period. No family could escape illegal activity of some sort, if only through the need to have recourse to the 'black market'.

For the Italian anti-fascists, whether veterans of the struggle or more recent converts, an armed Resistance offered, in the absence of Allied recognition of Italy as a full member of the United Nations, the only way to recover a legitimate national identity and dignity, and to remove the stain of Italy's primacy as a Fascist state. Most of them were convinced that there was some deep connection between the rise of Fascism and the character of the preceding Liberal State. They conceived of the Resistance therefore not only as the means 'to work their passage', as Churchill put it, but also, in a not very clearly defined way, to lay the foundations of a new type of democratic society and politics in the post-war Italy. If the Liberal State had spawned Fascism, then the source of national renewal had to be sought in a movement and an idea which represented a completely new beginning.

It is for this reason that the authentication and interpretation of the Resistance has assumed a central place in Italian political polemics since the war and is still capable of arousing strong feelings even among those who were not born at the time. Paradoxically, the struggle to appropriate the acknowledged source of retrieved political and national legitimacy served largely as a stage across which the contentions and oppositions which had characterised both the pre-fascist and Fascist period were once again rehearsed. The Italian Left in particular claimed that its numerical preponderance in the movement awarded it the right to claim the moral high ground on every issue of political principle, while the Right uneasily shifted between counter-claims of its own principled participation in the Resistance and the insinuation that the movement and its post-war legacy had been fatally vitiated by Communist strategy and tactics intended to make the Resistance the springboard for a Stalinist seizure of power, accompanied by a mass vendetta against all former 'Fascists'. Not without reason, in the light of the behaviour of many Communist bands towards their non-Communist rivals during the Resistance period, they suspected that the term might come to be applied to anyone who opposed the Communists. In fact, these fears were only marginally borne out by events: once the immediate urge to take revenge on hated persecutors and spies played itself out (albeit with the clandestine illegal execution of some thousands of Fascist small fry in certain 'red' areas of the north) the leadership of the Communists asserted a strict discipline, publicly opting to direct its aspirations for office to the democratic structures which, with its participation, were installed to succeed the Fascist régime's. Privately, nevertheless, it maintained some capacity to choose an insurrectionary option, and certainly never abandoned the Leninist concept of the inevitably violent struggle without which power could never be won by the working class.

How far this 'double game', as it was dubbed by the party's opponents, was inspired by instructions from the Soviet leaders of world Communism that the Communists should for the foreseeable future respect the division of Europe resulting from the defeat of the Axis powers and sanctioned by the secret terms of the agreements reached between Stalin, Churchill and Roosevelt, and how far it was the expression of the devious strategy of the leader of the Italian Communist Party, Palmiro Togliatti, is an open question. There is considerable evidence that he wished to distance himself, as far as was compatible with retaining the fervent support of his Stalinist rank-and-file, from the Soviet model of political action which he had experienced during his long years of exile in Moscow and to devise an alternative 'Italian road to socialism' based upon the theories of 'hegemony' over 'civil society' which had been the fruit of his predecessor Gramsci's long years of reflection in Mussolini's prisons.[9]

It is certain, however, that Togliatti and the rest of the leadership sought, as a counterweight to the criticisms levelled at them by others who depicted

---

9. Gramsci died in Fascist custody in 1937. His hundreds of pages of notes on philosophy, politics, history and literature, are very markedly heretical in relation to Leninist and Stalinist orthodoxy. Togliatti came into possession of the manuscripts, which had been smuggled out of Italy by Piero Sraffa, the Cambridge economist, while he was still in exile in Moscow, but did not allow any publication of them until 1948, when an abridged and bowdlerised version appeared. It took the Communist Party a further 30 years to produce a full critical edition with the title *Quaderni del carcere* (*Prison Notebooks*). Cf. also D. Sassoon, *Togliatti e la via italiana al socialismo. Il Pci dal 1944 al 1964*, Einaudi, Turin, 1980.

them as a mere tool of the Kremlin, to legitimate the Party as a patriotic, Italy-centred political force which had proved itself to be precisely such through its disproportionate contribution to the Resistance. Their success in doing so obliged their political opponents on the Right and their rivals on the Left to respond in kind, staking their own claims to have been the hearts and minds of the Resistance even if they could not match the Communists as its sinews.

One of the most serious penalties inflicted upon Italian political life by this mythologisation of the Resistance has been the absence of any form of political legitimacy for an unequivocally conservative party, with the consequence that intransigent conservatives have taken refuge in other parties nominally dedicated to programmes of social and political action based on 'the values of the Resistance' with the sole intention of frustrating all such missions. A further consideration for the parties of the right and centre, even when they were firmly entrenched in power as a consequence of the Cold War, was that circumstances might imaginably arise in which 'the unity of the Resistance' might need to be recreated in defence of the Republic (an eventuality which was in fact judged to have occurred more than once in its history).

On the other hand when, in 1960, the main Christian Democrat centre party risked officially turning for support in parliament to the neo-Fascist Italian Social Movement there was serious rioting with loss of life in several major cities, its own supporters rebelled, and for a few weeks it unwittingly forged a renewed unity between the other parties of the 'constitutional arc' which raised the spectre that it would lose its pivotal role as the largest party in any possible coalition. The Italian Social Movement thus remained merely an unusable reserve army of political and social outsiders of the type attracted by the prospect of street violence and terrorism. Even more extremist groups of the far right, in and out of which individual supporters of the Italian Social Movement readily moved, were, however, formed and sustained by the official intelligence services of the Italian Republic, with the knowledge of at least some of its ministers and presidents, for the purpose of carrying out terrorist activities directed at the creation of a political climate in which political collaboration with the Communists, and still more any attempt to bring it into government coalitions, could be readily frustrated.[10]

These later developments undoubtedly had their roots in the structure of party participation in the Resistance movement, reflecting a strong Left-wing tendency (with the Communist formations known as '*garibaldini*' representing some 50 per cent of the total), accompanied by much rhetorical fire-eating,

---

10. It has recently been suggested (June 1992) that the kidnapping and murder of Aldo Moro in 1986 by the Red Brigades (ostensibly an extreme left group) was also orchestrated by *Gladio*, the cover name for the intelligence service's anti-communist operation; whether this particular theory is true or not, there can be no doubt that a 'secret State' existed (exists?) in Italy as in most other Western European countries, including the United Kingdom.

and a corresponding basis for a repeat, in 1945–48, of the 'great fear' which had preceded the rise of Fascism in 1919–22.

Part of the appeal of 'communism' in 1943–45 must be attributed to the fact that years of Fascist propaganda had instilled the idea that the only real enemies of Fascism were the Communists. In the new circumstances, to declare oneself a Communist was thus often no more than shorthand for defining oneself unequivocally as an anti-fascist. The long-term solidarities which stemmed from the shared experiences of being on the same side of a bitter civil war also persisted and were an important countervailing influence on the anti-communist tone of Italian domestic politics, even at the height of the Cold War. Nevertheless, the more or less open acknowledgement on both the left and right extremes of the political spectrum inherited from the Resistance period, that violence was an inevitable component of politics and that, in the cause of revolution or counter-revolution, it was a legitimate tactic in given circumstances, meant that the 'continuity of the state' so assiduously pursued by the Italian establishment and the Allies was fully matched by a 'continuity of the anti-state' whose historical origins went back, through anarcho-syndicalism, *nazionalismo*, *squadrismo*, anti-fascism and the Resistance to the conspiracies of the *Risorgimento*.

The social composition of the Resistance movement was fairly remote from the general pattern of Italian society: factory workers and artisans constituted some 40 per cent of the movement, but peasants and rural workers only 20 per cent, while middle-class intellectuals comprised more than a quarter of its numbers. Most of the leaders at local as well as national level were drawn from this latter segment, effectively reproducing in the Resistance movement precisely the top-down political process which had characterised the *Risorgimento* itself, even if the ideological component differed considerably. One consequence of this was that, despite the accumulating evidence of the horrors of Soviet domination of Central and Eastern Europe, most of the most talented and prominent philosophers, historians, social scientists, writers and artists of the post-war generation remained members or supporters of the Communist Party: long after their peers in other West European countries had been disabused of their wartime enthusiasm for the 'socialist sixth of the world', Italian intellectuals continued to see in a Resistance which had fore-shadowed a socialist Italy the only firm guarantee against a creeping recrudescence of Fascism and, equally, a bulwark against the Americanisation of Italian culture. A further consequence of this highly critical attitude to democratically constituted authority on the part of the intellectuals was to reinforce the already powerful traditions within Italian culture of polarisation around issues of public morality and total distrust of politicians as a class. It is thus an irony of historical interpretation that the Resistance has often been referred to as a 'second *Risorgimento*'.

Similarly reminiscent of the 'first' *Risorgimento* were popular attitudes to the high politics of Fascist war and anti-fascist Resistance. Although few peasants were strongly influenced by the official ideologies of either Fascism or anti-fascism, their 'common sense' provided models of interpretation and response which reflected a long history of exploitation and more or less successful passive resistance to it, while they possessed a traditional technique of survival through concealment and displacement, and a framework of values tending to legitimate such behaviour.

The mass of the peasantry never went beyond passive resistance to the exactions of the German and Fascist authorities, in particular by withholding food from enforced collections, a phenomenon not unknown in the 'liberated' south, where conditions were even more conducive to a black market in food supplies. In partisan-dominated areas of the north most peasants regarded the guerrillas as 'our lads', but if their activities aroused too much interest by Germans and Fascists, their willingness to keep them supplied with food and intelligence became problematic: defence was preferable to attack, and non-aggression arrangements with the enemy were generally supported.

Support for the Resistance by factory workers was also problematic, though less so. A spontaneous strike in the 'industrial triangle' between Turin, Milan and Genoa in March 1943 quickly spread to almost one million workers, changing from a protest against hunger into a demonstration against the war. The anti-fascist precursor of the Resistance, in the shape of a nucleus of Communist militants surviving from pre-fascist times, claimed to have instigated it but could not possibly have had the numbers or organisation to do so. But the strike was a success in that it was far too large for immediate mass repression to be effective and after a week of anxiety the employers, encouraged by the authorities, granted increased wage-rates in response to it. At the time it merely strengthened the hand of the Fascist dissidents already casting about for a way to defenestrate the *Duce*. A less equivocal success, in terms of the rallying power of the Resistance was a strike of some 100,000 workers in June 1944, which was clearly directed against the German occupiers and their stripping of Italian industrial resources for their war-effort. It led to severe reprisals and mass deportation to forced labour in the *Reich* itself. Finally, in April 1945, with the Allies and Russians already in the heart of Germany, a 'general insurrectionary strike' called by the Resistance in the north was a euphoric success as a gesture to speed the departing occupiers on their way. At no time previous to this, however, were the factory workers available simply as a weapon in the Resistance armoury.[11]

None of the foregoing analysis should be taken to imply that the Resistance was militarily ineffectual, still less politically insignificant. There is no question that it was a force in being which tied down almost 25 per cent of

---

11. The memory of the abuse of the strike weapon which had assisted Mussolini's rise to power had perhaps persisted in the popular mind, linked to an older distrust of the propensity of the Italian middle class to play at revolution at the expense of its disadvantaged followers lower in the social scale.

German and Fascist forces in the north, and inflicted notable casualties as well as receiving them. Its political importance as the representative of new and renewed values and attitudes needed for the reconstruction of the democratic system can hardly be overstated, since it was the training ground for the future leaders of the six parties which, under various names, subsequently dominated the country's political life for half a century. At the time it was both encouraged and feared by the Allies, who wished to exploit its military potential but equally feared the obvious Communist preponderance within it. Eventually its most prominent non-Communist leader, Ferruccio Parri, with the support of the Allies, was to become Italy's first post-war prime minister despite the fact that he led a coalition in which the Communists were one of the two leading forces.

The 'Allies' to whom the Resistance movement, both locally and centrally, addressed its proposals for collaboration and its pleas both for political recognition and for material and moral assistance were in practice the undercover agencies attached to the fringes of the Allied forces to carry out specific clandestine tasks above and beyond the normal functions of operational intelligence and counter-intelligence.[12]

All the undercover agencies working in Italy were supposedly controlled by G-3 (Special Operations) at AFHQ and coordinated by an inter-services committee known as SOMTO, located first in Algiers and later at Caserta, which in turn supposedly coordinated its activities with Middle East HQ in Cairo, the War Office in London and the War Department in Washington. Nevertheless, all three of the latter also conducted relations directly with the armed Resistance in the north through the more convenient channels of their intelligence networks in Switzerland, sometimes neglecting to keep their representatives elsewhere as well-informed as they wished, and needed, to be for the proper discharge of their duties. In practice, moreover, virtually the whole of the Allied military and political establishment regarded Italy, Italians in general, and the Italian Resistance in particular, as little more than a side-show, any undesirable or distasteful aspects of which could be easily tidied up at the post-war peace conference. For the duration of hostilities, and away from the hustings of the 1944 US presidential election, the consensus was expressed in the common acronym found in marginal annotations on official policy papers of the time: KID and MIP ('Keep Italy Down'; 'Make Italy Pay').

---

12. British and mixed-nationality units and services specifically created or adapted for use in Italy included such agencies and units as the various branches of Military Intelligence, the Special Operations Executive, the Long Range Desert Group, 'Phantom' (a signals-interception unit related to ULTRA), Special Service Brigade (commonly known as Commandos), Special Air Service, Special Boat Section and No.1 Demolition Squad (also referred to as Popski's Private Army). They were often given cover names such as No. 1 Special Force (the local designation of SOE), ISLD (MI6), and MI9's prisoner-of-war and evader rescue service was referred to successively as 'SIMCOL', 'N' Section of 'A' Force and IS9; for the Americans, the newly created OSS, known to its British counterparts as 'Donovan's Cowboys', covered most of the same functions.

In short, between the 'disunited nations' on the one hand and the shattered fragments of the Italian nation-state on the other, opportunities for muddle were virtually unlimited.

It was against this background of almost total confusion, of demoralization of the Italian establishment and the growth of a Resistance movement which was determined to supersede it, that the overlapping alien bureaucracies attempted, in the Allied-occupied area, to make their contradictory writs run on the basis of minimal use of Allied resources and maximum exploitation of whatever Italians might have to offer by way of manpower, expertise and allegiance to the 'common cause', while in the looking-glass world behind enemy lines, they strove to carry out a multiplicity of clandestine intelligence, tactical and rescue operations.

In the German-occupied area an even more ruthlessly exploitative régime was operating, with every human and material resource of an already straitened economy being stripped, pillaged and vandalised for the use of the Nazi war machine and its Republican Fascist collaborators. As the fighting drew near to an area, all movable equipment was sent north, often directly to Germany, and what could not be moved was sabotaged. Stores of food and clothing, livestock and, too often, civilian labour were requisitioned and removed. Even stocks of Italian metal coinage were shipped out for use as washers, while cattle, sheep and horses were driven north by auxiliaries in German uniform recruited from the occupied areas of the Soviet Union.

As the Allied armies advanced slowly northwards the Royal Italian government led by Badoglio also edged further up the peninsula, first to Salerno, then to Rome after the city's capture on 4 June, two days before the Normandy landings. Until March 1944 all the anti-fascist parties, which unanimously claimed the exclusive right to represent the 'liberated' Italian people, refused intransigently to take part in any government which had allegiance to Vittorio Emanuele, although not all of them were republicans.

Stalin now stepped in with typical cynicism, turning the tables on everyone concerned by giving the Badoglio government official *de facto* recognition as a partner in the struggle against Nazi Germany. This forced the British and Americans, who had continued to treat the Italians as a conquered enemy and had been postponing any widening of Badoglio's Royal Italian government until the fall of Rome, to match this opening to the Italians by accepting such widening at once. Two weeks later, moreover, on 26 March 1944, after an unexplained ten-day stopover in Algiers, seat of Allied Force Headquarters and a Soviet mission to it, the leader of the Communist Party, Togliatti, was permitted to return to Italy from his exile in Moscow (where he had been the secretary of the Communist Third International, conveniently just disbanded by Stalin).

He had no sooner stepped ashore at Salerno than he declared, without prior consultation with his comrades of the Resistance who had been leading the clamour for the abdication of Vittorio Emanuele before any participation by the anti-fascist parties in Badoglio's Royal Italian government, that national unity must be the overriding consideration while the war was on and that therefore the Communist Party was prepared to join a government led by Badoglio forthwith and without preconditions concerning the future of the monarchy. This *svolta di Salerno* ('U-turn of Salerno') at once transformed the political situation. It short-circuited the sterile discussions of the 'institutional question' which had for six months dominated the proceedings of the Central Committee of National Liberation and quickly forced the other parties to declare themselves ready also to take part in a wartime government of national unity.

The British, following Churchill's expressed scorn for the 'political ghosts' of the anti-fascist parties, had not been concerned at the lack of any popular support for the Royal Italian government. Although grudgingly prepared to let an alternative anti-fascist establishment emerge provided that it was willing to assume the extremely onerous burdens of secret armistice terms binding Italy to a state of humiliating subordination for the foreseeable future, the British on the whole preferred to deal with a dependent monarchy and an opportunistic residual civil service. The Americans, however, with an election looming in the autumn in which the Italo-American vote would be critical to Roosevelt's return to the White House, welcomed the development and insisted that, once Rome was taken, the Italian government should resume much more extensive powers in the liberated areas and that clear recognition should be accorded to the progress being made towards the re-integration of Italy into the camp of democracy. After a good deal of bad-tempered secret diplomacy, Churchill was forced to accept that, upon the fall of Rome, 'the old King', as he usually referred to him, should be required to step down in favour of his relatively untainted son Prince Umberto, who would assume the title of Lieutenant of the Realm until the Italian people should have the opportunity after the war to make a decision upon their constitutional arrangements and so settle the 'institutional question' once and for all.

Italy was thus divided for this period between a backward south, where there was no experience of either the military or the political mobilising processes associated with the Resistance movement, reluctantly and inadequately administered by the Allies, and a more advanced north where the population, though still subject to the Nazis and their Italian surrogates, was proving to be capable of generating an increasingly self-confident potential leadership for the country. The division was not only to intensify the old political and economic cleavages which had dogged Italy's development since unification, but also to add new dimensions to them in terms of relative participation or passivity in the events which were shaping the future institutions and political culture of the country.

In any case the south was the poorest part of Italy and had grown accustomed to being managed and subsidised from far away. The experience of Allied administration and control did little to challenge the dependency culture which already afflicted it. Worse still, the Allied policy of minimal direct involvement in civil administration coupled with rigid insistence that the old-style mainly ex-Fascist bureaucrats to whom the latter was delegated take no initiatives without prior Allied consent, emphasised the powerlessness of the Italian state in conditions which could only encourage the re-emergence of the Sicilian *mafia*, the Neapolitan *camorra* and the Calabrian *'ndrangheta* as the alternative powers capable of 'protecting' the weak. In Sicily this process was materially assisted by the collaboration between the American intelligence services and the *mafia* at the time of the Allied invasion of the island, when the OSS arranged for the return of American *mafiosi* such as Luciano Liggio, cancelling out the one benefit that Fascism had brought in its two decades of rule. The connection was strong enough to encourage a Sicilian separatist movement, closely connected with the *mafia*, whose populistic goal was to become one of the United States of America, although its real *raison d'être* was to call violently to heel those peasants who were attracted by the Communist Party's policy of large-scale land redistribution, an aim acceptable to all official and unofficial forms of authority in a part of Italy still untouched by industrial development, where most agriculture was carried on by landless day-labourers toiling without mechanisation on the great estates of absentee landlords.[13]

The leaders of the Resistance movement, and particularly those of the anti-fascist parties which had been brought into the Royal Italian government in March 1944, made much play in their public statements of their plans to reform completely the backward aspects of Italian rural life, to redistribute the unused or under-used lands of the great estates in the south and to enable the share-croppers of the centre and north to become independent peasant proprietors, or at least to have a more genuine equality in their contracts with the landowners. The shorter-term motivation, as much as any wider consideration of social justice, was to find a means of persuading both landowners and peasants to deliver their produce to the official collecting centres and not to the black market. In the longer term, all the parties, including the Communists, uncritically assumed that Italy's future economic development not only would not involve any large-scale urbanisation of the rural population, but required the bulk of it to stay on the land.

Although black market phenomena were common to every one of the nations involved in the Second World War, in a country such as Italy they quite clearly had more than a contingent and temporary significance which the return of peace and adequate supplies would eliminate. Here, the black market not only had significant outcomes in terms of changed attitudes among those who produced for it and those who managed its mechanisms at the time, it

---

13. The movement was also connected indirectly with the bandit Salvatore Giuliano, whose story is graphically recounted in Gavin Maxwell, *God Protect Me From My Friends*, Penguin, Harmondsworth, 1957. When Giuliano had served his purpose he was delivered, dead, to the authorities.

also provided a new social context for economic behaviour which amounted to a training ground in the entrepreneurial activities which became possible as soon as the battle-front had passed. In a real sense it was an important plank in the developmental springboard for areas of intense post-war economic activity of an unprecedented type, leading to the formation of industrial districts characterised by the preponderance within them of mutually support-ive small enterprises. As we shall see, both the basic stability of the local civil society in the post-fascist period in the centre and north of Italy, and the inadequacies of the political system and the political class which simulta-neously emerged at national level, appear to be deeply rooted in the contradictory experiences of Resistance and black market.

To understand fully these post-1945 phenomena, they must be also seen as an outcome of longer-term factors operating in the historical development of Italy, reaching back certainly to the origins of the unitary state, and in some cases to local mercantile cultures dating from the time of Francesco di Marco Datini, the 'Merchant of Prato'.

Mussolini's 'ruralisation' and demographic policies, the end of mass emigration in the early 1920s and the religious inhibition on birth-control had prevented any significant depopulation even of the areas most marginal for agricultural production. In 1943 it was still a crowded countryside in which a stranger could not move for more than a mile or two without being observed by many shrewd eyes, and where industrialised zones existed within a few miles of archaic agricultural backwaters. Townspeople of all classes habitually looked down upon farm-labourers and peasants, and the latter as habitually suspected the motives of the former. Every rural area had its own distinctive social stratification deriving from the historical accumulation of forms of ownership, tenancy, inheritance and occupation of the land, and of exclusion therefrom. Neighbouring villages and households were often in permanent feuds over customary rights or festering ancient torts. Outside the towns few could speak standard Italian with confidence and some not at all. Confined within their mutually incomprehensible dialects, illiteracy was still common, especially among women.

An immediate and highly disruptive effect of wartime conditions upon communities so anchored in their local past was that the traditional trading advantage of the city over the countryside had been unexpectedly reversed. Firstly, with the virtual collapse of the official purchasing and distribution system for agricultural produce and its substitution by the black market, the peasant with a surplus of food or other home-produced goods (either his own or what he could conceal from the landowner) was able to generate a much larger cash income than before; secondly, the price of land was not rising as steeply as inflation in general, since many small town-dwelling landowners

---

Figure 8.2 A Fascist family decorated for 'numerous offspring', 1934.

were being forced by inflation to realise some of their assets. Peasants who had formerly been unable even to dream of buying land or converting share-cropping tenures to freehold now glimpsed the prospect of doing so. Dealings in land, even during the German occupation, accelerated rapidly, due both to the greater money incomes of the agricultural classes and to the relative lack of investment opportunities in other sectors.

The conventional wisdom of Italian historians concerning the 1943–45 period axiomatically assumes the mass of the population to have been from the start active supporters of the 'liberation movement' led by anti-fascist élites and parties. This was, however, true only in the sense that, for the great majority, to survive was itself to resist, in the course of its more ancient struggle to baulk all oppressors and exploiters, and now also in many cases to take advantage of the economic conjuncture to achieve a measure of upwards economic mobility.

For days, and in some districts for weeks, after the armistice, almost every aspect of organised civil life ceased to function. Although, amazingly, many trains, trams and buses continued to run, food stores in town and country were raided and emptied *en masse* (accounting perhaps for some of the easy generosity in foodstuffs experienced by the hundreds of thousands of assorted fugitives including tens of thousands of Allied prisoners-of-war released by the armistice, who were roaming the countryside in the early weeks after the surrender); the few public servants, from Prefects to town hall clerks, who had remained at their posts, were unclear about what, if any, rules they were to apply. The rationing system went into free fall, many banks, offices, shops and factories were closed. On the other hand, barter instantly began to replace the money economy.[14]

The economy, as always, was also a moral economy. Although the black market (which it would be better to define as the 'real market') not only came to dominate economic production and distribution, it provided legitimacy for creative lawbreaking, opportunities for upwards mobility, and most importantly the margins necessary for hospitality and assistance to those with whose cause an instinctive identification and a symbolic appropriation was possible. It was far from being the case that those producing for it normally bore out the stereotype of the corrupt and corrupting black marketeer. On the contrary, most of them merely extended the age-old system of exchange of favours between those within the village or neighbourhood to a wider spectrum of those in need, responding to the demand expressed by the continuous stream of town-dwellers who cycled or walked into the countryside in search of something that would eke out the meagre, or non-existent, official rations. Their peasant suppliers were able to rely on tried and tested techniques for

14. For a full account and analysis of this remarkable episode of migration, cf. Roger Absalom, *A Strange Alliance. Aspects of Escape and Survival in Italy 1943–1945*, Leo S. Olschki, Florence, 1991.

mitigation or frustration of the exactions of authority which were as old as the peasantry itself, ranging from illicit appropriation of produce and tax-evasion to collective insistence on 'ancient rights' of pasture in inaccessible places where livestock might be concealed from requisition.

The spontaneous outburst of entrepreneurial activity constituted by the black market was also underpinned by the peasant community's social cohesion and capacity to create spaces for survival in conditions of emergency which were themselves partly due to an implicit conspiracy for self-defence against 'outsiders' and were reinforced by the observance (more fervently than ever) of local feast-days and the maintenance of old customs which strengthened the sense of collective identity and solidarity of those living in a given settlement. Both individually and collectively, fending for themselves was second nature.

As the military and political organisations of the Resistance movement gained ground against the enemy, extensive, though strategically secondary, areas of the Italian outback were 'liberated' by partisans, sometimes for several weeks at a time. The partisans set up their own improvised civil administrations, rich in high principle but inevitably lacking significant resources, to operate within them, regulating the distribution of necessities, dispensing rough and ready justice, even collecting taxes in some cases. The vast majority of the populations of these 'partisan republics' established in the summer and autumn of 1944, were, inevitably, peasants. Where the partisan leaders attempted to involve them in these activities and functions, more or less explicitly as an exercise in 'political education', friction was often very near the surface as they discovered that peasant concepts of 'justice and liberty' were closer to the Old Testament than to Rousseau and Marx. In other areas, where strategic conditions did not allow the setting up of 'partisan republics', partisan bands provided not so much a promise of political emancipation as a hope of refuge for those wanting to evade conscription and for deserters from it, and a useful threat of retribution to overzealous officials, representing future legitimation of present disobedience.

In general, however, the experience of living in these 'partisan republics' did not lead the peasants to seek political forms of expression for the practical imperatives of self-defence and survival, nor for the cultural impulse to solidarity. Their brief exposure to a greater degree of formal participation in the public administration of their lives does not seem to have been perceived by them as constituting as important a turning-point as was the conquest of relative economic autonomy through the black market.

A considerable distance thus remained between the largely town-bred partisans and Resistance politicians on the one hand, and the peasants on the other. The very presence of partisans in an area tended to transform the peasants who inhabited it into targets for reprisals, hostage-taking and systematic military activity which was guaranteed to inhibit normal patterns of cultivation and husbandry. Though partisan–peasant relationships were often close and occasionally heroic, they were subject to the usually grim fortunes of civil war and therefore more fraught with apprehension and fear than charged with enthusiasm for any form of 'new politics'. In a number of cases where reprisals had been especially harsh after apparently irresponsible provocation of the enemy, the adequate logistical and intelligence support normally provided by the host population dried up completely, forcing the partisans to abandon the territory concerned.

All this points to a resilience, a power of initiative and a flexibility of response which do not at all match conventional ideas of 'the mediocrity of rural life'. The wartime experiences of Italian peasants in the centre and north of the country, whether as purveyors of the means of survival (and apprentices in micro-economic management), or helpers of Allied escapers and others on the run from authority, seem, on the contrary, to show that here, at least, was a peasantry capable of accommodating within the cognitive-affective maps of its manifold wisdoms almost any unfamiliar proposition or intrusion, appropriating symbolically both disaster and the millennium, both war and tyranny on the one hand and the 'world turned upside down' on the other. Despite formal ignorance and widespread illiteracy, their understanding of the human predicament was comprehensive, and those in trouble with authority were never regarded as alien.

The peasantry's categorical imperative was survival and to traumas of every kind it had a repertory of practical responses which gave it a better chance of achieving it than those more dependent on the servicing mechanisms of modern states and societies. Though peasants' explicit judgements may sometimes appear to be simplistic and reductive, they are generally able in practice to appreciate the contradictory and complex nature of human behaviour. Thus, although they normally sympathised with, and often materially supported, the partisans, especially if a proportion of them were of local origin and peasant stock, it was usually their sons who were conscripted into the ranks of the Italian Social Republic's forces, and who had in any case long provided the bulk of the lower ranks of the *carabinieri*. In this sense they were still, as always, on both sides, and on neither, of the social and political conflicts precipitated by those sectors of the population to which they were subordinate.

This complex peasant subjectivity is part of the explanation of the later shipwreck of so many high hopes which were raised among the politically aware by the Resistance movement: their fulfilment depended on the creation of a relationship of unprecedentedly stable reciprocal trust with the world of the town, of the gentry, of the social groups to which the peasantry was traditionally subordinate, and whose social superiority was concretely and specifically personified in other men who dressed, spoke, ate, drank, and worked in ways clearly distinct from the peasant's but with whom he had always had to share the worlds of nature and production, and always at a disadvantage, in terms of self-perception when not of fact. Eighteen months of resistance, however heroic, could do little to bridge this age-old chasm.

182

On the other hand, it is not a coincidence that the areas of the most dynamic entrepreneurial activity based on small and medium firms in the 30 years following the war corresponded closely to those subjected for the longest time to the disciplines and opportunities of production for survival. It was in the areas particularly where conditions of economic 'emergency' prevailed for longest that the total conjuncture of these, taken with the social and political expectations formed by large-scale resistance, contact with the Allies and an underlying tradition of millenarian rebelliousness going back for centuries, all combined to create the archipelagoes and islands of 'red capitalism' which were to become a unique component of the post-war recovery of Italy.

It was not in this perspective, however, that Italians viewed their situation when, after the Allies had occupied the whole country in May 1945, they turned with immense relief from the horrors of war and civil war to the problems of economic and political reconstruction. The only objective on which the country's new leadership, drawn from the anti-fascists who had guided the Resistance movement and ranging from the Communists to the Liberals was agreed, was that Fascism and all its works should be dismantled and never allowed to rise again. But the government of national unity formed in March 1943 had already been through a series of convulsions even before the war was over and had lost much credit in the course of them. Badoglio had soon been replaced by an elderly pre-fascist prime minister, Paolo Bonomi, who, despite having been the unanimous choice of all the anti-fascist parties, had manoeuvred to force the Communists out of the coalition in the hope of achieving greater bargaining power with the Allies, and also to reassert the authority of the Royal Italian government over the National Liberation Committee for North Italy based in Milan which had been the real power behind the Resistance in the north.

Pursuing their own military and political priorities, the Allies had preferred to deal directly with the latter, effectively cutting the Royal Italian government in Rome out of the process. They agreed to provide material and financial support for the northern Resistance on condition that its leadership accepted their total authority after the Allied troops arrived and, in particular, agreed to disarm and disband their formations as and when instructed by Allied Military Government. At the same time, in central and southern Italy, they continued to interfere arbitrarily and irresponsibly whenever their short-term interests appeared to require the subordination of Italian reconstruction to the immediate and often trivial benefit of the Allied forces.

Whatever the Allied intentions in this last manoeuvre of their divide and rule approach, in practice they achieved the reinforcement of the authority of the National Liberation Committee for North Italy not only in the regions in which their partisans were operating but also at national level. Despite the fact that the military leader of the Resistance in the north, Ferruccio Parri had been arrested by the SS in February, by April 1944 the *vento del nord* (the wind from the north) was already blowing through the whole of Italy, raising hopes

and fears: hopes of a complete cleansing and healing of the wounds left by Fascism, fears of a vendetta which might leave very few unaffected in a population which had willy-nilly been obliged to make its accommodations with the Fascist régime for more than a generation.

Thus, by the time the north was finally clear of the Germans and their satellites, the way seemed clear for a genuinely historic transformation of the basis of Italian politics: for the first time since the fall of the *destra storica* the north had produced a group of determined and committed men who, having personally fought for the resurgence of Italy, could be expected to govern it firmly and fairly, rejecting both the shoddy compromises of transformism and the false idealisation of the state which the *nazionalisti* and the Fascists had so disastrously pursued.

At the same time as the Resistance had, it seemed, forged a new political élite capable of giving a decisive impulse to the construction of a genuinely popular and democratic Italy, as the war ended the wealthy, the conservative and the well-born who had compromised themselves with the Fascist régime, initially held back from the political fray for fear that their antecedents would catch up with them. Most were prepared to make large concessions to the *vento del nord* and its principles of socialism and democracy in order to save what they could from the collapse. In the end, however, their apprehensions proved unwarranted: within three years the revolutionary wave had passed, leaving scarcely any trace in the real structures of power, even though the leaders of the winning party in the political contest between the left- and right-wing legatees of the Resistance movement, the Christian Democrats, sincerely stood for their version of liberty, democracy and social justice. Below that principled tip of iceberg, there was by then a much larger and more ramifying lower part, whose actions and entrenched practices harked back not to the Resistance but to the far less inspiring traditions of transformism and demagogy.

Figure 8.3 The Socialist leader Sandro Pertini at the Liberation celebration in Milan, 1945. He later became Italy's most popular President.

185

The consolidation of republican Italy

On 25 April 1945, the call by the National Liberation Committee for North Italy for a 'general insurrection' in the north was answered by hundreds of thousands of Italians who had not until then been active participants in the Resistance. The partisans came down from the hills and took over the towns as the Germans fled north and for a few days were mandated by the Allies to administer public affairs until military government could be established. For a few heady weeks it seemed to Italians and outsiders alike that Italy had indeed finally 'worked its passage' back into the fold of democratic nations forging their own destiny. It was easy to forget that, while a large minority had been involved in or at least supported the Resistance, the much larger majority had not.

The Resistance parties in the north were especially left-wing in their policies and attitudes. It was not surprising therefore that the temporary administrations set up by the Committees of National Liberation there all had a distinctly socialist tinge. In the factories of the industrial triangle, workers were encouraged to build upon the legislation passed *in extremis* by the Italian Social Republic which in effect provided for the workers to form joint management committees with the owners. In most cases their first actions were to demand punitive sanctions against managers, technicians and proprietors who had collaborated with the Fascists, which was a recipe for large-scale expropriation.

To some extent, this was an attempt by the political leaders of the Resistance to channel into some kind of manageable procedure the raw desire for revenge upon the defeated remnants of militant Fascism. Drastic purges were promised, to clean up the civil service and local government, but the necessary legislation had still to be introduced and the processes of justice, applied by judges who had been appointed under Mussolini, were slow and not usually drastic enough to satisfy the more vindictive of the partisans. In some areas, notably in Emilia-Romagna, the most politically militant

186

Communist partisans, believing that the 'third war', of workers against their capitalist oppressors would soon begin, anticipated its results, and settled old scores, by 'executing' in considerable numbers locally known former Fascists, both older-generation *squadristi* and supporters of the Italian Social Republic returning from the wars.

When Allied military government was established, and the partisans had been disarmed with ceremonies and speeches, it had absolute powers to override sanctions applied by Factory Councils and local Committees of Liberation, and normally did so, since the underlying policy remained to repress 'disease and unrest', which in practice meant that such political direct action had to be prevented. As for the violent settlement of scores, this was a matter for the Italian authorities, since the Allies had no intention of becoming involved in trying to police crimes by Italians against their fellow countrymen.[1]

At the national level, however, the National Liberation Committee for North Italy had greater success at the start. The spokesmen of all five parties comprised in it (Christian Democrats, Communist Party, Socialist Party, Liberal Party and the Action Party) were adamant that the day of the super-annuated pre-fascist parliamentarians and other relics of the Liberal State who formed in large part the 'timid and reactionary' Royal Government in Rome had now passed. Bonomi's second administration did not even contain the Socialists and the Action Party. Bonomi counted on the Allies to support him in the name of continuity, but, given the Labour Party's crushing victory in the British elections, and having still the Japanese to beat and many more pressing problems than propping up a shaky Italian monarchy, they maintained a studied indifference. After six weeks of tortuous bargaining, the National Liberation Committee for North Italy succeeded in imposing its own leader as the new prime minister of a five-party anti-fascist coalition, in which the parties of the left outweighed those of the right.

This was Ferruccio Parri, whose party affiliation was with the Action Party, the least revolutionary of the three main forces of the northern Resistance. Nevertheless, the aim he set for his government was far more radical than anything conceived by its post-fascist predecessors. It was no longer merely to restore the parliamentary system of the Liberal State in its last manifestation before Mussolini but to extend to all Italy the spirit, and some of the practice, of the Liberation Committee rule which had been temporarily established in the north, deriving its legitimacy not from royal appointment but from the presumed will of the Italian people, as the precondition of a total reorganisation of the Italian state and Italian society, a reorganisation delayed for a quarter of a century.

---

1. The only Allied-run war-crimes prosecutions were against Italians and Germans who had killed escaped prisoners-of-war or evading aircrew knowing them to be unarmed and willing to surrender. Cf. Roger Absalom, *A Strange Alliance. Aspects of Escape and Survival in Italy, 1943–45*, Leo S. Olschki, Florence, 1991, pp. 295–6.

In the spring and early summer of 1945 it certainly appeared that Italy was ready for precisely such a radical approach. All the main parties were talking fervently of basic social change and the tens of thousands of partisans in the north and centre had risked their lives already in the cause. In reality, however, the Resistance was a rapidly waning force. Not only was it prepared to be peacefully disarmed by the Allies, but most of its rank and file, particularly in the non-communist formations, were far more interested in rebuilding their private lives than in building a new Jerusalem.

Although the Allies lacked the resources to rule the north directly, the few hundred Allied Military Government personnel (Ancient Military Gentlemen, as they were derisively termed by their combatant colleagues) who represented the victorious Big Three nations initially enjoyed a remarkably high level of local cooperation from the National Liberation Committees which they found running every town, and there were few serious incidents of civil disorder. The very triumph of the National Liberation Committee for North Italy in securing the appointment of Parri as the new prime minister had, however, the effect of demobilising the local committees. In the name of orderly reconstruction of the economy the Allies quietly sidelined the Workers Management Councils in the factories and restored the prerogatives of the employers. As Allied Military Government asserted its local control, largely through the personnel and institutions of the Italian state, the temporary ascendancy of the Committees was quickly negated and they became a shrill and vexatious lobby of militants always, it seemed to most Italians, causing trouble in the name of vast, but locally irrelevant, universal principles and allegiance to abstractions.

The only party with the rigid discipline to be able to avoid a north–south polarisation was the Italian Communist Party. Togliatti was in a position to be thoroughly informed of Stalin's thinking, which at this point was aimed at consolidating the division of Europe along the boundaries agreed at Yalta rather than driving still further westwards. Italy was in the Anglo-American sphere of influence and it was made amply clear to the Italian Communist leadership that the Red Army would not be available to back them if they tried to make a revolution. The fact was less plain to those below them, and many rank and file militants still believed that Togliatti was playing a crafty double game by constantly asserting the democratic and parliamentary strategy of the Communists while secretly preparing for an insurrection. But, apart from one or two romantic, and very limited, local attempts to restore the partisan republics of 1944, the party's discipline remained firm, sustained as it was by the fervent belief that Communism was the 'wave of the future', destined to sweep across the whole world.

Togliatti's strategy was based on a long-term plan to reconcile the demands of the Soviet connection, from which much of the fervour of the rank and file was derived (the 'Socialist sixth of the world' had a charisma almost impossible to describe, far less recapture, since 1989), with the realities of the external and internal conditioning of Italian politics. One essential tactical feature in it was for the Communists to remain in the coalition government, whoever might be its prime minister; a second was to ensure that henceforth the only parties allowed to count in Italian politics should be the 'mass parties' (Christian Democrats, Socialists, and Communists); the third was that, in the long run, a kind of 'power-sharing' should be worked out between the parties of the left, representing the working classes (and thus, in Leninist theory, the inevitable inheritors of power), and the party representing the independent peasants, artisans and petty bourgeoisie, the Christian Democrats. All the other minor parties, including the Action Party whose contribution to the Resistance had been second only to the Communist Party's, should be allowed, or induced, to decline, since they represented only a handful of doctrinaire intellectuals, class traitors or big business.

For this reason, when in November 1945 the forces of conservatism both within and outside the coalition government joined together to bring down the high-minded but ineffectual Parri, Togliatti remained indifferent. His Socialist allies, led by Pietro Nenni, romantically convinced that there could be 'no enemies on the left', did not object, although they had been in opposition with the Action Party during the second Bonomi government, and had an equally libertarian tradition.

In a typically noble, but ultimately futile gesture, Parri, who had lived throughout his ministry in his office, sleeping on a camp bed for no more than three hours per night, called an unprecedented meeting of his colleagues, with journalists present, to explain his reasons for resigning:

> With sober detail and in a gentle, monotonous voice, he told them
> how a Fifth Column within the government, after systematically
> undermining its position, was now going to restore to power the social
> groups that had formed the basis of the Fascist régime. In a moment
> Alcide De Gasperi was on his feet. As the leader of the Christian
> Democrats and Parri's logical successor, he hotly denied the assertions
> of the outgoing Prime Minister and pleaded with the foreign
> journalists present not to report what they had heard. But the
> journalists refused to be convinced; they knew – and most Italians
> knew with them – that the militant opposition to Fascism had passed
> into history.[2]

A few days later, with the foregone support of Togliatti and Nenni, De Gasperi formed his first ministry. He was to dominate Italian politics for the next 12 years, presiding over the most critical and formative phase of the Italian Republic.

---

2. H. Stuart Hughes, *The United States and Italy*, 3rd edn, Harvard University Press, Cambridge, Mass., 1979, p. 140. Hughes was at the meeting.

It is an indicator of the subtlety of De Gasperi's approach both to his own party and to those of his coalition partners that his first move was to re-create the six-party government whose overthrow he had helped to contrive. This first ministry lasted for seven months and allowed the arrangements for the popular referendum on the 'institutional question' of whether Italy was henceforth to be a monarchy or a republic, and the elections for a constituent assembly charged with the task of drawing up a new Constitution, to be carried through with relatively little trouble, even though the referendum was fairly close-run (54 per cent to 46 per cent) and the vote reflected clearly the continuing north–south divide, with the north decisively republican and the south equally for the monarchy. The King, Vittorio Emanuele, abdicated in April so that his son Umberto could represent a relatively untainted monarchy, and the vote was close enough for some of the latter's advisers to press him to refuse to accept the result on the grounds that the votes had been tampered with, still hoping that the Allies would intervene in his favour. De Gasperi, who may himself have voted for a monarchy and whose party had certainly been in the majority pro-monarchy, would have no truck with this manoeuvre to elude the will of the people: after an icy interview with him, Umberto boarded a plane to exile in Portugal.

The elections for the constituent assembly which followed the institutional referendum reflected a pattern which had already emerged in March, when the first local elections were held, and the Christian Democrats had won in almost half the communes, with the united left close behind them, while all the other parties combined managed to win in only 16 per cent, with the Action Party winning less than 2 per cent. In the elections for the constituent assembly, where the voting was not on a territorial basis, the voting was, for the Christian Democrats, even more alarming: they won only 35 per cent of the popular vote against the Socialist Party's 20 per cent and the Communist Party's 19 per cent. The Liberal Party, which in 1921 had won 47 per cent of the votes cast, was reduced to less than 7 per cent, while the Action Party gathered a derisory 1.5 per cent. A further unpleasant surprise was provided by the performance of an outsider party, dubbed the *qualunquisti* ('the Man in the Street Party') led by a satirical journalist. This 'party' had no real organisation and no message except to call a plague on all politicians, but it won over 5 per cent of the votes, and had clearly attracted the votes of covert but unrepentant Fascists.

It thus appeared that at least two of Togliatti's assumptions had been fully borne out: Italian politics would henceforth be dominated by the three 'mass parties', and none of them would be able to rule without the others. His preferred configuration was obviously for the left parties to be the dominant influence and he therefore continued to press strongly for the maximum unity of policy and action with the Socialists. Nenni appeared to be happy to endorse this, despite the rumblings of discontent from the right in his own party concerning the loss of its political independence to a party with a record of U-turns in its attitude to other parties of the left.[3]

The left–right polarisation of Italian politics revealed by these results has not greatly changed over the half-century since 1945. Only in April 1992 did a significant variation occur. The Christian Democrats remained the largest single party in domestic elections and the combined total of Communists and Socialists never exceeded 45 per cent. Just as significant a fact, however, is that some 20 per cent or more of the votes were always divided between an array of small parties covering the whole political spectrum, and coalition with one or more of them was a necessity for the formation of a government.

The regional distribution of the votes for each of the mass parties in 1946 also tended to confirm Togliatti's analysis: the Christian Democrats gained the highest percentages in rural areas, particularly in the south and the islands, where they approached 40 per cent, while in the north the left parties were much stronger, with over 50 per cent, but only 20 per cent in the south. The implication was that the Christian Democrats were essentially a peasant party, as their ancestor the Popular Party (in which De Gasperi had also been a young leader) had been in 1921, and that therefore the concept of a structural alliance between the left and the Christian Democrats would be likely to appeal to the latter.

Within the Christian Democrats there was certainly a faction prepared to heed such a possibility: the heirs of the social-reformist tradition of the Popular Party's trade union and peasant league wing, led by Giuseppe Dossetti. A year later he was to reflect, with a certain bitterness, that

> The historical significance of three-party government [i.e. the De Gasperi coalitions with the left from July 1946 to May 1947] was less the sharing of power with the Marxist parties, which the latter demanded out of desire to exercise an influence on policy and the Christian Democrats accepted for fear of something worse, than what was (or should have been) a greater feeling of solidarity among the people and of convergence in practice between real attempts by the mass parties to take the first steps towards the structural reforms which would provide our democracy with a coherent content.[4]

Dossetti's words highlight some of the main issues to be faced in any

---

3. All West European Communist Parties had, during the 1930s, followed switches in the Soviet line from denunciation of social democratic parties as 'social fascists', to 'popular fronts' embracing the whole left, and, during the Nazi-Soviet non-aggression pact, a return to attacking them as 'imperialist lackeys'. After the German attack on the Soviet Union, the line reverted to 'popular fronts'.
4. Giuseppe Dossetti, 'Fine del tripartito?', in M. Giusenti and L. Elia (eds), *Cronache sociali (1947–1951)*, Luciano Landi editore, Rome-S Giovanni Valdarno, 1961, p. 35.

interpretation of this critical post-war period: the preponderance of the mass parties, the divergence between the readings of the situation by the protagonists, the popular expectation of a structural reform which would transform the content of Italian politics and make the state an expression of the nation, and not vice-versa.

In approaching each of these aspects the overriding conditioning of the Italian political scene by a series of external and domestic factors must always be borne in mind.

In the first place, the attraction and power the Church possessed as a focus, after the removal of Fascism and its institutions, for all the forces of reaction in Italian society, whether defeated monarchists, Fascist-trained bureaucrats, landowners fearful of dispossession, or industrialists threatened by the new militancy of their workers. In the Church they sought and found, at this point in its history, a doctrine, an organisation and a legitimation for opposing all the pressures for social and economic change: insofar as the Church secular political representation was the Christian Democrat party, it was inevitably to that party that they turned, without much regard for its declared policies.

Secondly, there was a diffuse but still powerful *nazionalismo* which found ample scope for grievance in the Peace Treaty negotiations between the Big Four, which effectively relegated Italians in international terms to the status of defeated enemy, despite their contribution to Allied victory between 1943 and 1945. Parri and De Gasperi alike resisted as far as they dared the decisions being taken in their absence not only to deprive Italy of her colonies (including those acquired before the First World War) but also to redraw her eastern and northern frontiers (ceding large areas to Yugoslavia and small ones to France) and to impose harsh reparations upon her (including the transfer of much of her fleet to the Soviet Union).

Thirdly, there was the challenge of uncontrollable popular social movements among the landless peasants of the south and the share-croppers of Tuscany and Emilia-Romagna, intent upon the immediate satisfaction of extreme demands, and which, in the well-established traditions of agrarian violence going back to the 1860s, were resorting increasingly to mass-occupation of uncultivated land, *jacqueries* against property, and even brigandage. In 1946–47 these phenomena were so widespread that they threatened basic law and order in large areas of the country.

There were also the external pressures which affected all the Italian protagonists: the continued presence of Allied forces and the implied threat, even after they had handed over control of all Italy (except the areas bordering Yugoslavia) in December 1945, that they would intervene in cases of serious civil disorder. Italy was at this point totally dependent for food, basic raw

Figure 9.1 Hunger-demonstrators in Naples, 1947.

materials for industry, and for fuel, on the Allies, especially the United States, where by late 1946 the anti-communist hysteria which would culminate in Macarthyism was already building up the domestic pressure for an end to aid for governments which included the Communists. Conversely, the Communist Party was the object of increasing insistence from Moscow to manifest unswerving loyalty to the 'anti-imperialist' line, with the implied threat that the existing leadership would be by-passed unless it did so.

Each of the three 'mass parties' responded to these complex constraints by exhibiting a form of political schizophrenia. The Communist Party, while continuing to call for a broad class-alliance to install 'progressive democracy' through the electoral process, and to acknowledge the need for collaboration with the Christian Democrats as the representative of large sectors of the middle class and peasantry in the cause of creating a socially harmonious nation, nevertheless continued to maintain and to proclaim its Leninist identity, with an explicit commitment to proceed to the 'dictatorship of the proletariat'. At grass-roots level, the old 'conspiratorial' cadres and the newly-recruited mainly peasant millenarians made no secret of the intention to 'seize power' (and, by implication, 'property') in a forthcoming revolution. To complicate matters, almost every week large caches of arms and munitions, hidden by Communist partisans against the 'great day', were discovered by the police and widely publicised.

Even if Togliatti was not intentionally playing a double game, these evident contradictions were widely perceived and interpreted as being evidence of a deep-laid plot to Sovietise Italy. Togliatti's cautious approach was not assisted by the re-establishment in September 1947 of an explicit Moscow-centred coordination of Communist activities throughout the world: the Cominform was different only in name from the old Comintern which Stalin had closed down in 1943 in order to reassure his Western allies. Although ostensibly only a clearing-house for information, this organisation soon began issuing rebukes to the West European Communist Parties for not pursuing more vigorously the struggle against capitalism and 'bourgeois democracy'. Suspicion of the aggressive political content of the Cominform could only be confirmed by statements by the French and Italian Communist Parties to the effect that the workers would welcome the Red Army in the kind of circumstances in which their counterparts in Poland, Czechoslovakia and Romania had done so.[5]

The Socialist Party also had two souls: the old division between maximalists and reformists quickly reasserted itself and was made more acute by Nenni's insistence on the policy of seeking a complete merger with the

---

5. Cf. the statement made by Maurice Thorez to the French Assembly in February 1947: 'If the Soviet army came to pursue an aggressor on our soil, the workers and people of France could not act towards the Soviet army otherwise than the workers and people of Poland, Romania and Yugoslavia' (cited in S. Neumann (ed.), *Modern Political Parties*, University of Chicago Press, Chicago, 1956, p. 123.

Communist Party. After the collapse of the Action Party in the elections of April 1946, many of the latter's members moved into the Socialist Party, strengthening the reformist wing, and in January 1947 the reformist wing, in a replay of the cleavages of 1921, defected from the party and formed a new one, the Italian Social Democratic Party, led by Giuseppe Saragat. The new party looked to the British Labour Party for its model, and was decisively anti-communist. The rump Socialists went into the next election, in 1948, in a joint list with the Communists, and lost half of the votes they had attracted two years earlier.

The Christian Democrats' strength lay precisely in their lack of any clear ideological position. Despite the efforts of Dossetti and those who agreed with them, they were a classic 'catch-all' party which provided an umbrella for a wide range of social and political forces united by little more than fear of Communism. De Gasperi was an astute politician and strongly resisted the pressure from his own right wing and from the Vatican to allow it to become simply the 'clerical party'. He insisted on including in his coalitions as many of the minor 'lay' parties as he could persuade to join, even if he did not technically need their votes in parliament, warning the Pope that this was necessary in order to forestall the formation of any anticlerical alliance which might be exploited by the Communist Party. He also used this tactical device to reward those among these minor parties supported by significant numbers of the industrial bourgeoisie with important concessions on economic matters, thus also keeping at bay his social-Catholic left wing, which saw collaboration with the Communist Party on social and welfare issues as being in the interest of the 'harmony' which had been at the heart of Catholic social doctrine ever since the *De Rerum Novarum* encyclical.

An important constraint on all the parties during the period between 1945 and April 1948 was that everyone was conscious that Italian politics, despite the tremendous ferments experienced at the grass roots, were in an interregnum. The elections to the Constituent Assembly had defined the political preferences of the population but had not given any mandate for a programme of concrete measures. In a real sense all De Gasperi's coalitions in this period were caretaker governments. The Constituent Assembly itself was not empowered to make policy or take executive decisions; its sole task was to draw up a Constitution. De Gasperi probably understood the laws of this situation better than Togliatti, who evidently believed that concessions to Catholic opinion (such as the re-endorsement of the Concordat of 1929 and the consequent entrenchment of the special status and privileges of the Vatican and the Papacy) in the constitutional arena would incline the Christian Democrats to political compromise in the Cabinet. But in fact his unprincipled acceptance of clerical pretensions was accepted by De Gasperi with equal lack of principle and had only the result of exacerbating the tensions within the traditionally anticlerical Socialists and eroding their electoral support while not increasing that of the Communist Party.

Between 1945 and 1947 the left in Italy, with the strong initial momentum gained from its role in the Resistance, seemed quite irresistible, but within a year of joining De Gasperi's three-party coalition it found itself increasingly on the defensive.

The parties of the democratic left and centre had lost disastrously to Mussolini in 1921–25 and in hindsight attributed their failure to prevent the dictator's rise to their own lack of unity and their doctrinaire refusal to collaborate with the Catholic Popular Party. After the Second World War the strategy of the two Marxist parties reflected an obsessional determination to avoid any repetition of this experience. They therefore sought unity of action with a view to eventual unity of organisation, and at the same time were prepared to make considerable concessions to the Christian Democrats in order to keep the coalition in being.

As often happens after a catastrophic defeat, the 'lesson' learned proves to be inappropriate at the next strategic turning point. The left's strategy was a response to a challenge that was not being posed: the real risk of a return to Fascism was not that a new Mussolini might arise to exploit the disarray of the democratic parties in order to overthrow democracy itself, but rather the creation of conditions in which politics could be permanently dominated by a 'catch-all' party operating well within the democratic rules of the game. The Christian Democrat Party was the only one which fitted this description.

In practice the period of the three-party coalitions in the name of 'anti-fascist unity' gave an unsolicited opportunity of reassertion to the two social and economic forces in Italy whose implicit division of the spoils of political control had already lasted since unification: the industrialists of the north and the great landowners of the south. The 'spoils system' built up during the next decade by the Christian Democrats constituted a renewal of the original 'historic compromise' of the 1860–76 period, but this time strengthened by the active collaboration and sanction of the Church (whose social 'anti-capitalism' had been and remained ambivalent at best). In the circumstances of the first and harshest period of the Cold War, with the Red Army to the north and Tito's forces to the east threatening the end of American economic aid and the incorporation of Italy into Stalin's Asiatic empire, the left's alternative was less appealing, as was dramatically revealed by the results of the April 1948 election, when the single list of the left lost a quarter of the total vote its two component parties had achieved only two years earlier.

The period leading up to the elections of 18 April 1948, the first held under the new Republican Constitution of Italy, was thus marked by the rapid ebbing of the tide of change which had seemed in 1945 to be on the point of sweeping Italy into a radical social transformation. As for the new Constitution, apart from the institution of the monarchy, replaced by a largely ceremonial presidency, the parliamentary framework was remarkably similar to the original *Statuto* of 1848 (as modified in 1919 in order to introduce fully proportional representation). Local government was also little changed from

Figure 9.2 Waiting for Utopia: Italians after the foundation of the Republic, 1948.

the pattern prevailing in 1919: the power of the Prefects, responsible to the Ministry of the Interior, was undiminished, in order to discourage any tendency towards separatism.

Almost the only real and lasting gain made by the left during these critical years was, nevertheless, in the field of the Constitution, where certain key principles were enshrined which remained for decades the unfinished business of the country. The most important of these in relation to the subsequent pattern of political and economic development was the provision for the creation of Regions which, at least in the centre and north of the country, virtually coincided with historic boundaries of the states of pre-unification Italy. Of great long-term significance, too, were the provisions in the Constitution relating to the supremacy of parliament (which was responsible for the election of the President of the Republic), the provision for an independent

197

Constitutional Court, the role of the presidency in the appointment of the Prime Minister, the independence of the judiciary, the institution of popular referendums, and (on the debit side) the entrenchment of the 1929 Concordat, which effectively barred women from exercising important civil rights in the fields of marriage, divorce and abortion. All these provisions were to furnish significant occasions for inducing and resisting political and social change in the decades which followed.

The Constitution was, however, the only field where, in this period, the left was able to impinge upon the patterns of the future political development of the country. In terms of actually coming to power (or at least to office) within the democratic and parliamentary framework, as both the Communists and the Socialists declared to be their goal, they were from the beginning of 1947 forced continuously on to the defensive by the external conditioning due to the Cold War, and the successful mobilisation by the Christian Democrats of all the forces opposed to the radical social programme the left proposed. One key factor in this long-term marginalisation of the left as a protagonist of political life at national level was undoubtedly the astute leadership of the Christian Democrats by De Gasperi. Another was the direct influence on Italian internal affairs exerted by the United States, particularly during the campaign leading to the elections of April 1948.

It has usually been assumed by the left in Italy that De Gasperi was little more than an American puppet. A year after he took office he made a visit to Washington to confer with the Truman Administration about how best to reconstruct the Italian economy. He was given assurances that aid would be provided (the Marshall Plan, under which Italy would receive more than $1.5 billion in aid, was already in the making); he was also left in no doubt that the United States would prefer a government which did not include the Communist Party.

Looked at in another perspective, however, it is clear that De Gasperi was the manipulator at least as much as he was the subject of manipulation, seeking in effect American support for what he already planned to do: force the left parties out of his coalition, while countering their likely response in the streets, in the form of strikes and demonstrations against the severe anti-inflationary policies being pursued by Luigi Einaudi, his stern Minister of the Budget. By installing the tough-minded and efficient Christian Democrat Mario Scelba of impeccable anti-fascist antecedents in the Ministry of the Interior he first made sure that the State once again had the monopoly of coercive force. Togliatti and Nenni threatened that the country would be ungovernable without them and organised a wave of strikes during the autumn. But the stabilisation of the economy was already taking effect psychologically as well as economically: while street violence was put down ruthlessly, United States aid was already beginning to flow with visible effects in terms of supplies of raw materials and capital equipment with which the manufacturing sector could begin to raise production and productivity. The strikes quickly collapsed since there were no obvious concrete alternative policies for the left to put forward. It was not after all possible convincingly to advocate at one and the same time the dismantling of the economic control mechanisms of the Fascist régime as the main instrument of the exploitation of the labouring masses, and the imposition of new, equally top-down state restrictions upon the management of production in order to protect the workers.

By the end of 1947 the battle-lines for the forthcoming elections were already clear: on the one hand the left, consisting of a 'people's bloc' of the Communists and the Socialists in a single list; on the other, a coalition of parties ranging from the newly-formed Social Democratic Party created by the dissident Socialists, to the small but influential Republican Party and the conservative Liberal Party, all led by a Christian Democrat Party which had succeeded in reabsorbing most of the protest votes which in the 1946 elections for the Constituent Assembly had gone to the parties of the far right. This second grouping was powerfully backed by the Catholic clergy, explicitly instructed to do so by Pope Pius XII, and by officially supported Italo-American pressure groups in the United States which organised a flood of letters and food parcels to kith, kin and complete strangers belonging to the vast informal network created through generations of emigration. The United States embassy in Rome, particularly through the person of the energetic and fanatically anti-communist ambassador Clare Booth Luce, took a prominent part in the high tide of exhortation directed at the Italian electorate.

In the arena of foreign policy, too, a series of anti-communist cards were played by the United States, backed by Britain and France. The Peace Treaty of February 1947, punitive in intention (mainly at Soviet insistence, although not without an element of vendetta from the British), had aroused disappointment and resentment in Italy and a certain recrudescence of *nazionalista* feeling, was quickly overtaken by events: less than three months after its signature the Truman doctrine of containment of communism became the official policy of the Western powers and within a year the latter had already abrogated *de facto* their claims devolving from it. Upon Italy now depended the security of southern Europe and the country was at once included in the Atlantic Alliance, with all that implied for its military and naval strength and dispositions.

The furious resistance to this 'war-mongering' on the part of the Italian left was deprived of much of its effectiveness by the latter's obvious schizophrenia in relation to the claims of communist Yugoslavia to the whole of Istria, including the port of Trieste. The negative symbolism for the Italian middle-classes, brought up in the lay religion of the *Risorgimento* demand for the 'redemption' of Trento and Trieste, of the Communist Party's apparent ideologically inspired willingness to cede control of this emblem of Italy's 60-year struggle for unity and freedom from foreign oppression can hardly be overstated and was certainly exploited to the full by De Gasperi and his allies, new and old, at home and abroad. At the critical moment, one month before

the 1948 elections, the Western Powers proposed that the whole of the disputed territory should be transferred to Italian sovereignty, since the previous compromise plan to create a Free Territory of Trieste had proved to be unworkable because of Soviet and Yugoslav intransigence.[6]

These blatant interventions in Italy's internal affairs appear to have had the desired effect, although the opinion poll evidence upon which the Americans based their fears can hardly have been reliable. Two months before the April 1948 elections they were convinced that the Communist-Socialist alliance might win, and were strongly encouraged in this belief by De Gasperi and other leading Italian politicians. In all probability, however, there was never the slightest chance that they would do so. A large majority of Italians had no desire for their country to go the way of Czechoslovakia, where the Communists, under Soviet 'protection' (loudly endorsed by the spokesmen of the 'People's Bloc') had illegally seized power only two months earlier. Nor, with the years of privation still deeply ingrained in their memory did they wish US aid to be cut off, as the United States spokesmen made abundantly clear would be the case if the Communists came to power.

The Communists and the Socialists had assumed that 'Resistance values', with their stress on 'national' solidarity for liberation and reconstruction, would easily overcome the deep-rooted traditions at every level of the population of 'looking after the family' and distrusting 'authority', even the leadership to which one had given one's vote. They mistook the powerful but ephemeral currents of millenarian expectation in their 1946 electorate for a permanent state of militant political mobilisation, when it most often expressed no more than a temporary enthusiasm for an ideal which, in the voter's heart of hearts, was felt to be unattainable (and perhaps the more cherished for precisely that reason).

By polling day, too, the consistent misuse of the two Parties' dominant position in the trade unions (revived enthusiastically by the Allies as a barrier to any recrudescence of Fascism) to call strikes and demonstrations for dimly understood non-economic goals, such as the campaign against the Marshall Plan, had already begun to be counter-productive: not only were improvements in pay and conditions not won (indeed, Togliatti and Nenni had agreed to wage-restraint in the cause of national reconstruction), but workers who displayed militancy at factory level were frequently penalised by their

---

Figure 9.3 A southern emigrant reaches Milan.

6. Ironically, only ten weeks after this exercise in the political use of diplomacy, Tito made his historic break with the Soviet Union, with the consequence that Yugoslavia then became the front line against Stalin. The United States then pulled back from the March 1948 proposal, complacently leaving the Trieste question to fester for another 27 years. Cf. Roberto G. Rabel, *Between East and West. Trieste, the United States, and the Cold War, 1941–1954*, Duke University Press, Durham and London, 1988.

employers, with shop-stewards sacked and blacklisted by the thousand. The error was compounded by the adoption of a union strategy based on the paternalistic assumption that the skilled workers of the traditional working class would form a natural leadership for incoming unskilled workers of peasant stock: in practice the skilled resented the unskilled as the vehicles of dilution and wage-cutting, while the unskilled regarded the skilled traditional workers, who provided the militant shop-stewards, as simply another layer of alien 'authority' obstructing their familial survival strategies.

In the last instance, moreover, there was no practical way in which the Communist Party could reconcile its policy of 'progressive democracy', signifying full cooperation with the state in the tasks of national reconstruction, with an effective defence against the blunt police and administrative repression by De Gasperi's government of any public disorder which they might stage. Since they knew that the Soviet Red Army would not come to their aid if they tried a violent seizure of power (even supposing they could mobilise the resources for it within Italy itself), the only response available to them was to issue threats and warnings of popular wrath to come when the polls opened.

On 18 April 1948, over 92 per cent of the Italian electorate went to the polls, and 48.5 per cent of the voters gave their votes to the Christian Democrats, with another 15 per cent going to that party's coalition allies. The 'People's Bloc' gathered just over 30 per cent, with a considerable transfer of votes directly to the Christian Democrats in addition to those lost to the dissident Socialists of the Social Democratic Party. The extreme right populists, who had seemed to threaten a resurgence of Fascism in 1946, were almost wiped out, their voters having heeded the warning that a vote for any party but the Christian Democrats would be wasted. For the only time in post-war history a single party had achieved an absolute majority in terms of parliamentary deputies and senators. The left, having renounced the extra-parliamentary roads to power in the firm expectation that the tide of popular support for the Resistance and for a radical programme of social transformation would sweep it there anyway, now found itself facing life in the political wilderness, perhaps permanently.

Two months later, as if to confirm that the Christian Democrats now had achieved full control of the situation, the Communist Party's outraged response to an unsuccessful assassination attempt against Togliatti by a deranged individual, which in Milan and Genoa took the form of a pre-insurrectionary mobilisation, and elsewhere resulted in protests and strikes ending in violence (in Turin the FIAT car-workers took the management prisoners), was firmly and decisively suppressed by the army and the police. But the leadership of the Party and the General Confederation of Labour on the whole sought to hold the 'base' back from any outright confrontation with the state, although it did call a general protest strike in an attempt to maintain some control of the outrage of the base. Complaining that this was a political use, and debasement, of the strike weapon, the small Catholic component of the Confederation walked out of it. Although this did not significantly weaken the trade-union movement in terms of membership, it was an important nail in the coffin of the anti-fascist unity upon which the Italian Republic was ostensibly founded.

In retrospect, the most remarkable fact about the results was less the triumph of the Christian Democrats than the solidity of the left vote, particularly that of the Communists. They confirmed rather than created the profound polarisation of post-war Italian society between the heirs of Garibaldi (under whose image the 'People's Block' had campaigned), demanding radical social change, and a real popular majority which feared it, or did not believe it was possible. Until 1994 between a fifth and a third of all adult Italians continued to support a party with no hope of achieving national office.[7]

The Communists buoyed up by the unwavering faith of its grass-roots supporters ('the base'), were not demolished, even as an organisation, to the extent that might have been expected. While the Christian Democrats had succeeded in aggregating sectional interests sufficient to crush it at the polls, they could not create for most of their voters the periodic surges of conviction and hope which the Communists continued to be able to generate among the deprived and dissenting elements in the population. They succeeded in retaining mass support in the north and centre of the country and slowly established the framework of an 'alternative hegemony' to that of the Christian Democrats. They were able to aggregate much of the discontent and dissent generated by the transformation of the Christian Democrat party into a régime dominated by narrow vested interests. In the conditions of what most Italian intellectuals regarded as the country's stultifying cultural provincialism, the Communist Party was able to present itself as an important channel for cosmopolitan outreach, successfully recruiting during its first decade as a mass party a large proportion of Italy's leading intellectuals and artists who resented the vulgarity of the consumerism which characterised the chaotic and socially disruptive

---

7. Psephological evidence clearly indicates that such support was in great part passed from parents to children over at least two generations, taking the form of an inalterable familial identification rather than being a matter of individual rational conviction periodically renewed through examination of issues and debate about policies. Such a system of attachment clearly possesses both the merits and the vices of any form of sectarian belief in a 'pillarised' society. In the Italian case, where the cement of national identification is particularly weak, what the Italians themselves refer to as 'the Communist Church' has been of considerable importance in underpinning the social stability generated by economic and cultural success and consequent self-confidence, while keeping within reasonable bounds the effects of militant conviction. Parallels of some limited relevance may be found in the formal and informal structures of politics in linguistically (Belgium and Switzerland), ethnically (USA), and religiously (Netherlands) divided societies, although it is also true that the supra-sectarian frameworks which inhibit recourse to violence are currently everywhere under great stress. There is a considerable amount of hearsay evidence that Togliatti himself welcomed the decisive outcome of the election, remarking to one colleague that the results were the best thing that could have happened for the Party.

post-war economic development of Italy. It also moved, albeit with painful slowness and frequent retreats, away from total subservience to Moscow. Although not a 'catch-all' party in the same way as the Christian Democrats, it had, in addition to its overtly political incursions into trade unions and the peace movement, a long-term policy of creating its own non-political outposts in civil society, ranging from a hunters' federation to a union of women.

Its main strength remained, however, the quasi-religious fervour and trust of 'the base', for whom it was the morally pure custodian of their dream of social justice, the local representative of the socialist heaven on earth, whose Mecca was the Soviet Union (to which the Party organised the cheap mass pilgrimages that were the only experience of foreign travel of much of the Italian working class for some 30 years). Its very remoteness from the possibility of national political power, after 1948, meant that it was not embroiled in the parcelling out of privilege and peddling of influence which characterised the practice of the parties in government and could always claim to be 'the honest party'.

At the same time, its pre-eminence in local government throughout a 'red belt' stretching from Emilia-Romagna in the north to Tuscany and Umbria in the centre, enabled it to become the vehicle of regional and local identification and to express the resentment of 'the thieves from Rome' (to use the phrase favoured by more recent autonomists in the north) of regions threatened, but not overwhelmed, by the flood of southern migrants to the factories of the industrial triangle which was the first and most obvious effect of the 'economic miracle'. Thus, in paradoxical contrast to its anti-racist and egalitarian platform of 'workers' solidarity', the Communists in these areas took over the leadership of a powerful traditional conservatism stemming from dislike (historically well-founded) of central authority and attachment to local allegiances and family-based social networks which automatically excluded outsiders.

Although in the last 20 years it has consistently sought to prepare itself for a share in office at national level, the Communist Party has always had to measure the trade-off between floating votes attracted by such efforts, and the depressive effect that any major compromise with the established order was certain to have on its conviction supporters. It is a measure of the complexity of the patterns of Italians' identification with and against their nation-state that even in the post-Soviet epoch the Communist successor parties retained the unswerving allegiance of nearly one fifth of the electorate: precisely the level of support that Togliatti's party enjoyed in 1946.[8]

The Socialist Party, on the other hand, never recovered fully from the self-inflicted wounds of the period of its partially consummated marriage to

---

8. The vote of the two successor-parties (Democratic Party of the Left and Communist Re-Foundation) totalled nationally approximately 21 per cent in the April 1992 elections.

the Communist Party, even when its leader Bettino Craxi was a successful prime minister in the 1980s and its elder statesman Sandro Pertini was for seven years the Republic's best loved president. It never regained the status of a mass party: in 1992 it had still not succeeded in overtaking the Communists in terms of the popular vote, despite the latter's profound post-1989 crisis. From 1951, when Nenni made a visit to newly-Sovietised Prague, it became evident that the ties between the two mass parties of the left were gradually weakening. The process was accelerated by the appalling revelations of Stalin's misrule which surfaced in Khrushchev's 'secret' speech to the Twentieth Congress of the Soviet Union Communist Party in 1956, and by Nenni's evident anxiety to enter, before the end of his political career, what he called 'the control room' of government.[9]

It was, however, to be another eight years before the Socialist Party was invited to follow the other minor parties of the centre into a further experiment in coalition government with the Christian Democrats. In the interval critical changes had occurred in the political configuration of the country which were the expression much less of the overt clash of views and policies between the major parties than of deeper processes of social aggregation and disaggregation. These, in turn, can be understood only in terms of far-reaching developments in the economic and cultural spheres which created in the minds of many outside observers an incomprehensibly paradoxical impression of permanent instability and total paralysis in Italian politics in the context of an 'economic miracle' which within a generation catapulted Italy into the ranks of the seven most powerful industrial nations of the world.

As well as a defeat for Togliatti's political tactic of 'progressive democracy' (based on the left parties, representing the worker and peasant masses, taking power irreversibly through electoral means), the April 1948 results refuted his basic analysis of the underlying economic conjuncture faced by the country. The theorists of the 'People's Bloc' believed that the reform of political institutions under the pressure of mass-participation was itself the *precondition* of any radical restructuring of the economic and social system and a redistribution of wealth in favour of the 'exploited'. It was for this reason that they took the constitution-making process so seriously and failed to perceive that Italy could no longer be regarded as a closed system in which the main motor of change would be the domestic class struggle. They thought that the nation-state's administrative machinery could be taken over and used to control and direct the development of capitalism in post-war Italy, through planning and taxation, more or less independently of external pressures from stronger capitalist systems, and the internal pressures from the personnel and traditions of the state's bureaucratic machine.

---

9. The secret speech was, of course, read by Italian communists and socialists, but not in their own party newspapers: the Communist daily *'L'Unità'* only published the speech, finally, in 1990.

This theory failed to take account of the real nature of the state machine itself, of the domestic and world market situations, and the psychological disorientation of the masses. The State machine was not designed to control the economy: on the contrary, under Fascism, the 'captains of industry' had learnt how to penetrate and dominate its decision-making processes to their own advantage. The country's dependence on the United States, the world's main capitalist power, for raw materials, food and improved technology meant that the outside market situation was the principal factor for recovery: to pursue anti-capitalist policies would invite immediate retaliation. Most intractable of all were the inappropriate expectations encouraged by the left in its supporters: the masses expected quick results in terms of improved standards of living directly attributable to social and political reforms ('the expropriation of the expropriators' was a favourite Marxist formulation). When these failed to materialise, while not losing their basic political allegiance, people had to develop personal strategies for surviving within the existing system, for all its inequities.

The Italian economy in 1945 had been reduced to 29 per cent of the level of industrial production, and to 36 per cent of the agricultural production of 1938. Real wages had over the same period been cut by 40–50 per cent for shop-floor workers and 65–70 per cent for public servants. Best off were those independent peasant farmers and landowners whose land was not sown with mines and who still had seed and breeding livestock; those who had no such good fortune were nearest to penury, particularly the already landless labourers.

War damage, especially to infrastructures and civilian housing, was massive. As Einaudi described it on taking up his post as Minister of the Budget, there were:

> two million dwellings destroyed [...] five million damaged [...] railways lacking 50% of their rolling stock and 20 per cent of their other plant compared with pre-war [..] the merchant fleet had only 10% of its pre-war tonnage left [...] machinery had been requisitioned from factories, agricultural stock, especially livestock, drastically reduced [...] at least three billion *lire* needed for minimum essential reconstruction.[10]

Stocks of raw materials and finished goods were near zero and most of the population depended for mere subsistence on shipments of basic necessities from the United States, which until the end of the year was still formally an occupying power and accepted a basic responsibility to 'prevent disease and unrest'. Had this assistance been withdrawn and Italy left to its own devices

---

10. The *lira* was then worth 400 to the dollar, thus the sum required (at 1947 prices) was about $7,500 million; the aid received by Italy under the Marshall Plan amounted to about 20 per cent of this sum.

there would undoubtedly have been widespread starvation, epidemics and civil strife, notwithstanding the joint efforts of the anti-fascist parties to keep the situation under control. There was thus, in 1945, a very real material basis for American apprehension that the country could either be swept into the Soviet camp by a wave of revolutionary desperation, or revert to an authoritarian régime along Fascist lines. At the time of the massive United States interference in the 1948 election this perception was still dominant in American policy-making. In fact, however, the critical corner had already been turned by then, and the basis for this success had already been laid in 1946 and 1947.

In general the national debate on economic reconstruction, which had begun even before the liberation within the National Liberation Committee for North Italy, was long on abstract theory and short on empirical knowledge of the real economic situation. Proposals for economic reform and reconstruction therefore tended to be scholastic and abstract, whatever their political origin. The demands of the left for nationalisation and land reform were inspired by a vague belief in the benefits of social engineering but were so inadequately operationalised that the old guard of academic free-trade economists, led by Einaudi, easily demolished them as woolly and impractical.

This led rapidly to a dilution of Togliatti's and Nenni's proposals to the Constituent Assembly for wholesale nationalisation, the declared aim of which was to eliminate the 'inevitable' war-mongering tendency of capitalism. All the parties were in practice intent on courting the middle classes and the small and medium entrepreneurs who were universally assumed to be the key to the economic reconstruction of the country: for the Christian Democrats the aim was to create the conditions for a stable competitive capitalism as a bulwark against any reassertion of corporativism, while the left saw it as necessary to detach the 'middle classes' from 'big business', which they thought to be innately imperialistic and aggressive. 'Monopolies' were bad, but 'healthy' small or medium capitalists extracting only 'normal rates of profit', would naturally tend to be firm supporters of classically democratic political framework. When a Socialist member of the Constituent Assembly proposed that the Constitution should guarantee only property managed by workers, peasants and cooperatives, Togliatti opposed him on the grounds that

> the struggle is not against free enterprise and the private ownership of the means of production in general, but only against those forms of property which inhibit the initiative of broad strata of producers, against monopolistic forms of private property.

All three mass-parties advocated a degree of economic planning and 'control' to serve various social and economic ends but the control they called for remained a moral commitment incapable of implementation. Throughout the period 1945–47 the dominant theme was that individual economic activity should somehow be constrained to achieve social goals as well as private benefit, but no one had any concrete suggestions as to how this might be brought about.

With few exceptions the professional economists who had remained aloof from Fascism were unwilling to allow political considerations to enter into economic debate: it was impossible to refute their objection that this was precisely what the Corporate State had been about. The only antidote was old-fashioned 'free market' economics, in which government had only a minimally regulatory role and all significant decisions were technical rather than political. When the Communists proposed a constitutional provision that the state should 'coordinate and direct' (later amended to 'foster') production in order to 'guarantee the right to work' while simultaneously ensuring 'maximum benefit to the community', it was easy for a trained economist such as Einaudi to demonstrate the logical and practical incompatibility of these goals in economic terms. Not even Togliatti could persuade the Assembly to challenge the authority of Einaudi, Italy's only internationally recognised economist.

The failure to carry through structural reforms as part and parcel of the post-war reconstruction of the Italian economy, and the progressive erosion of any demand for such reforms from the left, reflected an assumption by all the political parties that the existing social structure could not radically be changed. The real task as they perceived it was to restore and increase output, as the only path to improvement of living standards. Since in 1945–47 all the mass parties regarded themselves as parties of government committed to this common task it was for them to minimise all obstacles thereto. Every measure which might have had the effect of reducing the willingness of industrialists, landowners and entrepreneurs to commit their capital to investment in production had to be avoided.

Of particular significance was the rejection of a currency substitution which would have enabled the government to identify precisely by whom liquid capital was held and thus to apply taxation measures efficiently (including the confiscation of profits illegally acquired under Fascism, which was a nominal commitment of the coalition). Strongly supported by the left as part of a package which included effective exchange controls, a capital levy and enhanced state investment in heavy industry, it was intended to cut off export of capital, reduce the money supply (thus curbing inflation), and lead to some redistribution of income by fairer taxation. It was finally rejected because, it was argued, it would shift control of capital investment from the private sector to the state: it might lead to an 'investment strike'. The left, which fought hard for the measure as a way of achieving some palpable proof to show the 'base' that the profiteers, hoarders and speculators who preyed upon them would finally be penalised, had to give way because its leaders, by proclaiming that the working class was now 'at the centre of the new national society, of which it is the basic force', had made it impossible to make any such 'technical issue' a matter of principle, and of resignation. Instead, in order to consolidate the image of the working class as the new protagonist of national life, the left accepted in autumn 1946 a 'wages truce', in effect voluntary wage restraint by the unions they controlled, as a way for it to take the lead in national recovery. The General Confederation of Labour (which, significantly, had now added 'Italian' to its title) declared that the interests of the unions 'coincided with the national interest'.

The net effect was to 'liberate' a mass of capital, however ill-gotten, from any possibility of state intervention and therefore make it available for any form of investment which might produce a quick return: for Italy it was the 1945 'big bang'. The availability of this type of capital, the re-creation by economic means (essentially the threat of unemployment) of a fiercely competitive labour discipline in industry and large-scale agriculture, and above all the 'responsible' wage-restraint exercised by the trade union movement at the behest of its political controllers on the left, produced an economic conjuncture in which a self-fuelling 'economic miracle' could take place. Even before Marshall Plan funds began to arrive, the basic components of the 'Italian economic miracle' which followed in the 1950s were already in place. Profit margins increased, exports rose (also because of the extreme devaluation of the *lira* imposed by the Allies during their occupation), inflation slowed, and investment, however chaotic in character, proceeded apace.

When De Gasperi expelled the left from government in mid-1947 and thus removed the political reason for wage-restraint, the political as well as the economic initiative had passed decisively to the Christian Democrats who could now present themselves as the standard-bearers of the 'order and continuity' of a national society in which the interests of the most disadvantaged (the southern peasantry) were threatened by the disruptive and selfish wage-grabbing of the northern working class. Meanwhile, Einaudi, the persuasive advocate of economic freedom and financial orthodoxy, was at last offering a coherent economic policy which anyone could understand: the stabilisation of the currency and the end of the controls inherited from the war period. In effect this was a recognition that the black market was the real market and that there had to be a balance between what the government received in revenue and what it spent.

Einaudi's policies were quickly perceived to have brought results. Price increases were slowed or halted; the *lira* was stabilised at about one fiftieth of its pre-war value, creating the conditions for export-led growth. Gradually people in work had more to spend on life's necessities, if not yet on luxuries. The negative aspects were the continuing high level of unemployment and the fact that investment was almost entirely without effect on the deep-seated structural problems of the Italian economy: the north–south disparities in development and culture, outdated technology, lack of indigenous energy resources, and the drain on state revenues of a bloated and irrelevant bureaucracy. It is of course an open question how far some of these problems were really susceptible to cure by government intervention. The suggestion that an

Figure 9.4 Resistance ... to the Marshall Plan for economic recovery: the Cold War polarises Italian politics in 1948.

Italian version of Jean Monnet's plan for the modernisation of the French economy through the channelling of the post-war recovery effort towards long-term goals could and should have been attempted begs the fundamental question of the technical capacity of the state to impose its will through administrative action carried out by well-trained and impartial technocrats in its service. At the very least, the Italian bureaucracy, as it emerged from fifty years of transformism followed by twenty years of Fascist manipulation, and two years of civil war, was unlikely to have been capable of accomplishing successfully such a demanding task. As for its massive over-staffing, it would have been difficult if not impossible for the Christian Democrats to have imposed mass redundancies on the very core of its own constituency, especially since the victims would have found vocal defenders in a clergy dedicated to the Catholic doctrine of the family.

The immediate effect of these unresolved structural weaknesses underlying the Italian economy was to reduce the capacity of large-scale industry to respond flexibly to changing conditions in the market-place and to create the basis for improved productivity through technical innovation rather than intensification of labour. The European Recovery Programme (known as the Marshall Plan) was intended to be the key to solving this problem. The thrust of the Programme was that the United States should provide the raw materials and capital equipment (i.e. American technology) that would enable Italy to expand its production far beyond anything previously achieved and thus permanently exorcise the nightmare prospect of a 'hunger revolution' led by the Communists.

Statistically at least, during the four years during which the Marshall Plan was running, the objective was achieved. By mid-1952 Italian industrial production was at 140 per cent of the pre-war level (although at only 125 per cent, if the increase in population was taken into account). By the same year the Italian merchant fleet had been rebuilt to its 1938 strength, which meant that the transport abroad of the exports which were driving the recovery were not a burden upon the foreign exchange reserves. But the issue of the long-term restructuring of Italian industry on American lines was not addressed, despite the urgings of the Marshall Plan advisers. While paying lip service to the ostensible aims of the Programme the Italians contrived to divert the funds intended to trigger increased capital investment in the modernisation of industry to the goal of financial stability, for all Italians concerned with guiding the recovery, from Einaudi downwards, were determined to avoid a repetition of the hyperinflation which had destroyed the value of money during both world wars, with disastrous consequences in terms of social destabilisation.

The Marshall Plan certainly helped to maintain the momentum of recovery at a critical moment when it might have faltered, and the arrival of the shipments was of great symbolic importance in restoring Italian self-esteem. It also provided the important political bonus of demonstrating both that the Communist Party was prepared to oppose an initiative clearly in the interest of ordinary Italians if it was regarded unfavourably by the Soviet Union, and that its resort to strikes and protests could be defeated by firm government action. But once the Programme ended, in 1952, there were legitimate fears that the momentum might be lost, with unwelcome political consequences. For once, however, nature came to the aid of a country whose industrialisation had always been disadvantaged by its lack of natural resources and by its topography. Under the inspired leadership of an ex-partisan, buccaneering entrepreneur called Enrico Mattei who had been appointed to manage the vestigial state oil-prospecting agency set up as part of the Fascist policy of autarky, vast deposits of natural gas were discovered beneath the Po valley: for the first time in its history, Italy had abundant, cheap fuel.[11] By mid-1952 it was already being piped to industry in Milan and Turin. In addition the methane provided cheap raw materials for the petro-chemical industry which sprang up along the northern Adriatic shoreline. Substantial oil-fields were discovered shortly afterwards in Sicily. In the space of a decade Italy's consumption of energy, mainly from these sources, increased fivefold.

Thus several barriers to Italy's recovery and further development were clearly being overcome by the time the Marshall Plan came to an end. But much greater obstacles remained to be cleared. These were both of structure and of conjuncture. Although by 1951 employed northern industrial workers were already some 20 per cent better off in real terms than they had been in 1938, there were over two million registered unemployed, also mainly in the north, whose only income was what they could procure from the charity of relatives and from odd jobs, while almost half the country's population was still engaged in archaic forms of subsistence agriculture, mainly in areas dominated by *mafia* and similar traditional forms of extortion. Large sections of the middle classes on fixed incomes from pensions and non-speculative investments had been forced below the poverty line by the dramatic fall in the value of the currency. The early De Sica neo-realist films 'Bicycle Thieves' and 'Umberto D' still provide an unforgettable image of these conditions.

Despite the efforts of the left to keep the 'social question' at the top of the political agenda, the battlefront was increasingly being defined during this period in terms of the basic foreign policy choices forced upon Italy by the hardening of the post-war division of Europe between the Soviet Union and the Western Allies. Not only had Italy been assigned by the wartime 'Big Three' to the Western sphere of influence but in the post-war period its geographical position gave it a high strategic importance in the context of the new military alignments: those of the North Atlantic Treaty Organisation (NATO), normally referred to as the Atlantic Alliance, and of the counterpart created by the Soviet-led Cominform, referred to as the Warsaw Pact. Italy had clearly been absorbed into the United States sphere of economic dominance through its participation in the Marshall Plan, but this had no direct military dimension. The question confronting De Gasperi after his stunning victory in April 1948 was therefore how to ensure that Italy should become an inseparable and indispensable component of the United States-backed system of collective security.

It would be wrong to assume that in April 1948 Italy's incorporation into this system was in the forefront of American thinking. Initially De Gasperi had

---

11. Mattei went on to become the first of a long line of dynamic post-war Italian tycoons, single-mindedly ruthless and efficient in the pursuit of their goals. Mattei was exceptional in that he was uninterested in personal wealth; his ambitious plans to make Italy energy-independent were thwarted by his death in a crash in his private aircraft, probably caused by sabotage. (See also note 14.)

simply sought from the United States a unilateral guarantee of protection 'against any attack from the East'. The Americans were not, however, willing to extend this type of commitment to Italy in addition to Turkey and Greece. There had already been determined resistance by Britain, which was the most attached of the Allies to the symbolism of the punitive aspects of the 1947 Italian Peace Treaty, to the idea of admitting Italy to the Treaty of Brussels (the forerunner of the Western European Union) which was concluded by Britain, France and the Benelux countries in March 1948. The stereotypes generated by wartime propaganda (and experience) of Italian military incompetence were not easily laid to rest and it was not difficult to question how useful a member of the military alliance Italy could be.

The Brussels Treaty was not thought by the Americans to be likely to have the deterrent effect on the Soviet Union that they now increasingly sought. In June 1948 the Russians began the blockade of Berlin, to which the United States and Britain responded with a nine-month airlift. An immediate diplomatic consequence was greatly increased pressure for a much more comprehensive US-European defence arrangement. As the negotiations for this proceeded De Gasperi became convinced that it would be in Italian interests to participate, less because of real fears of a Soviet invasion from the east than from the desire to lock the country permanently into a US protective system which would deter those he called 'the Cominform's men' (i.e. the Communists) from challenging the pre-eminence of the Christian Democrats in the country's politics. He also had some hopes of using Italy's acceptance as a means to procure concessions on the terms of the peace treaty.

For this reason Britain continued strenuously to oppose any Italian association, but the French were prepared to sponsor Italian membership because they shared with Italy the problem of having a large, indigenous Communist Party whose allegiance to the restored nation-state was distinctly problematic in the light of the Czechoslovak events of February 1948. De Gasperi had, nevertheless, also to conduct a long and devious battle against those, both outside and within his own party, opposed to Italian membership. The people at large had little or no appetite for further talk of war, still less for its reality. For the most part they did not feel actively threatened by the individuals they personally knew to be Communists, as was clearly shown by the immense contemporary popularity of Giovannino Guareschi's 'Don Camillo' stories, which presented the village Communist – for all his bluster – as an archetypically warm-hearted Italian whose hostility to the Church was only skin-deep. This may have been, as the Communists asserted, an insulting stereotype, but it was the image which, for most ordinary Italians, most closely corresponded to the reality they perceived around and within them.[12]

---

12. Giovannino Guareschi, *Il piccolo mondo di Don Camillo*, Rizzoli, Milan, 1948; the book was reprinted dozens of times and was the basis of an equally popular film starring the French comic actor Fernandel.

De Gasperi and the centre and right of the Christian Democrats which supported his line, were, for a mixture of not necessarily coherent reasons, nevertheless determined to procure Italy's inclusion in whatever Western alliance might emerge. The most obvious inducement was that anti-Communism had been their trump card in the elections just held: it was the only truly unifying theme for all those who had voted for them, or rather, against the 'People's Bloc'. De Gasperi himself was convinced that, to avoid a resurgence of Fascist sentiment on the right, the Christian Democrats had to continue to take the lead in this respect. It was also a way to keep the intransigent clerical faction in his own party safely occupied rather than allowing them free rein to force through integralist policies and laws of the kind which the Vatican was demanding, including an outright ban on the Communist Party: the Church had declared the excommunication of all militant members. By insisting on the continuing importance of a broad anti-Communist alliance, and therefore of keeping the small lay parties in, or at least prepared to support, the government coalition, he was able to head off such attempts to subvert the new Constitution and to avoid the worst of the divisive polarising effect that outright clericalism would have had. It was a policy little appreciated at the time, and irritated Pius XII, in particular, to the point that not very veiled threats were made that the Vatican might be prepared to back an alternative Catholic party.[13]

Above all, De Gasperi was persuaded that Italy must remain under the United States' protective umbrella as the lesser evil in a world rapidly moving to a situation of permanent and perilous confrontation between two super-powers, both of which by 1949 had the capacity for nuclear warfare, in which the country could never hope to be more than a minor player. Italy in fact never became a significant contributor to the military deterrent provided by NATO, either in terms of men or of treasure: Italian appropriations for NATO were consistently lower than those of other members and were almost entirely expended on non-military matters. Membership was conceived primarily in terms of containing the supposed indigenous capacity for subversion of the Communists, most notoriously through the preparation of Gladio, a secret 'stay-behind' network funded and organised by the United States intelligence agencies, whose real function was to decapitate that party if it should ever risk a *coup d'état*. A collateral effect, which De Gasperi

---

13. The attitude of the Vatican during the final years of Pius XII's reign can only be described as fundamentalist: as well as the excommunication of Communists, the militant Catholics of the 'Civic Committees' led by Luigi Gedda (a man much admired by the CIA) were pressing De Gasperi to bring in censorship, 'moral' legislation and state sponsorship of religious activities. A flood of subsidised propaganda was produced by Catholic Action demonising not only Communists and Socialists, but all forms of 'materialism'. In 1953 De Gasperi was only just able to prevent Gedda from promoting a Catholic-Neofascist alliance to ensure that the local elections in Rome were not won by the left and the anticlericals.

may not entirely have foreseen, was to ensure that Italy, not unlike its former wartime partners, would become an economic giant while remaining a military and diplomatic pygmy, without the capacity to pursue an independent foreign policy.

De Gasperi had little difficulty in accepting a modest international role for Italy, and no moral reluctance to renounce the trappings of sovereignty where necessary in order to be in a position to restrain its more powerful allies from any taste for adventures. This was less true of several of his successors, who sometimes sought to impress the voters at home by executing grand gestures on the international stage, being particularly prone to rattle the skeleton of the Trieste issue. Italy's press, at the instigation of the foreign ministry, kept stressing the Italian 'presence' in international issues where in reality Italy's weight was negligible. The most extravagant of these examples of the *bel gesto* approach to foreign policy, offering Italian mediation where it was neither requested nor desired, was provided by President Gronchi's probably unconstitutional 'peace-making' visit to Moscow in 1960.

After the disastrous Anglo-French Suez adventure of 1956, some Italian politicians thought that Italy's limited colonial past in the Middle East qualified them to win the sympathy of the Arabs and to become the main broker between the West and the Arab world. At the economic level a real opportunity to win advantage certainly existed, and was seized by Mattei, who, to the fury of the Western oil giants, concluding historic deals with the Iranians, the Moroccans and the Egyptians which exchanged Italian oil technology for cheap oil supplies.[14]

Mattei's short-lived economic buccaneering nevertheless did not amount to an alternative foreign policy for Italy. After his unexpected death, the diplomatic and economic focus returned permanently to the construction of the European Community. All the fine gestures and experiments in foreign policy eventually led back to De Gasperi's insistence on the interests of Western Europe as a whole, with its implications of a relationship of equality between the Member States of the European Community and resistance to any attempt, such as De Gaulle's in the 1960s to give one of them a hegemonic rôle. Despite some uncomfortable memories of British intransigence in the post-war period, Italy consistently pressed for United Kingdom entry to the European Community.

The image projected by the Christian Democrats in the first two decades of the Italian Republic nevertheless remained that of a country whose newly-won democratic system and values were constantly under threat from without and within, however little this may have corresponded to the real situation. On the home front the police forces, energetically reorganised by Scelba, had made

---

14. His death in an air crash in 1962 was widely suspected to have been arranged by his enemies in the international oil business, possibly with the connivance of either or both the CIA and the *mafia*.

sure that any possible danger of a Communist insurrection arising from trade-union or protest activities was completely under control by 1950, when Togliatti indignantly revealed that in civil conflict, mainly with the police, during the previous three years, 48 Communists had been killed, 2,367 injured, over 70,000 arrested and 15,000 imprisoned.

It may be commented fairly that, regrettable as these figures are, they do not amount, in relation to a population of nearly 50 million, of whom some ten million had voted for the People's Bloc in 1946 either to a restoration of Fascism, or to a revolutionary opportunity neglected. Although De Gasperi has been accused of bringing about a 'creeping restoration' of the Fascist régime so persistently that the concept has become a commonplace of Italian non-Catholic historiography, the evidence for the assertion is far from conclusive if it refers to the creation of a police and propaganda state designed permanently to mobilise the population in support of goals of national aggrandisement and the permanent suppression of dissent from below. No comparison with Franco's Spain or even with Salazar's Portugal, begins to hold water, despite superficial resemblances in the field of Church–state relations.

That the Christian Democrats systematically abused their power and sought to maximise their control of every level of national and local public administration for the benefit of their party and the interest-groups which it served is beyond doubt; that for the most part their leaders turned their backs upon the idealism and the ideals in which they had participated during the Resistance is equally clear. But by 1953, when De Gasperi resigned, a basic democratic framework for political life had been established and was for the most part respected in practice; an independent judiciary existed and was functioning, even if significant numbers of magistrates were of a repressive cast of mind and deeply conservative in their interpretation of the law, including much surviving Fascist legislation; there was no official censorship of dissenting views, even if, with the ready assistance of the clergy, such views were venomously condemned and their authors demonised.

Though the Church was afforded unprecedented influence in civil administrative matters and still enjoyed the legally privileged status conceded to it by Mussolini in 1929, which it exploited to the full, the Italian Republic was not a theocracy and only a minority of the population in practice accepted clerical authority in their private lives, despite a few blatant attempts to impose it by law. The main thrust of the 'recatholicisation' of Italy attempted by the first generation of Christian Democrats (mainly survivors from the Popular Party) was to seek to promote a balance between material progress and traditional 'spiritual values'. In practice this meant the pursuit of top-down philanthropic policies designed to shape the 'just society', such as the planned redistribution of the land to needy peasant families, mainly in the south, and the revision of contracts of *mezzadria* in the areas where it was prevalent, with the backward-looking (and diseconomic) aim of preserving a traditional family structure for an agriculture based on a mass of independent peasant farmers.

216

It was a vision which had more to do with Catholic social doctrine than with the imperatives of modernisation implicit in other aspects of their programme for economic recovery and development based upon enterprise-led industrialisation.

The Republic consolidated by the Christian Democrats was not the one envisaged by the Resistance and to some extent enshrined in the Constitution, but it was in its essentials a parliamentary democracy and its citizens had their individual civil rights established in its fundamental laws. Despite the moralistic approach of some leaders, a real attempt was being launched, with the establishment in 1950 of the *Cassa per il Mezzogiorno* (Development Fund for the South), to tackle the fundamental structural problem of the Italian state, the economic (and hence social and political) discrepancy between north and south. In the field of international relations, De Gasperi's period of office saw Italy received once more into the comity of nations, and already making a commitment to the construction of a European Community which was to come to fruition with the signature of the Treaty of Rome in 1956.

In the circumstances of defeat, civil war, military occupation and armed Resistance, of the shattered economy and profound political polarisation orchestrated from powerful foreign sources, it was a far less negative outcome than might reasonably have been expected, reflecting underlying traditions of tolerance and solidarity embedded in Italian popular culture, as well being an expression of the unresolved tensions and unbridged cleavages of a nation-state which had so far never overcome its legacy from history. In an historical perspective the De Gasperi period may be compared, with all due allowances for changed circumstances, to that of the *destra storica*, when men of high principle and narrow vision also strove to shape their fellow countrymen to a grand design which never achieved full popular support, far less success, and by its methods paved the way for a system open to opportunism and corruption.[15]

---

15. Although it is marginal to the general developments with which this book is concerned, it is worth recording that De Gasperi, before leaving office, also negotiated with Austria the framework for a lasting settlement of the dispute about full cultural autonomy for the German-speaking population of the Sudtirol.

'Stable instability' and economic progress, 1953–1968

A characteristic shared, but not acknowledged, by both the dominant mass parties in post-war Italy has been that of being, apparently, always on the defensive. After the chastening defeat of April 1948, the Communist Party retreated into a citadel of meticulous and all-embracing organisation designed to prepare its members to meet every possible eventuality except that of taking office. Its ultimate objective was always to preserve the Party itself as a stronghold of both values and structures which would permanently provide a distinctive and satisfying identity to its members, and give meaning to every aspect of their lives. It is for this reason that it was often referred to as a 'church' comparable in many respects to its counterpart in the Catholic Church.

The party of the Christian Democrats, while not needing to operate in this way because the Church itself, assisted by its satellite organisations such as Catholic Action, Gedda's 'Civic Committees', its Catholic Working-Men's Clubs and so forth, already monopolised these functions for those of their supporters who felt the need for them, also behaved in an essentially defensive way. This was not because its hold on office, and ultimately on power, was seriously threatened by its political adversaries, but precisely because it did not possess any real measure of ideological autonomy and was therefore unable to develop any strong and coherent set of policies stemming from a clear world-view shared by all its supporters. Its declared *raison d'être* was essentially negative: to oppose Communism. Its hidden agenda, as is the case with any political party enjoying prolonged office, was that no means be neglected which might ensure its hold on power remained intact. Being a 'catch-all' party it was obliged to appease rather than enthuse its supporters, whose conflicting interests were represented, but not fully reconciled, in the numerous factions ('currents', in the Italian terminology) which composed its leadership. In practice therefore it was almost never able to carry through a policy in a decisive and consistent manner, but always found it expedient to trim. Its *modus operandi* as a permanently unruly coalition of interests inevitably created a fertile terrain for influence-peddling activities which easily slipped into corrupt administrative practices and connivance with organised crime, and again necessitated a defensive stance whenever evidence of scandalous or criminal activities surfaced.

The net effect of the dominance of Italian politics by two such parties for forty years was a condition which has been aptly termed 'stable instability'. To the outside observer such as the visiting foreign correspondent little versed in Italian history it appeared that Italian governments rarely lasted more than a year and that the legislative process was lengthy and uncertain, while the administration of the country was both heavily bureaucratic and highly inefficient.

At one level all these contentions were (and indeed remain) perfectly true, but at another they could be misleading. Although there was a constant rotation of ministers and under-secretaries, the same names just as constantly reappeared: some can be found in every government for decades. The delays in legislation and its patchy application, while certainly dysfunctional to a modern bureaucratic state, mattered far less in a country where individuals and groups traditionally developed strategies and customary practices which enabled them to pursue their activities without reference to the state, or in symbiosis with a 'parallel state' in which every problem could be smoothed out by private application to the appropriate persons of influence within the informal networks of the local and national political establishments. The 'instability' was, in effect, only the chaotic surface of a system of diffused power in which, provided one followed the unpublished rules of the game, anything could be 'arranged' by a *combinazione*, by 'playing the system'.

The 'rules of the game' were essentially those of *clientela* and *parentela*, of a dense and generally effective network of patronage based on the sale and bartering of favours, which could, at one end of the spectrum, be as crude as the handing over of a plain envelope full of used banknotes (*'la bustarella'*), and, at the other, an arcane process of mediation between interest groups which in effect divided a particular economic (and therefore political) domain between competing interests. Although no democratic system is ever entirely free of such a trade in influence, in Italy the ghettoisation of the opposition, in the form of the Communists, for over forty years, and the absolute dominance, in government coalitions, of the Christian Democrats for at least thirty years, led to a situation in which some form of patronage became a *sine qua non* for virtually any significant transaction between the state and the citizen.

There can be no question that this system had such profoundly deleterious effects on public life and upon standards of business conduct that, for a majority of ordinary Italians, politicians are simply 'those thieves in Rome'. Still worse, however, is the seamless robe that it created between political life and organised crime, most evidently, but not exclusively, in the south: it has recently been calculated that 12 per cent of the Italian gross national product is now controlled by the various species of *mafia*, and that organised crime now extracts some three billion pounds per year from state funds; honest judges and policemen who have seriously threatened this connection have regularly been assassinated. Yet it was only in April 1992, for the first time since the Second World War, that it appeared that the system was no longer a guarantee of electoral stability but was actually threatening to break down in political chaos. The issues raised by this development are discussed more fully in the concluding chapters.

In the period now under consideration, responsibility for the exercise of power fell, for better or worse, upon the Christian Democrats. They tacitly adopted a two-track approach: even at the moments of greatest political tension when their attacks upon the parties of the left as agents of international Communism, and possibly of the Devil, were fiercest, they maintained the convention that the Constitution must at all times be respected as the basic guarantee of a democratic system. The Communists and the Socialists reciprocated, never sabotaging the working of parliament as they had done in 1919–22, even when denouncing the Christian Democrats as mere US stooges. At the same time the Christian Democrats forged a working alliance with the old-fashioned free market liberals led by Einaudi, whose approach to the model for economic development they tacitly adopted notwithstanding the social doctrines they publicly proclaimed. The social basis of this alliance was a coalition of peasants and artisans, of the commercial, professional and *rentier* middle classes, of the managers and technocrats represented by the *Confindustria*, and of the undiminished army of bureaucrats at local and national level.

The need to represent such a multiplicity of interests over such a wide social and cultural spectrum led to a proliferation of factions within the party, held together less by shared beliefs than by the fascination of power. These ranged from De Gasperi's moderate reformists, who were convinced that the Christian Democrats must always occupy the centre ground of political debate and action, to a leftist grouping led by Giovanni Gronchi, a survivor from the days of the Popular Party, who had been the main leader of Catholic trade-unionism prior to the advent of Fascism, to the integralists, led by Dossetti, who were the custodians of activist Catholic social policies in favour of the disadvantaged and in opposition to 'materialism', to what was soon to become the largest faction, that of the pragmatic conservatives, primarily concerned with retaining power and minimising change of any kind. These broad groupings each contained a number of lesser currents, each in effect the following of a particular individual leader. The Christian Democrats thus did not appear as the representative of any one social class, but as a 'catch-all' party made up of a number of heterogeneous groups, alliances and lobbies which sought to bring together and reconcile within its own structures the different and conflicting interests which existed in real civil society. This process inevitably led to a dilution of any initial idealistic vision of what society should be like which the party may have had at the outset and opened the door to special interest groups inclined to exploit its control of the state for their own ends.

The local elections of 1952 revealed a sharp drop in the votes won by the Christian Democrats, from the 48.5 per cent of the 1948 elections to just below 36 per cent, almost exactly where it had started from in 1946. Even with its coalition allies, the Social Democrats, the Republicans and the Liberals, the government polled no more than a bare majority. De Gasperi was greatly alarmed by this, particularly fearing that the pattern would be repeated in the general elections in the following year. He therefore proposed to parliament a modified electoral law under which any party, or pre-announced coalition of parties, which polled 50.01 per cent of the vote would receive an electoral bonus of 85 seats in the lower house. By this device, it was hoped, the ruling party or coalition would always enjoy a comfortable majority of some 65 deputies and would not be subject to back-bench rebellions, or the delaying tactics of the opposition.

The proposal was fought tooth and nail by the opposition, which dubbed it the 'swindle law' (*legge truffa*), and was supported only half-heartedly by the small government parties. On all sides uncomfortable memories were aroused of the Acerbo Law of 1924 by which Mussolini had planned to secure total control of the parliament while having only a minority of votes. In January 1953, when the vote was taken after an unparalleled filibuster, a number of Social Democrat deputies rebelled, voted against, and were duly expelled from their party. Although the vote was narrowly won in both houses by the end of March 1953, the expelled Social Democrats, together with a number of prominent elder statesmen of the Resistance, led by Parri, established an independent electoral list of non-party candidates for the coming election, campaigning exclusively against the *legge truffa*, which became the dominating issue. On both the left and the right of the political spectrum there were important changes which also affected the outcome: the Socialists did not form a common list with the Communists and the Monarchists distanced themselves from the neo-Fascists of the Italian Social Movement, both calculating that if the *legge truffa* was not activated by the result of the election, a future government might well need to recruit them to its coalition.

In the event, by the narrowest of margins (which corresponded almost exactly to the votes won by the independent list), the government coalition failed to accumulate 50 per cent of the popular vote, although, with over 40 per cent, the Christian Democrats did better than they had feared, while their allies were almost annihilated. Both the Monarchists, an amorphous collection of anti-democratic traditionalists cemented together by the lavish funding provided by their populist millionaire leader, Achille Lauro, and Nenni's Socialists did extremely well, controlling between them almost one fifth of the seats in parliament. De Gasperi would have no truck with the Monarchists, whom he regarded as anti-democratic reactionaries, and Nenni, though hinting broadly at his readiness to share power, made it impossible for him to move towards any arrangement with the Socialists by refusing to make a clear break with the Communist Party with which he had been allied for almost twenty years.

With the Social Democratic Party in turmoil because of its heavy losses to the Socialist Party from which it had split in 1947, De Gasperi could not command enough votes in the lower house to form a centrist ministry with a parliamentary majority and therefore had, dispiritedly, to set about forming a one-party minority administration which parliament would accept. By the time he put forward his list of ministers in July 1953, his own party had turned against him, wanting to shake off his heavy political tutelage, his preoccupation with the Vatican's evangelical view of Italian politics, and the resented belief of the American Embassy that he was indispensable to the survival of Italian democracy. His speech was heard in hostile silence: the Christian Democrats voted for him half-heartedly; the parties of the left voted against, and the rest abstained. The point that he was no longer needed was forcibly made a month later, when the same formula was presented by his successor, Giuseppe Pella, and was voted through with the external support of the Monarchists.

External factors, too, had conspired against De Gasperi's survival. The initial, most acute phase of the Cold War, which had begun with the Berlin blockade in 1947, was coming to an end in the realisation by the superpowers that neither could destroy the other without risking its own destruction. In January 1953 Eisenhower succeeded Truman as President of the United States with a commitment to bring an end to the Korean War, while in February Stalin died, and his successors immediately began to talk of a thaw in East–West relations. Although the United States was still pressing hard for German rearmament within a European collective defence framework, it was already clear that there was little enthusiasm for the idea and much resistance still to be overcome. De Gasperi's crusading anti-communism was beginning to look out of season: even if it could never be entirely discarded by the Christian Democrats as the unifying theme of their propaganda, it was becoming necessary to present a less unilateral and defensive image, under the banner of 'progress without adventures', a slogan that might well have been coined by Depretis or Giolitti.

After his resignation as Prime Minister, De Gasperi continued, until his death at the age of 73 in August 1954, to serve his party as Secretary-General, from which position he sought to continue to guide his successors, particularly exhorting them to take up the cause of European unity, a policy which had been anticipated as early as 1948 in a customs union with France. Despite some backsliding into nationalistic rhetoric by his immediate successors, De Gasperi's consistent promotion of the European dimension proved to be his greatest posthumous service to his country and he is rightly remembered as one of the founding fathers of the European Community.

It was indeed the European Community which from then on provided the main focus of Italian foreign policy debates and initiatives. While the

Figure 10.1   Motorway engineering was a matter for national pride in the 1970s.

government parties sought a further source of anti-Communist legitimation in their fervent acceptance of the constraints and opportunities of 'building Europe', the Communist Party consistently denounced the Community as merely an anti-Soviet bloc which was bound to compress the economic interests of the Italian working man. The growing evidence to the contrary, in terms of the subsidisation of agriculture and infrastructures in the poorer areas of the country, and of the general economic benefit of untrammelled trade and mobility of labour, was dismissed as illusory for almost 20 years, until the general revision of Communist policy resulting from the growing rift with the Soviets, after the repression of the 'Prague Spring' of 1968, led to a reversal of this attitude and the adoption by the substantial contingent of Communist Members of the European Parliament of the slogan of a

223

'People's Europe' and, in due course, an acceptance of the need for Italy's membership of the North Atlantic Treaty Organisation (NATO). In this they were merely following the popular mood: no other population of a member state of the European Community has displayed as much enthusiasm as the Italians for progress towards a politically and economically integrated union, voting in massive numbers in European elections even while the parties for whose candidates they voted were officially deploring Italy's membership of this 'capitalist club'.

Similarly, the government parties, led by the Christian Democrats, sought in their enthusiastic endorsement of all things 'European' to compensate (symbolically, at least) for the increasing disillusion of the electorate with the domestic political system's incapacity to deliver honest and efficient administration, foreshadowing an integrated, efficient, welfare-Europe which would wash over Italy and miraculously bring it up to 'European standards'. It was a new variant of the old strategy, regularly used by Crispi and Mussolini, of distracting the electorate from real domestic woes by tensions abroad and dreams of utopian solutions.

Amintore Fanfani was elected as De Gasperi's successor as Secretary-General of the Christian Democrats in July 1954. During his term of office, the post assumed the king-making importance that it has had ever since as the ultimate centre of power within the party and as a strategic position from which to influence the conduct of public affairs at every level. Almost 30 years younger than De Gasperi, Fanfani had made a comfortable career as an academic economist teaching at the Catholic University of Milan and was not known as an anti-fascist. His position among the Christian Democrats was nevertheless to the left of centre, his sponsor being Dossetti. He saw his main task as bringing the party out of the unimaginative sterility which had settled over it after De Gasperi's departure from the scene and persuading it to pursue a strategy of social activism, with large-scale initiatives to upgrade and modernise public education and to seize some of the 'commanding heights' of the economy, in particular the power-generating industry. From De Gasperi he inherited the long-term strategy of seeking 'an opening to the left' by bringing the Socialists into a basically centrist coalition. Often impetuous, he had made an early attempt to form a government with this declared objective early in 1954, but his own party was unready for such boldness and failed to support him.

For the next three years a series of weak single-party or centre-coalition governments dependent upon support from the fickle or opportunistic minor parties of the centre and right attempted various versions of neo-transformism which were often reminiscent of the tactics of the *sinistra storica* under Depretis and Crispi, accompanied by persistent scandals and rumours of corruption in high places, by vehement denunciation of 'subversives' and by resort to populistic appeals to patriotism and nationalism. Nevertheless at least one of the Christian Democrat prime ministers concerned, Antonio Segni, with the support of the newly-elected President of the Republic, Giovanni Gronchi, who were both on the left of the party, achieved something positive, by beginning to implement the Vanoni land reform, and by the belated establishment of the Constitutional Court provided for in the 1947 Constitution, which at once energetically started to clear away the massive débris left by Fascist legislation, although it quickly came into conflict with the government over the abolition of some of Mussolini's security laws sanctioning administrative detention or internal exile, with the Minister of the Interior refusing to enact the Court's decision.[1] Another piece of Fascist legislation which, to the great satisfaction of the industrial lobby of *Confindustria*, was not revised, still less overturned, was the Institute for Industrial Reconstruction (IRI), the channel via which the Italian state subsidised ailing industries in the name of rationalisation.

It was, however, outside the legislative framework that the most significant changes were being made and consolidated during this period. Under Fanfani's leadership, the Christian Democrats set about a different type of rationalisation. This was the party's almost total occupation, by political appointment or 'arrangement', of every key state and parastatal position: in the civil service, in local government services, in public bodies, in national and local quangos, in nationalised and IRI-assisted industries, banks, and other financial sector services. In parallel with this process, the clientelistic system in the south was largely taken over from its traditional controllers, most of whom were happy to pass into the Christian Democrat fold where the return on favours was guaranteed. The system, little changed from the days of the *sinistra storica*, was well summarised by an Italian economic historian in 1976:

> A vast combination of heterogeneous interests and forces was formed,
> protected politically by the concentration of power in the hands of the
> Christian Democrats and by the impossibility of replacing them as the
> ruling party both in government and in public bodies, or simply
> magnetised by the party's lack of scruple and open-handedness in
> systematically diverting public funds to private gain. Although this
> combination produced a certain social stability through its extensive
> hold over its clients, it also had some fundamental limitations: it was
> either socially paternalistic, basing itself on integralistic social
> Catholicism, or completely lacking any clear political or moral
> principles and simply reacting pragmatically to events...[2]

---

1. Three years later the constitutional independence of the judiciary was finally confirmed by the establishment of the Higher Council of the Judiciary which, alone, had responsibility for the appointment and advancement of judges and state prosecutors. As the judges appointed under Fascism died or retired, this body became progressively more inclined to challenge ministerial abuse of power and its membership to reflect more accurately the spectrum of opinion in the general public.
2. Valerio Castronovo, *Storia d'Italia*, Vol. 4/2 Einaudi, Turin, 1976, pp. 27–8.

In seeking to make permanent in this way the Christian Democrats' dominance over Italian society, Fanfani, and Aldo Moro, his successor in 1959 as Secretary-General of the party, were interested in more than merely staying in power. Their grand design, which was shared in some degree by the whole of the left wing of the party, was to bring about that 'opening to the left' which would permanently marginalise both the extreme left and the extreme right and accomplish both the control and the consensus which, in his period of supremacy between 1903 and 1913, Giolitti had demonstrated was the most effective way to govern and stabilise a country so profoundly affected by its experience of uneven development.

During the second half of the 1950s three powerful external stimuli to pursue this approach and to relinquish the exclusive reliance upon the mobilising power of anti-communism which had proved to be an electoral trump card in 1948 and 1953 were provided by external events. In February 1956 Nikita Khrushchev, by then undisputed post-Stalin leader of the Communist Party of the Soviet Union, made his famous speech to its 20th Congress, in which he described in detail the crimes of Stalin. In October of the same year, the Red Army ruthlessly suppressed the Hungarian revolution. In 1958, Pius XII died and was succeeded by Pope John XXIV.

The Communists rejoiced at the prospect of greater autonomy apparently presaged by Khruschev's speech, and Togliatti came forward with a new formulation: the notion that international Communism should henceforth be 'polycentric', with each national party taking its own national 'road to socialism'. Only eight months later Togliatti promptly followed the Soviet lead, denouncing the Hungarian insurgents as Fascists and traitors, but to an unprecedented chorus of dissent from his own intellectuals. A large number of these left the party in the wake of its most prestigious 'young Turk', Antonio Giolitti, the grandson of Giovanni Giolitti. It seemed that the Communist Party was about to break up. Nenni and the Socialists believed their moment had come, not only to break away from the damaging alliance with the Communists, taking many dissidents from it with them, but also to negotiate a merger with the separated brethren of the Social Democratic Party as a preliminary to entering a coalition with the Christian Democrats in a stronger position than they would as separate parties. As for the Christian Democrats, the departure of the obsessional Pius XII would at last give the leadership more scope for developing their own policies without constant interference from the Vatican in support of the party's more reactionary members.

Although none of the expectations aroused by these events were quickly fulfilled, they can in retrospect be seen to have constituted a critical turning-point in the post-war political history of Italy. Apparently the most disadvantaged was the Communist Party, which continued to follow the basic Soviet line, despite lip-service to the Gramsci legacy of the slow conquest of hegemony rather than the revolutionary seizure of state power. As we shall see, however, there were, in the medium-term characteristics of Italian economic development, particular opportunities for it to consolidate its hold over its own faithful and even to improve its electoral strength.[3]

For the Socialist Party's leader, the presumed end of Stalinism seemed to provide just the chance he had been seeking for a divorce from the Communists. After declaring the Party's independence in the spring, he began to court the former Socialists who had split off in 1947 to form the Italian Social Democratic Party led by Giuseppe Saragat with the ultimate aim of recreating a unified party. Nenni now agreed to support Italy's membership of NATO in addition to abandoning the unity of action pact with the Communists. Saragat, however, wanted a full recantation and Nenni knew that this was likely to lead the left wing of his own party to walk out, particularly in view of the fact that the leadership of the General Confederation of Italian Labour was still equally shared by the two parties and if the Socialists extended the break to this area they would lose most of their working-class support.

By early 1957 it was clear that there was no immediate prospect of reuniting the two Socialist parties and that they would be in direct competition in the elections set for 1958. Nevertheless, Nenni's new flexibility, and his straightforward candour in admitting his past mistakes, had created a new political perspective for part of the electorate: the chance to vote for a real alternative to the Christian Democrats by making the 'opening to the left' not only more feasible but perhaps productive of a coalition government in which the Christian Democrats were not so totally dominant as hitherto.

In the latter party's preparation for the election, the theme of the indispensability of Christian Democrat rule was once again the keynote, but with an interesting variation. There was much less stress upon the need for national unity to combat 'World Communism', and much more upon the unique capacity of the Christian Democrats to oversee the modernisation of Italian society without sacrificing hard-won social stability, in short 'progress without adventures'. Fanfani brusquely pushed aside the older members of the party leadership both nationally and locally, installing his own brand of supporter in their place: young, aspiring and ascetic in their life-style. The idea was to present a public image of an efficient, pragmatic, forward-looking party of 'professionals in government'. Imperceptibly the election became a plebiscite: the voters were invited to endorse this new vision of a rejuvenated Christian Democrat party with an absolute majority, so that it could 'get on with government'.

In the event the election showed clearly that, with the pressures of the Cold War gradually easing, the Italian electorate was prepared to endorse more actively progressive policies, from whichever side they were proposed: while

---

3. In December 1956, Togliatti's policy formula of a unique Italian road to socialism prevailed at the Party Congress: there was virtually nothing in it, however, to offend the current Soviet leadership, which continued to subsidise the Italian Communist Party until 1972.

the Christian Democrats, with over 42 per cent of the votes, recouped most of what they had lost to the far right in 1954, both Socialist parties did well, their combined strength almost equalling that of the Communists who, surprisingly in view of the Hungarian events only two years before, maintained their existing level of support at almost 23 per cent. The Monarchists and the Italian Social Movement, together with the Liberal Party which had now openly become a party of extreme conservatives, together polled less than 10 per cent. Thus over 90 per cent of the Italian voters had indicated their readiness for change.

With the support of the Social Democrats and the Republicans the Christian Democrats were able to form a government with an overall majority and President Gronchi duly invited Fanfani to form a ministry. He presented an unprecedented list of ambitious reform plans to parliament, but all with the proviso that the economic situation should be tackled first, in particular the questions of the state deficit, the trade gap and the repercussions on Italian agriculture of the European Common Market which had just come into force and was already threatening the traditional family-farm basis of Catholic social policy. Unfortunately, too, Fanfani had offended many influential people in his own party by his tactics and attitude in reorganising it and creating its new 'progressive' image. The party was still a 'broad church' of fundamentally unreconciled sectoral interests (industry, agriculture, bureaucracy, clerisy) which could only be managed by compromise and mutual concessions, a process leading inevitably to political stagnation. The policies which would provide the dynamic 'progress' Fanfani had promised were not ready in detail, and he was widely suspected by his colleagues of harbouring dictatorial, or at least Gaullist, ambitions. Since the voting in parliament was by secret vote except on confidence motions (a system intended to baulk any future aspiring Mussolini), his critics, known as 'sharpshooters', regularly defeated government proposals.[4]

Within eight months Fanfani's second attempt at ruling the country came to an untimely end. Gronchi had by now understood that the time had not yet arrived for the 'opening to the left' to which he had previously been committed and, indeed, of which he had wished to be the main protagonist. He therefore chose another deflated ex-reformer of the Christian Democrat left, Segni, to take over as the prime minister of a single-party minority government supported from the outside by the Monarchists, and the Liberals. But in contrast to previous occasions when the Christian Democrats had accepted Monarchist support shamefacedly, Segni, strongly backed by *Confindustria*, now presented it as a stable and durable formula. This at least clarified the real meaning of Christian Democrat 'centrism': it was now unequivocally conservative and the party unambiguously stood on the right of politics.

---

4. There was a certain poetic justice in this, since it was a system which had enabled Fanfani and his supporters to bring down previous Christian Democrat incumbents.

Almost the only achievement of Segni's ministry was thus to confront his party with the necessity, finally, to make a choice between a centre-left and a centre-right alliance. It soon had the chance to discover the implications of the choice. Segni quickly lost the confidence of his right-wing allies because he failed to block President Gronchi's personal initiative of making a visit to Moscow in the cause of détente (and his own long-term goal of being elected President for a second term) and was forced to resign when the Liberal Party withdrew its parliamentary support.

Fanfani returned to the attack with a fresh proposal for an 'opening to the left' but met with a double veto from the *Confindustria* and its right-wing Christian Democrat supporters, and from the Vatican, where John XXIV had not yet fully imposed his more broad-minded attitudes to politics and international affairs. Gronchi then started the Christian Democrats on the biggest 'adventure' of their history by designating as prime minister of a 'caretaker' government his personal friend and political associate, Fernando Tambroni. Rejecting the advice of Moro not to accept extreme right support, Tambroni won the necessary vote of confidence with the votes of the Italian Social Movement.

Memories and apprehensions were immediately aroused: was this not a repeat of the way in which Mussolini's handful of deputies had succeeded in taking over the parliamentary process in 1922? When it became clear that Tambroni was aiming not simply to carry out his mandate as a 'caretaker' but was intending to consolidate his power and prolong the life of his government by popular measures such as reductions in the price of petrol and sugar (both still state monopolies) and by playing up a fresh Red Scare in the wake of the U-2 incident, several ministers from the left of the Christian Democrat party resigned in protest: Tambroni merely designated 'interim' replacements. In May and June, when there were popular demonstrations in Ravenna and Bologna against the installation of US missiles on Italian soil and strikes in Reggio-Emilia on wages issues, Tambroni displayed his new tough line on public disorder by ordering the police to 'act energetically', which they did with vicious enthusiasm, causing many injuries.

But the main agitation against the Tambroni government was aroused by his decision to allow his neo-Fascist parliamentary allies to hold their national congress in Genoa in the first week of July. Genoa was a self-liberated city in which the tradition of resistance to Fascism was still strong: overnight the spirit of anti-fascist unity was reborn. There were mass demonstrations there in protest, and all the parties of the CLN except the Christian Democrats declared they would never allow the Italian Social Movement to gather there. Clashes with the police ensued all over Italy; in Reggio-Emilia, in the worst incident, five demonstrators were killed and 21 wounded by police gunfire. Fisticuffs even spread to the Chamber of Deputies and the Senate, where the respected Christian Democrat President of the house, Cesare Merzagora, issued a national call for a truce, which the government attempted to censor.

Figure 10.2 Riots in Genoa against the Tambroni government's acceptance of an alliance with the neo-Fascists, 1960.

This was the last straw: the mass of Christian Democrats in parliament found themselves in complete isolation, shunned by all their previous respectably democratic allies, and quickly moved to force Tambroni's resignation, despite the fact that at the last moment he had persuaded the neo-Fascists to cancel their congress.

The Tambroni experiment lasted for less than four months but its impact was decisive: never again would the Christian Democrats veer so far and so cynically to the right in search of parliamentary survival, since the experience had shown that to do so would be to abandon the basic principle of being a 'catch-all' party: it ceases to be one as soon as the inclusion of a certain category of supporters implies the exclusion of others. Individual Christian Democrats, no doubt, remained attracted by the vision of a more authoritarian régime: with like-minded confrères in the other parties of the coalition, they could be recruited into organisations and associations of the 'parallel state', notably the notorious 'P2' masonic lodge headed by Licio Gelli. The party as whole, for all its inconsistencies and cross-currents, preferred to achieve its capillary control of Italian public and civic life through the well-tried methods of *clientela* and *parentela*. Its adversaries regularly denounced it as a 'régime', with ugly echoes of the Fascist system of attempted 'totalitarian' dominance, but this was to overstate its capacity for formulating and consistently pursuing objectives ulterior to its own survival. Precisely its propensity to prefer inertia and 'low' politics to 'grand designs' and grandiose activism was its best claim to continue to receive the acquiescence of most Italians, for whom anything more was likely to have been considered an excess of government.

After Tambroni, the Christian Democrat pendulum swung strongly back to the left and Fanfani was once again asked to form a government. This time he wisely included in his ministry no fewer than five former prime ministers from his party, which effectively left any residual 'sharpshooters' without leadership. There was no coalition possible, since the Liberal Party had now moved so far to the right that it could not agree to collective responsibility in the company of the Social Democratic Party, which had been extremely vociferous in its opposition to the Tambroni adventure. Both parties therefore supported the new ministry without joining it, while the Socialists abstained on the vote of confidence, breaking ranks for the first time with the Communists.

Fanfani's declared aim was still to form a working alliance with any party left of centre, with the obvious exception of the Communists, but this time he intended to carry the whole of his own party with him. His strategy was assisted by the success of the Socialists in the local elections in November 1960, and the readiness of that party, in a number of cities previously ruled by local Communist-Socialist councils, to swap partners and join forces with the Christian Democrats, and by the hints of approval for this development coming from John XXIV's Vatican. The principal trigger for Christian Democrat acceptance of the 'opening to the left' was, however, the subtle and persistent campaign conducted by Fanfani's chosen successor as party general-secretary, Aldo Moro. The crowning moment of this was a five-hour harangue to the party's 1962 conference in Naples during which he developed his theory of 'parallel convergences', a typically sybilline formulation which was intended to please those who wished for change, and equally to reassure those who wished to delay it. It was a triumph of logic and obfuscation which won him many admirers, but few friends: one of the more confusing elements in Italian popular culture is an admiration of 'cleverness', combined with glee when it overreaches itself.

Fanfani's long-awaited opportunity had now arrived: he reshuffled his cabinet, giving the Social Democrats key ministries and excluding the Liberals: the Socialists assured him of their support in parliament. In general, anticipating the general election of the following year, the policies pursued were cautious, with the single exception of the nationalisation of the electricity industry: a clear token of a new Christian Democrat determination to curb the great industrial monopolies. The agenda was thus set for the elections of April 1963, which coincided with the final splendid blooming of John XXIV's pontificate in the shape of his encyclical *Pacem in Terris*, in which he pleaded for international reconciliation and, in effect, turned the Church away from its obsession with the Cold War. Although conservatives, including some in the hierarchy itself, denounced him as the 'Red Pope', most Italians felt relief at the end of an epoch of Vatican interference in their electoral preferences.

The results of the voting surprised everyone. It had been generally assumed that, with general shift to the left of centre, the Christian Democrats and the Socialists, as the putative partners in the new centre-left coalition, would make considerable gains. In fact, although there was indeed a marked swing of votes to the left (apart from a conservative fringe which returned to the Liberal Party), the party which gained most from it was the Communist Party, which for the first time received more than a quarter of the votes cast. Despite the disappointment felt by the Christian Democrats, this confirmed the leftwards trend: with the four centre-left coalition parties scoring a total of 60 per cent, only 15 per cent of the electorate had judged the 'opening to the left' a dangerous or pernicious development.

This progressive loosening-up of Italian political life in the late 1950s and early 1960s owed something to the gradual accommodations reached between the mass parties as each side realised that, in view of the extraordinary stability of the electorate's political loyalties, final destruction of the adversary was highly unlikely. As international tensions eased and the Vatican's attention turned to issues wider than the Italian political situation, the external pressures (and justifications) for a confrontational approach to politics also relaxed. But these factors alone are not adequate to explain the 'opening to the left' and its final consummation in 1963, when the ageing Nenni was finally admitted, as Deputy Prime Minister, to the 'control-room' which he had waited so long to enter. It would be more correct to assert, indeed, that, as so often in Italian history, the political awareness and arrangements of 'official Italy' were lagging far behind the achievements, and the needs, of 'real Italy', where during this period an unprecedented process of social and economic transformation was in progress. Usually, if misleadingly, referred to as the 'economic miracle', this explosive experience was what inspired the politicians to try to catch up with the voters.

The Italian economy, as we have seen, produced in 1945 less than a third of the industrial output achieved in 1938 and little more than a third of the same year's agricultural output. Real wages had fallen by between one half and two thirds. These factors of extreme economic weakness were crucial in bringing about a rapid recovery to pre-war levels and then, after a pause coinciding with the harshest years of the Cold War, an even more remarkable acceleration, for certain regions and social categories, into what must be termed affluence at levels comparable with the most advanced and successful economies of the Western world. The 'miraculous' combination of an artificially low exchange rate for the *lira* against the dollar, the re-equipment of Italian industry with new US technology at the same time as Italian labour and energy costs remained exceptionally low, meant that exports were competitive and highly profitable. Given the low rate of domestic inflation, this quickly led to balance of payments surplus which, taken with the growing inflows of hard currency from emigrants' remittances and from a revived tourist industry, made it possible by the late 1950s for the Italian treasury to begin minting new silver coinage whose specie value was the same as its face value.[5]

Undoubtedly the most important factors were the abundance of low-cost, well-motivated labour, both skilled and unskilled, and the possibility of introducing the latest techniques of management without significant obstruction by craft unions, which had never taken root in the Italian labour movement. Because living standards at the outset were so low, because there was a very large reservoir of unemployed and underemployed labour, and because habits of frugality and 'saving for a rainy day' were so deeply implanted in the Italian psyche, the proportion of the extra income derived from the spectacular growth which was reinvested was at a level sufficient to make most industry self-reliant for finance: while income grew in the period of the miracle by 78.3 per cent, consumption increased only by 59.8 per cent despite an increase of almost a quarter in the number of Italians employed in industry and an even greater fall in the number engaged in agriculture.

The economic development of Italy in this period affected almost exclusively the traditional area of industrialisation: the 'triangle' enclosed by Turin, Milan and Genoa. The vast increase of productive capacity and of economic activity formed a vortex into which almost all the financial and human capital available in the country was channelled: millions of unskilled workers from

---

5. The price stability which had permitted this symbolic celebration of recovery did not last long and by 1960 the coins concerned had become collector's items.

Italy since 1800

the south moved into these cities and their hinterland, often having to live in third world conditions of squalor and lack of amenities. This human flood, part of which found an outlet, after 1957, in job opportunities in other countries of the European Common Market (as it was then known), was stark testimony to the failure both of earlier Christian Democrat attempts to maintain a 'traditional way of life' for the southern peasants by means of paternalistic subsidies, land reform and infrastructural development aimed at improving the conditions for family farming, and of the 'Vanoni Plan' for overcoming the historic discrepancy between living standards and economic development in north and south.

This ambitious plan had aimed at an annual rise of 5 per cent in the national income in order to invest disproportionately in the south and thus overcome its historical backwardness. While reducing unemployment nationally to 4 per cent, the plan assumed a million new jobs would be created in the south, where the per capita income was intended to rise at twice the annual increment planned for the north and where industrial investment would expand by 163 per cent in 8 years, as opposed to the 61 per cent foreseen for the north.

But to make such projections for the future – and in the absence of any means of ensuring that the plan was followed by investors – was to ignore the way in which the economy would be affected by external factors outside Italian control, by the operation of domestic market forces and by the expectations of the individuals who were supposed to benefit from it. Investment, whether from outside the economy or from within it, flowed into the proven sources of likely profit, where the advanced technology already existed, in the north. While per capita income rose in the north by 5.7 per cent per annum, in the south it rose only by 4 per cent, just half what the plan called for. The south made more economic progress than in any previous ten-year period but the gap between it and the north was widening, not closing: where the per capita income in the south had previous been about half of that in the north, by the beginning of the 1960s it had fallen to 46 per cent, even though it had risen in absolute terms.

The response of the government planners was to increase state and state-controlled investment in the south, attempting to stimulate diffuse economic development and promote entrepreneurial attitudes by implanting 'poles of growth' based on massive state investment in the development of primary industrial capacity. But this, too, was to prove over the next 30 years to have been little more than the construction of 'cathedrals in the desert', such as steel works whose distance from their raw materials and from the industries which might need their products made them incapable of ever achieving economic viability. The vehicle of the investment was the *Cassa per il Mezzogiorno*, through which over the next 25 years huge sums of public money were disbursed with the intention, officially, of overcoming the north–south development gap.

234

The original goals of the *Cassa per il Mezzogiorno*, comprising redistribution of land and the creation thereby of a class of independent, prosperous peasant farmers with access to reliable infrastructures (roads, irrigation works, drainage of marshes, clean water-supply), had already been partially achieved in the early 1950s. Unfortunately, it was by no means a suitable instrument for the task of radical industrialisation, being essentially a paternalistic technocratic organisation geared to grandiose projects planned to effect social and economic transformation on a large-scale universal model of development, with little or no reference to local conditions and cultural frames of reference. It was not the most effective way to solve what has been described as

> the problem of fusing together two societies which existed
> simultaneously and in tragic disequilibrium – the static, stratified
> society of an agrarian régime that had outlived its usefulness, and the
> advanced society of a modern industrial state which was itself
> damaged by the possibilities of exploitation afforded by the other
> society.[6]

In fact a great deal of the northern wealth poured into the vast funnel of the *Cassa per il Mezzogiorno* quickly returned to its source, in the form of commissions and orders for public works, subsidies to industrial investment, and fees and salaries for the technicians and experts required to conceive and apply modern technological solutions. The south produced very few such *cadres* from its own educated class, whose children largely followed the family tradition and studied law, medicine and humanities with a view to obtaining a position in the local or national bureaucracies. Where factories were set up with northern capital, the local labour force usually lacked both the technical skills, and the artisanal base for their ready acquisition, which characterised their counterparts in Piedmont or Lombardy. Productivity could only be maintained by intensification of labour input, which led to frequent industrial confrontation between a labour force with little experience of industrial bargaining, and managements largely staffed by northerners whose latent anti-southern prejudices were all too easily aroused by the combination of overt intransigence and covert corruptibility which they discerned in their interlocutors.

The statistics relating to the north–south gap during the 25 years from 1950 reveal the human reality behind the official attempt to rescue the south from economic underdevelopment. Despite the high demographic rate of increase, the population of the southern regions fell from 37 per cent to 35 per cent of the national total, due almost entirely to the mass exodus of adults of working age to northern industry, and after 1957 to other countries of the European Community. They left because the local economy, despite the

6. Francesco Compagna, *La lotta politica italiana nel secondo dopoguerra*, Laterza, Bari, 1950, pp. 137–8.

investments made by the *Cassa per il Mezzogiorno* was no longer able to absorb their labour power. Agricultural jobs fell by 60 per cent, although agricultural production more than doubled as a result of improved technology and applied crop science. Conversely there was a 73 per cent increase in the number of people employed in public administration, reflecting the spread of the Christian Democrat patronage system known as *clientelismo* whereby posts in public employment were distributed on a large scale in return for political support, each job representing the votes available from a whole extended family.

The relative failure of the attempt to implant industry and enterprise may be judged from the contrast between the increment in new industrial jobs: two million in the north as against only 370,000 in the south. More significant still, however, was the corresponding scissors effect in relation to small businesses: while in the north during the quarter-century concerned artisan family firms employing fewer than ten people rose by a quarter, in the south they fell by a fifth. Even more spectacular was the contrast in small and medium manufacturing firms: in the centre and north the number of employees in these firms rose by 70 per cent while in the south there was no increase at all, clearly signalling the inability of the southern economy and its workforce to respond to the market challenges of what on the whole was an unprecedented period of rising demand.

That the failure was relative needs to be stressed: the context is one of accelerated economic growth for the country as a whole, averaging 6 per cent per annum in the 1950s, with a doubling of imports and a trebling of exports. Growth continued at a steadier but still remarkable rate until the mid-1960s. In the period as a whole the agricultural population in the south was more than halved (from 57 per cent to 27 per cent) while the numbers employed in industry rose from 20 per cent of the working population to 32 per cent. Even though in the same period public employment, mainly as a function of *clientelismo*, rose from 23 per cent to over 40 per cent, the total picture was one matching the world trend towards modernisation. Between 1951 and 1962 the proportion of national investment going to the south was 15–18 per cent: 20 years later this had increased to 44 per cent. Overall economic output doubled in the period as a whole, yet actually fell slightly as a proportion of national production, and per capita income remained only 70 per cent of the national average, having scarcely increased proportionally since 1951. In practice the south developed economically at half the rate of the north and thus the gap widened, notwithstanding a total investment worth tens of billions of pounds (at 1992 prices) by the state alone. The most revealing statistic is that 79 per cent of total purchasing power in Italy over the period as a whole was spent in the north, and only 21 per cent in the south and the islands, where 35 per cent of the population lived on 40 per cent of the national territory.

The growth pattern of the economy was matched by urban development, mostly unplanned and with disastrous ecological (and often aesthetic) consequences. In a few years the major cities more than doubled their populations. Massive increases in car ownership and acquisition of consumer durables were accompanied by urban sprawl and environmental degradation. In the north and centre the expansion of urban conglomerations at least went hand in hand with the development of manufacturing industry and, to a lesser extent, of services, which provided jobs and a measure of prosperity for a wide spectrum of the population. In the south the urbanisation of a large proportion of the rural population was an end in itself, attracting speculative building of luxury accommodation, corrupt practices and crime. It was an ideal terrain for criminal organisations such as the *mafia, camorra* and *'ndrangheta* to extend and deepen their activities, dominating the building materials and labour markets and able to make local authorities into their willing accomplices in crime:

> The doubling of the urban population of the south during the last thirty years constitutes perhaps the most grievous and obvious aspect of the breakdown of society, of the gulf between rich and poor, of the abnormal growth in a poor country of 'conspicuous' consumption, i.e. of the worst economic and social inequities in the whole country.[7]

The most enterprising and dynamic among the southern population responded to this situation by voting with their feet: if the new prosperity was not going to reach them at home they would move north in search of it. Totally unplanned, a flood of more than five million people moved from south to north in the period concerned, with as many again moving from country to city in the south. All of them for a while lost their cultural and social bearings and suffered from the traumas always associated with urbanisation of a rural population. But those who went north, despite all the hardships endured and the disadvantages suffered from being dialect-speaking unskilled labour in a cut-throat market, began a long process of adaptation and acculturation which by the 1990s enabled their children and grandchildren to accept their new environment, and be accepted by it. Those who moved into the cities of the south received promises of progress but learned to despair of it, and were soon ready to be recruited as the foot soldiers of corruption and delinquency.

At the heart of this failure, in addition to the contingent causes mentioned, lay a limitation of vision. The problem of the south, the *'questione meridionale'* which had run like a dark thread through the history of Italy since 1860, had almost always been seen, by both southerners and northerners, as an economic one. Both believed that a change in material conditions would suffice to set off a process of modernisation which would bring the whole of the country up to the same level, create a truly national cultural heritage and lead Italians to see themselves as full members of a single society. Almost no attention had been given to culture in the anthropological sense of the word,

---

7. M. Rossi Doria, *Scritti sul Mezzogiorno*, Einaudi, Turin, 1982, p. 172.

to systems of motivation and values. This was the basic reason why, despite the not inconsiderable infrastructural achievements of the *Cassa per il Mezzogiorno*, the post-war 'miracle' in the north did more harm than good to the south, where the rapid erosion of the old checks and balances of an agrarian civil society were not compensated by a simultaneous blossoming of grass-roots entrepreneurial activity of the kind which was to occur in the not previously industrialised regions of the centre and north.

In the south, as the networks and habits of mutual dependence which had generally prevailed in a village-based subsistence agriculture and had provided a material and moral safety net for those struck by misfortune ceased to function, they were replaced by such welfare provision as the state could make. The latter was, however, represented by the omnipresent networks of *clientelismo* and the overlapping alternative civil society of the *mafia* and its clones. The vicious circle was already evident to the economic experts by the end of the 1960s and inspired a sense of profound and gloomy impotence: 'The Italian experience appears to prove conclusively that it is no longer possible to rectify a situation of uneven development once it has taken shape. As the same experience shows, the most that can be done is to prevent it getting worse'.[8]

The paradox was that the increase in production and profits, because it was so inextricably bound up with large-scale social and cultural problems which in turn were grist to the mills of politicians, had the effect of reinforcing a downward spiral of increasingly desperate remedies for an intractable social and economic condition which would eventually lead to the self-destruction of the system. Widespread *clientelismo* was caused by social and cultural backwardness and the consequent need for handouts to stem the effects of the destruction of traditional local communities and their systems of values. The inefficient local and national administrative structures were unable to cope and the chaos which ensued provoked generalised refusal of authority and endemic anti-social violence. Businesses which were continually a prey to unchecked vandalism and theft, and to extortion by *mafia*, *camorra* and *'ndrangheta*, could do little more than tick over, while the social security and health care systems were used as the main channels to pump public money into private pockets whether by assigning invalidity pensions to healthy people or through corrupt tendering for public works.

The state had to foot the bill for all this, which in practice meant that still more wealth had to be shifted from the thrifty north to the spendthrift south in order to buy off trouble. Since increased taxes were politically too risky, and in any case could not be reliably collected from the wealthiest

---

Figure 10.3 The not-so-hidden costs of rapid industrialisation: removing polluted topsoil after the Seveso dioxin disaster.

8. P. Saraceno, *Il Mezzogiorno nelle ricerche della Svimez*, Giuffré, Milan, 1968, p. 111.

tax-evading segment of the population, whose income could not be taxed at source, the state financed its social expenditure in the south by massive borrowing and the sale of treasury bonds. The economic consequences of this began to manifest themselves in acute form in the 1980s when the public deficit first approached the annual gross national product. This was not a temporary phenomenon but indicated a long-term trend derived directly from the developmental dualism which had afflicted the country since its formation. By 1992 the state's indebtedness was to reach proportions which seriously undermined its capacity to remain a full member of the European Community and threatened to lead to the break-up of the state created by the *Risorgimento*.

The surprising fact is that, despite the leaky sieve of the tax collection system and the widespread diversion of public funds into private pockets (often in untraceable Swiss bank accounts) which characterised the Christian Democrat administration of the southern regions, the north and centre of the country for some 30 years continued to produce enough wealth to sustain the stability of the system and at the same time propel Italy as a whole into the world's premier league of economic powers. The contribution to this result of the large super-modernised industries of the north such as Fiat in car-making, Olivetti in office machinery and computers, and Zanussi in domestic appliances, is evident. What is less well-known but at least as important in this achievement was the explosive economic expansion and success, in what has been called 'the Third Italy', of small and medium manufacturing and service businesses combining low unit costs with advanced technology.[9]

In these areas, during the post-war period, certain key economic factors were present in a variety of dynamic configurations. In all them there was a pre-existing network of small and medium towns which over many centuries had established themselves as centres of trade, craft manufacturing, banking and culture, which had strong traditions of local and external contacts and trade, mainly located within the Genoa-Milan-Venice-Florence quadrilateral which, in the fourteenth century, had already long been the centre of the world.[10]

There was also a pattern of agricultural production based on types of landholding (*mezzadria*, small independent farms or tenancies) which depended on the family as the basic unit of production and of management of labour, often prosperous enough to be able to plan ahead effectively and autonomous enough to be able to risk experiment and innovation in pursuit of greater economic success. They were also intrinsically stable enough over time to accumulate the experience needed to cope with changed conditions.

9. This seminal concept of a 'Third Italy' was first coined by A. Bagnasco, *Tre Italie. La problematica territoriale dello sviluppo italiano*, Il Mulino, Bologna, 1977. The term originally denoted Emilia-Romagna, Tuscany, Veneto, Alto Adige, Friuli, Marche and Umbria; more recently, and somewhat questionably, it has been extended to include Abruzzi and Puglia.
10. Cf. Fernand Braudel, *The Structures of Everyday Life: Civilization and Capitalism 15th–18th Century*, Vol. I, Collins, London, 1981.

Such family-managed farms were micro-cosmic mixed economies, and the ultimate source of the 'new entrepreneurialism' which flourished in the 'Third Italy' of the centre and north-east of the country from the late 1950s onwards.

It was not, however, upon agricultural production that the breakthrough depended, even if the general upsurge in local prosperity washed back into that sector as well. The extended family farms in the 'Third Italy' had long had important links with local manufacturing production, in sectors such as textiles and straw goods which could be effectively managed through some variant of the putting-out system. The segment of the population most involved were often the wives and daughters of the farmers, whose intensely active working days included many hours of hand-spinning, handloom-weaving or straw- and basket-work to supplement the family's meagre money income. In other areas of 'the Third Italy', independent peasant farmers had traditionally also been foresters and woodworkers, or had intermarried with village craftsmen making furniture, ceramics or hand-forged tools and utensils. Generations of low and discontinuous wages, compensated by the capacity to survive by collective effort, coupled with comparable generations of flexible manual skills and human resources management within the family productive unit, were ingredients only awaiting a recipe and a stimulus.

The circumstances which provided the latter varied notably from area to area. Politics were important but their particular colouration was not decisive, for the areas concerned were both 'red' and 'white'. More important was the absorption into post-war politics of pre-political cultures of self- and mutual help, of hard work, thrift and solidarity, which could be traced back to the Middle Ages, and which had formed an active part of political subcultures in the rise of the labour movement in Italy, whether catholic or socialist in their terminology. The memory of lost battles against Fascist *squadristi* in the 1920s, the experience, direct or indirect, of the Resistance movement of 1943–45, and the traumatic passage through the country of the massively mechanised Italian campaign had all served in some way to set these traditions fermenting once more, to generate expectations of change and improvement, to provide models of boldness leading to success.

In each case the critical factor was likely to be different, but would be such as to make possible the joint achievement of external economies by a whole local constellation of small enterprises taking in each other's washing, as opposed to economies of scale in the classical capitalist fashion where large firms could undercut and drive out smaller ones.[11] In Emilia-Romagna the well-established tradition of farmer cooperatives sharing out the benefits of mechanisation and market services provided the socio-economic infrastructure

---

11. There is a considerable literature on the hypothesis that in such areas Marshallian 'industrial districts' have been formed; cf. for all G. Becattini (ed.) *Prato. Storia di una città*, Vol. 4, Sansoni, Florence, 1994.

Figure 10.4 Female domestic piecework was one of the keys to the economic success of the 'Third Italy': but note the benefits to the family in terms of the acquisition of consumer durables.

for the development of a mass of small interdependent enterprises in food-processing and ancillary activities, while in north Tuscany the combination of established textile putting-out networks with the collapse of the large complete-cycle mills unable to adjust to new market conditions, provided a window of opportunity for a small army of ex-peasant entrepreneurs who bought up the individual machines from the factories closing-down and set up intrafamilial sweat-shops in their own homes.

A particularly significant feature of this development was the absence of any large-scale inwards immigration from the south to these areas, compared with the massive flow (already by 1963) of almost three million unskilled southerners to the established factories in the 'industrial triangle' formed at the turn of the century.[12] The recruits to the small and medium industries of 'the Third Italy' came from the areas around the towns concerned which had for generations had economic links with them through putting-out and local seasonal employment. They were therefore part of the 'moral' as well as the material economy of the town dwellers with whom they shared the industrial

12. Also to take over abandoned farms in the hill areas which formed its hinterland; this also happened in Tuscany where Sardinian shepherds replaced indigenous Tuscan hill farmers attracted to work in the furniture-making industrial district formed in and around Empoli.

242

district, which thus was able to avoid the additional external social and administrative costs of taking in large numbers of immigrants from other parts of the country.

The source of the greatest economic strength of these new or transformed industrial areas lay precisely in the flexibility they enjoyed in the face of rapidly changing market conditions. It was a flexibility which stemmed directly from the structural characteristics of the family firm, which could set wages and conditions without reference to national norms laid down by authority or in collective bargaining, and, by the same token, could more readily make investment decisions about acquiring new technology which involved initial sacrifices of living standards. At the same time, the strong local political cultures of these areas, whether focused upon left-wing alliances of Communists and Socialists (often against national directives), or on the social Catholicism which underpinned Christian Democrat support in the north-east and the Marche, supported the spread of the micro-capitalism of the family enterprise and kept individual wages and consumption below the national level. The micro-capitalists repaid the favour by continuing to vote, even at the height of the Cold War, for those who proclaimed anti-capitalist doctrines at election times.

The net outcome, for the national economy, of the blossoming of 'the Third Italy' was a dramatic increase in both production and productivity, an improved capacity to compete in international markets, and an astonishing propensity to save on consumption in order to invest in future success: in the period of the 'economic miracle' over 40 per cent of the corporate income of small and medium enterprises was reinvested. The success of 'the Third Italy' was not, however, fully reflected in national economic statistics: as well as peasant traditions of self-sweating for the sake of the family, those of resistance to taxation were also respected. The extent of this evasion is, in the nature of things, impossible to quantify accurately, but its importance may be judged from the fact that when, in the mid-1980s, the Italians jubilantly claimed to have overtaken the British gross national product, it was officially specified that the sum involved included the unreported income deriving from production within the 'hidden economy'.[13] The essential achievement was, of course, not the inflation of official statistics, but the real prosperity attained by millions of Italians who had emerged from a poverty-stricken agriculture only a few years earlier.

Many Italians assumed that their spectacular economic success, however patchy in terms of the north–south divide, and however distorted by patterns of consumption reflecting a preoccupation to achieve conspicuous luxury, would more than suffice to keep political problems at bay, indefinitely buying time for their rulers to devise ingenious compromises which would maintain

---

13. In 1992 the Italian Treasury estimated that the declarations by small and medium proprietors and industrialists represented no more than 25 per cent of their real incomes.

stability. The economy took a sharp downturn into recession from the mid-1960s, at precisely the moment when the 'opening to the left' finally became a reality. For 20 years from 1968, however, the classical notion that economics are the ultimate determinant of politics appeared to be falsified by the course of events in Italy: while the dynamic sectors of the economy continued to produce increasing prosperity for the numerical majority of the population who were involved in them, the degeneration of the state continued to worsen, and large segments of a previously apathetic or fatalistic electorate began to refuse vehemently, and then violently, to accept its defects. The 'years of the bullet' were approaching.

1968–1969 and 'the years of the bullet'

Social and political violence had remained endemic in Italy during the post-war period, reflecting a deep-seated tradition on both the left and the right of politics. In the 1950s and 1960s there was news almost weekly of protests and strikes, in both town and country, and on numerous occasions, as the cynical Italian phrase would have it, 'out popped a corpse'. Normally the dead and wounded were among the strikers and protesters, shot down, or deliberately run over, by the riot police created by Scelba to deal with such threats to 'law and order' with heavy-handed decisiveness. There was also a low-level running war, with its own tally of casualties, between militant followers of the Italian Social Movement and their counterparts on the extreme left who believed the Communists had betrayed the Resistance and surrendered the revolution. In Sardinia, Calabria and the Abruzzi, the tradition of sheep-rustling, kidnapping and social banditry was by no means extinguished.

In addition, and far exceeding these, there was organised crime in the south, the realm of the *mafia*, whose toll of victims far exceeded those already mentioned. Until 1948 the *mafia* supported the Sicilian separatist movement led by Finocchiaro Aprile by providing from its own resources a 'Free Sicily Army', led by the bandit Salvatore Giuliano, who had previously terrorised landowners in western Sicily. Its best-known exploit was the machine-gunning of a May Day procession of Communist peasants in 1947, killing 11 and wounding many more, but it, and other emanations of the *mafia*, waged a pitiless campaign against anyone opposing that organisation's power: in 1947 alone 46 *carabinieri* were killed and 734 wounded in clashes with its 'soldiers'. Politically motivated killings of trade-union leaders continued, even after 1948, when the *mafia* switched its support from the separatists and the Monarchists to the triumphant Christian Democrats after their sweeping victory in the April elections. The Christian Democrats were a tempting target for penetration not only because they now dominated the national stage and led the government, but because of their methods of conducting politics both nationally and locally.

Being convinced that economic development was the only long-term way to stem the tide of Communism, and at the same time that radical change in social structures was to be avoided at any cost, the Christian Democrats had launched the 'Vanoni Plan'. This massive paternalistic rescue operation for the south was intended to narrow the north–south gap and relieve population pressure through economic development while not altering the basic relationships between social classes. For this strategy to succeed, the national leadership needed powerful local allies in a position to channel the extra resources to the greatest effect politically as well as economically. The protean capacity of the *mafia* to adapt to any régime made it an obvious candidate for the rôle of the mediator whose offers are rarely refused. Once again in the history of the unhappy island 'everything had changed so that everything could remain the same'.[1]

The most direct impact upon everyday life in the south of the developing symbiosis between Christian Democrat control of 'legal' Italy and *mafia* power over the 'real' Italy inhabited by Sicilians, Neapolitans and Calabrians could be seen in the economic distortions resulting from the misapplication of funds from the *Cassa per il Mezzogiorno* intended for useful public works such as roads, water supply, schools and hospitals. Although the original intention of the 'Vanoni Plan' had been to foster the development of local industries, the bulk of the money, in regions almost totally lacking an industrial tradition and experience based on local enterprise, had flowed into the building industry and its allied trades. For the *mafia*, which had clearly understood that its prosperity now depended upon wholesale diversification out of its traditional activities in the agrarian sector of the economy, the building trades, whose workforce was largely unskilled and not more than one generation removed from agricultural landless labour, was an obvious target. Its main task was to develop a *de facto* alliance with those who now controlled the flow of funds for public works: the Christian Democrats and their allies in the minor parties, and the banks. The banks were also increasingly under Christian Democrat control because of the system of political appointments to head them which the Christian Democrats had inherited from the Fascist period, when many of them had needed to be rescued by the Institute for Industrial Reconstruction (IRI).

The typical pattern of southern patronage prior to the *Risorgimento* had been based on three elements: the patron, who was normally the wealthy owner of a great estate (*latifundo*), his steward or similar intermediary, and the

---

Figure 11.1 Ancient and modern: a typical Naples street in the 1970s.

---

1. Cf. note 62. The best analysis of the phenomena described relates to Calabria, but is perfectly applicable to Sicily: cf Pino Arlacchi, *Mafia, Peasants and Great Estates*, Cambridge University Press, Cambridge, 1983.

peasant mass of possible clients. The patron had the power to grant or withhold favours, through the intermediary. After unification the intermediary, who was frequently connected with the *mafia*, acquired greater and greater influence, in practice sharing power with the patron, who was increasingly unable or reluctant to use it in person, and increasingly reliant upon the capacity of the intermediary to act as both a semi-autonomous rent-collector and as an effective vote-gatherer. As the franchise was extended the importance of the latter role increased still further. The state stood well clear of the local manipulations involved, demanding only the parliamentary support of the southern 'native levies' (the *ascari*) as they were referred to under the Giolittian system.

During the Fascist dictatorship vote-gathering was no longer required of the intermediaries, who generally found other ways to make themselves useful to authority, often becoming leading figures in the local Fascist organisations, to which they had little trouble adapting. A police state did not require the services of the *mafia* as the guarantor of local order in the south. Although, as we have seen, the Allies had cynically restored the *mafia* in Sicily as a contribution to the island's liberation, after 1945 it was, as always, the government in Rome that ifound it could not rule the south without coming to an arrangement with the informal system of socio-political control based on *mafia* violence.

As the importance of the landowning interest as the fickle source of favours (and as the power that could withhold them) declined over the first decades of the post-war period, it was the Christian Democrat welfare state, ever ready to offer handouts in return for political support, which replaced the traditional patron. For the *mafia* the state was no longer the enemy, to be ignored or cheated, but the very source of patronage, access to which had to be secured by striking deals with its local intermediaries, or better still by becoming them.

Since the objective of this state was now to create in the south an 'enterprise culture', it was natural that those who typically assumed the role of intermediary should relinquish, at least in part, the characteristics of 'country gentlemen', ostensibly above the squalid business of trade, and present themselves as modern businessmen with political connections (or as politicians with business interests). The intermediary function remained necessary, however, precisely because of the gulf which still existed between the project of modernisation as expressed in the Vanoni Plan, and the social and psychological reality of southern life. The enterprise culture existed only in theory: in practice the 'entrepreneurs' concerned risked only the funds provided by the state, and lacked the classical incentive of personal financial risk in order to make a profit. The outcome has been well-described as the 'privatisation of profits and the socialisation of losses'.

The skills required for success in this rôle were essentially those forms of manipulation of national-local economic and political relations which could produce an even flow of state funds to non-accountable activities: the critical factor in such operations was a universal acceptance of corruption and cover-up – precisely the conditions which the *mafia* could provide through its monopoly of private violence and the imposition of the 'law of silence' (*omertà*).

To convert their operation to a mainly urban basis the *mafia* needed to effect a major restructuring of their organisation. Given that there was no single operational control of the structure, that there was constant, often lethal, rivalry between the various *cosche* ('clans'), and between generation within them, and that adaptation to an urban basis had important implications for *mafia* 'culture', it should not be surprising that the process lasted some 20 years. In a sense, and certainly not as the result of a deliberate policy of the Christian Democrats, the *mafia's rapprochement* with the new ruling class brought them into a higher culture of corruption and racketeering than before: alongside old-fashioned organised crime based on the threat of personal violence, more sophisticated activities were undertaken, some of them merging with 'legitimate' business. With their new connections, the more enterprising *mafiosi* could launder their illicit profits and invest them in apparently *bona fide* business activities. Had it been deliberate policy to tempt the 'new' *mafia* into legal (if still anti-social) activities, it may be speculated, the phenomenon might, in the longest term, have become more tractable and ultimately the descendants of the *mafiosi* might have merged into the general class of entrepreneurs. With the massive expansion of the market for hard drugs in the 1960s and 1970s, however, the rate of return on criminal activities deprived 'going legitimate' of its attractions.

For most Italians the *mafia* were, of course, simply criminals who had to be suppressed by the actions of the police and the judiciary, a process equally drawn out and signposted by spectacular defeats. Those unwilling to pay for 'protection' continued to be murdered by the traditional method (shooting with a sawn-off shotgun in order to inflict massive mutilation), as did policemen who proved too zealous and sought to reach beyond the small fry towards the bigger fish. As the *mafia* became 'industrialised' its ranks continued to swell and it acquired 'fellow travellers' throughout the political and economic system, no longer only in the south. In the 1970s the average annual murder rate by the *mafia* in Palermo city was almost one a day and a decade later it had more than doubled. Most victims were typical *mafia* targets: 'awkward' politicians, trade-union leaders and policemen, although there were often lengthy periods when these murders were suspended during bloody settlements of accounts between rival 'families'. By 1991 it was reliably estimated that the *mafia's* 'foot soldiers' (the *picciotti*) numbered 45,000 and its 'affiliates' over 100,000, divided between some 150 'families', each controlling between 100 and 300 men. Since 1950 it has carried out some 10,000 murders and in the 1990s it has averaged almost two killings a day. Despite special laws and police measures against it, its power appears to have grown rather than diminished.

Moreover, it has ceased to prey exclusively on the poor of rural Sicily: since the late 1970s it has set out to eliminate anyone in an official position who represents a serious threat to its interests. The names of this category of its victims are a roll-call of politicians who opposed it or, on the contrary, became too greedy, and of senior policemen, prosecutors and judges who fought it too successfully.[2]

The 'professional' use of violence by the criminal population, however greatly it may have been deplored by the respectable majority of Italians, was not a freakish anomaly in an otherwise law-abiding and non-violent society. The legitimation of violence had, from the *Risorgimento* onwards, been a central feature of the Italian experience. The violence of the *mafia*, differed from that of official 'national' (later, *nazionalista*) and unofficial 'internationalist' movements only in the choice of the arguments used to justify its use. For the 'honoured society' (its self-description in Sicily) and its counterparts elsewhere in southern Italy, the use of violence, often ritualised in its application, was shrouded in a seamless robe of mystifications ranging from a defence of Sicilian independence and of traditional family values to an assertion of personal worth through adherence to a code of 'honour' which embodied an impartial system of informal justice against malefactors (usually 'traitors' to the cause, and servants of the 'enemy State').[3]

These warped forms of 'patriotism' and 'justice' had their mirror image in the fanaticisms of imperialism, *nazionalismo*, and Fascism on one side of politics, and 'the struggle for the liberation of mankind' practised in turn by anarchist Bakuninists, anarcho-syndicalists, militant socialists of the peasant *leghe* in the 1920s and their partisan successors in the 1940s. None of them achieved a hold on the population as a whole and few ever attracted more than an exiguous minority of committed supporters, but like a Greek chorus they were always present to remind Italians that their nation was a recent political invention only held together by an unprincipled transformism, and that, because of their weak attachment to a unified civil society, it was incapable of instilling a robustly unchallengeable system of values. Writing in 1911 of the influence of the *camorra*, Sidney Sonnino had already put his finger upon the linkage between the practice of government as developed in Liberal Italy and the social permanence of organised crime:

2. 'Cosa Nostra secondo l'Ispes: criminali sempre più professionisti', *La Repubblica*, 6 September 1992, p. 18. The *mafia*'s most illustrious victims were the MP Pio La Torre, who gave his name to the first antimafia law, General Carlo Alberto Dalla Chiesa, police supremo for the fight against the *mafia*, and the judges Giovanni Falcone and Paolo Borsellino responsible for the mass prosecution of *mafia* bosses in the late 1980s.
3. The ritualised execution of its enemies is part of the *mafia*'s armoury: an example is *incaprettamento*, or 'goat-strangling', where the wrists and ankles are tied behind the back and at the same time around the neck of the victim, so that in attempting to break free he strangles himself. The practical advantage is that the corpse can easily be stowed in a car boot. Cf. Giovanni Falcone, *Men of Honour: The Truth about the Mafia*, Fourth Estate, London, 1992.

The *camorra* is not just a crime syndicate but the result of a whole attitude to life of the people of Naples, and not just the lower orders. It is also largely the result of the weakness and lack of moral sense of the government and of the corrupting influence which is inherent in elected bodies. When there is no effective defence of the official State, a kind of illegal State is formed and maintained, with exchanges of favours between its levels. The hard part is to find a remedy in such a debased moral climate as the Italian, especially where politics are concerned, where the rhetorical phrase is everything and the content does not matter. The only remedy I can see is to bring everything out into the light of day...[4]

The general public, especially in the north and centre of the country, demanded vigorous action against the *mafia* but did not generally have a clear understanding of how deeply rooted it was in the social and political history of Italy, nor of its growing symbiosis with the Christian Democrat system of patronage in the south. The image favoured by the media was that of the 'octopus', spreading its tentacles ever wider, an all-powerful but shadowy conspiracy of crime. Viewed, however, in the perspective of two centuries of Italian history, it has to be seen as part of the basic strategy developed by successive régimes to enable a small unrepresentative élite to control an almost ungovernable mass of peasants and urban poor, always close to economic desperation.

As we have seen, the strategy, for which the best name remains transformism, had had a history of its own. Starting from the parliamentary manoeuvring of Cavour and Depretis, it had developed through the 'active' transformism practised by Giolitti as a way to direct the patronage system of the south to achieve the modernisation of the north, and was then practised by Mussolini in his own version as part of an effort to harness Italy's unresolved social tensions and their potential for violence, to a grand design for conquest and empire. During the period of Christian Democrat hegemony it achieved probably its most pervasive manifestation.

The damage done by Christian Democrat policies which so distorted the post-war implantation of entrepreneurialism in Italy was not confined to the south, but could be observed in a less extreme form in other parts of the country, according to whether the local state (Region, Province or Commune) was dominated by that party and its allies, and to what extent the opposition parties were prepared to denounce it publicly and insist upon transparency. As we shall see, it could not be taken for granted that these parties, however distinct politically from the Christian Democrats and their partners, would pursue such matters to the logical conclusion of demanding concrete legal action against corrupt individuals. It was not merely a question of a 'mutual

---

4. Letter to P. Villari, 22 July 1911, first published 16 September 1992 in *La Repubblica*.

protection society of politicians': the opposition, and in particular the Communists, from the formation of the first centre-left coalition in 1962 onwards, were patiently pursuing a 'me-too' strategy intended, ultimately, to lead them into a grand coalition of some sort with the Christian Democrats. That there were cogent arguments for them to do so may be accepted, but the negative effect of a general failure to render the Christian Democrats' patronage system unviable (which was certainly in their power in many areas of the country) ultimately led them, in the public perception, to be equally tainted by its practices, and to bear a substantial part of the responsibility for the paradox that

> In the long run, the failure ever to complete the [bourgeois] revolution in Italy meant that the State did not 'rationalise' the south so much as be 'southernised' by it. *Le mort saisit le vif* [...] In the USA, machine politics may have served to socialise and integrate new groups (e.g. recent immigrants) into the social and political system without undermining their autonomy. In Italy the patronage system has lasted so long and has had such an absolute power while being so dependent on the protection of the State, that it left society even more inert than it was to start with. Politically speaking the patronage system [in Italy] did much less to foster multi-party democracy than to prop up governments fundamentally hostile to democratic process.[5]

The distortions of the democratic process induced by the reliance of the Christian Democrats on the patronage system to maintain their parliamentary pre-eminence quickly spilled over into the practices of their lesser coalition partners. During the three decades which followed the establishment of the centre-left coalition as the only viable political formula, every one of these partners became more or less tainted by corruption and by connivance with organised crime: in Sicily, in particular, the entrepreneurial *mafia* treated them all with cynical indifference as vehicles for obtaining access to public funds, even allowing on occasion the Christian Democrats to be by-passed in competitions for local political supremacy. There were honest men in all the parties who took no bribes for themselves, but very few indeed were able to resist the logic of the system when it came to obtaining 'contributions' from 'wealthy sympathisers' to assist their party's campaign at election times.

The impression left by this increasing trend, and the continual stream of gross scandals which marked Italian political life over this period, was particularly saddening in the case of those parties, notably the Socialists and the Republicans, which could boast of a tradition of incorruptibility and

---

5. L. Graziano (ed.), *Clientelismo e mutamento politico*, Franco Angeli, Milan, 1974, pp. 334 and 359. The words in French are a well-known quotation from Marx: cf. note 10, p. 55.

dedication to high principles of democracy and concern for social justice: it may be counted as a major political tragedy that the party of Matteotti, murdered in 1924 for denouncing electoral fraud, became the party of Bettino Craxi, whose personal entourage in Milan was the protagonist in 1992 of the greatest corruption scandal the 'capital of hard work' had ever witnessed. But the poison had entered their systems long before this: already by 1982 a disillusioned Socialist had analysed the process:

> The greatest example of this influence [of the patronage system] could perhaps be seen in the lightning conversion of the Socialist leadership as a result of the experience in the centre-left coalition: it moved from the concept of tightly-knit militant working-class group setting out to take power and to use it to bring about radical change just short of revolution, to a type of political leadership very close, if not identical, to that of the Christian Democrats, with their factions, their electoral manipulations, in their concept and practice of what government does, in their social connections, in the way they appear and act in politics.[6]

The members of the centre-left governments, from Fanfani onwards, would certainly have defended themselves by pointing to both their achievements and the unexpected constraints which were placed upon them by international events, notably the Vietnam war and the 1964 oil crisis, with its huge increase in energy costs and pump prices, and with the consequent discontent of the substantial segment of the electorate which had only recently become the proud owners of motor vehicles. In 1963 car sales rose by 45 per cent after having quadrupled in the previous eight years: the ownership of private cars had become the single greatest compensating mechanism for the miseries inflicted by chaotic mass migration, lack of services, and despoliation of both town and country by speculative building of the most obscene kind. The very rapidity with which the social and environmental impact of this frenzied motorisation of everyday life was felt made the sectors of the population which were excluded from its ostensible benefits even more resentful of the total inadequacy of the provision Italian society was making for them.

The governments of the 1960s continued to follow the centre-left formula, but were incapable of making any serious inroads on Italy's deep-seated problems, even if they understood them. The attempts at global economic planning which the Christian Democrats had developed during the late 1950s were abandoned or completely diluted by concessions to vested special interests, local and national. The business of government became no more than that of ensuring that state funds continued to flow into the bank accounts of the political, economic and criminal parasites whose capacity to deliver votes underpinned the stability of the system. The State became Italy's most successful *combinazione*, a ramified and complex

---

6. G. Galasso, *L'altra Europa*, Mondadori, Milan, 1982, p. 246.

deal which provided pickings for everyone who had access to influence within the system: even trade unions, even the parties of the opposition received their share.

No parliament in Europe passed as many laws and amendments to laws as the Italian, a fact of which the authorities publicly boasted. Yet this legislative activity, whether by parliament or by government decree, was mainly aimed at providing legalistic cover, by prescription or – more commonly – by well-designed loopholes, for corrupt or shady practices, while the attempts of the honest deputies in parliament to impose greater accountability were regularly filibustered into oblivion in parliamentary committees whose function was ostensibly to ensure it. A word was coined to describe this system of non-government: *immobilismo. Immobilismo* was a spoils system based on a guaranteed standoff between nicely balanced power groups and lobbies, whether parties or factions within them: it guaranteed the stability of the political system at the expense of the economy and social accountability.

The clearest proof that this 'kleptocracy' was, precisely, immovable, was the virtual nil-effect upon the stability of Italian politics of the continual scandals which in any other parliamentary democracy would have toppled governments. From 1950 onwards, when the first large case of diversion of public funds in return for political favours by the Christian Democrat senator Giuseppe Spataro was uncovered, followed by the revelation of the channelling of public money to the Christian Democrat farmers' association in a successful bid to head off further advances among the peasants by the Communists, the scandals came thick and fast. Besides those linking prominent Christian Democrats to corrupt planning permits and subsidies for *mafia*-controlled building firms, there were scandals involving massive slush-funds made available to the government parties by state-controlled and private-sector banks and enterprises, and even by foreign firms: in 1976 it was discovered that Luigi Tanassi, the then Minister of Defence, a Social Democrat, had accepted a huge bribe from the Lockheed Aircraft Corporation in return for arranging procurement of a number of 'Starfighter' aircraft with an extremely bad safety record. In other scandals illicit profits were made and transferred to party funds and private pockets from the import of bananas, tobacco and crude oil on which customs duty had been evaded. Probably the greatest scandal of all in this period, although it did not come to light for some fifteen years, was the use of over £22 billion pounds, a considerable portion of which was provided under various headings by the European Community, provided to repair the damage caused in 1980 by a series of disastrous earthquakes in Irpinia. When the newly-elected President Oscar Luigi Scalfaro in 1992 learned that after 12 years of 'reconstruction' 14,000 families were still living in mobile homes and makeshift accommodation and that more than half as many again of the dwellings declared to have been destroyed or seriously damaged had already been replaced with new buildings, he demanded to see the accounts of this operation, but none were available at the relevant ministries.[7]

Over and above scandals whose focus was money, a number of even more menacing episodes involved the secret services in attempts to by-pass the political process. In 1964, the general in charge of them Giovanni De Lorenzo, was discovered to have planned and all but implemented a political *coup d'état* intended to instal the authoritarian anti-Communist type of government which had loomed up during the Tambroni 'adventure' of 1960. The political ramifications of the plot were never fully clarified but there was no doubt in anyone's mind that De Lorenzo was acting on behalf of at least part of the political establishment which desired a more strongly repressive policy towards the Communists, after the latter, by raising their share of the vote to more than a quarter of the electorate, had been the unexpected victors of the 1963 elections which ushered in the 'opening to the left'. Without doubt, however, the greatest of the political scandals broke in 1981 with the discovery in a villa near Arezzo of a list of hundreds of names of leading politicians, officers, judges, journalists, bankers, and civil servants who were members of a Masonic Lodge called 'P2', and who were committed thereby to assist each other in all circumstances. The villa belonged to a certain Licio Gelli, whose whole career had apparently been devoted to furthering the interests of the Christian Democrat party. The Grandmaster also had a close relationship with members of the Vatican hierarchy, and with some in the Italian intelligence community who were suspected of master-minding the 'strategy of tension' which relied on indiscriminate right-wing terrorism to destabilise institutions and prepare the way for a *coup d'état*. That Gelli had powerful, and probably nervous, protectors may be deduced from the fact that eleven years later he was still a free man, disdainfully ignoring the criminal proceedings finally opened against him, despite the fact that new evidence linking his and other Masonic organisations to the *mafia* had come to light in the meantime.

Even the fact that a number of the grossest cases had connections with the Vatican was never more in Italy than a nine-day wonder, despite the assiduous efforts and revelations of investigative journalists which shocked opinion abroad: the two most prominent might even be regarded as merely the tip of a still undiscovered iceberg, their discovery being due to accident rather than design. These were the 1957 scandal which broke when the banker Gianbattista Giuffré (later known as 'God's banker') went bankrupt and his alarming speculations on behalf of the Church were revealed, and the even murkier episode in 1982 of Roberto Calvi, Chairman of the major Ambrosiana bank and chief financial agent for Cardinal Paul Marcinkus, the Vatican's

---

7. It subsequently emerged that local building contractors who were close relatives of Ciriaco De Mita, the then 'reforming' Secretary of the Christian Democrats, had profited hugely from the disaster funds concerned. In March 1993 his brother and brother-in-law were arrested by the magistrates conducting the 'Clean Hands' operation.

Figure 11.2 Well-dressed student protesters in 1969.

'finance minister'. Calvi was found murdered in London in circumstances which had the hallmarks of a *mafia* execution, after extracting a vast sum of money from the bank's depositors.

In May 1968 a totally unexpected tidal wave of social and political protest swept across Europe, starting in France and then rapidly spreading to every major democratic country as an inchoate but noisy student rebellion against antiquated university systems and facilities, and against the lack of graduate employment opportunities, but soon developing a momentum and ideological content of its own. The latter was a heady mixture of anti-militarism related to the Vietnam war, and assorted idealisms, mostly of the extreme left, with Trotskyists and Anarchists taking the lead, deliberately, in demanding the politically impossible. The repressive response of the authorities, not only in France but soon also in Germany, Italy, and even Britain had the inevitable effect of making martyrs of the dead and injured, and heroes of the leaders, many of whom seriously believed that a new 1789, or 1917, was at hand. A better parallel would have been with 1848, the *annus mirabilis* of revolutions that quickly faded away under the counter-attacks of the *anciens régimes*.

The May events in France of 1968, and their counterparts elsewhere undoubtedly did have long-term effects, both good and bad, in the organisation and atmosphere of university life, and even in Italy, home of perhaps the most resistant system of academic privilege for the professorate and of neglect of grossly overcrowded students, it ultimately brought some overdue beneficial changes and additional resources. A law was rushed through parliament in 1969 granting a free choice of curriculum and much broader access, theoretically similar to the US model, and over the next decade the number of university teachers was trebled to meet the 100 per cent increase in student numbers. But the fresh injection of resources was far too limited to ensure that academic standards could be maintained, quite apart from the inherently trivialising tendency of degrees based on 'open' curricula. Although the universities were able to provide little improvement in facilities for learning, and the discontent of students remained largely justified, the extreme ferment of 1968–69 was not repeated.

This was partly because the Italian militant student leaders had persuaded themselves that their 'struggle' could be the spark which lit the flame of a workers' revolution of world proportions. Che Guevara and Mao-tse-tung took over as their ideal heroes from Rudi Dutschke and Dany ('the Red') Cohn-Bendit. 'The struggle goes on', became their motto, but their capacity to rouse mass support in the streets steadily declined.[8] Their initial surge had nevertheless inspired much unrest in the north Italian factories, where the problems created by a mixture of mass immigration of unskilled workers from the south, the lingering effects of the oil crisis on living costs and inflation, and the inability of the divided Italian labour movement, based on industry-wide trade unions, to deliver higher wages, pay differentials, and better conditions at factory level, resulted in a series of mass wildcat strikes organised by leaders emerging spontaneously on the shop floor.

The workers participating in these largely successful strikes had, however, little more patience with the agitators sent by the student movement to exhort them to turn their disputes with management into a general insurrectionary strike than they had with the officials of trade unions whose real allegiance was to their party and not to their members in the workplace. The strikers wanted higher wages and shorter hours, and soon got them, for the

8. There was an interesting convergence between extreme right-wing and left-wing slogans in this period: in 1970 the Italian Social Movement led riots in Reggio Calabria yelling '*Boia chi molla!*' ('Never surrender!') while the left marched to the cry of '*Lotta continua!*'.

whole of the Italian establishment was running very scared. Within six months average wages in Italian large-scale industry had risen by well over a quarter.

The Communist Party would, traditionally, have been fully committed to controlling this situation and exploiting it, both to extend its organisational grip on industrial militancy, and to make electoral capital from it. Initially, however, it was relatively inattentive to the student rebellion because of its preoccupation with containing the backlash among its supporters against the Soviet suppression of the 'Prague spring' of February 1968. As the student movement assumed mass proportions, spreading also to secondary schools, the Communists became increasingly hostile to it because of the pre-eminence, within its leading groups, of Trotskyists, Anarchists and Maoists, their old and new sworn enemies on the left. With the onset of the 'hot autumn' in the factories, fearing that these rivals would begin to make real inroads among its working-class supporters, the Communist Party now hastily attempted to catch up with its own grass-roots, by endorsing the wages explosion as a legitimate response to the evils of the capitalist system. The attempted reassertion of its influence in the factories, however, had a perverse effect: the last thing the militant extremist splinter groups, with their pathetically provocative names ('Worker Power', 'Autonomy' and 'The Struggle Goes On'), really wanted was a re-invigorated Communist Party assuming once more the role of catch-all party of the discontented. Increasingly they began to theorise, if not yet to practice, the use of 'direct action', in other words their own version of the terrorism which they claimed was practised by the State.

Already on 12 December 1969 there had been the first major terrorist outrage, when a bomb exploded in a busy bank at Piazza Fontana in Milan. The police immediately attributed this to a little known, and completely non-violent, anarchist who was arrested, interrogated and then 'fell' to his death from an upper-storey window at police headquarters. In fact the bomb had been planted by a group of the extreme right, almost certainly in collusion with the secret services. Within a few months the extreme left also began to resort to 'direct action', as it preferred to call its terroristic activities, this time targetting property and individuals which it deemed to belong to 'reactionary capital', quite evidently in competition with the 'traitors' of the official 'reformist' left and the trade-union movement, which had eventually emerged from the 'hot autumn' of 1969 with enhanced support among the 'proletariat'.

Between the explosion at Piazza Fontana and 1975, over 80 per cent of the 4,384 acts of terrorist violence perpetrated in Italy were attributable to the right; 92 murders were among them, over two thirds of which were attributable to the far right groups (some 171 of them were counted, mostly local ephemera). The best known of these groups was 'Black Order', which had claimed the original outrage in Milan. They were certainly abetted by elements of the secret services, although no full official enquiry into this has yet been carried out, since it involved the top-secret *Gladio* organisation already mentioned, whose existence, but possibly not all of whose activities, were known to only a small number of ministers, including Francesco Cossiga, later the President of Italy.[9]

The strategy of the extreme right was the so-called 'strategy of tension', intended to destabilise the political system to the extent necessary to bring to power an authoritarian right-wing government pledged to roll back the 'red tide'. The tactics adopted were therefore intended to provoke maximum alarm in the general apolitical public by bomb outrages in public places against completely innocent 'civilians', or car-bomb booby-traps set for the *carabinieri*, in the hope of creating a 'great fear' such as the *squadristi* of 1919–22 had been able to exploit. Trains passing through long tunnels were a favoured target, as were station waiting-rooms. From 1976 onwards the leading groups on the right became even more extreme, apparently practising mass-slaughter for its own sake: the same few hundred exponents of this violence formed new groups, often borrowing the type of phraseology favoured by the extreme left.[10]

The extreme left, mainly grouped in the so-called 'Red Brigades', obsessed with its fantasy of a re-galvanised revolutionary working class demanding the 'sweeping-away of capitalism', operated according to a different theoretical analysis of how the 'system' worked. They believed that violence could be applied in an 'exemplary', even 'educative' fashion, by staging 'people's trials' of their kidnap victims among industrialists, journalists, union officials and politicians. At first the humiliated victims were released physically unharmed, but from the mid-1970s the 'trials' often ended in 'executions', while there was also a series of straightforward assassinations of troublesome policemen and judges. The 'years of the bullet' reached their climax in the period 1976–78. Each of the major cities, Turin, Milan, Genoa, Venice and Rome, had a 'column' operating independently, which set out to terrorise the 'cadres of capitalism', demonstrating to the supine working class that their oppressors could be punished, and also to 'strike at the heart of the State' by assassinating leading political and intellectual figures.

In 1977, in a move reminiscent of the attempt by Carlo Pisacane in 1857 to promote the 'national revolution' by mobilising the 'wretched of the earth' in the south, the left-wing exponents of violence decided to move the focus of their action away from their clandestine activities in the industrial heartland of the north to the desperate outcasts of the Roman suburbs, where they hoped to be able to recruit more support by organising violent demonstrations against deficient public services and unemployment which, masked and armed against the riot police, they could 'protect'. The 'world village' created by the media revolution provided apparently appropriate images of ghetto riots in the United States, Belfast and Berlin. The police seemed powerless to control either the riots or their organisers, and many Italian liberal intellectuals even applauded these manifestations of 'people power'.

---

9. Cf. note 5, Chapter 8.
10. The 'Armed Revolutionary Nuclei' and the 'Popular Revolutionary Movement' were among the most prominent.

Even worse was to come: on 16 March 1978, the Prime Minister, Aldo Moro, was ambushed by the 'Red Brigades' in broad daylight on a Rome street, his escort massacred, and himself abducted to a 'People's Prison', where he was kept as a 'hostage' until the day of his 'execution' on 9 May. His captors, leaving cyclostyled 'communiqués' in street-corner rubbish baskets, declared their intention of subjecting him to a 'trial' for his 'crimes against the people'. Wrapped up in a perverse mishmash of Leninist, Maoist and Guevarist rhetoric, these offered terms for Moro's release if the government agreed to negotiate with the terrorists, recognising them as a 'people's army' and agreeing to treat any of them captured as 'prisoners of war'. To heighten the effect of their coup, the terrorists issued photographs of their captive holding a news-paper which clearly showed he was still alive, and allowed him to write letters, which were duly posted, to his colleagues and family, appealing pathetically for them to agree to the terms offered in order to save his life. There was no response and on 16 May his corpse was left in the boot of a car, parked for deliberate effect half-way between the headquarters of the Christian Demo-crats and the Communists, both of which parties had rigidly refused to contemplate any deal with the terrorists.

This was by no means the end of the Red Brigades' offensive, nor of the terrorism of the right. More journalists and union officials were murdered in 1979, but in the following year the police finally achieved a breakthrough when Patrizio Peci, a prominent leader of the Red Brigades, 'repented' and confessed all he knew of the organisation and its members. From that moment it was on the defensive, despite a continuing series of political murders over the next three years, aimed at senior policemen and judges, university professors and others who publicly questioned its reason for existing. A law allowing less harsh penalties for genuinely repentant (and therefore cooperative) terrorists encour-aged many more to follow the lead given by Peci, and slowly the movement petered out as it became increasingly difficult for the militants to find protection among previous sympathisers. The extreme right terrorist movement was also affected by the repentance laws, but not before it had perpetrated two of its worst outrages with the bombing at Bologna station in 1980 and of a train (in a tunnel between Florence and Bologna) taking people home for Christmas in 1984.

At political level, the years of the bullet had increasingly dramatic repercussions, but little real effect upon the underlying character of the Italian system of 'stable instability'. Despite the fact that, spurred by the waves of popular discontent sweeping the country in 1969–70, the parliament brought in a Charter of Workers' Rights, finally enacted legislation provided for in the 1947 Constitution to set up the Regional Governments and also the legislative framework for the institution of popular referenda, and even introduced a limited form of civil divorce in response to the growing women's movement, the basic pattern of Christian Democrat dominance by patronage and Communist Party manoeuvring to become acceptable for national power-shar-ing were, if anything, more apparent than before.

Indeed, until the assassination of Moro in 1978, the gradual preparation of a further 'opening to the left', this time to embrace the de-Sovietised Communist Party, seemed to be well on course. The scene was set for this by the parliamentary elections of 1972, called a year earlier than scheduled by a Christian Democrat government frustrated by the increasing obstructionism and paralysis caused by the infighting of its own factions, broadly divided between the tendentially authoritarian wing led by Fanfani, which sought to change the Constitution to create a 'strong' presidency on the Gaullist model, the would-be reformers led by Moro, and the loose coalition of centrist trimmers whose *immobilismo* had dominated the party for 20 years.

The government itself derived no perceptible advantage from this move: the Christian Democrats merely maintained their support at just below 40 per cent of the electorate. On the left and the right of the political spectrum, however, there were significant changes, largely in response to the waves of agitation and violence which had been sweeping the country over the previous three years.

On the right, where the Italian Social Movement of neo-Fascists fielded a single list with the rump of the Monarchists, there was a perceptible swing towards those who demanded authoritarian solutions to the prevailing disorder and 'crisis of the State'. Gaining almost 9 per cent of the votes cast, the 'double-breasted right' won the largest number of seats it had ever achieved since the war.[11] It regularly disavowed the terrorist activities of 'both extremes', but still found space within its ranks for many of those who participated in, or at least sympathised with, the activities of Black Order. It recruited among its parliamentary candidates a number of frustrated senior officers of the armed forces, alarmed and affronted by the rampant anti-militarism of the student protest movement. Some Christian Democrats were, moreover, known to be still open to the idea of collaborating with this 'respectable' version of Fascism, especially since it had even changed its name to 'National Right'.

On the left, the Communist Party, raising its vote to almost 30 per cent of the electorate, had clearly succeeded in regaining at least the passive support of its traditional factory-worker vote, and had recouped some middle-class votes by the strong stand it had taken against terrorism of all varieties and by its newly-proclaimed independence from the dictates of Moscow. In 1972, after the death of Togliatti's contemporary and successor as Secretary of the Party, Luigi Longo, the Communists had appointed the much younger Enrico Berlinguer, offspring of an aristocratic Sardinian family, to be their leader. This taciturn, highly intellectual, totally unflappable man, with a reputation for probity and shrewdness, at once set about the long overdue task

---

11. Attempting to tone down the *squadrista* image associated with black shirts and knee boots, the leaders of the Italian Social Movement had taken to wearing 'respectable' double-breasted suits.

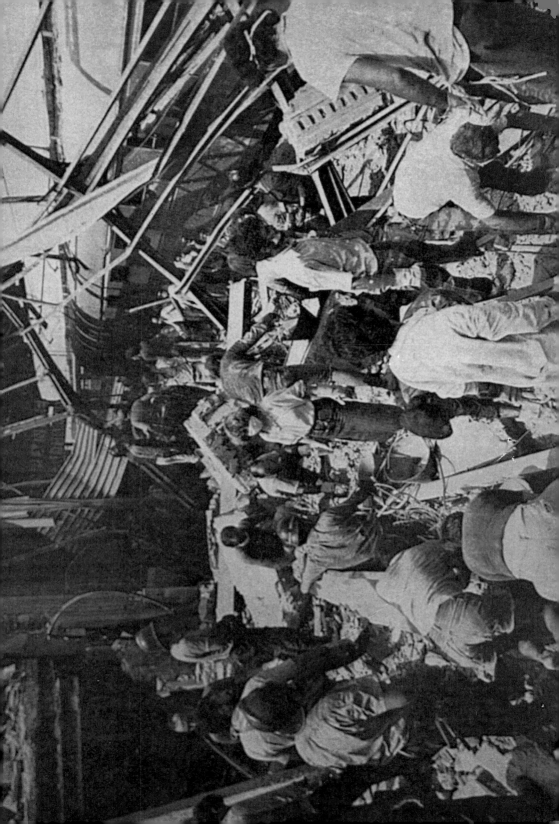

of levering the party out of the permanent ghetto to which it had been consigned by the Christian Democrats since 1947.

Berlinguer was convinced that his Party needed above all to confirm and demonstrate its readiness to share power within the existing political and economic framework. To detach the Party from its public subservience to the rulers of Soviet Communism was probably the least difficult of the tasks he had to confront, for the ground had already been prepared here by Togliatti's theorisation of 'polycentrism' in his famous 'Yalta Memorandum', written during the last weeks of his life. The revulsion caused by the brutal Soviet repression of the Prague Spring of 1968 had cleared most Italian Communist minds of any belief that this kind of 'real socialism' was a goal they shared. But the unassuaged quasi-religious longing for some form of 'real socialism' which was the emotional basis for the allegiance to the Communist Party of most of its militants and many of its voters could not be expunged so readily. To start the process, so that the Party could learn by doing, he proposed a 'different kind of opposition', eschewing the traditional root and branch hostility to whatever the government might do.

Taking seriously the injunction of the Party's founder and chief ideologist, Gramsci, to 'follow all the twists and turns of the real Italy', and deeply impressed by the harsh lessons to be learnt from the US-backed overthrow of Salvatore Allende the newly-elected Marxist president of Chile who had failed to achieve a consensus with that country's Christian Democrat opposition, Berlinguer started from fresh premises concerning the Party's path to power.

It could not, in the first place, correspond in any real sense to the Leninist prescriptions laid down in *State and Revolution*: if the Party's ascent to power was to be 'revolutionary' at all, the term would have to be completely redefined, and above all, the doctrine of the necessity for a 'dictatorship of the proletariat' to defend the revolution once achieved, would have to be rendered so anodyne as to lose all meaning. Simply to abandon it altogether, which would have been more logical, was, however, less easy, since it was an article of faith as significant for the Party's essential hard core of militants as the doctrine of the Holy Trinity for practising Christians.

Secondly, the equally fundamental tenet that 'proletarian internationalism' must always take precedence over local considerations, would also have to be redefined. On the whole this presented fewer difficulties since the Party's principled protest against the Soviet repression in Czechoslovakia had already loosened the ties of rank and file allegiance to the 'homeland of the workers' ruled from the Kremlin. Nevertheless, tens of thousands of Italian Communists continued every year to make their subsidised pilgrimages to the

---

Figure 11.3 Terrorism at work: Bologna railway station 1980. In 1993, although the Secret Services were widely suspected of this massacre of over eighty people, no one had yet been found guilty.

'countries of real socialism' beyond the Iron Curtain, and the Party secretly continued to accept substantial financial support from the Soviet government.

The third aspect of Berlinguer's new strategy was to seek increasing convergence between the world-view of a revised Italian Marxism and that of the Catholic clergy and laity, including those Christian Democrats who might be open to 'dialogue'. At the end of this process, it was hoped, there could be a political convergence as well, which would enable the Communists to enter a coalition government and enact 'elements of socialism' through the peaceful processes of parliamentary democracy.

The pursuit of these goals was assisted by some factors, both structural and conjunctural, and impeded by others. The Party's self-image as a disciplined and unitary force and own method of self-management by so-called 'democratic centralism' (in effect, the absolute authority of the leadership) were severe constraints upon the development of the genuine and far-reaching debate within the Party itself about goals and methods, which would have been the natural corollary of the strategy of redefinition. Since there was no room, while remaining a member, to disagree with the 'Party line', those who dissented had to resign.

A significant group on the left, led by one of the Party's women Members of Parliament, Rossana Rossanda, had already done precisely this in 1969, founding their own newspaper, *Il Manifesto*, to propagate their views. Unlike previous dissidents, this group was not easily snuffed out: it survived, encouraged by Jean-Paul Sartre, the guru of the French student movement, and supported by a handful of ex-Communist MPs. It attracted a considerable number of followers with its demand for the Party to return to a revolutionary tradition, which it had 'rediscovered' in the works of Gramsci, and its espousal of much of the 'impossibilist' agenda of the student movement. By 1972, however, even this had itself been outflanked on the left by *Lotta continua* and the 'autonomous' revolutionary mini-groups (*gruppuscoli*) which eventually coalesced into the Red Brigades. Although the success of these groups in recruiting support among the most marginalised of the urban population showed that the Communists no longer had monopoly control of radical dissent, it was also clear that in general they retained the mass following they had enjoyed since the war and that in a real sense they had shed an unnecessary burden with the departure of the totally intransigent protesters.

The Communists received a considerable boost, on the other hand, from the results of the first elections for the Regions which had finally been established in 1970.[12] In June 1975 they achieved a stunning success: their

---

12. The first Regions had been set up much earlier as a countermeasure to separatist tendencies in Sicily, the German-speaking Sudtirol (known in Italian as Alto Adige), and the French-speaking Valle d'Aosta. Progress on creating the Regions elsewhere had been blocked by the Christian Democrats, who, justifiably, feared the creation of a 'Red Belt' stretching from the Po to the Arno. By 1970, however, it was clear that Communist-controlled local governments were far from being subversive in their effects.

share of the vote, which had taken 30 years to creep up from 19 per cent to 27 per cent in national elections, suddenly rose to 33 per cent, only 1 per cent behind the tally of the Christian Democrats. In part this result was the outcome of their generally very creditable record of flexible and honest local government administration at municipal and provincial levels: the city of Bologna in particular, which they had controlled since the war, was beyond doubt the best run in the country and, because of their strict adherence to planning controls on building and their respect for the historic fabric of the city, the least damaged by the speculators. In the whole of central Italy they had fostered rather than held back the spontaneous development of local small and medium industries centred on such towns as Empoli, Prato, Modena and Reggio Emilia: for the mass of the electorate in these areas, to vote Communist was to vote for a stable and honest local government which encouraged enterprise. In 1975, to the areas they already dominated (Tuscany, Emilia-Romagna and Umbria), they added Piedmont and Liguria.

The Christian Democrats responded with their customary delaying tactics, proclaiming the unreadiness of the Communists to enter as trustworthy players into the democratic game, but at the same time giving unmistakable signs of interest, through their General Secretary, Benigno Zaccagnini, who was one of the rare Christian Democrats who had taken part in the armed Resistance, in the prospect of a 'grand coalition' in some indeterminate future, once their old enemies had finally rid themselves of all taint from their Stalinist past. The right wing of the Party, now led by Fanfani, was in considerable disarray because of the self-inflicted but historic defeat by a six-to-four majority of the referendum they had just promoted to abrogate the divorce law brought in by their own party only five years earlier, but it too was not entirely averse to having the implicit threat of an opening to the Communists to keep in check any unruliness in their left-wing partner in the coalition, the Socialists.

Despite the fact that the latter too had done quite well in the elections, they became thoroughly alarmed that the Christian Democrats would discard them in favour of the Communists, who were likely to be far less intransigent in matters of civil liberties. They therefore withdrew from the government, precipitating another early election, in which they hoped to re-establish their indispensability. Their calculations proved incorrect: in the June 1976 elections they lost heavily enough (to the Christian Democrats) to discredit the leadership which had chosen to seek the electoral contest: the elderly Neapolitan Francesco De Martino was replaced by the thrusting and ambitious 'young Turk', the Milanese Bettino Craxi.

The Communists had hoped finally to out-distance the Christian Democrats, but the very prospect of their doing so persuaded enough voters to switch from the right, as well as from the Socialists, to prevent it: though the Communists gained another percentage point, the Christian Democrats pulled away again to regain their previous unassailable position at almost 39 per cent. The only clear lesson of the elections, held against a continuing background

265

of left- and right-wing terrorism, was the confirmation that the existing political system was incapable of producing radical changes in the pattern of polarisation which had prevailed for three decades. Not even the adoption by the Communists of Berlinguer's programme of Eurocommunism abroad and the so-called 'historic compromise' at home had sufficed to propel the Party through the diffidence barrier at national, rather than local level.

At the time, both of these ideological and tactical initiatives had appeared to be of great significance and called forth a whole literature of exposition and analysis which was far from being confined to Italy. The idea that a distinctive, gentle, cultured and tolerant form of Communism might be developed in Western Europe, no longer tied to the crypto-Stalinist dictates of the Brezhnev régime (even being prepared to accept continued membership of NATO), and able to propose forms of socialism which did not depend upon the violent overthrow of the whole capitalist system, proved to be extremely attractive to many intellectuals throughout the West who were weary of Cold War attitudes and repelled by the image of US power and policies during the Vietnam and Nixon years.

The new approach to international relations was welcomed by Tito's Yugoslavia, bringing a renewed warmth after years of mutual hostility over Trieste. It had particular appeal to the Spanish Communists who were just emerging from the long night of the Franco régime into a restored democracy, and historically had had good reason to distrust the Soviet Union. They needed a new basis to establish their democratic *bona fides*: Berlinguer's mixture of gradualism and socialist idealism was precisely what they needed to replace the romantic but arid imperatives they had preached in the past. Although they did not excel in the first post-Franco elections, they outdid the Italians in the vigour of their rejection of subservience to Moscow.

The French Communists, too, showed interest in the new perspectives. The French party was then the only one in Western Europe with an electoral strength rivalling that of the Italian Communists. In November 1975, after a much-publicised meeting between Berlinguer and his French counterpart Georges Marchais, the latter declared that he now supported a democracy with the possibility of alternation of parties in power, thus abandoning the sacred doctrine of the necessity of the dictatorship of the proletariat. At the time the French Communists were preparing for national elections in alliance with the Socialists, and the polls predicted they would win.[13] With the three largest Western Communist Parties apparently converging on this new, open, independent programme for achieving their socialist objectives, and the smaller ones almost universally rushing to subscribe to the same club, Eurocommunism

---

13. In the end, the residual Stalinist tendencies of the French leadership destroyed any semblance of Eurocommunist convergence: in March 1987 the Socialist-Communist electoral alliance in France lost decisively at the polls, after months of disloyal sniping by the Communists against their partners, revealing they would prefer not to win at all rather than as a part of a Socialist-led coalition.

appeared to have arrived as a major initiative for peace and progress and centre of political attraction.

The corresponding domestic initiative, usually referred to as 'the historic compromise',[14] was apparently just as successful: within four years, the Communist Party had been accepted by all the other parties (with the exception of the neo-Fascists of the Italian Social Movement) as a respectable upholder of the democratic system and therefore one whose contribution to the governance of the country could also be accepted.

This new status was symbolised by the parliament's vote in 1976 to appoint Togliatti's widow, Nilde Jotti, as the Speaker of the lower house. It reflected the underlying strength of the Party as a provider in much of the north and centre of the country of sound local administration so well-tried that it had in effect become the 'establishment', controlling for the general benefit of the citizens the consumer and producer cooperative movement and the trade unions, and enjoying a cordial relationship with industrialists and businessmen. Their success as purveyors of clean local government had also contributed to changing the Communists' conception of the 'class struggle', whose role as the 'motor of history' was traditionally the basis of their ideology. They had broadened their constituency to include both the new technician and the old commercial, smallholding and artisan middle classes. By the 1970s they were frankly championing the interests of small and medium entrepreneurial capitalists (while still denouncing 'monopolists').

But although the new respectability of the Communists appeared to herald an early end to the isolation of the Party and an orderly approach to power-sharing with the Christian Democrats, it also had two negative collateral effects which Berlinguer had not foreseen. In the first place it provided the parties of the ruling coalition with an unrivalled opportunity to impose more or less vexatious conditions upon the way in which the Communists were to be integrated into the body politic: each time they sacrificed one of the sacred cows of Marxist doctrine on the altar of the new pragmatism, it was deemed insufficient to reassure those it was intended to impress, while at the same time reducing the Party's political room for manoeuvre by forcing it along a path of unilateral concessions.

Secondly, the Party was weakened by the growing discontent among its own followers about the real price of the 'historic compromise' in the currency of policy compromises: the tacit Communist support, in the name of 'national

14. The expression 'historic compromise' (*compromesso storico*) has often been misunderstood as meaning a 'compromise of historic importance'; what Berlinguer was referring to, however, was the way in which the historical development of the Italian State, reflected in the electoral system of the Republic, in practice imposed a 'grand coalition' government and inhibited the development of 'alternation' between parties or party-groupings within a general consensus about the nature of the 'national interest'. Togliatti's defence of Giolitti's 'transformism for progress' was cited as an example of 'historic compromise' from which Italy had benefitted.

solidarity' against terrorism, of the Christian Democrat governments between 1976 and 1979 brought neither political nor economic advantages to its electorate. In the local elections of 1978 they lost heavily while the Christian Democrats returned to over 40 per cent. In the 'anticipated' general election in the following year, even though Berlinguer had by then publicly abandoned the 'historic compromise', the Communists only managed to recoup half their losses, just reaching 30 per cent.

In fact, by transforming the image of the Italian Communist Party into that of a non-crusading, pragmatic party of reformers, prepared to abide by the rules of the parliamentary game and to join in the system of coalition-building based on compromise, Berlinguer had opened a Pandora's box which neither he nor his far less charismatic successors, Alessandro Natta and Achille Occhetto could hope to close. In a real sense the fate of the Communist Party in the most recent period of its existence corresponds very closely to that of the Soviet Communists after Mikhail Gorbachev introduced *perestroika* and *glasnost* into the USSR: once the 'historical inevitability' of a rigidly manichean system of belief and practice is opened to question, it becomes impossible to predict, far less to control, the process whereby it may change. The flexibility of the Italian Party over the period from 1968 onwards was, in fact, critically dependent upon the continued existence in an apparently indefinite perspective of Soviet Communism, and once the latter's structures and superstructures had crumbled, the 'uniqueness' of which Italian Communism boasted simply lost its relevance to the real world.

Early in 1978 the barely perceptible progress towards a new arrangement in Italian politics appeared to be changing pace. The patient groundwork of informal *combinazione* and terminological obfuscation carried out in their respective spheres of influence by Moro and Berlinguer seemed at last about to bear the fruit of an open agreement for Communist participation in government, at least in the form of a convention whereby parliamentary support for the ruling coalition would be forthcoming in exchange for firm commitments to reform in a number of policy areas. Even the scarcely veiled threat by the United States administration to deny any political or economic collaboration to an Italian government which included Communists was being quietly discounted.

Then, in its worst convulsion to date, the 'strategy of tension' again succeeded in its aim of blocking any such change. Moro's kidnapping was accompanied by a period of intense and very public collaboration between the Christian Democrats and the Communist Party to resist at all costs the pressures to do some sort of deal with the terrorists to save the statesman's life, and followed by a 'national unity' government led by Giulio Andreotti which the Communists supported from outside. Though initially these events appeared to precipitate the political process Moro had set in train, they proved almost immediately to be a massive political liability to Berlinguer's policy of 'historic compromise'.

Only two years after seeming to be ready to overtake the Christian Democrats, his party was once again trailing far behind them, while Berlinguer himself had been forced into making a humiliating U-turn, renouncing the policy of compromise in favour of a return to a far from clearly defined 'alternative', for and against which internal Party factions began to develop. Although Berlinguer survived this traumatic political experience, the new policy clearly represented the acceptance of a ticket back to the political ghetto from which the 'historic compromise' had been designed as the escape route. Berlinguer could not openly reverse the party's policies a second time without losing all credibility, although he directed most of his hostility against the Socialist Party, whose ambitious new leader, Craxi, was determined to beat the Communists at their own game by establishing the unbreakability of his alliance with the Christian Democrats. Berlinguer licensed senior members of the party to continue to advocate (and even informally to pursue) a renewed understanding with the Christian Democrats, but could not openly espouse the cause himself. He died of a heart attack which struck him down as he was addressing a mass rally in Milan. With cruel irony, the sympathy vote which had swung 40 per cent of the electorate back to the Christian Democrats after Moro's death, now produced a similar swing to the Communists in the European parliamentary elections of 1987, when they reached their historical electoral apogee of 35 per cent. This success was not carried over to the Italian national elections in the following year, when the Christian Democrat-Socialist alliance easily beat off the Communist challenge.

The political landscape for most of this period was well summarised by one of Italy's best-known experts on the south:

> A corrupt bureacracy accompanied by political corruption: a crash programme and its administration used as a game reserve or a bargaining counter with local and national political bosses as a function of the complex, often tortuous deals which underpin a 'Latin democracy', afflicted as it is in Italy by many of the old evils of squalid parliamentary wheeler-dealing and by the new evils of unthinking solidarity [...] The south has in fact called into question, and still does, the whole meaning of Italy: it has done so historically because of the way Italy was made and developed; it still does so politically and administratively today, and it is plain enough to anyone, it will continue to do so tomorrow'.[15]

The 'historic compromise' had failed to produce the sea-change in Italian politics which had been anticipated, while the Christian Democrats and their allies again enjoyed an unchallengeable tenure of political power and

15. G. Galasso, *Passato e presente nel meridionalismo*, Guida, Naples, 1978, pp. 217–18. A less charitable rendering of the 'Latin democracy', which has frequently been used in the Italian press more recently, would be 'a Banana Republic'.

269

patronage at national level. Yet, although the political system was less capable than ever of providing an efficient modernising state, the Italian economy once again began to provide the wealth needed to reconcile the majority of the population to allowing it to survive, despite the sea of corruption upon which it floated: private affluence appeared to be enough to compensate for public squalor.

Further, although all efforts to effect significant change at political level had failed, leaving the Italian electorate as rigidly polarised as it had been since the war, real shifts in public and private life had occurred. A programme of far-reaching social reforms was enacted, creating for the first time a comprehensive health service and the legislative back-up for genuine control of speculative development of urban areas. The implementation of these social provisions was entrusted to the newly-created Regional governments, which were finally provided with sufficient autonomy and finance to establish and run them. The aspects of these reforms which attracted greatest popular approval to begin with were the abolition of hundreds of 'useless quangos',[16] and the setting up of the Local Health Units, which were responsible for managing and coordinating all health services in a given area. Despite the fact that control of their activities was devolved to the Regions, the iron laws of *lottizzazione*, the party-system proportional share-out of jobs and favours, soon prevailed within the Health Units, and they became increasingly enmeshed in the same mechanisms of party influence and of direct and indirect corruption as the rest of the structures of the state.[17]

There was also a significant new trend, fostered by legislation, in the field of public information. Although, traditionally, most large cities in Italy had been the home to one or more daily newspapers of information, only a very small number of them had achieved anything like a national circulation. The political parties all had their own daily titles, but only the Communist *Unità*, achieved anything approaching a mass circulation, largely as the result of assiduous street-corner selling by faithful militants. The others, even the Socialist *Avanti!*, were 'loss-leaders' with minuscule circulations. The other media were just as hidebound and party dominated, preponderantly by the Christian Democrats whose appointees were in charge of their services which were largely devoted to game-shows, popular ballad festivals, and blandly boring news programmes. The most popular programme of all, watched regularly by young and old alike, was the nightly half-hour of advertising spots

---

16. Some of these, employing and providing pensions for thousands of clerks and administrators who had no work to do, were inherited from the pre-fascist and Fascist periods but had never been abolished because they provided a useful reservoir of favours in return for votes.

17. By 1992, public dissatisfaction with the totally inadequate performance of these units was being compounded almost daily by revelations not only of massive corruption in the award of contracts for supplies and building works, but of the direct involvement of the *mafia* in their running.

Figure 11.4 Laurel and Hardy come to the village cafe. The notice warns 'No watching TV without a purchase'.

which whetted the consumer appetites of a whole population.[18] Apart from this, public entertainment was still dominated by the cinema, where the enviable world reputation gained by neo-realists such as Vittorio De Sica, Roberto Rossellini and Luchino Visconti in the post-war years, had been confirmed by a whole new generation of *avant-garde* directors such as Federico

18. The impact of television on Italian social *mores* can hardly be exaggerated: one observer reported in 1958 that, on the evening when the most popular quiz ('Double or Quits') was broadcast, the population in and around a mountain village north of Florence, 'even decrepit peasants from the furthest farms, would come down the steep cart-tracks in the pouring rain, carrying a chair so that they could sit and watch' one of the 11 sets owned by the villagers (cited in Paul Ginsborg, *Storia d'Italia dal dopoguerra a oggi*, Einaudi, Turin, 1989, p. 328).

Figure 11.5 Emancipation by referendum: Italian feminists demonstrate, Milan 1976.

Fellini and Michelangelo Antonioni, who succeeded in combining a serious critique of Italian society and culture with a cinematic style which captured the admiration of a mass public.

After the social and cultural ferments of 1968–71, however, the public interest in and demand for a wider range of information sources and entertainment in printed and electronic media began to make itself felt more strongly in parallel with the mushroom growth of television ownership. The Constitutional Court ruling in 1974 that the state monopoly was illegal was immediately followed by an unregulated explosion of private broadcasting on both radio and television, some of it politically provocative, most of it at a depressingly abysmal technical and cultural level, but nevertheless hugely popular. The overnight passage from dismal uniformity to untrammelled cacophony was reminiscent of the great release of comment and gossip which swept the country in the heady weeks which followed the surrender of Italy to the Allies in 1943: a chance to express pent-up feelings and opinions was bound to be welcomed by a population so long frustrated by the paternalist repression of its subjectivity by Church and state.

Another result of the panic in government which followed the events of 1968–69 had been the implementation of the Constitutional provision for popular referenda with legislative effect, which could be initiated on the basis of a proposal bearing at least half a million signatures. It bore fruit very quickly, for it gave an opportunity to by-pass the party-dominated parliamentary system and put forward proposals intended to force the authorities into radical policies, which was seized upon by a number of fringe and pressure groups, such as Marco Pannella's Radical Party, spawned by the student movement, and the environmental and ecological groups. The proposals could easily gather half a million signatures, but were regularly voted down by the cautious majority of citizens. One of the referenda, however, was very different, and marked a major turning-point in Italian post-war history. This was the referendum launched by the Christian Democrats in 1974 to abrogate the 1972 law permitting divorce.

The Christian Democrats had until then been prepared to stand aside and allow, albeit with some reluctance, the women's movement and the lay forces in parliament to make the running in the matter. Within the party, however, the right wing and the integralists were chafing against this lax attitude. With the powerful encouragement of the Vatican and Catholic Action, Fanfani took up the cause, not only because he was sincerely convinced that divorce was morally unjustified, but also because if his campaign succeeded it would mean that he would be able to resume full command of the Christian Democrat Party which was being steered by Moro in a direction of which he disapproved, since it left him no space in which to promote his ambitions as a neo-Gaullist. But despite the fulminations of the bishops and the rabble-rousing appeals to southern *machismo* by Fanfani, three in five Italians voted to retain the law, with its progressive provisions which finally brought a European measure of emancipation to Italian women. It also, to almost universal relief, put an end to Fanfani's active political career.[19]

Italian literature also clearly reflected the national change in mood which occurred during this period, even if the Italian public continued to buy fewer serious books per head than any other population in Western Europe. The writers, such as Cesare Pavese, Italo Calvino, Giorgio Bassani and Giuseppe Tommaso di Lampedusa who had achieved world recognition and whose experience spanned the inter-war years as well as those of the Republic, were now joined by equally illustrious names whose success was won in a world cultural context which no longer accepted the traditional narrative or psychological novel as an adequate basis for literature. Leonardo Sciascia made brilliant use of the form of the detective story to penetrate the oppressive layers of Sicilian reality, while Umberto Eco, moving from linguistics to literature, became one of the European standard-bearers of 'deconstruction'.

Italian intellectuals had, throughout the Renaissance and modern periods

---

19. Nevertheless, the Christian Democrats, again influenced by fulminating bishops, successfully (with the support of the neo-Fascists) placed extreme limits on the provisions of the 1976 abortion law reform, prompting a 100,000-strong women's protest demonstration in Rome. This hint was taken and when, after the intervening election, the bill returned to parliament, the Christian Democrats introduced only minor amendments.

of European history, always been cosmopolitan, easily stepping beyond the local characteristics of their native culture. Their lack of parochialism now combined with their familiarity with the rich traditions of the arts and crafts which flourished in the peninsula to create a stylishness in every field, from fashion in clothing to car-body design and from cuisine to architecture. This capacity for acceptable originality in design merged increasingly often with the flexibility of response to market made possible by the high-technology small and medium enterprise which permeated the economic structures of the 'Third Italy' to enable Italian products to become world leaders in fields such as clothing, textiles, leatherware, interior décor and the multiplicity of personal accoutrements which characterise contemporary fashion: during the late 1970s and most of the 1980s Benetton, Armani and Versace products became the most imitated in the world. Their success rubbed off on other, less stylish, products simply because they were Italian-made: the overall effect was to create an export-led economic growth which lasted through most of that decade and greatly benefitted the national economy (and inspired an unjustified confidence in its prospects) at a time when the diseconomies of *clientelismo* were already creating distortions which in other circumstances might have become rapidly uncontrollable. As so often in the post-war period, the economy had come to the rescue of a flawed political system and an inadequate political culture. But there was no certainty that such a rescue could be repeated as the world recession gathered pace at the end of the decade.

Italy in the 1980s and 1990s

On 15 March 1980 Italo Calvino, one of Italy's best-known post-war novelists and the compiler of a classic collection of Italian folk tales and fables, published an article in the newspaper *La Repubblica* which he ironically entitled 'Apology for honesty in the country of the corrupted'.[1] Though not exactly an historical document, it clarifies perhaps better than any number of statistics or case-histories the precise nature of the relationship between private and public morality which from 1960 onwards has dominated political and civic life in Italy.

> Once there was a country which was built on what was unlawful. Not that it lacked laws, nor that the political system was not based on principles which most people said they agreed with. But this system, which was split up into a large number of centres of power, needed vast sums of money (**needed** them because once you get used to having lots of money you can't imagine life without it) and the only way they could obtain this money was by breaking the law, i.e. by asking for money from those who had it in exchange for unlawful favours. Or rather, those who had money to give away for favours had usually made that money because they had received favours earlier on. Consequently it was a somewhat circular and not inharmonious economic system.
>
> Though financing themselves unlawfully the centres of power were free of any sense of guilt because their own value system assured them that anything done for the sake of the group was permissible, indeed praiseworthy, inasmuch as the group saw its own power and the common weal as one and the same thing; breaking the letter of the law thus did not exclude a higher 'real' legality.

1. The article was reprinted as being of undiminished relevance in October 1992, in the same newspaper.

To tell the truth, in every illicit transaction in favour of collective bodies it is customary for a share to be kept by individuals as a fair recompense for their essential activities in seeking out and arranging the transaction: thus the law-breaking which their system of values assured them was permissible involved a margin of law-breaking which was not permissible in terms of those values.

But on closer inspection the individual who was in the position of pocketing his individual cut of the collective cut, was sure that he had only taken his individual cut in order to assist the group to take its collective one, which meant that he could quite sincerely persuade himself that his conduct was not only permissible but praiseworthy.

The country also had at the same time an extravagant official budget, fed by taxes upon every legal activity, and legally financed all those who legally or illegally managed to tap its funds. Since no one in that country was prepared to consider going bankrupt, nor even to be out of pocket (and it was far from obvious upon what grounds anyone could have been asked to do so), tax-payers' money was used to cover legally, in the name of the interests of the public, the deficits on activities which, still in the name of the interests of the public, had excelled in illegality.

The collection of taxes which in other times and cultures could rely upon the sense of civic duty, in that country amounted to no more than an act of coercion (just as, in some parts of the country, to the State's exactions were added those imposed by gangsters or the *mafia*) to which the tax-payer submitted simply to avoid even greater trouble, not with the feeling of relief at a duty well done but with the unpleasant sensation of having been a passive accomplice of the maladministration of public affairs and of having accepted that unlawful activities should enjoy the privilege of tax-exemption.

Now and again, when it was least expected, a court decided to apply the law, causing little earthquakes in a few of the centres of power and even the arrest of persons who until then had reason to think themselves beyond the law. In such cases the dominant feeling was not a sense of satisfaction that justice had been done, but the suspicion that one centre of power had simply got the better of another. So that it was hard to be sure whether the use of the law was now merely a tactical or strategic weapon in the feuds between illegal interests, or whether the courts, in order to justify the performance of their duties, now had to persuade people that they too were centres of power and illegal interests just like all the others.

A situation like this was, of course, also propitious for criminal organisations of the traditional kind, which through kidnappings and bank robberies jumped, when least expected, on to the 'lots of money' merry-go-round, sending some of it spinning down secret channels from which sooner or later it emerged in a thousand unexpected forms of legal or illegal finance.

Against this system terrorist organisations were gaining ground, using the methods of obtaining finance usually employed by outlaws, and following a well-thought out plan of regular murders among all classes of well-known and obscure citizens, and were putting themselves forward as the only all-embracing alternative to the system. But their effect upon the system was to strengthen it. Indeed, they became its indispensable prop, for they confirmed its own conviction that it was the best possible system and should not be changed in any way.

Thus all forms of law-breaking, from the slyest to the fiercest, were welded into a system which had its own stability, cohesion and consistency, and in which many people could pursue their own material advantage without losing the moral advantage of a clear conscience. The inhabitants of that country might well have considered themselves unanimously to be happy, had it not been for the existence of a still numerous class of citizens who did not appear to have any part to play in it: the honest.

The latter were not honest for any special reason (they did not claim to be inspired by high principles of patriotism, social concern or religious faith, for none of these were any longer current); they were honest by habit of mind, by upbringing, by reflex action. They just couldn't do anything to stop themselves from being like that, from thinking the things they cared about could not be bought for money, from having thought-processes still based on outmoded linkages between earnings and work, between esteem and merit, and on doing as you would be done by.

In that country where everyone had a clear conscience, the honest were the only ones to be so scrupulous as to wonder all the time what was the right thing to do. They knew that moralising at other people, getting indignant about them, telling them what was right and wrong are things that all too easily win general applause, whether sincere or not. They didn't think power was interesting enough to dream of having it themselves (not at least the power that the others were seeking); they did not delude themselves that the same evils did not exist elsewhere in the world, even if they were less evident; they didn't hope for a better society because they knew that something worse was always more likely.

Should they have resigned themselves to dying out? No, they consoled themselves with the thought that just as on the margins of every society for thousands of years an alternative society of highwaymen, pickpockets, petty thieves and confidence tricksters had

carried on existing which had never dreamed of replacing 'society' but
only of surviving in the crevices of the dominant society and of
maintaining its own style of life in the teeth of conventional morality,
so the alternative society of the honest would manage to carry on for
centuries, with no other desire than to live in its own different way, to
feel different from everyone else, and so perhaps in the end to mean
something important for everyone, to represent something which
could no longer be expressed in words, for which the words are not
yet ready and which we cannot yet define.[2]

This bleakly depressing moral analysis of modern Italian society has apparently
been confirmed repeatedly over the decade since Calvino's article was written.
A cynical acronym, formed from the initials of the surnames of the brash
Secretary of the Socialists and the Christian Democrats' evergreen Prime
Minister and Party Secretary, then Italy's three most powerful men, was coined
to denote the seemingly unbreakable bond between the indispensable master-
manipulators of the politics of patronage which dominated national public and
private life.[3] The 'CAF' (Craxi, Andreotti, Forlani) was always a jump ahead
of its critics, endlessly ingenious in buying or bullying parliamentary trouble-
makers into acquiescence, and apparently fireproof against all the evidence of
the corrupt practices which were the stock in trade of their parties. During the
second half of the 1980s they apparently enjoyed a charmed life, for despite
the huge and growing financial deficit due to the practice of government
borrowing at high rates of interest in order to fund the extravagant subsidisation of the southern patronage system (including pay-offs to the *mafia*, *camorra*
and *'ndrangheta*, whose takings amounted by 1990 to some 13 per cent of
total GNP), the economic motor of the north and centre, stimulated by the
prospect of the trading opportunities of the Single European Market, was still
pulling strongly in boom conditions.

Opinion polls revealed that the 'wily old fox', Andreotti, despite the
common belief that he was in league with the *mafia* to maintain himself in
power, was the most popular politician ever recorded in the post-war period.
He was particularly admired for his apparent ability to secure advantages for
Italy, or at least favourable notices, in the field of foreign policy without

---

2. Copyright © 1980, by The Estate of Italo Calvino, reprinted with the permission of
Wylie, Aitken & Stone, Inc. If poetic licence might be suspected here, the recent scandals
would have served to dispel it: in November 1993, for example, it was discovered that
the top echelon of Italy's main counter-espionage agency, SISDE, had been involved in
massive embezzlement of official secret funds both for their personal gain and to
subsidise terrorism and destabilisation within Italy. Of particular deviousness was the
practice of paying off the ransoms for selected *mafia*, *camorra* and *'ndrangheta* kidnap
victims, despite the law which explicitly prohibited all such transactions.
3. Craxi was frequently depicted by cartoonists as a neo-Mussolini, dressed in black
shirt, jackboots and fez, and carrying a whip, while Forlani was normally depicted
wearing a priestly *biretta* and Andreotti with a poker face distorted by a sly smile.

incurring any real costs. This sleight of hand was particularly evident during the Gulf War of 1990–91, when by the nominal commitment of a small air-force contingent, combined with carefully orchestrated hints that Italy was holding back the more hawkish members of the anti-Iraq coalition, he secured both United States approval and Arab sympathy. It was a carefully controlled exercise in making powerlessness respectable and even attractive.

By the end of the decade the well-tried political equilibria which had permitted the unbroken reign of Christian Democracy and its junior partners were, however, beginning to become unstable as the imperatives of the Cold War lost their cogency and the Italian electorate became less tolerant of their corrupt and inefficient welfare state. In the north the coalition of the Lombard, Piedmontese and Venetian Leagues, a new populistic movement of the middle classes, began to assert itself with increasing vehemence. It was politically inchoate but highly dynamic, gathering to itself the accumulated resentments of those in the north who regarded themselves as the wealth creators of the country dragged down by the burden of southern economic and social failure. Widely denounced by the shocked intellectuals of the left and centre as expressing the four-ale bar politics of anti-southern racism and pseudo-Fascism, its leader, an untidy, colloquial, Milanese called Umberto Bossi, was nevertheless elected to the Senate in the elections of 1988.

In the local elections of 1990, the movement made big gains, becoming the leading opposition party in several major cities. The conventional political wisdom remained, however, that it would soon lose its impetus, especially when it found itself obliged to take administrative responsibility through its electoral successes. Such critics had failed to appreciate the strength of feeling, among the 'little men' of the northern shopkeeper, professional and artisan classes, against what the Italian State had become since 1948 under the influence of the party system, the *partitocrazia*, which creamed off the wealth of the hard-working north to benefit its placemen and hangers-on elsewhere. Their most popular slogan, *Roma ladrona*, expressed their hatred of these 'thieves from Rome'. Insofar as the movement had a policy, it harked back to a populistic version of federalism, which for many, perhaps most, of its followers signified secession of the north. It threatened to organise a tax rebellion by its supporters.

Then, in April 1992, the Leagues made a historic breakthrough in the general elections, scoring more than 20 per cent of the vote in the three main northern regions, at the expense of Christian Democrats, Socialists and the Communists, now renamed the Democratic Party of the Left.[4] The Christian Democrats also lost votes on a large scale in Sicily to an anti-*mafia* party

---

4. The hardliners of the Party, who refused to abandon its Leninist name and tradition, founded a new party called *Rifondazione comunista* (Refounded Communism), which succeeded in retaining almost a third of the former Italian Communist Party's supporters.

created by a dissident former Christian Democrat mayor of Palermo, Leoluca Orlando, who threatened to become the southern equivalent of the *Lega*'s Umberto Bossi.

The overall results of the election already marked an unprecedented change in the Italian political landscape, with substantial losses for all the main traditional parties.[5] Craxi, who during the campaign had publicly proclaimed himself to be the only possible prime minister and had even gone to the lengths of naming the ministers he proposed to appoint to his cabinet, faced not a quick and easy return to power but a long struggle to bludgeon his potential partners into making way for it.

At this point, in May 1992, a criminal investigation (aptly code-named 'Clean Hands') into corrupt practices in the Commune of Milan began to reveal in all its squalid detail a picture of generalised malpractice and gross corruption in favour of the Socialist Party and its allies who for years had run the city where Craxi had his power-base and where the Socialist members of the administration (including his own son Bobo) had been hand-picked by him.[6] The former mayor, Paolo Pillitteri was at the centre of the web but it quickly became apparent that the soliciting of bribes from businessmen and contractors had for years been normal practice. In keeping with Calvino's analysis, all the political figures involved claimed to have accepted and handled the bribes only for the sake of the party (and therefore for the public good). Dozens of arrests were made, not only of Socialist councillors, but also of Christian Democrats and Communists who had been allied to them, and of the prominent industrialists who had given bribes in return for favours. Three of the Socialists committed suicide. Craxi himself was not yet directly implicated, but there was more than enough evidence to suggest that he could not have been ignorant of what his henchman had been doing.

Milan was not the south: its citizens had always proudly claimed the city to be the country's 'capital of honest hard work'. As the scandal bloomed,

---

Figure 12.1 A cartoonist's view of Umberto Bossi's first successful assault on 'Bribesville', when the *Lega* made notable gains in local elections in Milan: the 'troops' are wearing the *Lega* emblem, while the defenders are, from left to right, Forlani, De Mita, Craxi and Occhetto. The historical reference is, of course, to the 'Five Days' of the 1848 rising against the Austrians.

---

5. Although nothing to be compared with what happened only a year later in the local elections of June 1993, when the Socialist vote collapsed in Milan to less than 3 per cent and the Christian Democrat vote was halved.

6. The investigation had begun in February, when the peculations of Mario Chiesa, the principal Socialist go-between used by contractors to set up their deals with the Milan city council, were reported by his estranged wife. In an attempt to get his sentence reduced, Chiesa agreed to cooperate fully with the investigators. In November 1992 he was sentenced to six years imprisonment and a fine equivalent to £4,000,000. The total of corrupt payments received by him on behalf of his party was five times this amount.

fly-posters and graffitti appeared at all the entrances to the city proclaiming 'Welcome to *Tangentopoli* (Bribesville)' in ironic imitation of the more usual tourist welcome signs. Within a few days, Antonio Di Pietro, the most charismatic of the team of investigating magistrates conducting 'Operation Clean Hands', had become a popular hero for the whole population.[7] Craxi tried to counter-attack by publicly suggesting that the magistrates were part of a conspiracy of his enemies, but was unable to provide any evidence. His credibility sank even lower, but he still struggled to retain his position as party leader, evidently calculating that the storm would blow over and he would then be able to stake his claim to govern once more.

An immediate result of the electoral success of the *Lega* was to revive the long-running and generally sterile debate about the need for a revised constitution for the country, with particular reference to the electoral system and the rôle of the presidency and prime minister. There were deep divisions both between and within the parties on these issues, the deepest being those which separated the 'presidentialists' from the 'parliamentarists', and the supporters of proportional representation from the advocates of a British or French-style constituency system. The 'old guard' in all the parties preferred as little to be changed as was consistent with impressing the public that something had really been done to make the party-system less involuted, but not to loosen its hold on power. Above all they rejected any serious alteration to the principle of proportional representation, since it was the keystone of the party dominance of political life: through proportional representation the electorate delegated their choices of individuals to represent them to the party machines. Those who controlled, and benefitted from controlling, these machines were not at all eager to see them dismantled.

Others were convinced that the reason for the alarming dual success of the *mafia* and *Lega* was to be found in the disrepute which the professional politicians had incurred in the mushroom clouds of scandal which now shrouded a structurally imperfect welfare state which was no longer capable of delivering even basic services and amenities to the public. In short, they feared that the Italian electoral worm had really turned at last and that the democratic system itself might be fatally undermined if they persisted in their customary corrupt wheeling and dealing. Some of these dissidents, from parties across most of the political spectrum, came together to formulate a cross-party referendum campaign to promote the cause of radical constitutional change which would lead to a president elected by the people and a parliament no longer based on proportional representation of parties at national level. At this point, early in the summer of 1992, these reformers and the *Lega* were still looking askance at each other, although

---

7. The truth of this may be gauged by the fact that the traditional figurines produced by Neapolitan popular craftsmen to populate Christmas cribs in 1993 included several versions of Di Pietro. Only Garibaldi had previously enjoyed this honour.

objectively speaking their demands for structural political change were fundamentally convergent.

In the meantime, amidst all the tumult, the respected and patently honest Christian Democrat Oscar Luigi Scalfaro had, after a record number of ballots in the combined Chamber and Senate, become the successor to the increasingly eccentric Francesco Cossiga, who had resigned early after becoming a deep embarrassment to his own party because of his continual egocentric *ex cathedra* interventions in political matters and his acceptance of the political support of the neo-Fascist Italian Social Movement for his declared ambition to be re-elected as a French-style executive president.

Under intense pressure from the new president, who let it be understood that he was not prepared to instal as prime minister a man so evidently affected by scandal, and from all the prospective partners in a renewed coalition (which in any case could, after the success of the *Lega*, muster only a slim majority), Craxi reluctantly nominated one of his chief lieutenants, Giuliano Amato, to form a new coalition cabinet. After further extended negotiations Amato succeeded in forming what was in effect a transition government. Faced with the mounting pressure for a thorough clean-up of political life and a return to financial probity and stability in state expenditures (whose parlous condition led to a forced devaluation and ignominious exit from the European Monetary System in September 1992), the new government announced a drastic pro-gramme of new taxes and cuts in welfare expenditure. Most radical of all was the programme, reminiscent of the sale of Church lands in the 1870s, of privatisation of the 60 per cent of the Italian economy controlled directly or indirectly by the State, a move which would inevitably lead to the wholesale purging of the thousands of party placemen who currently controlled the industries and services involved. Through clenched teeth it was even foreshad-owed that the state-controlled media would be removed from party control.[8] Meanwhile a joint commission of Chamber and Senate would consider amend-ments to the Constitution which would make it possible to avoid the threatened referendum.[9]

The corollary of the federalism (or separatism) of the Leagues was the resurgence of the *mafia*, *camorra* and *'ndrangheta* in the south, once the alliance between them and the Christian Democrats had been broken at the end of the decade. This significant development was due primarily to the increasing independence and boldness of parts of the judiciary in fighting

---

8. There was considerable doubt, however, about the authenticity of the privatisation programme, since some Ministers appeared to believe that an all-embracing 'unit trust' in which the state would retain overall control of the sectors concerned would suffice, while others were demanding a wholesale sell-off of assets on the open market, in order to attract large-scale investment from abroad.

9. A provision of the law on referendums was that, if the parliament passed legislation substantially meeting the substance of the referendum concerned during the year before the date it was to be held, recourse to the popular vote was cancelled.

these criminal organisations consequent upon their increased involvement, from the mid-1960s onwards, in international drug trafficking. Italy's partners in Europe and, above all, the United States clearly signalled to the country's rulers that they expected results in the campaign against this scourge. It became increasingly problematic even for the best placed friends of the 'honoured society' to provide the protection from the processes of law which they had previously been able to dispense in return for control of the southern electorate.

The murder in 1982 of the newly-appointed special anti-*mafia* commissioner, General Carlo Alberto Dalla Chiesa, and his wife had set off a wave of revulsion and determination among the judicial community as well as the general public, and in 1987 his colleagues led by the judges Giovanni Falcone and Paolo Borsellino, brought no fewer than 456 *mafiosi* to trial at once, including some of the most famous bosses, such as Luciano Liggio and Michele Greco. Most were sentenced to imprisonment and 19 to life.[10]

The *mafiosi* were outraged, but Andreotti's chief political henchman in Sicily and the bosses' main contact in Rome, the former mayor of Palermo Salvo Lima, hastened to reassure them that they would be released on appeal, since it would be arranged that the appeals were heard by a judge who could be trusted to allow them on the slightest technical infringement of the rights of the accused during the investigations. In the meantime they would be released on bail. When the appeals finally came to be heard, however, the judge in question had been taken off the list, and all the appeals were turned down.[11] True to its traditions, the *mafia* immediately 'punished' the man who had failed it: Lima was gunned down in a busy Palermo street. There were, of course, no witnesses. The pact with the *mafia*'s friends in the state was suspended: in the summer of 1992 judges Falcone and Borsellino were assassinated by massive bombs in two separate incidents which were clearly intended to demonstrate that the *mafia* still controlled the streets of Palermo.[12] There is no reason to

---

10. Dalla Chiesa was widely respected for his effective work in suppressing the left-wing terrorism of the 1970s.

11. The Supreme Court of Appeal judge involved in these acquittals, Corrado Carnevale, known as 'the sentence-quasher', was forced to request his own transfer from the criminal to the civil section of the Court in December 1992.

12. In October 1992, one of the main *mafia* supergrasses, Leonardo Messina, alleged that Andreotti had been the recipient of *mafia* requests for favours via his most trusted lieutenant in Sicily, Salvo Lima. This first piece of concrete evidence against Andreotti was quickly followed by further allegations by many of the *mafiosi* 'penitents' helping the judiciary. In March 1993 Andreotti was formally accused of complicity in *mafia* activities, and in May, after the landslide victory of the 'Yes' vote in the referendum on electoral reform, his parliamentary colleagues lifted his immunity from prosecution, despite his vehement protests that there was a conspiracy against him between the *mafia* and the Palermo magistrates. Wilier than Craxi, Andreotti – having lost the argument – voted with the majority, declaring that the only court he really feared was that of the Last Judgement.

Figure 12.2 On trial behind bars: some of the 456 defendants in the marathon Mafia court case in Palermo, 1987.

doubt, moreover, that it still controls enough of the electorate of the south to ensure the success of any party it chooses to support there: the implication for its former political friends is crystal clear. Northern secessionism may soon be rivalled by a Sicilian movement aiming at a Cypriot or Maltese solution, '*Cosa nostra*' being replaced by a '*Cosa vostra*' in the shape of a tailor-made political party.

These recent strongly centrifugal tendencies in Italian politics lead directly back to the central issue underlying so great a part of Italy's troubled unity. An Italian government based on the *partitocrazia* which has dominated political life for over 40 years is very unlikely to be able to summon up the moral resources, and hence the credibility with a thoroughly disillusioned electorate, to tackle the immense problems which now confront the country. The air, at the end of 1992, was thick with proposals and counter-proposals for constitutional and electoral reform, for a thorough clean-up of public life, for an in-depth renewal of party structures and personnel, as well as with the heady rhetoric of populistic movements (above all the *Lega*) demanding the break-up of Italy, or at least its conversion into a federal, or confederal, state. Only the last of these programmes appeared to be achieving any real measure of popular support, but in the absence of any clearly articulated and realistic policy for achieving the ends proclaimed by the *Lega*, that support was thought likely to be short-lived. The party system had lost the confidence of the people, but no obviously viable and confidence-building alternative vision had emerged. For half a century most Italians had been voting against what they disliked rather than in favour of any set of policies or persons. Some observers felt that the continued withholding of their confidence in what they irreverently call *la compagnia del papocchio*[13] could well lead to a situation in which the old *nomenklatura* remains at the controls of an administrative machine which has completely stalled.

The similarities with the conditions prompting Pelloux's attempted monarcho-military coup of 1898, the Tambroni adventure of 1960 and, of course, the rise to power of Mussolini in 1922, were for most Italians too uncomfortable to ignore. Yet there were no obvious candidates for any forcible seizure of power in the name of 'law and order', indeed the bulldogs of the state, whether *carabinieri* or the other branches of the forces of order, at last earning the applause of the public, were palpably enjoying their work of tracking down and arresting *mafiosi* and corrupt politicians, no longer trammelled by the demoralising necessity to temper their professional activity to the sensitive interests of an all-powerful *nomenklatura*. At the same time, despite the continuing tide of *avvisi di garanzia* (notices of investigation) directed at hundreds of politicians and businessmen, prominent or scarcely known, it was equally clear that those under investigation or threatened by it were determined to outlast their accusers, using every parliamentary and legal means available to cling to their power and privileges. Well-informed observers, both domestic and foreign, were shaking their heads and foreseeing only worse trouble to come, whether in the form of an authoritarian *revanche*, or endemic and unlimited anarchy. The international markets reflected this unease, and the Italian currency, effectively free-floating since its exit from the European Monetary System, continued to slide towards the cliff-edge of inconvertibility: even the Italian economy, whose pulling-power had previously always counter-balanced political crises, seemed to teeter on the verge of collapse.[14]

At the end of 1992, in the joint parliamentary committee considering the framework for constitutional (and above all electoral) reform, the ex-Communists (now Party of the Democratic Left) found themselves once again on the horns of their classical dilemma, but in a new guise. Should they use their current parliamentary weight (deriving from the results of an election considerably divergent from subsequent poll findings, and the actual results of local elections) to tip the balance towards a 'grand coalition' solution (Christian

---

13. A rough equivalent might be 'The Fudge Conspiracy'.
14. It was reported, during one of the increasingly frequent market panics of November 1993, that an Italian central banker who asked a London counterpart why the international markets were selling Italian stocks and shares at knock-down prices, received the brutal response: 'Would you want to book a holiday in Croatia just now?'.

Democrats, Italian Socialist Party and the ex-Communists of the 'Party of the Democratic Left')? This would satisfy their 45 years of longing to return to a power-sharing government (Achille Occhetto referring to the 'Party's duty to govern'), but would also effectively prop up the existing *partitocrazia*. Or should they use it to deal a knock-out blow to that system by assuring a parliamentary majority for proposals to replace it by an English or French constituency electoral arrangement? This would, however, tend to eliminate minor and splinter parties, and would probably divide Italy into a *Lega*-dominated north, a central area (Emilia-Romagna, Tuscany, Umbria, the Marches and even parts of the Abruzzi) where the Party of the Democratic Left would be the natural party of government, and a *mafia*-assisted Christian Democrat south.

Such an outcome would be likely to prompt the groups dominant in each segment to press for a federal, or even a confederal, arrangement rather than a unitary 'national' one. It would be a possible answer, in the north and centre, to the problems of national identity, but probably not to those of politics and economics. It seemed likely that the choice made by Occhetto and the Party of the Democratic Left would, however, confirm the ex-Communist party's traditionally conservative, centralist propensities as against its recent flirtations with ideas of systemic innovation.

The consequences of either choice were difficult to predict. If the Party of the Democratic Left opted for consolidation of the existing system (even if embellished by cosmetic changes to win over protest voters), it might end by being swept away with the other components of the *partitocrazia*, particularly if the electorate's toleration of corruption in high places (calculated by then to amount to the equivalent of over two billion pounds per annum) were replaced by the total revulsion which would seem to be the most appropriate response to revelations that not only were prominent local and national politicians involved in corrupt deals with the *mafia* but that some had actually employed *mafia* killers to remove politically or financially 'inconvenient' rivals and associates.[15]

On the other hand, if the Party of the Democratic Left chose the path of supporting the radical innovators, including a few mavericks among its own deputies, who wanted the electoral system reformed to enforce the personal accountability of those elected, it perhaps risked becoming no more than the political 'establishment' of a Central-Italian 'Slovenia', a geographically limited area whose economic viability might be questionable and with virtually no weight in the international arena.

---

15. Magistrates investigating the murder in 1989 of Lodovico Ligato, former Chairman of the Italian State Railways (himself earlier found guilty of corrupt practices), after three years of fruitless enquiries baulked by a complete lack of witnesses, arrested 11 leading members of the ruling municipal council of Reggio Calabria for conspiracy to have him murdered by the local *'ndrangheta*. It was clear from the detailed evidence in the indictment that almost overnight a large number of witnesses had become available. The irresistible question was: for what reason at this juncture?

What remained certain was that the process of reconciling Italians to the implications of a renewal of a centralist national state would be far more problematic than ever before – and the alternatives scarcely more attractive. The confusion surrounding the proposals for systemic reform by a parliament which could no longer claim any legitimacy after the latest election and referendum results reflected the imperfection of Italy both as a nation and as a state. It could not reasonably be supposed that the members of such a parliament could correct it.

The pessimism which this spectacle inspired in the hearts of most Italians (and of those non-Italians who have formed a loving attachment to Italy's history and the hopes of its long-suffering people) was recently expressed by an eminent and widely respected elder journalist and may serve as a fitting last comment upon the country's present and its past:

> the ancient vice, the ancient weakness of a country which knows how to recover from lost wars and get a devastated economy running again, this vital yet morally soft country which cannot stomach the word revolution, whether democratic or violent, but has to drain the cup of the mistakes and misdeeds of its princes and tyrants and its own complicity and fatalism [...] though the innocent be slaughtered and our dearest and most treasured possessions be destroyed, yet our bitter cup we still must drain to the very last drop, even unto Mussolini hanging by his feet in Piazzale Loreto [...] Our revolutions and our subversive coups have always loomed up clearly for years, when they happen we already know them by heart, we always hope against hope that something will turn up, hiding behind caution and ambiguity. We are a vital but morally soft country and our rulers, cultivating cleverness far more than dignity, know what we are, and trample over us to the bitter end, until it takes only the least puff of wind to knock them off their perch.[16]

In the context of Italian history, the question that loomed ever larger was: what, and who, could possibly take the place of these institutions?

There was, however, one hopeful sign, if somewhat negative in character: the vast mass of Italians (in electoral terms never less than 80 per cent of the voters) still flocked to the polls whenever there was any opportunity to express political feelings, even though the unreformed proportional system still normally failed to produce any immediate resolution and still enabled the parties to dominate in tortuous post-election bargaining. The only acts of violence, fearful though they were, remained clearly the currency of organised crime and

---

16. Giorgio Bocca, 'Un cumulo di macerie' ['A heap of rubble'], *La Repubblica*, 16 December 1992, leading article commenting upon the indictment of Bettino Craxi, the longest-serving prime minister since De Gasperi, on a long series of charges of corruption, receiving bribes, and breaking the law governing the financing of political parties.

not of politics.[17] Mass rallies and demonstrations, though often angry and usually inflamed by rabble-rousing oratory, did not lead to significant violence against persons or property as they had in the 1960s and 1970s. Underlying the furious popular reaction to the revelations of *Tangentopoli* and *mafia* involvement in politics, there was nevertheless perceptible a deep-seated faith in the political process and in the resources of a democratic system equipped with an independent judiciary. Sooner or later the moment of decision would be reached, and it still seemed likely that it would occur through the ballot-box.

17. Evidence emerged in late 1993, however, that the corrupt leadership of the SISDE counter-intelligence agency may have been involved in organising some of these outrages, or at least claiming responsibility for them through a mysterious terrorist group known as the 'Armed Falange' in order to destabilise the political system. It was widely assumed that they were likely to have been prompted to do so by political forces eager to defend the *status quo*.

Afterword

However hazardous it may be for an historian to suggest so predictive a view, the events of the first six months of 1993 appear to represent a truly rare occurrence in Italian history: a genuine turning-point. To justify this assertion, it is necessary to place it in the context of a more global interpretation than any so far put forward in this book. This risky venture is attempted in the following addition to and enlargement of the original text (completed late in 1992). It is to be hoped that, in 1994, hindsight will not make it necessary to warn the reader to ignore it.

In the wake of the turbulent years of student protest and trade-union militancy between 1968 and 1971, a large-scale attitude and opinion survey was carried out among the 14–25 years age-group to try to measure what changes had occurred as a result of the experience. It was generally assumed that there must have been significant mutations in value-systems, amounting perhaps to a 'cultural revolution'. When the results were analysed, however, the researchers discovered that, underlying the new catch-phrases adopted by young people, the predominant pattern of attitudes were those long familiar to observers and historians of contemporary Italian society, usually denoted as 'amoral familism', 'authoritarian indifference to others', 'xenophobia', 'political and economic conservatism', 'political apathy' and 'individualistic protest'.

Essentially the picture which emerged was one of a generation concerned only with private values, usually in traditional terms of family solidarity, coupled with a negative attitude to authority in any form, and most particularly in the form of the State. Although this was the general picture, there were also significant variations within it, in relation to the economic, geographical, social and cultural locations of the respondents. These variations, in turn, corresponded to the known cleavages in Italian society and the differential paths of development followed by different areas of the country. In other words, the survey results could also be read as a map confirming the conflicts and tensions between urban and rural, between industrial and agricultural sectors and between north and south.[1]

It may be argued that these tensions also reflected a seething energy for individual betterment in that large segment of the population which provided the ingenuity, the persistence and the sheer hard work which was expressed in the 'economic miracle' and the later advances of the 'third Italy'. It was, in this view, precisely because of the ineptitude of the state, and of the remote and abstract character of its official values, that a large number of the inhabitants of the country chose to make their way in life without reference to them, relying upon the strong traditions of family and personal survival strategies and the micro-solidarities imparted by centuries of having to fend for themselves, while minimising the dependence upon and contact with anything official.

Any attempt to write the contemporary history of Italy, and in particular to relate the present to the past, must in the end grapple with the questions implicit in this analysis. They can, somewhat reductively, be brought together into a single puzzle:

> Why, in fact, has the intense economic development of recent years failed to strengthen the system, appearing on the contrary to have fragmented society, brought about a crisis of values, paralyzed the government and made the State itself a mere sham? Do historical 'flaws' exist which account for all this?[2]

One answer which has been given to this question is that Italy has never developed a dominant, decisively modernising middle-class capable of imprinting its value-system on the population as a whole and providing the progressive civic culture which would counteract the regressive tendencies noted. A prime characteristic of any such dominant middle-class culture is its capacity to inculcate a deeply-felt popular allegiance to the nation-state and then to draw upon it at times of crisis.

The historical absence of any such middle-class explains a great deal about Italy's current problems, but itself needs to be explained if it is not to become an 'uncaused first cause' to which all responsibility for failure can be assigned. While other European democracies have been profoundly influenced by the existence of such a class and the moral and material leadership it has provided, the processes which elsewhere led to its formation and the dominant role it exercised were not fully reproduced in the course of modern Italian history: Italy did not experience the effects of the Reformation, with its emphasis on the work ethic, nor of a powerful centralising absolutism native to the country as a whole. Its contact with the Enlightenment and the French Revolution was a derivative

---

1. Cf. C. Tullio-Altan and A. Marradi, *Valori, classi sociali e scelte politiche*, Bompiani, Milan, 1976; C. Tullio-Altan and R. Cartocci, *Modi di produzione e lotta di classe in Italia*, ISEDI-Mondadori, Milan, 1979.
2. G. Carocci, *Storia d'Italia dall'Unità ad oggi*, Feltrinelli, Milan, 1982, p. 9.

Figure 13.1 The heart of northern industry: workers coming off shift at the Pirelli factory in Milan, 1980.

of the history of other national formations; its *giacobini* were members of a restricted educated élite and, with the exception of a few untypical northern cities, the only mass popular movements which arose were profoundly reactionary: the urban poor of Naples, already organised by the *camorra*, were easily led by Cardinal Ruffo to butcher the liberal idealists of the Parthenopean Republic in 1799, and when in 1860 Garibaldi landed at Marsala the Sicilians who rallied to his support against the forces of order loyal to the King of Naples were the foot-soldiers (*picciotti*) of the *mafia*.

Political and social leadership in pre-*Risorgimento* Italy was, on the contrary, exercised by ruling groups whose power in their own areas was closely connected to ownership of land within social and cultural frameworks (*latifundia, mezzadria*, tenant-farming) largely incompatible with one another. Such industry as existed had grown up not in relation to a national Italy-wide market, but to geographically limited and backward economies closed off from one another by archaic forms of protectionism. Even after the making of Italy as a unified nation-state by a minority among the existing ruling groups, the political and cultural steps taken to 'make Italians' were conceived and framed at least as much to entrench the existing sectional interests of the social groups controlling northern industry and southern agriculture as to foster a unifying development of human and material resources in terms of a single national concept. No genuinely 'national' leadership could emerge under these conditions of permanent trade-offs between conflicting interests. The position of the unreconciled Papacy as a source of legitimation for non-participation in the nation-building project compounded the factors already gravely retarding it.

Once the political and administrative unification of the country was completed, the rigorous but narrow-minded idealists of the *destra storica* ceased to represent any clear developmental path and could no longer command even a minimal consensus. When Depretis took over, basing his parliamentary majority on the support of the southern deputies, national politics became a series of fleeting tactical alliances between the separate interest groups which held economic and (through patronage) political power in the different parts of the country. This 'asystemic system' was consolidated under Crispi by the support his policy of protectionism elicited from all the interests concerned: in effect, the south became the economic colony of the north in return for permanent subsidisation of the patronage system which underpinned the power of the local ruling groups. In Sicily, the groups concerned already included the *mafia* in its pre-industrial phase.[3]

3. Like many colonies in history it always absorbed more resources from its would-be colonisers than it produced returns on their investment: the population of the regions in the south which currently produce no more than 15 per cent of Italy's national wealth, and contain barely 10 per cent of its entrepreneurs, nevertheless enjoys, in quantitative terms, an average standard of living almost two thirds of that of the population in the Po valley which, as a region of Europe, ranks second in average income per head after Bavaria (cf. Giorgio Bocca, *L'inferno. Profondo sud, male oscuro*, Mondadori, Milan, 1992, pp. 268–77).

The breakdown of the economic basis for the Crispi compromise, signalled by the bank scandals of the 1890s was followed by the rise of organised labour and peasant mass movements and the failure of the attempt to repress them by political and military means during the end-of-century crisis. The fear and disquiet generated among the political class by these traumas created an opportunity for a new approach: the generation, by means of a rapid industrialisation, of sufficient margins of prosperity to enable the central government to direct strategic resources into the task of nation-building through socially directed economic amelioration.

Such a strategy required, above all, the reconciliation of the new mass-movements of the left (both Socialist and Catholic) with the liberal wing of the existing coalition of ruling groups. This was the policy pursued, with considerable effect, by Giolitti during the years of his dominance of Italian politics, but it contained a fatal weakness: the fact that no truly 'national' middle class yet existed for which Giolitti could really act as the representative. Moreover, because of the inevitable gradualism of his approach, those who demanded that Italy should already behave as a fully-fledged nation-state on equal terms with those to the north-west of it, were easily able to hijack the project, precipitating the country into a destabilising colonial war in Africa and then engineering its intervention in the tragic blood-letting of 1915–18.

The polarisation of popular feelings around the issue of intervention in the First World War opened a Pandora's box of political consequences. Intransigent revolutionary extremists irrevocably seized the control of the labour movement from the parliamentary moderates, who had believed that it would be possible to substitute for the missing 'national' middle class a broadly unifying worker–peasant alliance which could bring about socialism through reform. The extremism of the left was matched by, and mingled with, that of the *nazionalisti* and their Fascist successors. A predatory régime was installed, determined to make Italy into a 'great power' by repression at home and conquest abroad, but it proved incapable of establishing either the economic or the military strength to sustain the rôle. Since no geo-political space was available in Europe for such a project, a new colonial war was launched in Africa, whose very success made Italy even more vulnerable to pressure from without, since it had now to behave as if it had the resources to match the imperial mission it claimed.

When, in 1939, general war broke out once more in Europe, the Italian ruling group again sought to recoup domestic weakness by joining what appeared to be an easy ride to success abroad, but this time with military and political results so disastrous that, far from having established Italy as one of the 'great powers', they revealed the Fascist régime's utter failure to modernise and unify the nation-state inherited from the past. Although the country's consequent defeat and military occupation definitively discredited the coercive-militaristic approach to nation-building, the replacement political class which emerged in 1945, despite its claimed legitimation in a mass popular movement of anti-fascist Resistance, pursued (or at least tolerated) a developmental path which tended radically to increase the political and economic divergences between the different components of the Italian nation-state, most notably those between the north and centre on the one hand, and the south on the other. Although it was a multi-party rather than a one-party system, it nevertheless closely approximated its Fascist predecessor in the tendency to impose a permanent occupation of the state itself (and the 'local state') by the placemen of the dominant parties.

It has been suggested by some Italian historians that a substantial continuity links the three main phases of the history of unified Italy. In this view the Liberal State bred the Fascist régime, which (after the brief parenthesis of the Resistance) passed on to the post-1948 Christian Democrat-dominated governments the torch of repressive reaction against the deeply felt wish of the Italian people for democracy and socialism. A rather more convincing counter-interpretation sees in the post-unification history of Italy no real evidence of a permanent conspiracy to block progressive social and political change but only a continuity of fragmentation, marked by the occupation of the state by a series of temporary alliances of interests operating through the machinery of representative government based upon pure proportionality as a way to evade accountability in practice while claiming it in theory: the so-called *partitocrazia*.

The massive energy and innovative vitality displayed since the mid-1950s by the protagonists, large and small, of Italian private sector industrial development is, in this interpretation, to be seen as the positive aspect of a civil society whose main tradition is a negative 'particularism' already evident in merchant writings of the fourteenth and fifteenth centuries:

> By nature, love and charity make my family dearer to me than all else.
> And to maintain my family I seek wealth; and to protect my family
> and my wealth, friends are needed who can advise me, and help me
> both to bear and to avoid ill fortune; and to enjoy the fruits of my
> wealth, of my family and of friendship, it is well to find out some
> fair-dealing and honourable authority.[4]

A civil society which thus promotes the exclusive pursuit of private interest, and sees politics only as a subsidiary component of the wealth-creating environment in which the pursuit can produce its benefits, implies a weak form of social solidarity and the lack of an accepted ethical framework for political action. It thus forms a social and political reality which is profoundly paradoxical: hugely vital in some respects while at the same time being self-destructive. Such a system is seldom able to generate a leadership capable of uniting the population of a modern pluralistic state in the cause of an effective 'national' solidarity, rather than dividing it into separate

---

4. Leon Battista Alberti, *I libri della famiglia*, Einaudi, Turin, 1972, p. 226.

constituencies in each of which an élite group can rely upon an electorate made captive by whatever coerced or voluntary forms of patronage are locally available, or can appeal to a widely-felt resentment of the central state.

Social solidarity in these circumstances is most keenly experienced in relation to a *longue durée* territorial form of identification. This, in Italy, is focused upon the *paese*, whether a village or historic city-state, or upon a newly-formed but still territorially-defined 'imagined community' (such as Piedmont, Lombardy, Veneto, or even 'the North' in general). Wider solidarities are also still experienced in terms of identification with a religious or political faith, or an economic or social interest group, but the evidence is that the gravitational field exerted by these is growing steadily weaker and nowadays rarely goes beyond family voting habits.

In the absence of any compelling and broadly-experienced social solidarity stemming from a nationally-defined 'imagined community', the logic of a party system conceived and legitimated simply as a means to occupy a portion of political power through the exercise of a vested influence is clear. Whether in terms of ministerial or parliamentary seats, or at intermediate and lower levels of power derived from the abuse of the authority and resources of the national or local state, from television channels to state-supported banks and from nationalised industries to district health units, such a system of fragmented solidarities will be far more functional than one which depends on overarching identifications and preferences at national level. Insofar as the latter are in any way present and effective they will tend to be parasitic upon the more dynamic, if more incoherent, system based on local and sectoral interests and allegiances.[5]

The entrenchment of mediocrity is one of the heaviest costs of this version of 'transformism'. Since 1860, the Italian 'political class' has produced only two leaders who might remotely claim the status of 'popular hero': Garibaldi and Mussolini. Both of these had a declared desire to remould Italy and a belief that they could do so. Yet, in addition to their manifold personal failings, both were disastrous failures as national leaders because they lacked two essential qualities of modern statesmanship: firstly, a clear and concrete vision of what they sought to achieve, accompanied by an unwavering moral seriousness and intelligence in its pursuit; secondly, a full awareness of the complexity of the historical processes within which they were bound to pursue their objectives, together with the capacity to adapt their plans to changing conditions. Garibaldi, who never achieved power, remained in the realm of popular legend to represent a hope unfulfilled. Mussolini, who achieved too much of it, left a popular hope betrayed and a legacy of cynicism about ambitious leadership:

5. For a valuable and illuminating theorisation of 'bargained pluralism' in Italian politics, see David Hine, *Governing Italy: The Politics of bargained pluralism*, Clarendon Press, Oxford, 1993. For a interesting comment on the most recent interpretations of the current situation in Italy, see Stephen Lukes review 'Against corruption' in *TLS*, 8 October 1993, pp. 8–9.

the profound hostility among both élites and masses towards anything that could be construed as strong leadership thus became one of the major penalties inflicted by Fascism upon post-fascist Italy.

A decisive consequence was that the 1947 Constitution was deliberately structured in order to prevent any recurrence of leaders capable of transcending their parties and appealing directly to the people as a whole: virtually pure proportional representation created a system of permanent coalition, dependent upon party machines dominated by factions constantly jostling for primacy. In terms of the government's capacity to govern, the result was oligarchical paralysis: the leader who momentarily came to the top as prime minister had to play down to a constantly changing series of self-appointed king-makers, both in his own party and in those of its coalition partners, all of whom in turn were busy promoting their electoral position by appeasing an equally incoherent set of local interests. The apparent exception to this rule, the Italian Communist Party during its long Stalinist period of 'democratic centralism', was never allowed to share political power, and the real political independence of its leaders, and hence their capacity to defend Italian national interests, was always in question until the collapse of the Soviet empire in 1989. The system thus generated a political alternative which was unrealisable at national level and could therefore remain largely immune to the endemic corruption of the ruling parties. It could present itself as the 'party of the honest', occupy much of the high moral ground in local domestic politics, and consolidate its own control of the 'local state' across an important swathe of the country. Where it could combine pragmatism with this public image it often achieved a symbiotic relationship with the local entrepreneurial economy, producing the curiosity of a 'red capitalism'.

The most striking aspect of Italy's post-war history, the outstanding economic performance of both large and small-scale private industry, must, then, be measured against the wretched inadequacy of this political system in terms of the strategic management of the economy, above all in the sectors directly controlled by it: nationalised and state-subsidised industry, agriculture and services. The scale of the economic success achieved by hard-working Italians against these odds can be judged from a few statistics: between 1951 and 1961 Italian national income grew to three-and-a-half times the level it had reached during Giolitti's period of dominance prior to the First World War. The dynamism of industrial development was matched by, and clearly linked to, the virtual relocation of almost a third of the population: between 1948 and 1990 the proportion of the latter engaged in agriculture fell from 48.7 per cent to 14 per cent. On several occasions since 1961, despite the vast unproductive State expenditure in the south, the growth rate of the Italian economy as a whole equalled or outstripped that of its European competitors. In 1987 two significant facts about the Italian economy were revealed: Italy's average living standard in statistical terms (which of course conceal wide differentiation between areas and social groups) overtook Britain's, and a fifth of Italy's GDP was accounted for by the 'black economy', outside the tax system.

The political class inevitably sought to take credit for the greater affluence of the voters. In reality not only had Italian governments neither planned the economic take-off nor taken strategic action to maintain its momentum, they were also unable to regulate the economic and social changes which it brought about, with profoundly damaging results for both the physical and social environment. Social theory would predict, nevertheless, that the effect might be only temporary, and that the dramatic increase in personal wealth and life-opportunities would, over a fairly brief time-span, more than compensate for the psychological costs of the disruption of long-established patterns of local solidarity, replacing them with new forms of collective consciousness and action. Part of the prosperity might even become available for repairing the damage to the natural environment caused by economic expansion.

In the north, and to a considerable extent in the centre, of the country such compensatory mechanisms do appear to have been at work, although very unevenly (and in the case of the environment, lagging far behind the problems). In the south, however, despite the improved money-income of most of the population deriving from the massive subsidisation of the southern economy, the dominant civic culture has remained *mafioso* in the broad sense. There, the unevenness of economic and cultural development which has characterised the history of united Italy for 130 years seems to manifest itself most starkly and most intractably as a general acceptance of anti-social public values and tolerance of the behaviour which they legitimate. At the heart of this dissonance between private and public values has lain the weakness of popular attachment to the state which claims to embody the nation. It is a weakness which the political class has at best studiously ignored, at worst actively connived with, for half a century.

It could still be argued perhaps that the re-birth of Italy leading to the remarkable economic achievements between 1956 and 1964, like the successful damping down in the immediate post-war years of the separatist movements, nevertheless proved the viability of the re-established Italian nation-state. The case that a real consolidation of a popular identification with the concept of an Italian nation had occurred might even be strengthened, paradoxically, by reference to the existence in Italy of the strongest Communist Party west of the Iron Curtain. By apparently threatening to dissolve Italian nationhood in an 'internationalist' brotherhood of Soviet satellites, the Stalinist Communists did the shaky Italian nation-state of the 1940s and 1950s the great service of acting as a magnet for countervailing interventions. These in turn brought substantial benefits: security from a Soviet takeover, and crucial economic assistance, first in the Marshall Plan from the United States, and subsequently through membership of NATO and the European Community.

ASTA
l'immunità
rlamentare
RETE
BASTA
con l'immunità
parlamentare
RETE
razia La Rete
MONZA

It could also be argued that the process of 'Americanisation' of popular culture, so deplored by traditionalists and radical intellectuals, actually strengthened the new national cohesion beyond any possibility of a reversion to disunity, by the homogenisation of the popular imagination throughout the country, through mass-addiction to the consumption of standardised goods, and by the extension to previously excluded social groups of the powerful cultural and linguistic cements supplied by the mass media.

Yet the consolidation of Italian nationhood was always, and increasingly, contradicted by the dysfunctionality of the Italian State. Nowhere in the Western world (with the possible exception during the 1950s and 1960s of Franco's Spain and Salazar's Portugal) was there so little carry-over as in Italy from the popular sentiments of national identity and enthusiasm for the flag which were readily, and raucously, expressed in World Cup or Olympic sport, to willingness to pay through taxes for the activities of the state which was supposed to be the formal and administrative expression of that identity.

As to culturally induced reinforcement of a deep-seated national identi-fication, there are too many recent examples of the lability of such superficial, top-down social engineering for the argument to carry much conviction. It was, if anything, likely that the 'belly nationalism' to which the Communists attributed their electoral rout in 1948, had as little influence on real political behaviour as the 'belly communism' which inspired the Americans to invest in aid to Italy: the commitment of Italians to either of the political 'churches' was far more likely to derive from attachments or repulsions related to strongly localised perceptions of class, property and family.

These latter intuitions appear to have been confirmed by the most recent events. The referendum on institutional reform held on 18 April 1993, though referring only to the creation of a first-past-the-post electoral system for the Senate (albeit with 25 per cent of the seats still being allotted by proportional representation), received an overwhelming endorsement from the electorate. With a turn-out of almost 90 per cent of voters, the majority in favour of the change was a massive 87 per cent. It precipitated the fall of the Amato govern-ment, which almost daily was losing ministers because of judicial investigations into corruption (and worse: by this time Andreotti, now popularly nicknamed Beelzebub, was formally under suspicion of having been an accomplice in murder and an associate of the recently arrested *mafia* super-boss Toto Riina).

The referendum result, although numerically decisive, had been widely anticipated by opinion polls, and all the established parties which had origi-nally opposed any departure from proportional representation, with the exception of Italian Social Movement and its left-wing mirror image of the unreformed rump of the Communists (rebaptised *Rifondazione comunista*),

Figure 13.2 May 1993: one of the hundreds of angry demonstrations nationwide after the rump parliament voted against lifting Craxi's parliamentary immunity.

had all jumped on the bandwagon of reform, thus depriving the result of political decisiveness.

In May, reform of the electoral system formally became the top priority of a new government headed, as the personal nominee of the President of the Republic, Scalfaro, by the President of the Bank of Italy, Carlo Azeglio Ciampi, who chose his ministers largely without reference to party allegiance.[6] Though by mid-June the almost 150 deputies who had been officially notified by the judiciary that they were suspected of corrupt practices had formed a cross-party group which vowed to oppose any early dissolution (well aware that once parliament had been dissolved they would immediately lose their immunity to arrest), a further development occurred which seemed to point to the impossibility of further protracted delay.

On 6 and 20 June 1993 some 5 million Italians went to the polls to elect local councils and mayors throughout the country. The elections were held under an already reformed system (originally intended to be a long drawn-out experiment preliminary to a parliamentary reform), requiring the mayoral candidates to present themselves to the electorate prior to the vote and to specify their alliances, if any. If no candidate scored more than 50 per cent of the votes cast, there would be a run-off election between the two highest-polling candidates two weeks later. Moreover, the winning candidate would receive a proportionate number of councillors, thus guaranteeing a working majority for a four-year term of office.

The results proved to be a crushing defeat for all the parties of the former government coalition: Socialists, Social Democrats, Republicans (despite their belated move into opposition) and Liberals almost disappeared from the political map, while even the Christian Democrats were reduced to the same level of incumbencies as the neo-Fascist Italian Social Movement. The *Lega del Nord* won in 25 cities and large towns in the north, including Milan, while the ex-Communist Party of the Democratic Left confirmed its supremacy in the centre of the country. In a few cities, including Turin, where the Party of the Democratic Left had joined forces with a moderate Democratic Alliance composed of dissident ex-members of the establishment parties, it also did well.[7] Only in the deep south did the Christian Democrats manage to hold on

---

6. His other main objective was to rein in the deficit by increased taxes and other fiscal measures; essentially, however, Ciampi was heading a caretaker government whose only *raison d'être* was to pave the way for early elections under a new system.

7. Albeit to loud cries of 'foul' by the *Lega del Nord*, which insisted that its own candidate in Turin, who just failed to enter the run-off, had been foiled by vote-rigging organised by the 'old gang'. Colour was added to these complaints in November 1993 when the Rome official sent to supervise the administration of the election in Turin was arrested and charged with massive embezzlement of secret service funds and leadership of a group of 'deviant' security chiefs bent on destabilising the political system in order to delay fresh parliamentary elections. In December, however, to Bossi's embarrassment, the court ruling on the legality of the Turin mayoral election found that the ballots not included in the original count would not have altered the outcome.

to a few small towns; in the same areas the Italian Social Movement also unexpectedly beat the 'clean government' alliances in some cases, enabling their leader to claim that his party was now the only real barrier to the Communists.[8]

The only dispute for most of the political establishment, as for the opposition, was now whether early elections were technically possible in October 1993, or would have to be delayed until the spring of 1994. Those who only longed for a little more time to pass in the hope of postponing their day of judgement or even surviving the promised electoral holocaust pressed for 1994, or even 1996, with the 'party of the suspected' trying to insist that the existing parliament should run its full four-year term.[9]

The only rational course of action, if only to save what could still be saved of the Italian Republic and its institutions, would have been to accept an agreed procedure for early elections, but by mid-1993 there was little evidence of any such consensus emerging between the discredited

---

8. In the aftermath of their trouncing, the Christian Democrats' General Secretary, Mino Martinazzoli, who had been brought in as a 'Mr Clean' to replace the totally discredited Arnaldo Forlani after the first wave of scandals in 1992, proposed that the party should dissolve itself and reform, as the Italian Communist Party had successfully done two years earlier, under a new name (the 'Popular Centre'). At which, the southern faction threatened to secede, taking the old name with them. Martinazzoli quickly tried to retreat, but in any case the party was already irrevocably split, having lost its central *raison d'être* as the bulwark of anti-communism, and having been deserted by most of its remaining idealist militants.

9. Ironically, it was the incorruptible but unreliable maverick Marco Pannella, who had earned the enmity of the established parties by heading some of the successful (and most of the unsuccessful) referendum campaigns in the 1970s and 1980s, who now organised the 'party of suspects', a cross-party collection of deputies and senators most of whom were already under investigation, or feared they soon would be. His stand may, of course, have been influenced by the fact that his exiguous personal party-list was highly unlikely to reach the 4 per cent threshold needed for representation, even within the 'Indian reservation' of 25 per cent of parliamentary seats to be determined by proportional representation which was established by the new electoral law. Of particular opacity, even for the Italian parliament, was the controversy which raged for several months about the issue of giving a vote to the millions of Italians of the emigrant *diaspora*, whether or not they had become citizens of another country (as the great majority had) to elect 20 extraterritorial deputies and 10 senators. All parties initially supported this unrealisable plan, presumably because they believed there were extra votes to be garnered, and in most cases in an effort to capitalise on a facile nationalism in order to offset their loss of popularity in the wake of the 'Clean Hands' enquiry. When it became apparent that, in order to deny it a two-thirds majority and thus ensure several further months delay to the fresh national elections stridently demanded by the opposition parties, the parliamentary procedures for adding these provisions to the new electoral law would be exploited by tactical abstentions organised by some of its most judicially-vulnerable supporters, the *Lega* and the Party of the Democratic Left unexpectedly withdrew their support and the measure failed to achieve even the 50 per cent majority necessary for further discussion of any measure intended to change the Constitution.

parliamentarians in Rome. Moreover, the *homines novi* of the *Lega del Nord* were busy stoking up the fires of popular disgust with such delaying tactics, clamouring for immediate elections, even under the old rules if need be, and denouncing all attempts to calm the political atmosphere as a continuation of the conspiracy of the old parties to hold on to their power at all costs and to prevent 'the people' from having the final say in its own affairs. Their adversarial parliamentary and rhetorical style, and their plebeian epithets, extending to denunciations of the President of the Republic and the Prime Minister as 'swindlers', which would hardly raise an eyebrow in the rough and tumble of a Westminster 'question time', was found to be particularly disgraceful and shocking. Such outright populism broke the conventions of 'national solidarity' in defence of anti-fascist constitutional propriety which since 1945 had underpinned the *partitocrazia*, prompting mournful forecasts by intellectuals of all persuasions that a return to Fascism was imminent, despite the evident contradiction between the grandiose 'Greater Italy' imperialism of the neo-Fascists and the *Lega*'s declared intention to weaken Italy's national state for the benefit of its separate regions. On the contrary, such a robustly aggressive expression of accumulated popular disgust for the 'old gang' of politicians, was more likely to represent the arrival, for the first time in the history of Italy, of a politics which called a spade a spade and did not swathe issues of policy, power and decision-making in multiple veils of mystification.

So what is the outlook, at the end of 1993, for the Italian nation-state? It is undeniable that since 1860 Italy's rulers have signally failed to create the deeply rooted awareness of collective national identity which elsewhere serves as a reservoir of goodwill and potential self-sacrifice for the 'imagined community' of the single nation. The 'second *Risorgimento*' claimed in the 1943–45 Resistance, and the Republican Constitution which sprang from it, for a brief moment appeared to promise a greater measure of success in terms of a consensual 'nationalisation of the masses'. Yet it, too, was quickly followed by the descent into a *partitocrazia*, which faithfully echoed the worst features of the system of transformism, and some of those of Fascism. The disenchantment of most Italians with the corruption of public values and the consequent misgovernment, which were the outcomes of a century of this system, is not hard to understand, and their scepticism about its capacity for self-reform appears fully justified.

The 'political class', with honourable exceptions, is not, however, even now so much disenchanted with the flaws of the system, as fearful of losing its power within it. In the course of all the scandals, and worse, involving its members over recent decades, not one tainted politician has voluntarily resigned a seat in parliament, although many have been publicly discredited. The few sincerely disenchanted simply withdraw from political life; with their withdrawal the power of mediocrity is confirmed.

In November and December 1993, in two rounds of voting for majors and city councils, according to the new system which eliminates all but the two leading candidates and ensures they have a working majority on the council, an unprecedented electoral earthquake occurred. It had been widely expected that the traditional ruling parties most besmirched by the 'Clean Hands' investigations would be severely punished by the voters, and this duly happened, although to an extent which went far beyond their worst fears: the Christian Democrats lost 30-50 per cent of their former support and quickly showed signs of final disintegration, while the Socialists practically disappeared from the map. It had also been assumed that the *Lega* would further strengthen its grip upon the northern plain, which it duly did, and that the Democratic Party of the Left, the former Communists, would also do well. More surprising to observers was the sudden transformation, especially in the area between Rome and Naples, of the neo-Fascist Italian Social Movement from a fringe party of protest into one enjoying a relative majority, and with a good chance of winning the mayoral contests in the run-off ballots in Rome and Naples. Although they eventually lost these contests, in both cases they succeeded in gathering almost 50 per cent of the votes cast; in Rome this meant that over a million of its inhabitants had decided that they should cast their vote for a party whose very name had been chosen to echo the most politically divisive period of Italy's recent history, the civil war of 1943–45.[10] Similarly threatening for future developments at national level was the general advance of the *Lega* in the whole of the north, which, despite its narrow failure to win any of the run-off contests for mayor in the large cities, left it the largest single party in every constituency. If that position were maintained at a general election, the party would have over 150 seats in parliament and its collaboration would be indispensable to any government.

Until this earthquake in the local elections of December 1993, it had generally been assumed that the Christian Democrats would largely maintain their traditional grip upon the southern electorate even if they lost heavily in the centre and north of the country. At the end of 1993, however, the prospect suddenly loomed of a parliament divided more or less evenly between the Democratic Party of the Left, leading a probably ephemeral rainbow alliance of voters mainly concentrated in the north and centre of the country who from habit, tradition or considered judgement remained resistant to the surge to the right, and the two populist right-wing parties representing fundamentally incompatible regional interests.[11] After the electoral disaster for the former government coalition, there was no longer any realistic prospect of averting early elections as soon as the relevant legislation was in place, which meant, in practice, in early spring 1994 and promised a prolonged and exceptionally

---

10. The name of Italian Social Movement (*MSI* in Italian) is clearly, and intentionally, redolent of the Italian Social Republic (*RSI*), Mussolini's last gamble on a Nazi victory in the Second World War.

11. The first systematic scholarly study of the *Lega* has recently appeared: Ilvo Diamanti, *La Lega. Geografia, storia e sociologia di un nuovo soggetto politico*, Donzelli Editore, Rome, 1993. There is no recent study of the Italian Social Movement.

violent electoral campaign. Meanwhile, the 'Clean Hands' team of prosecutors, as the first trials of major corrupt politicians, businessmen and industrialists finally came to court, continued to make the headlines and kept the alienated portion of the electorate acutely aware of the reasons why it should register a vote clearly against the parties which had not only broken the law, but also the rules of the game and could no longer deliver expected benefits to its electoral clients.

In a rapid evolution, which nevertheless was in keeping with its long Togliattian tradition of seeking compromise with the 'healthy forces of capitalism', the Democratic Party of the Left became the main standard-bearer of moderation in all things, promising to maintain the Ciampi government's programme of privatisation and fiscal propriety, and clearly seeking to occupy the middle ground of politics and woo voters who only a few months earlier would probably never have dreamed of giving their ballots to even the most reformist party of the left. The serious press in Europe and America now took a fresh look at the Democratic Party of the Left and liked what it saw: a well-intentioned social-democratic party apparently no further to the left than its British or German equivalents, and equally capable of leading a 'broad church' of moderate politicians untainted by 'Bribesville'.

Equally determined to claim this centre ground was the *Lega*, which soon (albeit inconsistently) began to moderate its secessionist message in favour of a more respectable federalism. The Italian Social Movement, too, sought to demonstrate its centre-right vocation: its leaders wore sober business suits for their press conferences and published lists of names of intellectuals, mostly little-known, who had declared their support for Gianfranco Fini, the Movement's national secretary, who was in the run-off for the post of mayor of Rome. Many of their more embarrassing followers, however, again donned their black shirts at night and roamed the streets of Rome looking for 'long-haired lefties' to beat up. In Naples, where the run off was between a worthy but dreary ex-Communist and Benito Mussolini's incoherent but charismatic platinum-blonde grand-daughter Alessandra (formerly a soft-porn actress), there was little need to marshal such support.

At the time it was far less clear that the Italian electorate would reject the extreme right-wing parties, even for reasons of self-preservation. The dangerous blend of pent-up anger, resentment and disappointment seemed unlikely to be discharged in a single round of local elections. The abrupt ending of Christian Democrat clientelism and the related market for votes in the south could not be replicated by a Democratic Party of the Left dedicated to dismantling precisely that system, leaving a mass of voters with only their outrage to motivate them and an easy target for neo-Fascist populism. The *Lega* equally had no chance of persuading them to adopt a federalist solution which would enable the north to cease subsidising the south. On the other hand, no coalition between the two right-wing parties could be convincing, given the contrast between their constituencies as well as their programmes.[12]

Italy could thus easily slide even further into ungovernability, despite the electoral reform. If the relative strengths of the three main contenders for power were to be maintained at the forthcoming parliamentary elections, the only formula for effective government might well be a deal between the Democratic Party of the Left and the *Lega*. This might take the form of a *quid pro quo* arrangement whereby the *Lega* was guaranteed a federalist solution to the constitutional question while the Democratic Party of the Left was allowed to rule meanwhile through benevolent abstention on its programme of decentralisation and privatisation. But after the anathemas traded between these two protagonists over the years since the *Lega* achieved its breakthrough, it appears highly problematic that any such deal could be made by their current leaderships.

The situation has been further complicated by the impetuous irruption into the political arena of Italy's biggest media tycoon, Silvio Berlusconi, who owns a large number of magazines, newspapers and television channels. In November 1993 this Citizen Kane of Milan offered his moral and financial backing to anyone prepared to join him in forming a new party which would represent the necessary conservative pole in the system of alternation in office now ushered in by the electoral reforms, the Christian Democrat-led coalition having been dismissed from the role of champions of free enterprise values. He plunged at once into the thick of the post-Bribesville turmoil by announcing his support, in the mayoral contest in Rome, for the neo-Fascist Gianfranco Fini, although in the storm of protest which followed, he sought to stress that this did not commit him to supporting Fascism as such. The protest led to a significant fall in the viewing figures for his TV channels, which may perhaps have more influence on his future actions than the anguish of the intellectuals. Nevertheless the appeal of his media outlets, particularly TV, is to that portion of the Italian electorate which feels most alienated from the existing system and is most likely to register protest and anti-system votes, precisely the segments which have switched massively to the *Lega* and the Italian Social Movement, neither of which previously had any friends in the established media. If the vast resources of Berlusconi's publishing and media empire are now to be placed at the disposal of such parties, they might induce an even greater disruption than the latter have achieved with their own resources.

As one unhappy liberal intellectual wrote on the eve of the second and decisive round of mayoral contests early in December 1993:

---

12. Many foreign commentators have carelessly assimilated the *Lega* to the Italian Social Movement as a party of the extreme right. In pondering the likely evolution of the two, however, it is important to take account of the markedly differing social character of their mass support: while the *Lega* is a party of a disgruntled middle class which resents the predations of a centralising state, the Italian Social Movement's new strength is derived from the discontent of an 'under-class' no longer able to trade votes for favours and thus on the way to perceiving itself as an 'out-class' of despised no-hopers.

The unity of our nation is, in terms of historical time, a recent development. It was shaped by two events: the *Risorgimento* and the Resistance. Is it really wise and responsible of us to entrust the fate of the country to forces which, implicitly or explicitly, are attacking the two main pillars of this still fragile bridge?[13]

In the light of the most recent indications, it appears that less than half of the Italian electorate would share this view.[14]

---

13. Giorgio Ruffolo, 'Se domenica Fini e Bossi', in *La Repubblica*, 1 December 1993, p. 10

14. In the general election held on 28 and 29 March 1994, an electoral alliance consisting of Berlusconi's new party *Forza Italia*, the *Lega del Nord* and the neo-Fascists in their renamed party of *Alleanza nazionale* won 360 seats out of the total 630 in the Chamber of Deputies, with an aggregate of over 50 per cent of the votes cast, while the Senate was evenly divided between left and right alliances. Within the winning alliance, baptised the 'Pole of Freedom', the largest grouping was that of the *Lega*, which had benefited most from the first-past-the-post system even though its aggregate vote was substantially lower than those of its partners and its success was due in large part to local electoral pacts in the north with Berlusconi's new party. Berlusconi's personal popularity far outdistanced that of the other two leaders. Although two months later the victors were finally able to agree on a government, they did not produce a set of policies which would satisfy the federalist commitment of the *Lega* and the centralist intentions of the other two partners, nor even put forward a coherent package of measures to meet the immediate economic situation or to carry forward their commitment to wide scale privatisation of state enterprises. The popularity of the *Lega* and its leader quickly declined in the opinion polls and in the Euroelections of June 1994, mainly because they were perceived (probably correctly) as deeply hostile to their partners' authoritarian tendencies and already preparing for a reversal of parliamentary alliances. Berlusconi's popularity also declined sharply in July when he attempted to force through a decree depriving the 'Clean Hands' team of public prosecutors of their powers to arrest politicians and business men suspected of corrupt practices when they were about to indict a number of trusted collaborators, including his younger brother, in his Fininvest business and media empire. This stupendous tactical blunder provoked the threatened resignation of the team, led by Antonio Di Pietro; Bossi and the *Leghisti* immediately pounced, threatening to walk out of the government, and were soon joined by Fini, whose own rank and file were equally outraged. At the beginning of August 1994, Berlusconi finally agreed to seek through parliament a means of divesting himself of control of his investments and TV channels. While Berlusconi's ratings slumped, and Bossi's failed to recover, Fini's rose significantly, showing clearly that Berlusconi's support among right-wing voters was quite fragile. Meanwhile, the former Christian Democrats who had formed the successor Italian Popular Party were paralysed by a leadership contest whose outcome made it impossible for it to rally to the government (thus reinforcing Berlusconi's dominance) in the forseeable future. Bossi remarked that Berlusconi was now 'a hostage' (whether to the judges or to his partners was not clear). The left opposition, whose principal component party had just installed a cautious *apparatchik* as a replacement leader for Occhetto (who had resigned after the abject failure of his Euroelections campaign), was unprepared to take the initiative, for fear of being accused of trying to flout the verdict of the polls where it had been soundly defeated only weeks earlier. Some commentators were already predicting fresh elections in a year's time or less. What is clear is that the upheavals of the last few years have still not cleaned the Augean stables of Italian politics.

Does this mean that Italy can henceforth be written off as a serious and stable member of what used to be called the 'comity of nations'? Or does the discrediting of most of the Italian ruling classes, both political and economic, open up undreamed-of perspectives for change? Could Italy even become a model of such change for other European Community countries? In almost all of them, commentators frequently note, the principle of democratic alternation in office has become seriously weakened over the last two decades by the apparently permanent tenure of power, and occupation of the 'commanding heights' of the economy, of the media, and of influential quangos, by one party or coalition of parties. *Partitocrazia* is certainly not confined to Italy, nor is popular resentment and distrust of politicians as a class. Perhaps the latest turmoil in Italian politics is yet another example of that 'litmus quality, indicating good and bad to come' once identified by Peter Nicholls, the distinguished Rome correspondent of 'The Times' newspaper, as the special characteristic of Italy (or the Italies) and its people (or peoples).

Bibliography

Absalom, Roger, *A Strange Alliance. Aspects of Escape and Survival in Italy 1943–1945*, Leo S. Olschki, Florence, 1991.

Alberti, Leon Battista, *I libri della famiglia*, Einaudi, Turin, 1972.

André, G., 'La politica estera fascista durante la seconda guerra mondiale', in Renzo De Felice (ed.), *L'Italia fra tedeschi e alleati*, Il Mulino, Bologna, 1973.

Acquarone, A., and Vernassa, M., *Il regime fascista*, Il Mulino, Bologna, 1974.

Are, Giuseppe, *Alle origini dell'Italia industriale*, Guida Editori, Naples, 1974.

Are, Giuseppe, *Industria e politica in Italia*, Laterza, Bari, 1975.

Arlacchi, Pino, *Mafia, Peasants and Great Estates*, Cambridge University Press, Cambridge, 1983.

Bagnasco, A., *Tre Italie. La problematica territoriale dello sviluppo italiano*, Il Mulino, Bologna, 1977.

Becattini, G., (ed.) *Prato. Storia di una città*, Vol. 4, Sansoni, Florence, 1994.

Blackmer, Donald and Tarrow, Sidney, (eds), *Communism in Italy and France*, Princeton University Press, Princeton, 1975.

Bocca, Giorgio, *Palmiro Togliatti*, Laterza, Bari, 1973.

Bocca, Giorgio, *L'inferno. Profondo sud, male oscuro*, Mondadori, Milan, 1992.

Bocca, Giorgio, *Storia d'Italia nella guerra fascista 1940–43*, Bari, 1976.

Bonomini, Luigi, Fagotto, F., Micheletti, L., Molinari Tosatti, L., Verdina, N. (eds), *Riservato a Mussolini*, Feltrinelli, Milan, 1974.

Bosworth, R., *Italy, the least of the Great Powers: Italian Foreign Policy before the First World War*, Cambridge University Press, Cambridge, 1979.

Braudel, Fernand, *The Structures of Everyday Life: Civilization and Capitalism 15th–18th Century*, Vol. 1, Collins, London, 1981.

Carocci, G., *Storia d'Italia dall'Unità ad oggi*, Feltrinelli, Milan, 1982.

Carsten, F. L., *The Rise of Fascism*, Batsford, London, 1967.

Castronovo, Valerio, *Storia d'Italia*, Vol. 4/1, Einaudi, Turin, 1976.

Cervi, Mario, *The Hollow Legions. Mussolini's Blunder in Greece 1940–41*, London, 1972.

Churchill, Winston, *The Second World War*, 6 vols, Cassell, London 1948–1953.

Clough, Shephard, *An Economic History of Modern Italy*, Columbia University Press, New York, 1964.

Coles, H. L. and Weinberg, A. K., *Civil Affairs: Soldiers become Governors*, The United States Army in World War II: Special Studies, Department of the Army, Washington, DC, 1964.

Compagna, Francesco, *La lotta politica italiana nel secondo dopoguerra*, Laterza, Bari, 1950.

Davis, J. A., and Ginsborg, P., (eds), *Society and Politics in the Age of the Risorgimento*, Cambridge University Press, Cambridge, 1991.

Davis, J. A., *Conflict and Control: Law and Order in Nineteenth-Century Italy*, Macmillan, London, 1988.

Deakin, F. W., *The Brutal Friendship*, Weidenfeld & Nicolson, London, 1962.

De Felice, Renzo, *Le interpretazioni del fascismo*, Laterza, Bari, 1969.

De Felice, Renzo, (ed.), *L'Italia fra tedeschi e alleati*, Il Mulino, Bologna, 1973.

De Felice, Renzo, *Mussolini*, 8 vols, Einaudi, Turin 1965–1990.

del Boca, Angelo, *The Ethiopian War, 1935–1941*, Chicago University Press, Chicago, 1969.

Delzell, Charles, *Mussolini's Enemies*, Princeton University Press, Princeton, 1961.

Dossetti, Giuseppe, 'Fine del tripartito?', in M. Giusenti and L. Elia (eds), *Cronache sociali (1947–1951)*, Luciano Landi editore, Rome-S Giovanni Valdarno, 1961.

Ellwood, David W., *Italy 1943–1945*, Leicester University Press, Leicester, 1985.

Falcone, Giovanni, *Men of Honour: The Truth about the Mafia*, Fourth Estate, London, 1992.

Galasso, G., *L'altra Europa*, Mondadori, Milan, 1982.

Galasso, G., *Passato e presente nel meridionalismo*, Guida, Naples, 1978.

Gambino, Antonio, *Storia del dopoguerra*, 2 vols, Laterza, Bari, 1978.

Ginsborg, Paul, *Storia d'Italia dal dopoguerra a oggi*, Einaudi, Turin, 1989.

Gramsci, Antonio, *Quaderni del carcere*, edited by V. Gerratana, Einaudi, Turin, 1975.

Gramsci, Antonio, *Passato e presente*, Einaudi, Turin, 1951.

Graziano, L., (ed.), *Clientelismo e mutamento politico*, Franco Angeli, Milan, 1974.

Guareschi, Giovannino, *Il piccolo mondo di Don Camillo*, Rizzoli, Milan, 1948.

Guarneri, Felice, *Battaglie economiche tra le due grandi guerre*, 2 vols, Garzanti, Milan, 1953.

Guicciardini, Francesco, *Opere*, UTET, Turin, 1970.

Harper, J. L., *America and the Reconstruction of Italy 1945–1948*, Cambridge University Press, Cambridge 1986.

Harris, C. R S., *Allied Military Administration of Italy 1943–1945*, HMSO, London, 1957.

Hearder, H. and Waley, D. P., *A Short History of Italy*, Cambridge University Press, Cambridge, 1963.

Howard, Michael, *The Mediterranean Strategy in the Second World War*, Weidenfeld & Nicolson, London, 1969.

Hughes, H. Stuart, *The United States and Italy*, 3rd edn, Harvard University Press, Cambridge, Mass., 1979.

Kertzer, David I., *Comrades and Christians: Religion and Political Struggle in Communist Italy*, Cambridge University Press, Cambridge, 1980.

Knox, MacGregor, *Mussolini Unleashed 1939–41*, Cambridge University Press, Cambridge, 1982.

Kogan, Norman, *Italy and the Allies*, Harvard University Press, Cambridge, Mass., 1956.

Kogan, Norman, *A Political History of Postwar Italy*, Praeger, New York, 1966.

Tommaso di Lampedusa, Giuseppe, *Il gattopardo*, Feltrinelli, Milano, 1958.

Ledeen, Michael, *The First Duce: D'Annunzio at Fiume*, Johns Hopkins University Press, Baltimore, 1977.

Levi, Carlo, *Cristo si è fermato a Eboli*, Einaudi, Turin, 1947.

Lewis, Norman, *The Honoured Society*, Collins, London, 1964.

Ludwig, E., *Talks with Mussolini*, Little, Brown, Boston, 1933.

Lyttleton, Adrian, *The Seizure of Power: Fascism in Italy 1919–1929*, Weidenfeld & Nicolson, London, 1973.

Macmillan, Harold,*The Blast of War*, London, 1968.

Mack Smith, Denis, *Victor Emanuel, Cavour, and the Risorgimento*, Oxford University Press, Oxford, 1971.

Mack Smith, Denis, *Cavour*, Methuen, London, 1985.

Mack Smith, Denis, *Italy and its Monarchy*, Yale University Press, New Haven and London, 1989.

Mack Smith, Denis, *Italy. A Modern History*, University of Michigan Press, Ann Arbor, 1959.

Mack Smith, Denis, *Mussolini's Roman Empire*, Penguin Books, Harmondsworth, 1976.

Maier, Charles S., *Recasting Bourgeois Europe*, Princeton University Press, Princeton, 1975.

Mammarella, Giuseppe, *Italy after Fascism 1943–1965*, University of Notre-Dame Press, Notre-Dame, Indiana, 1966.

Marx, Karl, *Capital*, J. M. Dent & Son Ltd, London, 1974.

Maxwell, Gavin, *God Protect Me From My Friends*, Penguin, London, 1957.

Miller, J. E., *The United States and Italy 1940–1950. The Politics and Diplomacy of Stabilization*, University of North Carolina, Chapel Hill and London, 1986.

Molfese, F., *Storia del brigantaggio dopo l'Unità*, Feltrinelli, Milan, 1964.

Neumann, S., (ed.) *Modern Political Parties*, University of Chicago Press, Chicago, 1956.

Nizza, Enzo, (ed.) *Autobiografia del Fascismo*, La Pietra, Milan, 1962.

Origo, Iris, *The Merchant of Prato*, Peregrine Books, Harmondsworth, 1963.

Pavone, Claudio, *Una guerra civile. Saggio storico sulla moralità mella Resistenza*, Bollati Boringhieri, Turin, 1991.

Plato, *Theaetatus*, Loeb (James).

Quazza, Guido, *Resistenza e storia d'Italia*, Feltrinelli, Milan, 1976.

Quazza, Guido, *et al. L'Italia dalla liberazione alla repubblica*, Feltrinelli, Milan, 1977.

Procacci, Giuliano, *A History of the Italian People*, Weidenfeld & Nicolson, London, 1970.

Rabel, Roberto G., *Between East and West. Trieste, the United States, and the Cold War, 1941–1954*, Duke University Press, Durham and London, 1988.

Romeo, Rosario, *Risorgimento e capitalismo*, Laterza, Bari, 1957.

Rossi Doria, M., *Scritti sul Mezzogiorno*, Einaudi, Turin, 1982.

Salvati, Mariuccia, *Stato e industria nella ricostruzione*, Feltrinelli, Milan, 1982.

Salvatorelli, G., *Il nazionalfascismo*, Einaudi, Turin, 1977.

Salvemini, Gaetano, *Under the Axe of Fascism*, Viking Books, New York, 1936.

Saraceno, P., *Il Mezzogiorno nelle ricerche della Svimez*, Giuffré, Milan, 1968.

Sassoon, Donald, *Togliatti e la via italiana al socialismo*, Einaudi, Turin, 1980.

Sassoon, Donald, *Contemporary Italy. Politics, Economy and Society since 1945*, Longman, Harlow, 1986.

Scarano, E. L., (ed.), *Francesco Guicciardini. Opere*, UTET, Turin, 1970.

Schmidt, Carl T., *The Corporate State in Action*, Victor Gollancz, London, 1939.

Scoppola, Pietro, *La proposta politica di De Gasperi*, Il Mulino, Bologna, 1977.

Scoppola, Pietro, *L'Italia dei partiti*, Il Mulino, Bologna, 1991.

Seton-Watson, C., *Italy from Liberalism to Fascism, 1870–1925*, Methuen, London, 1967.

Spriano, Paolo, *Storia del Partito Comunista Italiano*, 5 vols, Einaudi, Turin, 1965–75.

Taylor, A. J. P., *The War Lords*, London, 1976.

Tranfaglia, Nicola, *Dallo stato liberale al regime fascista*, Feltrinelli, Milan, 1973.

Tullio-Altan, C., *La nostra Italia. Arretratezza socioculturale, clientelismo, trasformismo e ribellismo dall'Unità ad oggi*, Feltrinelli, Milan, 1986.

Tullio-Altan, C.; Marradi, A., *Valori, classi sociali e scelta politiche*, Bompiani, Milan, 1976.

Tullio-Altan, C.; Cartocci, R., *Modi di produzione e lotta di classe in Italia*, ISEDI-Mondadori, Milan, 1979.

Tyler, M. A., 'A Dissenting Voice in the *Risorgimento*: Angelo Brofferio on mid-Nineteenth century Piedmont', in *Historical Journal*, 33, 2 (1990) pp. 403–15.

White, Caroline, *Patrons and Partisans: A study of politics in two southern Italian Comuni*, Cambridge University Press, Cambridge, 1980.

Woolf, S. J., (ed.), *The Rebirth of Italy*, Humanities Press, New York, 1972.

Index